SCHOOLS, POLITICS AND SOCIETY

ELEMENTARY EDUCATION IN WALES, 1870–1902

by
ROBERT SMITH

*Published on behalf of the
History and Law Committee
of the Board of Celtic Studies*

CARDIFF
UNIVERSITY OF WALES PRESS
1999

© Robert Smith, 1999

British Library Cataloguing-in-Publication Data
A catalogue record for this book is available from the British Library.

ISBN 0-7083-1535-6

All rights reserved. No part of this book may be reproduced, stored in a retrieval system, or transmitted, in any form or by any means, electronic, mechanical, photocopying, recording or otherwise, without clearance from the University of Wales Press, 6 Gwennyth Street, Cardiff, CF2 4YD.

The right of Robert Smith to be identified as the author of this work has been asserted by him in accordance with the Copyright, Designs and Patents Act 1988.

Jacket design by Chris Neale
Typeset at the University of Wales Press
Printed in Great Britain by Dinefwr Press, Llandybïe, Dyfed

EDITORS' FOREWORD

Since the Second World War, Welsh history has attracted considerable scholarly attention and enjoyed a vigorous popularity. Not only have the approaches, both traditional and new, to the study of history in general been successfully applied to Wales's past, but the number of scholars engaged in this enterprise has multiplied during these years. These advances have been especially marked in the University of Wales.

In order to make more widely available the conclusions of recent research, much of it of limited accessibility in postgraduate dissertations and theses, in 1977 the History and Law Committee of the Board of Celtic Studies inaugurated a new series of monographs, *Studies in Welsh History*. It was anticipated that many of the volumes would originate in research conducted in the University of Wales or under the auspices of the Board of Celtic Studies. But the series does not exclude significant contributions made by researchers in other universities and elsewhere. Its primary aim is to serve historical scholarship and to encourage the study of Welsh history. Each volume so far published has fulfilled that aim in ample measure, and it is a pleasure to welcome the most recent addition to the list.

CONTENTS

EDITORS' FOREWORD	v
ACKNOWLEDGEMENTS	xi
ABBREVIATIONS	
INTRODUCTION	1
I THE EDUCATION ACT OF 1870: THE DEBATE IN WALES	20
II THE BATTLE FOR THE BOARDS	47
III HIGH PRINCIPLES AT THE PARISH PUMP	93
IV DIFFICULTY AND PROGRESS	132
V 'TO EDUCATE AND NOT TO PROSELYTISE'	158
VI THE WELSH LANGUAGE	179
VII 'I CAN LEARN HIM BETTER MYSELF AT HOME'	213
VIII THE TEACHER IN WELSH SOCIETY	237
CONCLUSION: RESTING ON LAURELS: EDUCATION AT THE TURN OF THE CENTURY	261
BIBLIOGRAPHY	282
INDEX	294

ACKNOWLEDGEMENTS

This study considers the implementation of the 1870 Elementary Education Act in Wales and its relevance to the political, social and educational development of the country in the closing decades of the nineteenth century. It considers the importance of elementary schools in the evolving Welsh education system; second, it analyses the debate concerning the establishment of School Boards in the context of the wider discussion about the democratization of Welsh local government; third, it considers the effect that religious differences had on the elementary schools; and, fourth, it examines the experiences of those who sought to build the Welsh elementary school system. The work is based on my thesis entitled 'Elementary education and Welsh society, 1870–1902', which was undertaken at the University of Wales, Swansea, and awarded the degree of Ph.D. by the University of Wales in 1995. During the research period, I received invaluable assistance from the staff of the National Library of Wales, the County Record Offices of the then counties of Clwyd, Gwynedd, Dyfed, Gwent and Glamorgan as well as the West Glamorgan Archive Service and the City of Swansea Archive. Mention should also be made of the assistance received at public libraries in Cardiff, Merthyr, Swansea and Llanelli and at the libraries of University of Wales Swansea, and University College of North Wales, Bangor. The staff at the Public Record Office, London, operated with admirable efficiency as did the archive staff at NUT headquarters, also in London.

My greatest debts, however, are personal. My efforts at Swansea were encouraged by my supervisor, Dr David Howell, who inspired my interest in nineteenth-century Wales and who provided fascinating insights into the period as well as giving freely of his time. The late Professor David J. V. Jones took a keen interest in the work and I shall always be grateful to him for his guidance and his eager willingness to share his knowledge and understanding of modern Wales. More recently, at the

ACKNOWLEDGEMENTS

University of Wales Centre for Welsh and Celtic Studies at Aberystwyth, I received generous support and encouragement from the Director, Professor Geraint H. Jenkins. Professor Ieuan Gwynedd Jones, Professor Glanmor Williams and Professor Gareth Elwyn Jones read various versions of the original manuscript and made many, immensely valuable, comments about how the work could be improved. I owe a special debt of thanks to Mrs Dot Jones of Aberystwyth, not least for her assistance with the statistical evidence contained in this volume. Colleagues at the Centre for Advanced Welsh and Celtic Studies have been a much-valued source of support and fellowship during the period in which I have been writing this work. Particular thanks go to David Llewelyn Jones, Mari Williams and Gwenfair Parry, all of whom opened my eyes to new themes and fresh avenues of scholarly research. I discussed various aspects of the work at length with Professor Hywel Teifi Edwards, Matthew Cragoe, Eryn White, Paul O'Leary, W. Gareth Evans, Neil Evans and Huw Walters. Professor Ralph Griffiths and Dr Chris Williams gave freely of their time and this volume would be much poorer were it not for their generous advice and guidance. Ceinwen Jones and other staff at the University of Wales Press steered the book to publication with great patience. I should like to record my gratitude to my parents for their selfless help over many years and I thank my father for his observations, especially in the closing months of this work. My wife's parents also gave much practical help that was invaluable in bringing this work to fruition. The greatest debt of all is to my wife Ann for her patience and forbearance, and to our son, Alun, who has brought so much love and happiness into our lives.

April 1999

ABBREVIATIONS

CDH	*Carnarvon and Denbigh Herald*
CRO	County Record Office
DWB	*Dictionary of Welsh Biography*
LLG	*Llanelly and County Guardian*
NLW	National Library of Wales
NUET	National Union of Elementary Teachers
PP	British Parliamentary Papers
PRO	Public Record Office
THSC	*Transactions of the Honourable Society of Cymmrodorion*
WHR	*Welsh History Review*

INTRODUCTION

'The present educational system of Wales is a distinctively Victorian work, and is the chief practical achievement of Wales in the Victorian era.' The words of T. F. Roberts, Principal of the University College at Aberystwyth, written in 1897, expressed the pride, shared by the nation's political leaders, in the creation of an edifice that rose from elementary schools, through the intermediate schools to the colleges of higher education and the University of Wales.[1] His words are echoed by others such as J. Herbert Roberts, who referred to the University of Wales as the 'crown and coping stone of the educational edifice' and who concluded that 'a new spirit has walked the land; new hopes of the future, new ideas of public duty have appeared; our young men have seen visions, and old men have dreamed dreams, and we face the future with courage and with confidence.'[2] Historians have also commended the conspicuous achievements of the years of Liberal ascendancy which had ensured a coherent educational system and the formulation of that distinctive meritocracy which has been identified as a defining characteristic of the modern Welsh nation. Yet, although the provisions made at intermediate and university level have attracted much appreciative appraisal, the achievements in elementary education, despite their unquestioned importance, have been somewhat neglected in modern historical commentary.[3] It was at this level, none the less, that basic instruction would be provided, and for the overwhelming

---

[1] T. F. Roberts, 'Sixty years of education', *Young Wales*, III (August 1897), 145–52.

[2] J. Herbert Roberts, 'The century's progress in Wales', *Transactions of the Liverpool Welsh National Society*, 15 (January 1899), 23–39.

[3] For the aspirations focused upon the foundation of a University and the provision made for secondary education, J. G. Williams, *The University Movement in Wales* (Cardiff, 1993), pp.1–19; T. I. Ellis, *The Development of Higher Education in Wales* (Wrexham, 1938), pp.21–54; idem, 'The development of modern Welsh secondary education', *THSC*, 1932–3, 1–39; E. L. Ellis, *The University College of Wales Aberystwyth, 1872–1972* (Cardiff, 1972), pp.1–32; G. E. Jones, *Controls and Conflicts in Welsh Secondary Education, 1889–1944* (Cardiff, 1982), pp.1–12; J. R. Webster, 'Welsh intermediate schools: creating the system', in W. G. Evans (ed.), *Perspectives on a Century of Secondary Education in Wales, 1889–1989* (Aberystwyth, 1990), pp.29–42 with references cited.

majority of Welsh children this limited provision would constitute their sole experience of formal education. Commentators on the state of Welsh society, from the early years of the nineteenth century onwards, were agreed that a comprehensive provision of rudimentary educational facilities was essential for society's regeneration. Elementary schools were perceived as the vital instruments in the effort to inculcate a reasonable level of literacy and numeracy in the population at large, quite apart from providing the essential foundation from which pupils might proceed, possibly in some number, to more advanced institutions of learning. It was almost inevitable that the issue of elementary education should stimulate a prolonged and tenacious argument, a protracted debate between, on the one hand, those who emerged as representatives of their society and, on the other hand, those who exercised authority in central government and its agencies. It also stirred vigorous argument within Welsh society as the search for solutions exposed the doctrinal and social distinctions that characterized the nineteenth century in Wales. The creative tension of these several processes and the achievement, after exceedingly long neglect, of a system of elementary education worthy of the children of Wales are the subjects of this volume.

By setting up an inquiry into the state of education in Wales in 1846, the government took an initiative which could conceivably have established the basis for a broad agreement on a comprehensive system of elementary education.[4] Government concern at the serious inadequacy of elementary schooling was certainly shared by public opinion in Wales. Equally there was an acute consciousness of the fact that educational neglect and the serious social problems apparent in Welsh society were connected, and the appointment of the Commission was itself a reflection of these concerns. Shaken by the unrest of the Rebecca Riots and the Chartist disturbances, the government initiated a review which sought to address the immediate issue of schooling in the context of deep-rooted social concerns, matters which had, indeed, been

---

[4] PP 1847, XXVII, Report of the Commissioners of Inquiry into the State of Education in Wales.

INTRODUCTION

discussed in earlier reports.[5] But, in the event, the Reports published in 1847 proved deeply divisive. The investigation found incontrovertible evidence of the sorry state of elementary schooling and set the deficiencies within a wider social dimension. The Reports also contained a damning indictment of the moral comportment of the Welsh people.[6] The charges of prodigality and dishonesty, and especially the accusation of unchastity among Welsh women, ensured that the publication of the Reports was met in the Welsh press with an outpouring of anger which marked a turning-point in nineteenth-century public opinion.[7] Patently inaccurate in many of their comments, the Reports reflected a failure on the part of the Commissioners, who professed the Anglican communion, to comprehend informed opinion on issues which required objective and sensitive consideration. Aggrieved by the slur upon their fellow countrymen who were largely of a Nonconformist persuasion, and resentful of the fact that their views had been discounted, the leaders of Nonconformity reacted with indignation and vehemence to the calumny.

If the affront to moral sensibilities embodied in the Reports elicited a fierce and unambiguous rebuttal from a broad swathe of Welsh public opinion, the response on other issues was far more equivocal. The role of the Welsh language in educational provision had been a major issue in the inquiry. The government

---

[5] This point is highlighted by G. E. Jones, 'Llyfrau Gleision 1847', in P. T. J. Morgan (ed.), *Brad y Llyfrau Gleision* (Llandysul, 1991), pp.22–48. While the intention of the 1847 Report was to consider the state of education provision, it also offered an opportunity to undertake a wider survey of the political and social condition of Wales. The alarm felt in government circles concerning disturbances such as Rebecca and the Chartist movement cannot be underestimated, particularly in view of the situation prevailing in Ireland. Thus, as Jones argues (ibid., p.24), the Report was influenced by the government's desire to increase its authority in Wales. Key studies include D. J. V. Jones, *Rebecca's Children* (Oxford, 1989), esp. pp.199–255; idem, *The Last Rising: The Newport Insurrection of 1839* (Oxford, 1985), esp. pp.7–84; David Williams, *John Frost: A Study in Chartism* (Cardiff, 1939), esp. pp.95–164; idem, *The Rebecca Riots* (Cardiff, 1955), pp.90–157, 289–91.

[6] I. G. Jones, *Mid-Victorian Wales: The Observers and the Observed* (Cardiff, 1992), pp.1–23, 103–65; idem, '1848 ac 1868: Brad y Llyfrau Gleision a gwleidyddiaeth Cymru', in Morgan (ed.), *Brad y Llyfrau Gleision*, pp.49–73. William Williams, MP for Coventry, a native of Llanpumpsaint, Carmarthenshire, prompted the inquiry into education in Wales which was conducted in 1846–7.

[7] The inspectors responsible for the Report, R. R. W. Lingen, J. C. Symons and H. V. Johnson, had respectable academic qualifications yet were hampered in their inquiry, not only by their lack of knowledge of the Welsh language, but also by their use of methods which might have been appropriate in England but were not so in Wales. This is particularly the case with their reliance on the evidence of members of the Anglican Church to the virtual exclusion of representatives of Nonconformist denominations. In the case of Symons, the difficulty was exacerbated by an abrasive turn of phrase. Jones, *Mid-Victorian Wales*, pp.149–65.

had been persuaded to appoint a Commission to inquire into 'the state of education in the Principality of Wales, especially into the means afforded to the labouring classes of acquiring a knowledge of the English language', and the Home Secretary himself had referred to the 'peculiar difficulty from the existence of an ancient language'.[8] In the Commissioners' Reports the language was portrayed as an impediment to pupils' advancement and a barrier to a broad-based social improvement. Moreover, language and Nonconformity were perceived as twin disadvantages which stultified progress.[9] The constructive efforts of the Welsh people to express their beliefs and aspirations in an expanding body of literature and in a vigorous periodical press in the Welsh language were largely ignored. Yet, whereas the obloquies on the nation's morality could be refuted in forceful and often eloquent terms, the issue of the Welsh language evoked ambivalent attitudes even among the most stalwart defenders of the nation's honour, and the substance of the Commissioners' comments would influence opinion on educational provision throughout the period considered in this present study.[10]

Equally revealing of the profound fissures within enlightened opinion in Wales were the denominational rivalries which were laid bare in the responses to the Reports. The Nonconformists were, not unnaturally, deeply antipathetic to Church schools for it was feared that the Church would seek to use its schools as a means of inculcating doctrines at odds with cherished Nonconformist beliefs. The Nonconformist riposte could reasonably concentrate on the unsuitability of the three young Anglican lawyers to undertake their commission, unfamiliar as they undoubtedly were with the communities that they investigated. They could be seen to have compounded their difficulty by limiting themselves to the evidence of those of their own persuasion – Anglican clergymen and landowners – who had an ideological antipathy towards the Nonconformist denominations at a time when pronounced doctrinal differences were entrenched in rigid denominational postures. Moreover, the efforts of the Sunday schools to provide a measure of formal instruction had been little

---

[8] These are the terms in which William Williams moved the motion for an inquiry in the Commons in March 1846; Jones, *Mid-Victorian Wales*, pp.123–7.
[9] Ibid., pp.137–8.
[10] Ibid., pp.109–23.

regarded and much adverse comment made on the role of Nonconformist ministers. But the issues of religious instruction in schools had fostered deep divisions within the Nonconformist denominations themselves. A vociferous group advocated totally secular schools while an increasingly large number sought a non-denominational form of religious instruction that would be acceptable to all Christians. The principle of state aid in education, a long-debated issue in Welsh Nonconformist ranks, was, likewise, a source of division and many of those who influenced opinion remained fearful that such assistance would place the schools under the control of a state which was inextricably linked to the established Anglican Church. Such issues divided the critics of the Reports of 1847 and, although united in their condemnation of the Commissioners, the fault-lines, visible not only between Nonconformist and Anglican but also within Nonconformity, were not easily bridged and remained a stubborn and almost insurmountable barrier to concerted action.

Yet, despite the marked response, even the most resolute critic of the Reports would have had to concede that education provision in both the rural and industrial communities of Wales fell lamentably short of what was necessary for the social and economic well-being of a civilized society. For, despite the determined efforts made by Welsh leaders to challenge many of the Commissioners' conclusions and to demonstrate the fragile foundations on which they were based, it was also the case that those who sought to promote education in Wales acknowledged the accuracy of much of the findings. Lewis Edwards, in his erudite and considered response to the Reports of 1847, while on the one hand offering a strong vindication of the moral probity and spiritual character of his countrymen, also laid stress on a need for basic educational provision. The three Commissioners, while not equally perceptive nor indeed prudent in their observations, had highlighted the gross inadequacy of existing facilities in their extensively documented Reports. R. R. W. Lingen, in an appendix rightly described as one 'of extraordinary power and import', identified educational need as one of the main difficulties confronting Welsh society.[11] Moreover, much of the substance of the Reports, when shorn of the gratuitous

---

[11] I. G. Jones, *Mid-Victorian Wales*, pp.1–23. Lingen was to have a distinguished career as an educational administrator and alderman of the London County Council.

rhetoric which so incensed the nation's defenders, was entirely in accord with the sentiments of earlier investigators who, far from revealing an antipathy to the people of Wales, were acutely sensitive to the social conditions which framed their lives. Particularly penetrating enquiries had been made into the state of education in the industrial areas of south Wales in the work of G. S. Kendrick and Seymour Tremenheere, while Joseph Fletcher, a school inspector, was likewise representative of those who offered informed and sensitive comment. Long before the Commission of 1847 embarked on its task, the backward state of education at the most elementary level had been identified as a factor which not only reflected but also perpetuated adverse social conditions. The social circumstances of industrial communities had been described in especially graphic terms, but those in rural areas also inspired poignant criticism. Indeed, when the educational provision available to Welsh children before 1847 is examined without prejudice, it is difficult to avoid the conclusion that Wales was a land whose children and young people were seriously and culpably disadvantaged.

What the Reports of 1847 had, in fact, brought to the fore were the almost intractable problems and limited progress achieved in providing even basic educational opportunities. In many areas educational facilities were entirely absent and in others sorely inadequate, testimony to the failure of both the National Society of the Anglican Church and the Nonconformist-led British and Foreign School Society to meet the community's needs. This failure had much to do with the mutual hostility, based on religious and social differences, between the societies. But, as has been noted already, it was also in part due to the reluctance of Nonconformist denominations to accept government assistance for education provision, and those parents who were concerned to educate their young children often had no choice but to ensure that their offspring availed themselves of whatever instruction could be gained from existing private and adventure schools.

None the less, the Reports served to galvanize the leaders of Welsh opinion into action on education.[12] On the Anglican side,

[12] These points are made by Frank Price Jones, *Radicaliaeth a'r Werin Gymreig yn y Bedwaredd Ganrif ar Bymtheg* (Cardiff, 1977), pp.48–64. Jones rightly points to the serious deficiencies in educational provision in Wales in 1847, a fact which was lost in the general furore which followed the publication of the report. PP 1870, XIII, Report of the Commission on the Employment of Children, Young Persons and Women in Agriculture, Vol. 3.

efforts were again made to expand the provision of National schools and training centres, exemplified by the opening of colleges in Carmarthen in 1848 and Caernarfon in 1849. The British Society redoubled its efforts to build schools, not least through the endeavours of William Roberts (Nefydd), who was appointed to join Thomas Phillips as organizer for the society. The teacher-training institution, Bangor Normal College, was expanded, and any reservations harboured by the older dissenters about the propriety of accepting government grants were removed. Just as important in preparing the ground for later initiatives was the remarkable transformation in the attitudes of those Nonconformist ministers who emerged as assertive political as well as religious leaders. The expansion of the Nonconformist press, and the increasingly radical statements of editors such as William Rees (Gwilym Hiraethog) and Samuel Roberts, enriched and sharpened the political consciousness of the Nonconformist community in Wales. Along with an increasing sophistication in their organization, the denominations developed into an effective religious force with a potential for political action through democratic institutions which would have been unrecognizable to earlier leaders of dissent.[13] Moreover, in the two decades following the publication of the Commissioners' Reports a measure of economic prosperity was witnessed. Although conditions in rural society remained difficult, this was a period of increased prosperity in the agricultural sector. The expansion of the iron and coal industries likewise generated a confident, vibrant society and one which offered new opportunities for those born in rural Wales who provided a steady flow of thousands of workers to the coalfields of the south. The advent of wealth-creating industries and varied commercial enterprises created new opportunities for an expanding and young population. Economic deprivation was, in some measure, alleviated and social legislation eased some of the dire hardships which had afflicted so many families. Partly as a result of the economic expansion, the militancy represented by Chartism and by Rebecca receded and the atmosphere of sedition, which had once permeated a whole society and

---

[13] I. G. Jones and D. Williams (eds.), *The Religious Census of 1851: A Calendar of the Returns Relating to Wales*, 2 vols (Cardiff, 1975–6).

tarnished its language, was dispelled. A new political leadership drawn from a middle class of business leaders and professional men was emerging. Centred on the Nonconformist chapel, attuned to the needs and aspirations of their societies, and distinct from the landed gentry who had traditionally dominated Welsh politics, an alternative leadership, dedicated to Liberal politics and determined to achieve political recognition, came to the fore. Elementary education, hitherto sorely neglected, became a focus of a new political will expounded by a new and articulate leadership.[14]

On the eve of the introduction of the Liberal government's legislation for elementary education for England and Wales in 1870, Welsh education was again subjected to scrutiny as evidence was gathered by the Commission engaged in the preparation of the Report on the Employment of Children, Young People and Women in Agriculture. Specifically concerned with the rural localities, the Commissioners were asked to make recommendations on how the Factory Acts could be amended to meet the needs of children in rural communities, to seek means of providing better educational facilities for those children and to ensure that they attended school on a regular basis. The enquiry provided an opportunity to assess the progress made since 1847 but refrained from unnecessary indulgence in sententious and provocative comment. At the same time, it furnished the government with information which could guide its approach to the drafting of new legislation, not least by canvassing a broader swathe of opinion among those in Wales who were concerned with the provision of educational opportunities.

The Report, when it was published in 1870 after a three-year inquiry, reflected some of the gains which had undoubtedly been made since 1847. Schools had been built through voluntary effort, and teaching had improved as greater numbers of qualified teachers had been attracted. Moreover, the Revised Code, introduced in 1862, had initiated a system whereby the annual grant to schools was determined according to pupils'

[14] I. G. Jones, *Explorations and Explanations* (Llandysul, 1981), pp.83–216.

performance in the annual examination. Despite the serious problems which this system created (not least by excluding Welsh as a grant-earning subject and therefore ensuring the neglect of the language by the majority of schools), teachers had been required to develop a style of teaching which could result in satisfactory examination results and to address a curriculum which was laid down by central government rather than by their own predilections. The Report also found that a significant number of Welsh public leaders were satisfied with the system of providing the voluntary bodies with financial assistance for school-building and with a system for their voluntary management. Indeed, some individuals such as the Revd J. W. Ellis, rector of Llanaelhaearn (Caernarfonshire), went so far as to claim that the system already in place had ensured that each child had access to a place in a school.

Even so, his confident assertions were belied by the mass of evidence which the Commissioners collected. The advancement of educational facilities in the rural localities was hampered by the geographical isolation of remote hamlet communities and dispersed and secluded farmhouses whose children were unable to reach even those schools located within reasonable proximity to their homes. Demographic change introduced new considerations as the pattern of settlement in Wales increasingly revolved around new industries and new centres of commerce. The continued migration from rural to urban areas denuded the rural schools of their constituency of pupils and this caused acute difficulties for existing establishments. School managers were denied the capitation allowance that was earned by each pupil who passed the annual examination, and reduced numbers in these areas also meant that the amount accruing from the school pence was lower and that fewer donations were made by the parents in support of the schools.

If difficulties were evident in those rural localities where a measure of schooling was already provided, still greater challenges were presented by those areas where educational provision was lacking. Many populous neighbourhoods were deprived of a school through the absence of wealthy patrons or other means of subsidizing school-building. Such drawbacks proved serious, especially in view of the fact that a significant portion of the cost of establishing a school had to be raised locally in order to qualify for a government grant to assist with remaining costs. Even the financial support which the National Society and the British and Foreign School Society could provide proved inadequate to surmount the problems faced by the more impoverished districts which found themselves unable to raise the necessary resources, a point noted by the Revd John Pugh, vicar of Llanbadarn Fawr, who observed that 'a great many parishes are really too poor to find the requisite amount to entitle them to government assistance'; furthermore, he questioned whether the educational needs of such areas could possibly be met without government initiative.[15] Indeed, in neighbouring Aberystwyth, where the resources of a business and professional class might conceivably have provided a measure of financial assistance, the deficiencies of the town's educational provision were described by John Davies, a solicitor and land agent in the town, in evidence to the Commission. Noting the location of the single school hitherto established in the north of the town and the total absence of provision for the large number of children resident in the harbour area of Trefechan, he claimed that, although considerable expenditure had been incurred by the leaders of the town's Nonconformist society in other directions, most notably in the erection of magnificent edifices, the construction of day schools had not figured high among their priorities.[16]

While the issue of poverty and its consequences for educational provision may have imparted a measure of unity among Anglican and Nonconformists alike, other issues left them deeply divided. Admittedly, instances of co-operation between the representatives of the diverse denominations were by no means uncommon. John Pugh, for example, noted that there was 'every disposition on the part of the clergy to co-operate with dissenters in establishing schools' and emphasized the atmosphere of mutual tolerance which prevailed.[17] In later times, too, when divisions had hardened, several communities could recall a period of understanding between Nonconformists and Anglicans when rigid conventions had been discarded for the greater good of providing a school. Such magnanimous attitudes, however, were hardly the

[15] PP 1870, XIII, Report of the Commission on the Employment of Children, Vol. 3.
[16] Ibid.
[17] Ibid.

norm. In too many cases British and National schools were locked in a vain competition, with the result that while some areas were amply provided with schools others were left destitute. By 1870, indeed, Nonconformist opinion was becoming convinced that an independent body, free of sectarian motives, had to be charged with the provision of elementary schools and that the state alone could properly undertake the role. They looked to the legislation proposed by the Liberal Party as a means of overcoming the religious divisions in education, and while they were to be satisfied by initiatives such as the ending of denominationally based school inspection, they were to be disappointed by the failure to end the Church's role in the management of state-aided schools. This failure in the legislation was to ensure that the question of elementary education occupied the minds of yet another generation of Welsh leaders, never to be resolved to the entire satisfaction of either Nonconformist or Anglican.

Poverty and sectarian division were undoubtedly inhibiting influences. But the Employment Commission of 1867–70 noted a further difficulty, namely the failure of those responsible for education provision to ensure that existing facilities were used to the full. True, George Cully's report on Carmarthenshire and Pembrokeshire and Edwin Portman's account of Breconshire testified to a burgeoning sense among parents of the value of educating their children. Both noted that the presence of large industrial conurbations nearby had stimulated the rural population to take full advantage of the opportunities available, and, with regard to Crickhowell, Portman was of the opinion that parental demand was of such an order of magnitude that 'nothing more was needed than to establish efficient schools'.[18] But the more common impression was that formed by Tremenheere who, in his report on Cardiganshire, Montgomeryshire and Merioneth, painted a very different picture. He wrote at length of the difficulties caused by children who attended school during the winter months only and who spent the summer engaged in all manner of menial tasks. Parental apathy and the use of child labour were, in fact, cited as often as financial exigency as a cause of irregular attendance. Tremenheere, for instance, concluded:

[18] Ibid.

> In Cardiganshire it is usual for children to attend school between the ages of 9 and 13 but to be absent for half that time in gainful employment as seasonal agricultural workers. This is also true in the eastern portion of Montgomeryshire despite the fact that there is less poverty there than in Cardiganshire, indeed the general rate of wages is comparatively high.[19]

The report also cited the comments of Owen Jones, a land agent in Caernarfonshire who, aside from appreciating the difficulties caused by a failure to establish schools, noted the negligent attitude of many parents:

> I don't think that the state of education at present is satisfactory. There are not enough schools and the children are taken away too young. There is an immense number of children now growing up without the power of reading and writing. There is no agricultural work which really interferes with the education. The main obstacle to education is the indifference of the parents. Education never will be satisfactory as long as it is left to the option of the parents whether they send their children to school or not.[20]

His observations were echoed by J. D. Jones, master of Ruthin British School. While admitting that many children were expected to find work at an early age in order to supplement family income, he doubted whether financial necessity was the main reason why Welsh parents failed to take full advantage of the opportunities that were available to them:

> There was really no work which the boys did for the farmers which interfered with their education. It is very rare for a boy to stay away to scare birds, but they sometimes remain at home, with my leave, to assist their parents in planting potatoes,

the sons of tenant farmers being 'more likely to absent themselves than were the sons of agricultural labourers'.[21] The Report discovered a pattern of irregular attendance, even in those areas where wages were comparatively high, the situation being made worse by the early leaving age prevalent in most areas.

[19] Ibid.
[20] Ibid.
[21] Ibid.

Educational provision in the urban areas was also clearly inadequate other than in older towns such as Cardiff, Swansea, Cowbridge, Abergavenny, Neath and Aberafan. Seymour Tremenheere found the number of schools in western Monmouthshire wholly unsatisfactory in his report in 1840, and the 1847 Report demonstrated the extent of educational deprivation in Glamorgan.[22] In both Monmouthshire and Glamorgan educational need was continually increasing due to a steady inflow of people, especially young people, from Wales and further afield. Numerous schemes had been developed to provide at least some educational opportunities to Glamorgan's pupils. The 1847 Report identified over one hundred schools associated with the Anglican Church in Glamorgan; the assistance of industrialists such as the Guest family in Dowlais and the Vivian family in Swansea, sometimes combined with contributions from workers, maintained commodious schools staffed by trained teachers. Moreover, the era of the Nonconformist industrialist, associated with the expansion of the coal industry, saw the foundation of numerous British schools such as those which were to satisfy the educational need of the Rhondda until the mid-1870s. In addition, efforts to promote educational opportunities in the coalfield benefited from the more structured work carried out both by the Anglicans and the representatives of the British and Foreign School Society. Prominent churchmen such as Alexander Stammers, John Griffiths and Connop Thirlwall sought to co-ordinate the provision of Church schools and Thomas Phillips and William Roberts were engaged in unsparing efforts to supply some of the needs of the mainly Nonconformist community in west Monmouthshire and the eastern part of Glamorgan. Such initiatives were, however, not adequate to satisfy the needs of Glamorgan's children. Attendance was irregular, buildings were often of poor quality, overcrowding was rife, equipment was substandard and, despite some notable exceptions, many teachers had little more than the most basic training. The Revised Code of 1862 based central government's contribution to the maintenance of a school on a more stringent annual examination and this again exposed the

---

[22] E. T. Davies, *Monmouthshire Schools and Education to 1870* (Newport, 1957), pp.78–9; Gareth E. Jones, *The Education of a Nation* (Cardiff, 1997), p.35.

inadequacies of many schools in Glamorgan and Monmouthshire. The schools also suffered from more fundamental defects. A system of education that was dependent on the patronage of industrialists and private sponsors inevitably suffered as economic fluctuations affected the ability of those companies to contribute to the maintenance of schools. The system was unaccountable, and the emphasis placed by many schools on an Anglican form of religious instruction was clearly liable to offend a large section of the population. At the same time, the curriculum of the schools was often limited to the most basic instruction. There were few opportunities to develop courses to prepare pupils for the requirements of an industrial society, and technical education was largely neglected.

The Report of the Employment Commission between 1867 and 1870, combined with the evidence of the school inspectors, made disappointing reading to the generation of Welsh educationists who had made a determined effort to overcome deficiencies identified in 1847. In the first place, the limited progress achieved in creating a coherent system of elementary education was undoubtedly frustrating. The standards attained in Welsh schools were a source of anxiety and school inspectors had regularly criticized both the poor examination results and the standard of discipline. Untrained masters teaching in inefficient and unsatisfactory schools provided the only education available to many and the instruction obtained was too often equated with the rote learning of enough facts (and, indeed, sufficient passages of English) to qualify for capitation grants. Despite some exceptions, pupils were regularly subjected to the strictures of teachers who lacked proper training and who, in some cases, had made little effort to acquire the best teaching methods. For their part, the teachers themselves worked in classrooms where children could not be relied on to be present and in localities where there was little parental support for their efforts. Moreover, poorly remunerated for their labours, their social status in the neighbourhoods where they lived was ill-defined and uncertain. Many were regarded as 'failures' who had been unable to secure work in more established professions or as skilled workers. The teacher's low social status undoubtedly reflected the fact that many in the profession were of limited intelligence, were often untrained and had little aptitude for their work, yet it also ignored the presence of many able and committed teachers. As is seen in chapter 8, these factors continued to influence public perceptions of teachers long after the passing of the 1870 Education Act.

Second, although the Commission of 1867–70 certainly points to a more sympathetic analysis of the needs of society than had been the case in the earlier Reports, its findings none the less indicate that some of the prejudices manifested in 1847 continued to colour the views of public servants and, indeed, of a significant body of opinion in Wales. The Welsh language was deprecated and identified as the biggest obstacle to educational progress. Social and economic well-being, it was stressed, depended on the Welsh acquiring a thorough knowledge of English. It was claimed that the advent of railways had stimulated the Welsh people's desire to learn English and even in the heart of the Welsh-speaking county of Merioneth, as Tremenheere had noted, the farmers had 'expressed strong desires that as a living language Welsh would soon become extinct' and that its inconveniences were felt daily. Acutely aware of the fact that such knowledge of English that had been acquired through the elementary schools was limited and, in the rural areas, 'seldom more than the most imperfect and mechanical kind', the Commissioners considered the failure of Welsh education to ensure that children gained fluency in English to be its most serious deficiency; no attempt was made to assess the intrinsic value of Welsh or the advantages of a bilingual proficiency. The assumptions that English was the language of learning and of national progress and that its diffusion should be the mission of Welsh schools were deeply embedded in official circles and among a significant portion of Welsh people. Such sentiments were undoubtedly influenced by the climate created by the report of 1847 and were to continue to play their part in the debate surrounding education in Wales in the late nineteenth century.

The atmosphere of religious rivalry and occasional bitterness likewise continued. The mid-nineteenth century in Wales may have witnessed the climax of the doctrinal arguments and thereafter theological differences would occupy less of the public's attention. Even so, Nonconformists and Anglicans became embroiled in an often acerbic debate as the privileged position of the Anglican Church became a political issue. Opposition to the payment of tithes to what was, for the majority, an alien church, and support for the disestablishment of the Anglican Church, became an essential part of the Liberal Party's programme. Alarmed by the rise of High Anglicanism, the Nonconformist denominations argued that the control of education by the Anglican Church was abhorrent and constituted an unacceptable manifestation of the privileges of a minority. Propagandists, among whom Henry Richard was a persuasive figure, offered a particularly daunting depiction of conditions in Wales; at the same time they accepted that the Nonconformist denominations lacked an abundance of wealthy patrons and sufficient charitable endowments and did not possess the financial resources to match the performance of the Anglican Church.[23] These considerations were critical in engendering the Liberals' manifesto commitment in 1868 to legislate on elementary education, even though the legislative proposals that were subsequently brought forward failed to satisfy an important section of Nonconformist and Liberal Wales.

Introduced by W. E. Forster in February 1870, the Education Bill received its third reading on 22 July 1870 and the royal assent on 9 August. It proposed to create machinery that would enable the deficiencies in the existing school provision to be addressed. Accordingly, it stipulated that England and Wales should be divided into school districts based on boroughs and parishes. Where a parish was partly within and partly without a borough, the part outside the borough was to form a parish by itself for the purposes of the Act, and, in certain cases, parishes or boroughs could be amalgamated to form a united school district.[24] The

---

[23] In 1867, Richard published a collection of essays written to W. E. Gladstone, *Letters on the Social and Political Condition of Wales* (London, 1867). The contents of that volume were republished in 1884 as *Letters and Essays on Wales* (London, 1884).

[24] In order to ascertain the exact needs of each locality, the school inspectors were dispatched to undertake a detailed survey of the extent and quality of the existing school accommodation. The requirements were assessed by taking the population of each parish and estimating the child population as one-eighth of the total. The inspectors also had the responsibility of estimating whether schools which were not of an acceptable standard could be improved and whether the voluntary agencies were capable of doing so. The information is recorded in PRO, ED2 files 577–640.

government would determine the amount of accommodation required in each parish, based on a formula that assumed that provision would need to be made for one-eighth of the population of each area. All schools which did not charge more than nine pence per scholar per week would be assessed in terms both of efficiency and of suitability of premises, and if they were found to be inadequate in any way their managers would be given an opportunity to make good these deficiencies. In those areas where there was a serious shortage of accommodation, the voluntary agencies would be given a period of grace to attempt to provide a school and, in accordance with the practice in existence since 1863, they would be entitled to a government grant to assist them with the task. Those grants would, however, cease after December 1870, and after 31 March 1871 no school which was not recognized by the Education Department under the criteria of the 1870 Act would be eligible to receive a government grant.

In those areas where a dispute arose concerning the assessment of educational need or the condition of the existing schools, the Education Department could initiate an inquiry. If no action had been taken to remedy the deficiency within six months of the announcement of the Department's final decision, it had the power to order that a School Board be formed without further consultation. Where a deficiency existed, a vestry meeting was to be held to discuss ways in which the needs of the parish could be met and the meeting had the power to request the establishment of a School Board. If no agreement was reached, at the request of ten ratepayers a poll of the parish would be held in order to settle the matter. In certain cases, it would be possible to establish a School Board in parishes where no deficiency existed but where the managers of one of the voluntary schools which provided accommodation declared that they were unwilling or unable to continue to maintain their school.

Where School Boards were established they were to be elected on a triennial basis and to consist of no fewer than five members and no more than fifteen. Members were to be elected by the ratepayers on a cumulative voting system, whereby every voter was entitled to cast as many votes as there were members to be elected, and the votes could be given to one candidate or be distributed among several. The Boards were authorized to build a school and had the power to compel landowners to sell land upon which a school was to be built, although this power could only be exercised with the sanction of the Education Department and after a procedure for appeal had been exhausted. Under certain conditions, relating mainly to schools that were burdened with a heavy debt, voluntary schools could be transferred to Board control.

The Act enabled the Boards to make by-laws to compel children to attend schools, creating a situation whereby initially there was no means of compelling attendance in those areas where no Boards existed. At the same time, Boards were empowered under Section 25 of the Act to pay the school fees of children whose parents were unable to do so, or to waive the fees for the entire district. They were not empowered to instruct those parents who did receive such assistance as to the school to which they should send their children, and in consequence Board resources, derived from the ratepayers, could be used to pay fees for instruction in voluntary schools. Significantly, however, the parents who were in receipt of such assistance were not deemed to be in receipt of poor relief and therefore did not suffer loss of civic rights, as was the case with other forms of relief.

The Act made specific rules concerning religious instruction in all elementary schools which were in receipt of a parliamentary grant. No child was to be compelled to attend any Sunday school or place of religious worship as a condition of admittance to school. Parents were given the right to withdraw children from religious instruction and the lessons were to be given at the beginning or at the end of the day (or both) in order to facilitate the withdrawal of the children concerned. The times for all religious services or lessons were to be inserted in a timetable which had to be approved by the Education Department and kept permanently in a conspicuous position in the school.

All schools were to be inspected by members of Her Majesty's Inspectorate (HMI) on an annual basis. Their reports and the results of the examinations undertaken would be the basis on which the annual grant to the school would be assessed. Unlike the situation which prevailed before the Act, however, no inspector was permitted to inspect religious instruction and, although schools were permitted to invite independent examiners to assess religious instruction, no pupil could be forced to take part in that examination and the enquiries could only take place twice in every year. Board schools would face more stringent regulations in that no religious catechism nor any form of belief distinctive to any particular denomination could be taught in them. If no religious provision was desired by the School Board, the school could be completely secular.

Such, in broad outline, was the content of the Act of 1870. Its clauses stimulated a debate of outstanding importance in late nineteenth-century discourse on political and social issues in Wales. Along with tithes, the disestablishment of the Anglican Church and the land question, the issue of educational provision highlighted by the Act featured conspicuously in Liberal politics in Victorian Wales. Yet, education differed from the other issues in two vital respects. Whereas tithes, disestablishment and the land question were largely issues of concern to rural society, education was a matter which touched rural and urban communities to an equal degree. More than any other issue, education was relevant to the needs of Welsh society in its entirety. Education was different also because, more clearly than in other issues, it was a matter in which legislation by central government would need complementary action in individual localities. It placed on elected representatives in the rural and industrial communities a responsibility to implement, after a period of woeful neglect, a programme of educational reform deemed essential to the well-being of the nation. In short, it demanded that Wales embark on its apprenticeship in political democracy. The commitment of the people of Wales to learning and the growth of a true meritocracy is often regarded as signalling the emergence of a Welsh democratic society. Taking the whole of Wales as its field of study, this volume examines the creative interaction between the preoccupations of the political leadership and the aspirations and the constraints which shaped the course of events in the localities. The development of elementary education offers an exceptional opportunity to examine how ideals and reality were reconciled in a distinctive and crucial aspect of the making of modern Welsh society.

I
THE EDUCATION ACT OF 1870: THE DEBATE IN WALES

The Education Bill introduced in 1870 was a cornerstone of the legislative programme of the Liberal government that had been elected two years previously. The return of the Liberals had been assisted by the selfless determination of their adherents in Wales, many of whom risked their livelihoods in order to ensure a Liberal victory; some, indeed, suffered dispossession for the constancy of their political beliefs in the aftermath of the election. The Education Bill reflected the conviction of the Liberal leadership that education was an essential facet of improvement in a society that was gradually basing its government on democratic principles. Equally, it was realized by those who aspired to political authority that Britain's position as the pre-eminent industrial power was being challenged by the growth of foreign economies, such as those of France and Germany, whose success lay partly in their endeavour to develop an effective education system.

Before the Bill came to be presented to the Commons, the principles upon which it would be based had initiated a wide-ranging debate throughout England and Wales.[1] It certainly generated vigorous argument in Wales, both on account of its bearing on the interests and convictions of the increasingly vociferous Nonconformist community, and, particularly, due to the commitment to education which characterized its leaders. The Nonconformists were acutely aware of their own strength. The religious census of 1851 had pointed to the great preponderance of members of their denominations among the religious worshippers of Wales. Of the total recorded as being present at the evening service on the census day, the Calvinistic Methodists accounted for 29.2 per cent, the Congregationalists for 23.4 per cent, the Baptists for 18.6 per cent, the Wesleyans for 13.0 per cent, the Anglicans for 9.6 per cent and other groups for 6.2 per cent. Although there is some reason to doubt the

---

[1] Gillian Sutherland, *Policy Making in English Education* (London, 1973), p.115.

accuracy of these figures, it is clear that the Anglican community was very much a minority, and while the total number of people who claimed an association with any form of religious body was by no means overwhelming, the Nonconformists' ranks contained the majority of Welsh society. Education gained an added significance for the leaders of Nonconformity for a second, equally important, reason. A majority of them regarded education as a means of furthering the process of emancipation which had been commenced by the chapels and their Sunday schools and was a vital element in the evolution of a democratic spirit in Wales. Such aspirations were by now deeply embedded in Welsh society. As Nonconformity became a mass faith, its adherents became increasingly concerned with material betterment as well as spiritual salvation and, in the estimation of those who influenced opinion, education was the best means of achieving social progress.[2] At the same time, the Nonconformist leadership in Wales had abandoned the stance that had led its early leaders to reject government involvement in the provision of education. The denominations came to accept the need for government grants, though they came to this view only gradually. The weekly newspaper *Baner Cymru* declared in 1857 that the role of the government was to be supportive of a voluntary endeavour in which the congregations had a central function:

> Pa beth bynag a wna y llywodraeth mewn ffordd o gynhorthwy, dylai wneyd hyny bob amser mewn dull darostyngedig i'r egwyddor wirfoddol, fel ag i beidio rhoi dim rhwystr neu ddigalondid i'r ymdrechion a'r trefniadau lleol a phersonol hyny pa rai ydynt yr anghreifftiau a'r profion mwyaf gwerthfawr o grefydd ymarferol yn mhlith cymmydogion.

> [Whatever the government does to support education should always be done in full acknowledgement of voluntary principle, so that no obstacle nor discouragement is given to those local and personal efforts and arrangements which are the most valuable examples of practical religion among neighbours.][3]

This standpoint was acknowledged by 1870 as the Nonconformists increasingly demanded government provision of education

---
[2] David Jenkins, *The Agricultural Community in South-West Wales at the Turn of the Twentieth Century* (Cardiff, 1971), pp.209–10.
[3] *Baner*, 4 March 1857.

rather than assistance with its maintenance. This clearly indicated that the liberal doctrine that the state should have only a minimal influence on the life of the individual had been tempered quite considerably; although it was not yet asserted that the state should be the servant of its people, there was certainly a greater acceptance of the desirability of action by the state. However, the principle that there should be no connection between the state and the provision of any particular form of religious instruction remained a cardinal feature of Nonconformist belief. As a great proportion of the existing educational provision was made under the management of the Anglican Church, and in view of the bearing of this upon the education of Nonconformist children, the precise provisions of the 1870 Education Bill were matters of major concern for their leaders.[4]

During the period from the 1868 election to the close of 1869, many of the concerns of the Welsh Nonconformists had been articulated through organizations such as the National Education League, based in Birmingham. Established by Joseph Chamberlain and Jesse Collings, the League had formulated an approach whereby local authorities would be granted the power to establish schools in the areas where none existed, schools financed by the rates and wherein no religious dogma could be taught.[5] This scheme, formulated by the autumn of 1869, was not accepted by a significant body within the League's Welsh branches, however. In January 1870 the Merthyr branch withdrew from the League and declared itself a separate organization, forming the basis of the Welsh Education Alliance.[6] The secretary of the Merthyr branch, Evan Williams, in a letter to

---

[4] These issues are discussed, in detail, in M. V. George, 'An assessment of the contribution of Henry Richard to education', M.Ed. thesis, University of Wales, 1975.

[5] Ryland Wallace, *Organise! Organise! Organise! A Study of Reform Agitation in Wales, 1840–1886* (Cardiff, 1991), pp.146, 185–97. Jesse Collings (1831–1920) was MP for Ipswich and a member of the Birmingham Corporation. Closely associated with Joseph Chamberlain, he was a founder of the National Education League and served as its secretary at the time of the debate concerning the Forster Bill.

[6] The Birmingham Education League had operated as a leading Nonconformist pressure group on the issue of education. In 1870, however, the Merthyr Branch seceded from the League, under the leadership of its secretary, Evan Williams, owing to the willingness of the Birmingham organization to accept the compromises included in the Forster Bill. Although merely a splinter group, the decision of the Merthyr branch to reject the compromises made by the Birmingham organization suggested that Wales intended to pursue a more radical set of policies than did England.

Jesse Collings, declared that his Association was totally opposed to the League's policy on three issues: the compulsion upon some children to attend denominational schools and the likely impotence of the conscience clause; the provision for non-denominational religious instruction rather than secular schools; and proposals to increase grants to the existing denominational schools.[7] Indeed, so concerned were the Nonconformist leaders in general with proposed legislation that a conference was called at Aberystwyth in January 1870.[8] Two broad subjects were placed on its agenda: the prospects for education in Wales in view of the country's special needs and the hopes for the establishment of a University of Wales. Delegates were invited from municipal corporations and congregations, with ministers of religion invited in an *ex-officio* capacity.[9] Seven papers were received as topics for discussion, each of them concerned with the central themes of the conference, namely, what proposals could be accepted by Nonconformists as part of a system of education, and what system was most appropriate for the needs of Wales. The matter of religious instruction was considered along with the critical issue of compulsory attendance at denominational schools. At the meeting, attended by over three hundred people described as 'Cyfeillion Addysg' (Friends of Education), Dr Lewis Edwards, principal of the Calvinistic Methodist College at Bala, noted that, although Nonconformists were no longer opposed to state intervention in education, considerable dangers remained while the Anglican Church remained an Established Church. He expressed concern that the state could be seen to be patronizing the religious indoctrination of children by providing grants to schools that included religious instruction as part of the curriculum.[10] The Revd Josiah Jones of Machynlleth roundly denounced the conscience clause as inadequate, especially in Nonconformist communities such as those of Wales, and he urged support for the resolution of Professor William Morgan of Carmarthen that the meeting

---

[7] *Y Tyst*, 28 January 1870.
[8] L. Hargest, 'The Welsh Educational Alliance and the 1870 Elementary Education Act', *WHR*, 10 (1980–1), 172–206.
[9] *Y Tyst*, 28 January 1870.
[10] These issues are discussed, in detail, in H. G. Williams, 'A study of the Kynnersley Educational Returns for Caernarfonshire', *WHR*, 13 (1986–7), 299–327.

should advocate a system of education that was free, universal, non-denominational and compulsory.[11]

The gathering was virtually unanimous in its support for a provision financed by the rates and government grants, totally free of charge and compulsory. However, the question of religious instruction divided the conference. It eventually advocated a secular policy for rate-aided schools but conceded the right of voluntary schools to provide religious instruction on condition that it was taught at the beginning or the end of the day. This would allow parents to use the provisions of the conscience clause with minimum disruption either to the school or to the child's education. Those from Merthyr and Cardiff who advocated the total exclusion of religion from the schools were in a minority, not least because a significant number of those present envisaged a system which permitted the reading of the Bible while remaining opposed to 'religious teaching'; these differences, already apparent before legislation was introduced, were to be the focus of heated debate for the remainder of the period under consideration here.[12]

The Bill was introduced on 17 February 1870. Yet, as soon as its contents became clear, it was evident that several key matters remained unresolved. The Bill noted that more schools had to be provided and it certainly envisaged co-operation between the voluntary sector and elected bodies in satisfying those needs, but it was unclear how that co-operation could be achieved. Originally, Forster advocated the concept of vestries or select vestries as opposed to directly elected school boards as governing bodies. The question of whether voluntary schools should be entitled to some assistance from the rates was initially unclear, as was the question of whether voluntary agencies could continue to receive grants to build entirely new premises. Undoubtedly the most contentious issue, however, was that of religious instruction. The Bill presented at first reading sought to address the problem, but the process by which parents could withdraw their children from religious instruction was cumbersome and unclear in the original proposals and the provision for parents' rights applied only to new voluntary schools, thus leaving those already in existence untouched.

[11] Ibid.
[12] Ibid.

It was this Bill which became the topic of discussion on almost a weekly basis in the editorial columns of Nonconformist newspapers such as *Y Goleuad* and *Y Tyst* and in political publications such as *Baner ac Amserau Cymru*. From then until the following September, *Y Tyst* devoted some twenty editorials to discussion of the Bill[13] and some twenty-two appeared in *Y Goleuad*.[14] Early in the year, *Y Goleuad* undertook a detailed assessment of the options that were available and, stating its conviction that the government had a wholehearted commitment to education, it concurred with W. E. Forster, vice-president of the Committee of Council on Education, that the Bill should be regarded as merely the first in a series of measures designed to establish a comprehensive education system.[15] The Bill that was published failed to match the expectations of Welsh Nonconformist leaders, however, and a determined effort was undertaken to secure radical changes to what was proposed in two ways. Nonconformists sought to influence the views of the government and, having failed to gain any concessions, they launched a second campaign to try to prove to the Education Department that Anglican schools were incapable of providing for the educational needs of Wales and to convince Wales of the desirability of opting for the School Board method of making good the educational deficiency.[16]

The extent of the religious divide had been underlined by the rise of the High Church movement within the Anglican Church in Wales. The principles associated with High Anglicanism were abhorrent to the Welsh Nonconformist community, and the fears now aroused were especially pronounced when it was realized that the education of so many Nonconformist children was to be left to the Church. The conscience clause introduced by William Cowper-Temple was regarded as an ineffective defence that failed to provide adequate guarantees against the victimization of those children whose parents chose to take advantage of its provisions. *Y Goleuad* went further, stating that though a conscience clause might be acceptable in those areas of the country where the Nonconformist element was a minority in the community, it was not acceptable in Nonconformist Wales as a

---

[13] *Y Tyst*, January to September 1870.
[14] *Y Goleuad*, January to September 1870.
[15] *Y Goleuad*, 26 January 1870.
[16] Ibid.

whole. *Y Goleuad* asserted its view that a system of education designed for Wales had to take account of the particular religious features of the country and, for the system to succeed, religious freedom had to prevail in the schools.[17] *Y Tyst* claimed that the provision of a conscience clause constituted an extension of forbearance to the Nonconformists reminiscent of the Act of Toleration (the Repeal of the Test Act in 1828), insisting that the only just solution was to recognize the rights of Nonconformist groups rather than to tolerate their 'deviation'. At the same time, *Y Tyst* argued that the Bill failed to take advantage of the opportunity that existed to create a comprehensive system of School Boards rather than leave their establishment to local referenda, a situation that would be detrimental to Nonconformists in those areas where a strong gentry and clerical influence existed.[18] For its part, *Baner ac Amserau Cymru*, owned by Thomas Gee and edited by William Rees (Gwilym Hiraethog), openly declared its belief that an Education Act and the establishment of School Boards should be an opportunity both to remedy the educational deficiencies of Wales and to seize control of education from the Church. It was argued that the changes should seek to strengthen local democracy in Wales through the establishment of elected School Boards. Ever conscious of the wave of evictions which had occurred in the aftermath of the previous general election, the paper was determined, too, to establish the principle of secret ballot at School Board elections and led a successful campaign to insert this provision in the Bill during the later stages of the process.[19]

The Welsh periodicals were equally concerned. *Y Cronicl* called for the establishment of a Welsh Board of Education, mainly on grounds of economy but also in order to secure a more sympathetic treatment of Welsh peculiarities than it envisaged would be received from the Education Department.[20] Fears were expressed that because the educational needs of the children might be met by totally different agencies in areas where two such conflicting schools operated in close proximity to one another, attempts would be made by the one side to undermine

---

[17] Ibid.
[18] *Y Tyst*, 25 February 1870.
[19] T. Gwynn Jones, *Cofiant Thomas Gee*, 2 vols (Denbigh, 1913), pp.243–69.
[20] 'Nodiadau'r mis', *Y Cronicl*, 28 (March 1870), 81–4.

the other. These concerns were highlighted in *Y Traethodydd*, which welcomed certain provisions, such as the insistence that trained teachers should be responsible for each school, but was critical of the government for not providing greater resources for the training of teachers. It confidently predicted that the demands on resources would be such that the Anglican provision would not be sustained and that School Boards would therefore be inevitable in due course.[21]

The response to the Bill was not confined to the pages of the Welsh radical press. Public meetings held to consider the Bill expressed similar sentiments. Meetings at Pwllheli,[22] Llanberis,[23] Porthmadog (Caernarfonshire)[24] and Dolgellau (Merioneth)[25] reiterated the Nonconformist objections, especially those provisions dealing with religious instruction and the conscience clause. The interest in these meetings reflected the concern for education that was prevalent in Wales and genuine enthusiasm for the creation of an educational system. Yet the anxieties expressed represented the unease and disappointment which were felt within the Nonconformist community with regard to the proposals. It is clear that attempts by Forster to reach a compromise with the Anglican Church and to allow the Church monopoly over education to continue in several districts, was abhorrent to many, and it is equally apparent that the Nonconformists' lack of faith in the conscience clause was a particularly pertinent issue.

Shortly after the publication of the Bill, a meeting of the Welsh Education Alliance held at Llanidloes launched a determined campaign to persuade the government to make significant amendments. A petition was circulated throughout Wales which was then presented to W. E. Gladstone by a deputation sent by the Alliance.[26] Their submission expressed the view

> That the religious education of Children should be left entirely in the hands of their Parents, their Ministers, and Friends and that no attempt

[21] D. C. Rowlands, 'Byrddau ysgol', *Traethodydd*, XXV (April 1870), 244–50; idem, 'Deddf Addysg 1870', *Y Traethodydd*, XXVI (May 1871), 90–119.
[22] *Y Tyst*, 3 September 1870.
[23] *Y Tyst*, 17 September 1870.
[24] *Y Tyst*, 22 October 1870.
[25] *Y Tyst*, 17 September 1870.
[26] *Y Tyst*, 27 January 1870.

should be made to relieve them of this feeling of responsibility by delegating any part of their duty to either the Masters or Inspectors of schools.

That the Bill perpetuates and even encourages the present Denominational System of Schools in England and Wales, and will make it impossible to continue the Undenominational Schools in Ireland, the effect of which must be prejudicial to that feeling of unity and concord which should pervade all classes of Her Majesty's subjects.

That the clauses which relate to the election and appointment of School Boards, and of Managers of Schools, will create and promote sectarian strife in almost every town, parish, and district, in a far greater degree than has been hitherto known in this Kingdom.

That the Bill, by enacting the Payment of rates for religious purposes, introduces the principle of Concurrent Endowment, which was so emphatically condemned by your Honourable Houses last Session of Parliament.

That it renders a Conscience Clause necessary which must create invidious distinctions amongst Parents and Children, and which your Petitioners also considers to be indefensible in principle, and impossible in practice.

That it recognizes a principle which has never yet been acknowledged, either by your Honourable House or your Constituents – that of levying rates for the erection of buildings which may be used for Religious Worship.[27]

The majority of these criticisms, and those voiced in public meetings and in the pages of the Welsh press, were equally appropriate to English Nonconformists. Indeed, throughout the campaign that followed the publication of the Education Bill there had been considerable co-operation between the leaders of Welsh and English Nonconformity, most notably through the Nonconformist Central Committee.[28] What was crucial, however, was the fact that these difficulties were more pronounced in Wales, where the preponderance of the Nonconformist denominations was so great and where only a minority of the people worshipped in the same place as their landowner. The evictions of Liberal farmers less than two years previously had accentuated divisions within Welsh society, and the role of the Church and gentry in that experience meant that fewer people

---

[27] *Y Tyst*, 11 March 1870.
[28] George, 'Henry Richard', pp.39–86.

trusted the Church and the gentry to honour arrangements such as adherence to the conscience clause in denominational schools. T. Selby Jones of Tre-wen (Cardiganshire), writing in *Y Tyst*, reflected the frustration that was felt by many in Wales who feared that religious equality, a key element of the programme on which the Gladstone administration had been elected, was in danger of being jettisoned. He warned that the government would face immense resentment unless it satisfied the aspirations of those who had endeavoured to secure its election, asking:

> ai trwy daflu holl blant dyfodol y blynyddau ddaw i ofal a chrafangau culion cefnogwyr y deugain erthygl ond un yr ydym i gael ein talu am ein gwasanaeth yn ystod y blynyddoedd a basiodd ac yn neilltuol yn adeg yr etholiad diweddaf?
>
> [is it by throwing future generations of children to the care and clutches of the supporters of the thirty-nine articles that we are to be repaid for our services over past years and especially during the last election?][29]

He claimed that the Education Bill as then proposed was unjust and expressed his earnest hope that the government would listen to the entreaties of its more radical MPs, such as Henry Winterbotham, a leader of the Nonconformist members, Edward Miall, the Liberationist leader, and Henry Richard.[30]

Commentators expressed the view that the preponderance of Nonconformity in Wales created particularly acute problems. At a meeting in Caernarfon in February 1870, the Revd E. Williams quoted the comment made by the *Daily News* that the Education Bill was a good deal for England, and went on to lament that it was not so for Wales. His claim that the Bill needed to take account of the special circumstances that existed in Wales, and the unsuitability of the Church schools in Nonconformist Wales, won considerable support.[31] Similarly, an

---

[29] *Y Tyst*, 15 April 1870.
[30] Henry Selfe Payne Winterbotham (1837–73) had emerged as the leader of the advanced, Nonconformist Liberals. Edward Miall (1809–81) had been a life-long advocate of Church disestablishment and a leading proponent of voluntaryism in elementary education. He had, however, become converted to the principle that the provision of education was the responsibility of the state.
[31] *Y Goleuad*, 5 March 1870.

editorial in *Y Tyst* urging non-sectarian provision highlighted the unsuitability of the Church schools, on account of the different nature of the community:

> Byddai yn fuddiol i bob cynulleidfa i anfon deiseb at ysgrifenydd cyngor addysg i ddymuno arnynt roddi eu cefnogaeth i ysgolion rhydd ac ansecteraidd, ac mai y fath ysgolion sydd yn ateb angen Cymru yn arbenig.
>
> [It would be beneficial if every congregation were to send a petition to the Secretary of the Committee of Council on Education in favour of free and non-sectarian schools as it is such schools that fulfil the particular needs of Wales.][32]

Few, however, contemplated specific alterations to accommodate the needs of Wales. Undoubtedly, the hostility of the government to any suggestion that Wales should be treated as a case separate from England meant that such arguments would be futile. Yet the reluctance to make demands for Wales from a specifically Welsh standpoint was also influenced by the commitment of the Welsh Nonconformist leadership to a joint approach with their colleagues in England that was calculated to secure amendments of general application rather than for Wales alone.[33] The 1870 Bill was debated in a period when the concept of the coherence of Welsh and English aspirations, as advocated by Hugh Owen, was at its most persuasive.[34] This inclination extended to co-operation with both the government and the leaders of the Nonconformist denominations in England. Under these circumstances, those advocating an education system for Wales, separate from that of England and considerably different in its provision, had little hope of success. The response of the Nonconformists of Wales to the Forster proposals may have been motivated by specifically Welsh concerns, yet, unlike the trend that was to emerge in public debates over legislation to establish intermediate education in 1881, it did not lead to their advocating any special treatment for Wales.

[32] *Y Tyst*, 11 April 1870.
[33] Wallace, *Organise! Organise! Organise!*, pp.68–76, 84–5, 115–21, 127–36.
[34] Gwyn A. Williams, 'Hugh Owen (1804–1881)', in Glanmor Williams et al. (eds.), *Pioneers of Welsh Education* (Swansea, n.d.), pp.57–82.

Acknowledging Nonconformist interest in the creation of an education system, and taking account of the extent of the concerns in Wales over the Forster Bill, it was natural that Welsh representatives should take an active role in the debate in parliament. Members such as Henry Richard, George Osborne Morgan and Watkin Williams were already assuming a role as tribunes of the Welsh Nonconformist community. Henry Richard was notable for his commitment to the development of an education system for Wales as well as for his wider endeavours. He had been a leading critic of the attitudes expressed in the 1847 Report on the condition of education in Wales, and he had highlighted the educational needs of the country in 1867. Richard advocated a system of schools that were free and where attendance was compulsory, and schools which, if not secular, would certainly be non-sectarian. As secretary of the Liberation Society, Richard regarded the exclusion of the denominational influence from school as a key element in establishing religious freedom and believed that religious instruction should be left to parents and the efforts of the churches, acting without state subsidy and outside day-school hours.[35]

In conjunction with other radical Liberal MPs, Richard opposed the continuation of grants for voluntary schools and, in June 1870, he moved an amendment at the Committee stage of the Bill:

> that the grants to existing denominational schools should not be increased, and that, in any national system of elementary education, the attendance should be everywhere compulsory, and the religious instruction should be supplied by voluntary effort and not out of public funds.[36]

Richard further maintained that the conscience clause was an insult to the principle of religious equality:[37]

> [The conscience clause] is at best, a bungling and unsatisfactory expedient. It might have done very well for a time of transition, while the Churches

---

[35] These ideas were explained in detail in Richard, *Letters*, pp.8–15; I. G. Jones, *Explorations and Explanations* (Llandysul, 1981), pp.236–68; Wallace, *Organise! Organise! Organise!*, pp.189–90.
[36] *Hansard*, 203, 1870, p.29.
[37] *Hansard*, 200, 1870, p.269.

were unlearning the notion of which they had become possessed, that they had a sort of divine or prescriptive right to control the education of all the children of the country. The Conscience Clause was useful in letting them down gently from that high pretension. But I should be sorry that it should become a permanent part of our educational legislation. For what is it but a kind of educational Toleration Act?[38]

While paying tribute to the great work done by voluntary agencies and the efforts of the clergy of the Church of England, he felt that the reason the Church authorities outshone other agencies in this work was the fact that they represented the wealthiest section of the community.[39] Moreover, Richard expressed his belief that the exclusion of religion from the day school had been shown to be beneficial to the creation of religious feeling. He noted that in Prussia there was a considerable irreligious feeling despite rigorous religious instruction in the schools, while in the United States, where secular education prevailed, religious observance was buoyant. According to Richard, the role of the state in education should be to provide literary and scientific instruction, and religious teaching should be left to the religious bodies, giving freedom of choice to the individual and preventing the state subsidy of religious teaching. Richard advocated secular education for two main reasons. On the one hand, as a leader of the Liberation Society he had a principled objection to state subsidy of religious instruction and he maintained that any form of religious instruction would be objectionable to some element in the community: Jews, Roman Catholics, Nonconformists (and among the Nonconformists, the Unitarians) would all have objections that would need to be respected. On the other hand, his objections reflected his experience of the Welsh Sunday school.[40] The Nonconformist Sunday school in Wales was at the height of its influence, with an efficient system for teaching Biblical knowledge. In addition, the quality of the teaching was high and there was a thorough system of inspection. This system was the product not of government

[38] Ibid.
[39] Ibid.
[40] Richard, *Letters*, pp.25–35; see below, ch. 5; D. Ben Rees, *Chapels in the Valleys: A Study of the Sociology of Welsh Nonconformity* (Upton, 1975), pp.86–101; Jenkins, *Agricultural Community*, pp.216–18.

sponsorship but of the zeal and enthusiasm of members of religious denominations, and the faith that Richard had in the Sunday school system was such that he regarded the provision of religious instruction in day schools as superfluous. Support for the arguments put forward by Richard came from varied sources. An editorial in *Y Tyst* for April 1870 quoted misgivings expressed by Lord Russell, who reiterated the point that the dominance of the Church, especially in rural areas, meant that it was likely to exert undue influence in such districts.[41] Yet there was a lack of clarity in the Nonconformists' demands. One group advocated the establishment of non-denominational schools; a second group was in favour of secular schools; and a third group advocated Bible reading (though not teaching) even in secular schools. This meant that no clear policy existed on which the Nonconformist body in Parliament could agree. Liberal members such as Samuel Morley and Lyon Playfair argued for a modicum of religious teaching that was voluntary and not based on any creed distinctive to a particular denomination, acknowledging that the strength of the Sunday school in England was by no means sufficient to provide for the spiritual needs of children. Similarly, although a cordial reception was extended by Gladstone and Forster to both Richard and the delegation sent from the Aberystwyth conference, the government refused to agree to any of their demands. And, despite Richard's protestations that the government was yielding too much to the Church and Tory opposition while ignoring the wishes of its own supporters, his amendments to the Act were opposed by the government and won no acceptance in the House.

The failure of even some of the more radical members on the Liberal benches to support the amendments advocated by Henry Richard in favour of a totally secular system of education was not surprising. Although there is evidence that Gladstone initially subscribed to the principle of secular schools, his own cabinet was hostile. The suggestion that Nonconformist ministers should be allowed access to the school to teach the children of their respective members was unacceptable to the Anglican Whig members and others, including those of an evangelical persuasion, who felt the total exclusion of Biblical instruction from day

[41] *Y Tyst*, 1 April 1870.

schools would deprive many children of their only opportunity for religious instruction. Gladstone was also opposed to the concept of universal School Boards and had committed himself to the defence of the voluntary schools where those could be proven to be effective providers of education, a feature of the Bill which was wholly objectionable to Nonconformist opinion in Wales.[42] As the representatives of the religious majority, the Nonconformist advocates naturally took the most prominent part in the educational debate in Wales. However, the reaction of the Anglican and Conservative forces to the Bill was also of critical importance, not least because of the disproportionate influence that they exerted over education in Wales. While Forster was attacked by the Nonconformist leadership as being too conciliatory towards the position of the Church, his proposals failed to gain the acquiescence of the Conservatives in Wales. Undoubtedly, the programme of the Liberal administration (especially the legislation to disestablish the Irish church, passed the previous year) led many Anglicans to take a defensive position against all Gladstonian enactment. This instinctive reaction was evident over the question of education. In Wales, the numerical superiority of Nonconformity threatened the pre-eminent position of the Anglican Church.[43] Moreover, the association of the Welsh landowners with the Anglican Church in this society, together with divisions in language, ensured that the landowning interests perceived themselves to be increasingly isolated and threatened not only by broad social trends but also by the proposed legislation of the Gladstone government. Despite the cordial nature of relationships at a personal level, and the fact that there were few Welsh instances of the excesses demonstrated by their Irish counterparts, there remained a wide gulf between landlord and tenant and this was taking an increasingly political form.[44] It was accentuated by the events of 1868 and the subsequent introduction of the secret ballot (in no small part a direct response to the actions of the Welsh gentry),

---

[42] Roy Jenkins, *Gladstone* (London, 1995), pp.321–3.
[43] Jones and Williams, *Religious Census*, I, xi–xxxv.
[44] On the cordial relations which prevailed on large numbers of Welsh estates, see D. W. Howell, *Land and People in Nineteenth-Century Wales* (London, 1978), and idem, *Patriarchs and Parasites: The Gentry of South-West Wales in the Eighteenth Century* (Cardiff, 1986); M. F. Cragoe, *An Anglican Aristocracy: The Moral Economy of the Landed Estate in Carmarthenshire, 1832–1895* (Oxford, 1996).

which demonstrated that the overt exercise of gentry power in 1868 was unacceptable in modern society.[45]

These trends were especially important in determining the reactions of landlords to the detailed provisions of the 1870 Education Act. In general, landowners adopted a low profile, invariably attending vestry meetings to oppose the establishment of Boards, yet finding that their hostility to the Board system did not in itself constitute sufficient reason for the community as a whole to withstand the setting up of a School Board. Indeed, fear of the financial costs of the School Board system had a greater influence in commending the rejection of the Board system than deference to the views of local landowners. The gentry reaction may be classified in two broad categories. A first group regarded the provision of a school as a means of asserting their authority in the countryside and of sustaining a deferential loyalty to their own political and religious beliefs.[46] A second, larger group opposed the establishment of School Boards not on grounds of principle but from a pragmatic and paternalistic desire to spare the tenantry from the rate burden which would inevitably follow the establishment of School Boards. In the Lampeter area, J. N. Harford expressed such concern in his opposition to the Board system, declaring that he felt 'desirous of relieving the occupying tenants as much as possible from the expense of building schools'.[47] This sentiment was echoed by Thomas Lloyd of Bronwydd, who confidently predicted that, whatever was included in the Forster Bill, the people of Wales would graciously remember the contribution of the landowning class to the provision of education and thus ignore the demands of the more radical political leadership.

> It is in my opinion a very wise principle in the Act that it is prepared to aid in maintaining existing denominational schools, thus recognising the great exertions made and the vast sums laid out in the cause of primary education. I feel convinced that the majority of my countrymen, to whichever class they belong (more especially those who are resident in

---

[45] Jane Morgan, 'Denbighshire's "Annus Mirabilis". The borough and county elections of 1868', *WHR*, 7 (1974–5), 63–87.
[46] NLW, Voelas and Cefnamwlch, C 190.
[47] NLW, Dolaucothi Correspondence, 2273.

rural areas) will feel a strong repugnance to imposing fresh burdens on the already overtaxed ratepayers of South Wales, and it is from this strong conviction that I would suggest to Churchmen and Dissenters residing in parishes wholly destitute of schools, that they should make mutual concessions for a common object, and follow the example of the people of Dinas in Pembrokeshire, who have combined, irrespective of sect, to erect a commodious schoolroom.[48]

Lloyd's reaction, however, demonstrated the extent to which the Welsh landowning class had misjudged the mood of the community in 1870, as it had in 1868. The Conservative interest may have expected the incoming Liberal government to pursue moderate Whig policies. In doing so, it underestimated the radicalism of the government and the perceptions of the wider community in Wales. Whereas a divergence had existed between the views of Conservative landowners and Liberal communities, this had been veiled by a perception that those Liberal policies were essentially moderate. The public debate over the 1870 Act was an early indication of the extent of the radicalism being nurtured within the Welsh community and demonstrated that what had previously been a gap was increasingly becoming a gulf. Despite this awakening to the true extent of radical opinion, it was clear that, in the case of Wales, no amount either of coercion or persuasion could overcome the determination of the community. It was openly admitted by Connop Thirlwall that sectarian bitterness was so intense in Wales that the general establishment of rate-supported schools would be attempted 'on account of the injury which they are expected to do to the church',[49] indicating a growing awareness that politics there was likely to follow a different and more radical path from that of England.

The growing impotence of the landowning interest in the face of a determined effort on the part of the Nonconformist adherence was reflected in a somewhat limited landed involvement in the debate concerning elementary education. Increasingly, it was the clergy of the Anglican Church, rather than the landowners, who made the most determined effort to oppose the

[48] NLW, Lucas papers, 346–68.
[49] NLW, Dolaucothi Correspondence, 3794.

implementation of the Act. The rejection of the Church by the majority of the Welsh population, in addition to the constant attacks on the position and privileges of the Church in Wales made by Nonconformist leaders, contributed to the further polarization of opinion in Wales. This occurred at a time when the Anglican Church was making a determined effort to revive its fortunes in Wales, particularly by attempting to overcome the charges of inactivity that had been levied against it by Nonconformist leaders a generation earlier. This determination manifested itself clearly in the field of education. The Revd J. D. James, Cadoxton, writing of Connop Thirlwall, notes the efforts made by the Church to provide for the educational needs of Wales prior to the passing of the 1870 Act.[50] As has been indicated already, much of this effort was due to the realization, after the publication of the Report of 1847, of the need for greater activity on the part of the voluntary agencies in Wales. There were certainly areas where the Church had provided a sufficient number of schools for those seeking education, albeit not sufficient for the needs of the entire child population of the districts. Thirlwall, it appears, maintained that school should not be a place for secular education alone but should also be concerned with the moral and spiritual condition of the child.[51] He showed genuine surprise at the way in which Nonconformist leaders were supporting secular education and believed that co-operation between the denominations was possible. The religious difficulty, he claimed, existed only in the minds of some Nonconformist leaders and contended that a majority of parents were perfectly happy with the education their children received in the National schools. Where these were sufficient for the educational wants of a district, he believed that they should be allowed to continue, and where a deficiency existed and could not be supplied by voluntary methods, School Boards should be established. Church representatives should actively seek election to these Boards and co-operate with the Nonconformists for the benefit of education.

[50] J. D. James, 'Connop Thirlwall', in J. V. Morgan (ed.), *Welsh Political and Educational Leaders in the Victorian Era* (London, 1908), pp.105–10; W. T. Gibson, 'Fresh light on Bishop Connop Thirlwall of St David's (1840–1875)', *THSC*, 1992, 141–58 and references cited.
[51] Morgan, *Welsh Political and Educational Leaders*, pp.110–11.

This position was unacceptable to the majority of Nonconformist leaders, who wished to seize control of education from the Church. Yet theirs was a conciliatory attitude by comparison with that expressed in Anglican journals such as *Y Cyfaill Eglwysig* which, in the spring of 1870, stressed the imperative need to retain the excellent system of Church schools as they currently existed, arguing that it would be folly to destroy good schools.[52] The journal attacked Nonconformist demands for a system of free, secular and compulsory schools and also expressed surprise at Liberal Party demands for compulsion.

> Gellid meddwl fod y gair 'gorfodaeth' yn swnio yn ddyeithr yng nghlustiau Rhyddfrydwyr, y rhai a gyhoeddant eu hunain yn gewri rhyddid.
>
> [It would have been thought that the word 'compulsion' sounded strange in the ears of Liberals, people who declare themselves the champions of freedom.][53]

By suggesting that police officers should enforce compulsory attendance, the journal expostulated, the Nonconformists were attempting to give to the constabulary the work which rightfully should be undertaken by ministers of religion. The Nonconformists were neglecting their duties and expecting support from others. The next edition was equally forthright. Ignoring the differences within Nonconformity on the question of religious instruction, it claimed that their attitude was comparable only to atheism:

> Y maent wedi myned i gynghrair ag anffyddwyr er cael deddf seneddol i wahardd ysgolfeistr i ddyweyd gair wrth blentyn am ei Grëwr a'i Brynwr o fewn muriau yr ysgoldy . . . dengys fod dirywiad mawr wedi cymmeryd lle yn nheimlad crefyddol yr Ymneillduwyr.
>
> [They have entered into league with atheists in order to secure a parliamentary Act which will prohibit a schoolmaster from uttering a word to a child about his Maker and Saviour within the school walls . . . it shows that there has been a marked decline in religious feeling among the Nonconformists.][54]

---

[52] *Y Cyfaill Eglwysig*, 4 (1870), 85–8.
[53] Ibid.
[54] Ibid., 113–17.

Thus, those who had been advocating *Beibl i bawb o bobol y byd* (a Bible for all the people of the world) were now in league with those who denounced the Bible and refuted its contents. Nonconformist opposition to rate-aid for religious purposes was denounced as hypocrisy in view of the fact that they had been happy to receive rate-aid for British schools which the Anglicans accused of promoting Nonconformity. Further, while Sunday schools did much good, they did not have the resources to provide religious instruction for the entire child population. Demands for free education, it was claimed, would place an unbearable rate burden on the community, especially those tenant farmers whom the Liberals sought to represent.[55] *Y Cyfaill Eglwysig* also paid tribute to the work of the Church in providing schools over the previous ten years, stating that the Church had done up to six times as much as other denominations in the same period. The voice of the Church, it claimed, should be heard as the major provider of education, while the Nonconformists were merely looking to the Act as a means of placing struggling British schools on the rates and thus relieving themselves of the burden of their maintenance.[56] By October 1870 *Y Cyfaill Eglwysig* was adopting the threat of the rate burden as the focus of its campaign. An editorial alleged that the prophecy that the average rate would be three pence in the pound was a deliberate underestimate and held that a rate of nine pence was a more accurate prediction in view of the likely cost of construction of schools, their annual maintenance, the cost of the triennial elections and the wages which would be paid to the various Board employees.[57]

Y Cyfaill Eglwysig was only one of a number of Church and Conservative papers to advocate such views. Local clergy and Church leaders throughout Wales, both ecclesiastical and lay, were active in denouncing the Nonconformist proposals and especially the attempts by Henry Richard to amend the Bill in committee. The vicar of Caernarfon, the Revd H. T. Edwards, together with the rector of Corris, the Revd Daniel Evans, gave voice to these concerns. Together they organized a series of public meetings throughout north-west Wales to attack the

[55] Ibid.
[56] Ibid.
[57] Ibid, 311–12.

Nonconformists for allying with atheists to exclude the Bible from the schools of Wales. In a letter to the *Standard*, Edwards stated:

> The unscrupulous leaders of political dissenters of Wales have been making great efforts, by means of a deputation that waited upon the Premier, and their agencies, to make it appear that the Welsh people are in favour of the Godless Education Scheme of the Birmingham League in preference to Mr Forster's Bill. That the leaders and agitators have taken that position is quite true, but the serious, sincere, religious dissenters (of whom there are many thousands in Wales) have declined to stand with them on the irreligious platform.[58]

The letter included the observation that a petition from Caernarfon contained the names of the more responsible members of the Nonconformist denominations, arguing that it was the Nonconformist leadership rather than the members who were not prepared to co-operate with the Anglican Church in the provision of education.[59] An editorial in *Y Tyst* was scathing in its reply. Pointing out that the Birmingham scheme provided for non-sectarian rather than secular schools, it reminded the vicar that the Aberystwyth conference had stated that the reading of the Bible was neither to be ordered nor prohibited. Strong exception was taken to the description of the leaders of Nonconformity in Caernarfon as agitators, and *Y Tyst* questioned how the vicar could decide who were the sincere Nonconformists when he had only been in the town a few months:

> Nid oes ond ychydig fisoedd er y daeth i'r dref fel y deallwn, ac er ein bod yn clywed ei fod yn myned gryn lawer o dy i dy, ond nid yn gymaint at y *serious*, y *sincere* a'r *religious* ag at y gwan, y gwamal, y difeddwl a'r prynedig ym mysg yr ymneilltuwyr.

> [Only a few months have passed since he came to the town, as we understand, and although we hear a great deal that he goes from house to house, he does not call as much with the serious, the sincere and the religious as with the weak, the fickle, the thoughtless and the corruptible from among the ranks of the Nonconformists.][60]

[58] *Standard*, 17 March 1870.
[59] Ibid.
[60] *Y Tyst*, 25 March 1870.

Nevertheless, as *Y Cylchgrawn* stated upon the passing of the Act, it was the Church which had the greatest reason to be joyful at its provisions.[61] Yet, although they had secured more concessions for their side than had been made to the Nonconformists, and despite the fact that the Anglican bishops had become reconciled to the Act, the lower clergy retained their hostility: an ominous stance that presaged a vigorous debate on the desirability of establishing School Boards.

Although they did not participate in public debate, the inspectors of schools were in a position to convey their views to the government and their influence could conceivably have a bearing on ministerial judgement; indeed, they were specifically invited to comment on the Act in their reports for 1870. Their denominational adherence could therefore be a matter of some import. Inspectors were mostly Anglican, although as members of the civil service they had to uphold at least an appearance of impartiality and they tended to underplay the extent of the religious divisions in Wales. Shadrach Pryce claimed that there was no religious compulsion in schools in Wales and that many clergy adopted such a conciliatory attitude that they went further than the provisions of the Cowper-Temple conscience clause in the existing schools. According to Pryce, the children of Welsh Nonconformist parents could feel perfectly happy in a Church school where the religious instruction given was wholly uncontroversial. No Welsh child, he claimed, was forced to learn the Church catechism, attend a Church on a Sunday or do anything which would be objectionable in the eyes of the Nonconformists. Pryce further insisted that any religious difficulty which did exist arose from the principle that a school was controlled by the Established Church. Many Nonconformists had a principled objection to sending their children to the school of a denomination to which they did not belong, and the leaders of Welsh Nonconformity regarded Church control of so many schools with a certain amount of jealousy. Yet this was due more to the fact that the Church possessed the power than to any specific use the Church made of that power. There were few actual accusations of misuse of power, only theoretical objections to what could be done. According to Pryce, the Act would bring

[61] 'Addysg y Werin', *Y Cylchgrawn*, 101 (September 1870), 172–8.

an end to these jealousies and would create an atmosphere of co-operation beneficial to the cause of education. He predicted that a number of the smaller or less viable National schools would be transferred to School Board control in order that they might benefit from rate-aid and that many clergy would be relieved to lose the burden of maintaining a school. They, in turn, would be elected to the School Boards by ratepayers grateful for the contribution of the Church to education in the past and who wished that the Boards be filled by experienced members.[62] E. T. Watts was equally hopeful in his assessment of the likely consequences of the Act. He felt that religious questions did not enter into secular matters in Wales and that the 'religious difficulty' was non-existent in his experience, except in the pages of the Welsh Nonconformist press. He reiterated the point made by Pryce that the conscience clause would not be used, not on account of gentry influence or fear of victimization but because the religious instruction given in the schools was in accordance with the wishes of the parents. The 1870 Act, he suggested, would disappoint both its supporters and its opponents by ending arguments over trusts and endowments which had dogged the progress of education in the past. Just as important, he believed that the coming of elementary schools would exert a beneficial moral influence on the community which would civilize the inhabitants of Wales.[63] William Williams alone expressed the Nonconformist reservations. As an inspector of British schools, he was one of the few Nonconformist inspectors and in his estimation it was morally wrong for the Church to retain control of education in so many areas of Wales when it was a church of a minority. He claimed that the conscience clause offered inadequate safeguards to the community, especially in isolated rural areas, and the mere fact that parents might not withdraw their children from religious instruction lessons did not necessarily indicate acquiescence in that education. According to Williams, what was needed was a compulsory system of education with totally non-sectarian schools throughout the country in order to be able to justify compulsory attendance. Such compulsion was morally wrong where the school was run

[62] PP 1871, XXII, Mr Pryce's Report. For Pryce, see below, p.52, n.10.
[63] PP 1871, XXII, Mr Watts's Report.

on principles which contravened the wishes of the parents, and consequently a non-sectarian system was required. The divisions between Anglicans and Nonconformists therefore permeated even the ranks of the inspectorate. Many were of the opinion that religious difficulties and divisions were a figment of the imagination of the Welsh Nonconformist leaders and were not genuine feelings within Welsh society. The operation of the Act was to show, however, that predictions that harmony would prevail were premature.[64]

Yet it would be wrong to depict the Nonconformist arguments in totally confrontational terms. The passing of the Act led to a discernible change in the attitude and tone of the Welsh Nonconformist press. Papers such as *Baner ac Amserau Cymru*, *Y Goleuad* and *Y Tyst* had a large readership, which usually included those local Nonconformist leaders whose participation was crucial to the implementation of the Act. The provision of information in the Welsh language concerning the Act brought its details and minutiae to the attention of local leaders, constituting an important exercise in political education. An early example was an article in *Y Goleuad* by Daniel Rowlands, principal of the Normal College, Bangor, and a leading promoter of British schools. He explained the provisions of the Act, the methods by which it could be implemented and the hazards which might threaten Nonconformists in attempting to establish School Boards.[65] Hugh Owen was also aware of the need to ensure popular knowledge of the Act. His barrister son, Hugh Owen, produced *Deddf Addysg 1870*, a step-by-step manual of the provisions of the Act, again emphasizing the pitfalls which could be anticipated.[66] Almost every journal of the period considered it to be its duty to join in this process, yet, despite these attempts to publicize the Act, considerable ignorance remained. So concerned was *Y Tyst* that the information contained in the articles was not being understood that it sought more varied methods. A question-and-answer session, 'Ymgom y Bwrdd Ysgol', in which 'Owen' questioned 'Morris' on the provisions of the Act, dealt with different aspects of the legislation in a series which extended over several weeks, a method

[64] PP 1871, XXII, Mr Williams's Report.
[65] *Y Goleuad*, 3 September 1870.
[66] Hugh Owen, *Deddf Addysg 1870* (London, 1870).

familiar to the Nonconformists of Wales because preparation for the Sunday school examination was conducted on similar lines.[67]

The Welsh press was not the only agency which sought to educate the community in the new provisions. The Pwllheli Methodist connection was involved in lengthy correspondence with the Education Department over the details of the Act,[68] as were several other denominational organizations. In addition, it must be remembered that the many public meetings which were held to discuss the Act not only expressed criticisms of the proposals but also spread popular knowledge regarding its provisions. Yet the press remained a formidable influence and its editorials and articles were naturally written from a pro-Board, Nonconformist point of view. Their intention was to enable Welsh Nonconformists to know every detail of the Act and to use the knowledge to their advantage. This attempt at political education reflected the concern among the editors that the Act should be explained as fully as possible to the population at large, and it was also an illustration of the genuine interest in education which existed within the Welsh community. An editorial in *Y Goleuad* for September 1870 noted the delight of the paper at the passing of the Act and stated that although many Nonconformists were disappointed that many of their demands had been rejected by the government, political expediency had forced the government to reject them. A more extreme bill, it noted, might have been rejected by the House of Lords and it was more important to have some form of an Education Act than risk denying the country the creation of an education system.[69] *Y Tyst* was equally conciliatory. It paid tribute to Forster as a man who had to face both Anglican and Nonconformist demands and create a system which was acceptable to both sides and urged a great effort to implement the current Act.[70] Despite the fact that few of the demands of the Nonconformists were granted and the government seemed willing to concede numerous points to the Anglicans, the leaders of Welsh Nonconformity sought to come to terms with the deficiencies of the Act and to highlight its

---

[67] 'Ymgom y Bwrdd Ysgol', *Y Tyst*, September to October 1870.
[68] Correspondence between Revd Roger Edwards, Secretary, Cymdeithasfa Methodistiaid Pwllheli, and H. S. Bryan, Education Department, London, reprinted in *Y Goleuad*, 3 September 1870.
[69] *Y Goleuad*, 3 September 1870.
[70] *Y Tyst*, 7 October 1870.

strengths. Certainly, much of the enthusiasm for the measure reflected their hope that even the present Act could be used to overcome Church control of education in large areas of Wales where the provision was at its most meagre. The positive response also reflected the view that the Nonconformists had to demonstrate their commitment to the creation of an education system and actively participate in its creation in order to be able to influence further legislation.

Even so, as predicted by E. T. Watts, the 1870 Education Act disappointed both its supporters and its opponents. For the Nonconformist community it left too much in the hands of the Church and did not go far enough. For entrenched Anglicans, the Act was yet another piece of legislation by a Liberal administration which, in the estimation of many of them, seemed determined to undermine the position of the Church. The Welsh gentry were also left fearful for their position when faced with a community which, being overwhelmingly Nonconformist, had an increasingly self-confident, assertive and articulate leadership. The provision of a school for their tenantry or their workers, in conjunction with the Church, was seen by many landowners not only as a paternalistic duty but also as a means of social persuasion. For them, the Act further undermined their influence and their role as the accepted leaders of the community. In the case of some landowners, the Act placed a heavy rate burden on them and their tenants, many of whom were already facing financial difficulties. They felt it their duty to protect their tenantry from a liability imposed by a government they opposed and which they believed to be supported by agitators whom they regarded as alien influences attempting to undermine the traditional features of rural life.

The leaders of Welsh Nonconformity subjected the 1870 Education Bill to rigorous scrutiny and were vocal in their criticism of some aspects of it. Their anxieties were a reflection of the deep social, religious and political divisions that existed in Wales and which were to dominate its public debate for at least a generation. Within a brief period of time, however, Nonconformist opinion became reconciled to the limitations of the Education Bill and a determined effort ensued to use the provisions of the Act in order to achieve what was possible under its – admittedly limited – powers. Yet the debate over elementary education was not concluded. It was to continue at a local level in arguments concerning the existing deficiency, in referenda and in elections to the School Boards, ensuring that the arguments over the control of education were a recurring theme of Welsh political life until the turn of the twentieth century.

II
THE BATTLE FOR THE BOARDS

The 1870 Education Act was concerned only with ensuring that a school was available for each child. It did not address the issue of how education would be provided. Indeed, the Act gave the voluntary agencies the opportunity to retain control in large areas of the country and also gave them a six-month period of grace in which to attempt to expand their role in the neglected parts. Only in the areas where the voluntary agencies had failed to provide school accommodation were School Boards to be established as elected local authorities charged with the provision of elementary education. To accomplish this, the country was divided into School Districts based on boroughs or parishes, with parishes that were considered too small to constitute an effective unit being amalgamated to form a United District School Board. The members allocated to each Board numbered between five and fifteen and were elected on a triennial basis. Owing to the concerns expressed by many that the elected Boards could be dominated by a particular sect or denomination, a cumulative voting system was adopted by which each elector had as many votes as there were seats on a Board, and voters could then distribute these as they desired, giving all votes to the one candidate if they wished to do so.

The creation of School Boards was thus dependent on two factors. First, it had to be established that a deficiency in school accommodation existed in a particular area and, second, that the voluntary agencies were unable or unwilling to remedy that deficiency. Where a deficiency in provision was found to exist, one of two processes could be invoked in order to establish a School Board. In borough areas, the borough council had the power to resolve in favour of the formation of a School Board. In the parish areas, however, a more complex arrangement was introduced. Vestry meetings were to be held to discuss the desirability of establishing a School Board. When a resolution to that effect was proposed it would be put to the vote by a show of hands, with the proviso that when ten or more ratepayers were dissatisfied with the result of the vestry meeting, they could demand a poll of the parish, to be held by secret ballot. In areas where no deficiency existed, the voluntary agencies were to continue to provide the school. As most of the voluntary initiatives had been National schools, it followed that in many areas, particularly rural districts, the education of the parish remained in the hands of the Anglican Church in what was an overwhelmingly Nonconformist community. This 'dual system' meant that there were variations in school management, often in neighbouring parishes, which were reflected in the financial arrangements of the schools. Board schools were to receive an annual grant from the Treasury on a *per capita* basis dependent on a favourable report from the school inspector. In addition, the school pence, charged upon each pupil for his or her education, were available to the Board school as well as the revenue from the School Board rates. For their part, voluntary schools also had capitation grants and the revenue from the school pence, but they had no support from the rates. The capitation grant for voluntary schools was increased, but it was felt that the amounts raised by voluntary means, such as contributions from wealthy patrons and the fund-raising efforts of local committees, would be adequate for the voluntary schools to survive without rate-aid.

The Act did not attempt to compel attendance at a school but rather sought to ensure that each child was provided with a school place should a parent require one for him or her. Local School Boards were, however, permitted to apply local by-laws to compel school attendance. The provision of religious instruction was also a matter for local discretion, with the Boards having to decide what, if anything, was taught in their schools and with a stipulation that religious instruction in Board schools had to be given on strictly non-denominational lines. With the majority of the voluntary schools being provided by the National Society, it was inevitable that Anglican objectives would form part of the remit of the greater part of this sector. The National Society's constitution proclaimed among its objectives its responsibility to 'educate the children of the working classes in the principles of the Established Church', pointing to a source of serious difference with the Nonconformists. A compromise was reached in the form of the conscience clause, introduced by

Cowper-Temple during the course of the parliamentary debate. This allowed parents to withdraw their children from religious instruction lessons in both Board and voluntary schools, and stipulated that those lessons had to be confined to specific periods of the day.[1] In addition, no child could be forced to attend a place of worship on a Sunday against the wishes of a parent. The denominationally based system of inspection of schools was ended by the Act. Rather than the divided system whereby Anglicans inspected Anglican schools while British schools were inspected by Nonconformists, inspectors were now to be appointed to districts and were to inspect schools within those districts irrespective of religious affiliation. The Act also precluded inspectors from examining religious instruction.

The 1870 Education Act, therefore, was a measure which sought to supplement rather than replace the existing education system. It did not seek to establish a system of compulsory schooling and considerable local discretion was allowed. By taking the parish rather than any larger unit (such as the Poor Law Union) as the basis on which to set the administration of the school, a principle of subsidiarity was adopted, which created considerable difficulties in imposing a centralized authority over the schools. Certainly, W. E. Forster regarded the Act as the first in a series which would create a universal system of elementary education. Throughout the passage of the Bill, he adopted a cautious approach, indeed demonstrating a willingness to accept amendments from the Conservative benches which he did not display in responding to his Liberal colleagues. What was crucial to Forster was the creation of an education system based on cross-party consensus, thereby ensuring that the Act he proposed would not be subjected to any radical amendment by a subsequent Conservative government. Ensuring the fulfilment of this aim, however, risked disappointing, if not alienating, the government's more radical supporters. This disappointment was profoundly felt in Wales, especially in the rural areas, where an overwhelmingly Nonconformist society was faced with continued dominance by Church schools.

---

[1] William Cowper-Temple (1811–88) had held various ministerial offices between 1846 and 1866. His main contributions had been in relation to local taxation and tenant rights. Part of the reasoning for a conscience clause was a desire to avoid the total elimination of denominational schools and to avoid a drift towards ending all forms of religious instruction in schools.

The task of ascertaining the exact number of school places required was undertaken by school inspectors. Assessments were made of the precise number of children of school age resident in each parish, of the extent and condition of existing educational accommodation and, if that provision were insufficient, whether it could be supplied by voluntary means. In order to calculate the deficiency, a formula was adopted by which one-eighth of the whole population of a parish would be taken as being of school age. After deducting 5 per cent, who would be assumed to be the children of gentry or professional classes (and thus likely to be attending private schools), and a further 2 per cent for those children who would be expected to be away from school at any given time, a figure indicating the number of places required could be ascertained. Thus, the parish of Loughor (Glamorgan), with a population of 878, would be expected to have a child population of 109 and would be required to provide education facilities for 102.[2]

Difficulties arose in adopting this formula. It was unsuitable in Wales, where the number of wealthy parents was small and where a larger proportion of the child population could be expected to attend schools provided by the Act. In addition, the rapid industrialization of south and north-east Wales meant that statistics were often outdated, in terms of both population size and age structure. As HMI William Edwards complained in 1881, the rapid increase in population meant that local authorities had the unenviable task of meeting an ever-increasing deficiency. He pointed to his own district of Merthyr Tydfil and noted that between 1877 and 1881 as many as 7,000 additional places had been provided, while in the Rhondda the number of places required had increased from 16,914 in 1871 to over 35,000 by 1881.[3] Although overcrowding was likely only on the rare occasions when full attendance was secured, the formula benefited the voluntary agencies by underestimating the deficiency in several areas. This enabled voluntary bodies to resist establishing a School Board by claiming that they were able to supply the deficiency. Defining efficient accommodation was a further problem facing the Education Department. Schools

[2] PRO, ED2 /607.
[3] PP 1881, XXXII, Mr Edwards's Report.

which were to be deemed efficient had to submit to government inspection and qualify in terms of buildings, playgrounds, facilities and teaching staff. Although private schools continued to exist, they were discounted as far as the survey was concerned. These regulations again presented difficulties in the schools subject to inspection. Whereas the regulations stipulated that the teaching staff were to be certificated, many voluntary schools, which were efficient in terms of buildings, had uncertificated masters or mistresses. Schools such as the one at Llanbister in Radnorshire, with excellent buildings but an uncertificated master, were threatened with being declared inefficient (thus suffering a loss of grant) unless a certified master was appointed.[4] As a result, several long-standing and experienced teachers were forced either to retire or to study for a certificate, simply in order to prevent a school from being judged inefficient. Many of these teachers had the sympathy of the inspectors. William Williams claimed that many of the untrained persons were better teachers than those with certificates, and he expressed concern that many good teachers would be lost to the profession on account of the code imposed by the Education Department.[5] The question of school buildings left much to the discretion of the individual inspector. He had to make an assessment of whether the building could be altered in such a way as to make it efficient and whether the voluntary agency responsible for the school had the resources for such improvements and, in areas where a deficiency was proved to exist, the inspector had to decide whether the agencies had to remedy that deficiency.

Dominance by the Anglican Church in the provision of educational accommodation prior to 1870 meant that a majority of inspectors were churchmen and many were suspect in the eyes of the Welsh Nonconformist leaders. B. J. Binns, inspector for Swansea and central Glamorgan, was accused of an over-sympathetic treatment of the Church schools, as was E. M. Sneyd-Kynnersley, assistant to E. T. Watts, who was responsible for Caernarfonshire.[6] An Oxford graduate, Sneyd-Kynnersley openly admitted that he owed his position to family connections

---

[4] PRO, ED2 /639.
[5] PP 1871, XXII, Mr Williams's Report.
[6] PRO, ED2/584.

rather than any knowledge of the situation in Wales.[7] Others were more attuned to the needs of Welsh society. John Rhys, inspector for Flint and Denbigh, combined outstanding academic ability with experience as a pupil teacher at a British school in Cardiganshire and as a master of Rhos-y-bol British School, Anglesey.[8] William Williams, inspector for Cardiganshire and northern Pembrokeshire, was a Nonconformist and a former inspector of British schools. He was one of the few inspectors to declare some reservations concerning the Act and especially the concessions to the Anglican influence, and he had considerable sympathy with the Nonconformist position in Wales.[9] The Revd Shadrach Pryce, a native of Dolgellau, was vicar of Ysbyty Ifan (Denbighshire) until his appointment to the inspectorate in 1867.[10] Despite his Anglican background, he was convinced that attempts to provide for the educational wants of Wales by voluntary effort were unlikely to succeed, and he maintained that the six-month period of grace awarded to the voluntary agencies was nothing but a period which would bring them to realize that the difficulties they would face were insurmountable. These inspectors were assisted by men such as the Revd H. Smith, T. W. Green, J. P. Palmer and H. M. Lindsell who, although men of academic capability, were Anglicans and lacked a knowledge of the Welsh language. The lack of educational opportunity in Wales meant that, as in the case of judges in Wales, few indigenous Welshmen were able to enter the ranks of the inspectorate and therefore the appointment of English inspectors was unavoidable. Yet, since the returns made by these inspectors formed the basis of the information on which the Education Department assessed whether further accommodation was required, it was inevitable that an inspectorate which was so closely associated with the Established Church was

[7] For a detailed assessment of the work of Sneyd-Kynnersley in Wales, particularly his relations with the Nonconformist community, see H. G. Williams, 'A study of the Kynnersley Education Returns for Caernarfonshire', *WHR*, 13 (1986–7), 299–327.

[8] John Rhys (1840–1915) was a pupil teacher at Pen-llwyn (Cardiganshire) and was later educated at Bangor Normal College. He served briefly as master of Rhos-y-bol school before proceeding to a distinguished career as a student at Oxford University. He served as inspector of schools, 1871–81, returning to Oxford as Professor of Celtic and Fellow of Jesus College (*Dictionary of Welsh Biography* (London, 1959), p.844).

[9] PP 1871, XXII, Mr Williams's Report.

[10] Shadrach Pryce served as vicar of Ysbyty Ifan from 1864 to 1867 and was an inspector of schools from 1867 to 1894, when he returned to the service of the Anglican Church (*DWB*, pp.802–3).

likely to arouse antagonism. The majority of inspectors thus differed from the community which they inspected in terms of background, religious affiliation and attitude to the Act. Their perception of the position of the Anglican Church in Wales was different from that of the vast majority of the community and they had a distinct tendency to underestimate the religious divisions. The inspectors' role in assessing the provision already made was itself a matter liable to create contention.

Table 2.1 Analysis of school places, 1870[11]

County	School places required	School places provided	Percentage provided
Anglesey	8587	6098	71.0
Brecon	8138	4744	58.3
Carmarthen	20482	15046	73.5
Caernarfon	18290	13900	76.0
Cardigan	11899	4510	37.9
Denbigh	17254	9067	52.6
Flint	10603	8316	78.4
Glamorgan	61365	35397	57.7
Merioneth	7690	5547	72.1
Monmouth	28585	17444	61.0
Montgomery	8722	5525	63.3
Pembroke	12784	5809	45.4
Radnor	2394	1174	49.0
Cardiff	7652	4077	53.3
Merthyr	10038	2236	22.3
Swansea	10755	6500	60.4
Wales	**245238**	**145390**	**59.3**

As the figures in Table 2.1 indicate, there was a huge variation in educational provision. In Wales as a whole, 245,238 school places were required but only 145,390 were provided, resulting in a situation whereby 59.3 of school-age children were afforded a school place. However, there were also significant differences within Wales: for instance, 78 per cent of Flintshire children had access to a school place compared with a mere 22 per cent in

[11] PRO, ED2/557–640; PP 1870, XXII.

Merthyr. The type of school that existed also merits investigation. According to the list of schools which were in receipt of a government grant in 1868–9, Wales had a total of 890 schools which between them provided places for 86,434 children. Of these schools, 274 (30 per cent) were maintained through the British and Foreign School Society. British schools were not Nonconformist schools and their curriculum deliberately avoided any matter that could arouse denominational controversy. However, although the denominations did not exercise direct control over the schools, the British Society and the British school committees were dominated by individuals of Nonconformist sympathies and they were the schools that were most acceptable to Nonconformists before the 1870 legislation. The greater part of the remainder of existing facilities was provided by denominational bodies, mainly the Anglican Church.

Table 2.2 Total number of schools and number of British schools and average attendance at those schools, 1868–9[12]

County	All Schools Number	Places available	British Schools Number	Places available	% provided by British schools
Anglesey	49	3124	21	1596	51.1
Brecon	51	2897	13	1065	36.8
Carmarthen	83	7195	35	3259	45.3
Caernarfon	77	7489	20	2610	34.9
Cardigan	57	3933	28	2254	57.3
Denbigh	74	6949	15	2318	33.4
Flint	59	5141	6	661	12.9
Glamorgan	168	30074	61	11841	39.4
Merioneth	47	2788	20	1518	54.4
Monmouth	85	8934	18	1992	22.3
Montgomery	55	3740	13	1431	38.3
Pembroke	67	3503	23	1467	41.9
Radnor	18	667	1	80	12.0
Wales	**890**	**86434**	**274**	**32092**	**37.1**

[12] PP 1870, XXII.

The number of schools in existence is less important than the number of places available, and it is clear from Table 2.2 that the British schools contributed more to the education of Welsh pupils than the total number of these schools would suggest. Although most schools were provided by the Anglican Church, a significant proportion of the school places was provided by the British Society, especially so in Anglesey, Cardiganshire and Merioneth. Yet despite the success of the British schools in several areas of Wales, the fact remained that Church or National schools were the only source of schooling available for Welsh Nonconformist children in several localities. Furthermore, many British schools were maintained only as a result of considerable effort by the Nonconformist community, a burden that many were increasingly unable to sustain. As a result, the majority of Nonconformist opinion sought to promote the establishment of School Boards, including the transfer of British schools to School Boards.

As the Act specified that the status quo would prevail in all areas where there was no educational deficiency, ascertaining the exact deficiency had substantial political as well as educational significance, and not unexpectedly these assessments were a source of considerable debate. Welsh Nonconformist leaders accused the inspectorate of deliberately underestimating the deficiency in several parishes in order to protect the interests of the Church schools, and accusations were made that inefficient schools had been deliberately classified as efficient in order to prevent the formation of a School Board. However, there were areas where the existing supply of school places was sufficient. Cricieth had an estimated need for 174 school places and was provided with 197 places at the Cricieth National School.[13] The accommodation was deemed sufficient despite the opposition of local Nonconformists. Although a vestry meeting called for a School Board by a vote of 105 to 84, the Education Department refused to sanction its formation on account of the existing provision.[14] The disappointment and distrust felt in Cricieth was

[13] PRO, ED2/585.
[14] PRO, ED2/585, and *Baner*, 22 February 1871.

a widespread phenomenon. Demographic considerations were said to have been ignored in Llanwinio, Carmarthenshire, where it was claimed that the educational deficiency of the parish had been underestimated by the failure of the inspector to take cognizance of the great influx of young couples into the parish and that the likely increase in the child population had been underestimated.[15] Accusations of conspiracy were also levied against the inspectorate. There were serious doubts in Caernarfonshire regarding the impartiality of E. M. Sneyd-Kynnersley who, it was claimed, was far too lenient in his assessment of the deficiency, in contrast to other more rigorous inspectors.[16] Criticisms of the inspectorate and their assessments were not limited to Nonconformist circles. The Anglican clergy and their supporters, for their part, engaged in lengthy correspondence with the Education Department in an attempt to convince the authorities that the deficiency in Wales had been overestimated.[17] The motives of those eager to prove that the existing provision was sufficient were two-fold: a low deficiency meant that the existing provision would continue, while a low estimated deficiency would mean less cost to the parish in meeting that deficiency. Yet despite the claims of the protagonists on both sides, the evidence points to the inspectorate's resolve. Revd Shadrach Pryce, for instance, insisted that his assessments should be adhered to and that arrangements aimed at passing on deficiencies to other parishes should be avoided, as they merely compounded problems in those particular areas. Clearly, for inspectors such as Pryce, finding a permanent solution to educational deficiencies was more important than short-term economies.[18]

A determined attempt to reduce the estimates of deficiency was made in Gelli-gaer (Glamorgan), where R. Laybourne, a director of the Rhymney Ironworks, reiterated the claims made by several others that, while shortcomings in accommodation did exist in terms of the total child population, the current level of accommodation was sufficient in terms of the total numbers of

[15] PRO, ED2/580. It seemed to have escaped the official agencies that an influx of young couples would normally be followed by the arrival of children.
[16] Williams, 'Kynnersley Educational Returns', 299–327.
[17] PRO, ED2/585, 604 and 607.
[18] PP 1871, XXII, Mr Pryce's Report.

children in attendance.[19] Laybourne predicted that the schools would be half empty and that their maintenance would constitute an unnecessary burden on the ratepayers. The arguments put forward by Laybourne and others were valid points in a period when compulsory attendance was a matter for local discretion. Yet these arguments ran contrary to the intention of the Act to provide school accommodation for the entire child population of the country. At the same time, they assumed that local by-laws to enforce attendance would not be implemented. Already, therefore, vested interests and a desire to keep expenditure to a minimum were threatening to hamper the progress of elementary education.

Insular feelings and local rivalries created further obstacles to increased provision for education. As parishes which were considered too small to become school districts were to be amalgamated to form united school districts, numerous disputes arose between neighbouring parishes. In Anglesey, according to the Revd E. T. Watts, there was a reluctance to amalgamate owing to the delicate diplomatic niceties of the relationship between neighbouring villages and the fact that certain villages 'treat the residents of the neighbouring village as a hostile, foreign tribe'.[20] Particular difficulty arose in areas where a school was built at a central location in a united school district, with the result that children from the contributory parishes had to travel to the neighbouring parish to receive an education. Discontent arose at paying School Board rates when it was claimed that the parish had no school, and the position of children living on the borders of a parish was a further source of disagreement. Demographic changes often resulted in a concentration of settlement at an extreme end of a parish, such as occurred in the parish of Llanedi (Carmarthenshire), where the two townships of Hendy and Tŷ-croes developed at either end. The Education Department envisaged that, in cases where it would be more convenient for a child to attend a school in another parish, arrangements could be made whereby the parish where the child was resident would pay the neighbouring parish for the child's education. Although the system envisaged was both sensible and,

---

[19] *Baner*, 8 February 1871, and PRO, ED2/604.
[20] Cited in D. Pretty, *Two Centuries of Anglesey Schools* (Cardiff, 1977), pp.177–81.

in theory, easy to administer, the reality proved otherwise as Boards demonstrated a marked reluctance to become involved in such arrangements.[21] Thus, it is clear that even in 1870 the parish was not the ideal unit for school administration in many areas and, while this was especially the case in the rapidly expanding urban areas, it was also a feature of a number of rural areas. At the same time, the problem of enforcing central government authority in the localities meant that a host of local irregularities continued for many years after the passing of the Act. In addition, regular periods of economic depression and the poverty of many districts meant that many parishes had genuine difficulties in achieving the criteria set by the Education Department. These factors were compounded by parochial rivalries and the conflict between the Anglican and Nonconformist groups in society, creating circumstances that were hardly conducive to the smooth implementation of the 1870 Education Act.

The political or denominational aspects of the debate had a much greater relevance than the administrative factors complicating the administration of the Act. The Nonconformist leadership in Wales regarded the monopoly of the Church in educational provision in so many parts of the country as grotesque. For the Anglican and landowning elements in Wales, retaining control of education was crucial to prevent a further decline in their influence and in their contribution to society. These concerns were compounded by the fact that the argument over the desirability of establishing School Boards was the first all-Wales political debate since the election of 1868; this served to increase the intensity of the exchanges and, in many instances, strengthened the resolve of the Nonconformist leadership to place education under the democratic control of the community.

The method by which School Boards could be established created a focus for a vigorous debate in many Welsh communities, particularly in the first five years after enactment. The

---

[21] PRO, ED2/ 575.

period from January 1871 to December 1872 witnessed the greatest activity, with 129 Boards established.[22] Of these, apart from thirteen established in the boroughs,[23] eleven were in Anglesey, seven in Breconshire, ten in Cardiganshire, eleven in Carmarthenshire, twelve in Caernarfonshire, twelve in Denbighshire, one in Flintshire, eleven in Glamorgan, nine in Merioneth, nine in Monmouthshire, nine in Montgomeryshire, twelve in Pembrokeshire and three in Radnorshire.[24] A further 107 Boards were established between January 1873 and June 1875,[25] with a reduction to fifty in the following year, six more in 1876–7,[26] thirteen in 1877–7,[27] three in 1878–7[28] and five in the period to June 1880.[29]

The decision as to whether or not to form a School Board in a borough rested with the councillors, although many sought to ascertain the views of the ratepayers before arriving at any decision. In those areas where the Liberals had control of the borough council, the issue was rarely put to the vote and resulted in speedy decisions to establish Boards in boroughs such as Aberystwyth, Beaumaris, Brecon, Cardigan, Carmarthen, Caernarfon, Haverfordwest, Newport, Pembroke, Pwllheli, Swansea and Wrexham, all of which had established Boards by June 1871.[30]

However, in the parishes the Nonconformist leadership had to make a determined effort to gain popular support for the establishment of a School Board. Where a deficiency was deemed to exist, it was normal for a vestry meeting to be held, at which a resolution would be proposed that the Education Department be requested to sanction the establishment of a Board for the parish. Those opposed to the initiative would usually propose an amendment that the matter be postponed in order that an attempt be made to remedy the deficiency by voluntary methods. Yet, whatever the decision at the meeting, it was possible for ten ratepayers to call for a poll of the entire

[22] PP 1871, XXII.
[23] Ibid.
[24] Ibid.
[25] PP 1875, XXIV.
[26] PP 1877, XXIX.
[27] PP 1878, XXVIII.
[28] PP 1878–9, XXIII.
[29] PP 1880, XXII.
[30] PP 1871, XXII.

parish to be held by secret ballot. These referenda were to be an early trial of religious and political strength in late nineteenth-century Wales, and one that gauged public opinion in both rural and industrial communities. The efforts to establish School Boards arose partly from the perceptions of social need among those who exercised Liberal and Nonconformist leadership in each parish, yet endeavours in the localities were also deeply influenced by the efforts of papers such as *Y Goleuad*, *Seren Cymru*, *Y Tyst* and *Baner ac Amserau Cymru*. The last named was the most determined advocate of the Board system, and its reporter, John Griffith, 'Y Gohebydd', was to play a key role in influencing the developments as well as reporting the news.[31] Despite this concerted campaign, however, the reactions of the communities involved were varied and differing attitudes on the questions posed by the legislation of 1870 provide a fascinating insight into the nature and predilections of Welsh society in a formative period in its political as well as its educational evolution. The ultimate outcome of the debate was a widespread adoption of the School Board system of provision in elementary education, but the debate itself reveals a complex web of often contradictory impulses.

The attitude of the Anglican and landowning influences varied. On the passing of the Act, the earl of Powis declared at a meeting in Oswestry that, in his opinion, Church and National schools should be allowed to continue to provide for the educational needs of parishes where they were already doing so and that, if deficiencies did exist, then every effort should be made to meet the need by voluntary effort. Only where such efforts failed should Boards be established and where this was necessary, churchmen should ensure that they operated effectively.[32] His attitude reflected the magnanimous paternalism of many landlords, yet his was not a viewpoint that was shared by the greater portion of Welsh landowners. Sir Watkin Williams Wynn, owner of the large Wynnstay estate which included swathes of Denbighshire, Montgomeryshire and Merioneth, declared in February 1871 that, as the patron of sixty schools, he intended to continue to support those which would still be

[31] J. Griffith, *Cofiant y Gohebydd* (Denbigh, 1905), pp.139–82. Griffith was a key participant in campaigns in Llangollen, Beaumaris and Dolgellau, among others.
[32] Cited in J. Davies, *Education in a Welsh Rural County* (Cardiff, 1973), pp.26–7.

maintained according to the principles of the Established Church.[33] The official position, represented by the inspectors of schools, was that Boards would be needed in the majority of towns in Wales, whereas the rural areas would continue to have their educational needs provided by voluntary methods, a view that was in accord with that of the earl of Powis. According to Shadrach Pryce, however, the deficiency which existed in certain rural areas was such that it would be impossible for the voluntary agencies to complete the task of supplying accommodation. As a result, the setting up of Boards was inevitable in a number of rural parishes.[34]

The debate concerning the desirability of School Boards thus manifested itself most strongly in the rural areas, where Anglican hopes of meeting the educational deficiency by voluntary means were highest. But although areas of rural Wales often witnessed vigorous campaigns over the education question, this was not invariably so. Certainly there were areas where the education question was settled amicably. In parishes such as Llanarmon (Caernarfonshire)[35] and Llanfihangel y Traethau (Merioneth)[36] a compromise was achieved, whereby the voluntary system would continue but on a non-denominational basis. In Llandinam (Montgomeryshire) a proposal to establish a School Board was made by the local clergyman and received unanimous support at the vestry meeting.[37] He was one among a small minority of clergymen who supported the establishment of School Boards, usually on account of the difficulty which they had experienced in raising funds by voluntary methods. The fact that many Nonconformists did not contribute to schools over which they had no control, coupled with the disinclination of many landowners to contribute for a variety of economic reasons, meant that many National schools faced serious financial difficulties and had been maintained only as a result of great exertions on the part of the local clergy. Many clergymen simply did not wish to shoulder such heavy burdens when an alternative was available.

---

[33] *Baner*, 8 February 1871.
[34] PP 1871, XXII, Mr Pryce's Report.
[35] *Baner*, 14 January 1871.
[36] PRO, ED2/615.
[37] *Baner*, 4 February 1871; J. M. Evans, 'Elementary education in Montgomeryshire', *Montgomery Collections*, LXIII (1970–3), 1–46, 119–66.

In other parishes a considerable measure of agreement was achieved on the education issue, with little, if any, opposition registered against the formation of Boards in parishes such as Llandwrog (Caernarfonshire)[38] and Llandrillo (Merioneth).[39] This spirit existed in other areas where opinion was often varied. Despite the objections of the Anglican element in the localities, large majorities were recorded in favour of School Boards in Llan-arth (Cardiganshire),[40] Llangollen (Denbighshire),[41] Llan-rug (Caernarfonshire)[42] and Llandegla yn Iâl (Denbighshire).[43]

In other localities, however, a more controversial picture emerges. In Tal-y-llyn (Merioneth) a vestry meeting voted unanimously in favour of establishing a Board, but objections were raised by the Anglicans to a proposal that the parish of Llanwrin (Montgomeryshire) should be joined with Tal-y-llyn to form a united district. Their reservations reflected the serious problem of seeking the amalgamation of parishes. Such combination was insisted on by the Education Department because of its advantages in reducing building costs in areas where surplus places were available in neighbouring parishes. However, problems could arise in areas such as Llanwrin because ratepayers would be faced with a School Board rate despite the fact that the education of their children was provided in a voluntary school. The parishioners would therefore derive no direct benefit from the rate, which would be spent on erecting and maintaining a school in the neighbouring parish.

The argument most often used against the formation of a Board was the fear that it would lead to an increase in rates. This was cited in a petition to the Education Department against the formation of a School Board at Aberdaron (Caernarfonshire).[44] There, however, matters were complicated by Lord Penrhyn offering to undertake the construction of a school, in association with other landowners; the reluctance of some of those to contribute and the fear that the school would be subject to the influence of the landlords provoked a determined response on the part of

[38] *Y Goleuad*, February 1871.
[39] *Y Goleuad*, 4 March 1871.
[40] *Baner*, 7 June 1871.
[41] *Baner*, 4 March 1871.
[42] *Baner*, 1 March 1871.
[43] *Baner*, 7 January 1871.
[44] NLW, Voelas and Cefnamwlch, B/6/20.

the Nonconformists.[45] In Cemais (Montgomeryshire) the local landowner adopted a policy of writing to each of his tenants, warning of the likelihood of high rates if a School Board were established and urging (unsuccessfully) that a Board be rejected.[46] The issue dominated the campaign in Penrhyndeudraeth (Caernarfonshire), where a vestry decision in favour of a Board was overturned by a majority of eight votes in a poll of the parish,[47] and in Corwen (Merioneth), where a vestry meeting and a subsequent keenly contested referendum produced a narrow vote against a Board.[48] Further defeats for the promoters of the School Boards were recorded at Nefyn (Caernarfonshire)[49] and in Llanidan (Anglesey), where the agitation in favour of a School Board met with vigorous opposition from Lord Boston. In a circular addressed to each household in the parish, he declared his willingness to extend the existing school in the village and to maintain a teacher at his own cost. He dubiously claimed that his sole motive was to save the ratepayers of the parish from the burden of the School Board rate, especially those who were his own tenants. The letter also stipulated that were the parishioners to opt for the School Board system, he would merely contribute the amount that he was legally compelled to pay.[50] The rates issue was also in evidence in Llanfihangel-y-Creuddyn (Cardiganshire), where the school was found to be inadequate in 1876, but where no School Board was established. A vestry meeting decided to levy a voluntary rate of one shilling per household in order to maintain the school, which would continue to operate under the supervision of the clergyman and be run as a National school. The Nonconformists protested that they had not been notified of the meeting, but attempts to persuade their ratepayers to withhold payment of the voluntary rate proved a failure.[51]

Less scrupulous methods than warnings of a heavy rate burden were deployed as a means of averting the creation of School Boards in other areas. The imposition of a 'screw', whereby landowners used coercive tactics to persuade their

[45] NLW, Voelas and Cefnamwlch, B/6.
[46] PRO, ED2/626.
[47] *Baner*, 1 April 1871.
[48] *Baner*, 19 April 1871.
[49] *Baner*, 22 February 1871.
[50] University of Wales, Bangor, Lligwy Papers.
[51] PRO, ED2/572.

tenants to vote as they desired, was cited as an influence in several cases. In Beddgelert (Caernarfonshire)[52] the School Board was adopted despite the alleged 'screw' imposed by the landowners, and at Llangelynnin (Merioneth) a poll of the parish resulted in a vote of 125 to 62 in favour of the establishment of a Board, notwithstanding the efforts of the rector, the Revd J. E. Davies, and the local landowner, H. J. Beckley, in opposing the proposal.[53] Similar results were achieved in Llanerfyl (Montgomeryshire), again despite allegations that a 'screw' had been imposed by the Wynnstay estate against the founding of a Board,[54] and in Llanfair Pwllgwyngyll (Anglesey) the bitterness occasioned by the outcome resulted in a boycott of a local tradesman by the opponents of a Board, an experience reflected in the literary work of his distinguished son, John Morris-Jones.[55] In Llandysul (Cardiganshire), a bitter contest resulted in defeat for the proponents of a Board in a campaign which witnessed allegations of threatening behaviour and undue influence on both sides,[56] a pattern that was repeated in the neighbouring parish of Newcastle Emlyn.[57]

Vigorous debate on the School Board issue was not confined to the rural areas. The town of Caernarfon had an honoured place in Liberal politics, serving as the home of several leading Liberal newspapers and being widely accepted as the fountainhead of radical politics in the north. The town had a sizeable working-class community centred on the harbour as well as an influential bourgeoisie of Liberal business and professional men. In common with a number of northern towns, Caernarfon was well endowed with voluntary schools, which led its Anglican community to assert with some justification that there was no need for a Board, as little, if any, deficiency in accommodation existed there. Caernarfon had over 2,000 school places, despite having an estimated child population of only 1,594,[58] yet over

---

[52] *Baner*, 10 May 1871; *Y Goleuad*, 4 March 1871.
[53] *Baner*, 4 March 1871; Denbighshire CRO, Ruthin, DD/Wy/5807.
[54] *Baner*, 29 April 1871.
[55] Personal information provided by the kindness of the late Professor Bedwyr Lewis Jones; J. E. Caerwyn Williams, 'Syr John Morris-Jones: y cefndir a'r cyfnod cynnar, Rhan 1', *THSC*, 1965, 167–206, see especially pp.180–2 and the poems 'Salm i Famon' and 'Cymru Fu – Cymru Fydd'.
[56] *Baner*, 1 April 1871.
[57] *Baner*, 1 February 1871.
[58] PRO, ED2/584.

1,300 of these places were provided by the Church, either at Caernarfon or Twthill National School, with a further 250 being ragged school accommodation. Fewer than 500 of the town's children were being educated at the Caernarfon British School, although the overwhelming majority of the town's people were Nonconformists. Another factor was the attitude of the vicar of Caernarfon, the Revd H. T. Edwards, the author of a volume on church endowments and a man who had alienated Nonconformist opinion by his pronouncements on the education question and his constant attacks on the congregations. Yet the initial reaction of the town's leaders was to urge delay rather than immediate action,[59] and it was on the question of school attendance that the supporters of a School Board based their claim. While acknowledging that the supply of accommodation was sufficient, the Nonconformists argued for a Board in order that rates might be levied to engage the services of attendance officers. The latter would combat the considerable problem of non-attendance in the town. Those of the Anglican allegiance sought to expose the Nonconformist ploy and claimed that the whole purpose of the establishment of a Board was to place the British school on the rates and undermine the National schools. Yet, notwithstanding their protestations and their argument that the rate burden was likely to become unbearable, a Board was established.

In several other northern towns, where a deficiency in accommodation did not exist, attempts were made by the managers to call for the establishment of Boards in order to relieve themselves of the burden of maintaining a school. In the majority of these cases, British schools had been opened merely to provide an alternative to the National schools and, as it was rare for them to have the support of wealthy patrons or a charity endowment, a number of the British schools experienced difficulty in remaining solvent. By declaring their unwillingness to maintain a school, the managers were creating an educational deficiency, thereby increasing the likelihood that the Education Department would sanction the formation of a School Board. The tactic was deployed in Porthmadog (Caernarfonshire), a seaport associated with the Ffestiniog slate quarries and a town

[59] Ibid.

with a strong Liberal presence. However, despite the efforts of Edward Breese, Love Jones Parry and Robert Rowlands, the voters rejected a Board on the grounds that the educational provision in the town was considered sufficient and that the ratepayers had no desire to incur an unnecessary rate burden notwithstanding their allegiance to the Nonconformist denominations and to Liberal politics.[60] The most controversial instance of the deployment of the closure tactic occurred in Bangor.[61] The city had a strong ecclesiastical tradition based on the cathedral, whose influence, though in decline, remained considerable. Moreover, the Anglican tradition was reinforced by the existence of several Church charities, including the Bishop Rowlands charity which provided a free grammar school. A large industrial presence in the town, associated with the slate trade (producing items such as school slates, tomb-slabs, roofing slates and chimney pieces), was controlled by Lord Penrhyn and the Assheton-Smith family, with varying degrees of influence on the workforce. It was in the light of this influence, and the knowledge that Bangor was a difficult area for the Liberals, that the managers of British and Wesleyan schools in Bangor sought to avoid a referendum by using Section 12 (2) of the Act, which stipulated that should the managers of a voluntary school decide to abandon their efforts and, should that decision create a large deficiency, the Education Department would be forced to order the establishment of a Board without a referendum. *Y Goleuad* strongly defended the action of the Bangor Nonconformists, arguing that the town was in the anomalous position of being a borough without a Borough Council and asserting that Anglican intransigence had provoked the decision of the managers of the British and Wesleyan schools to close their establishments so as to ensure that a Board was sanctioned for the parish.[62] It was clear that local Nonconformists were determined to avoid a referendum because of the experiences of other parishes. In the view of *Y Goleuad*:

> Yr oedd y ddau bwyllgor yn teimlo y gwrthwynebiad cryfaf i apelio at y trethdalwyr yn gyffredinol, canys yr oeddynt yn dwfn ffieiddio y

[60] *Y Goleuad*, 4 February 1871; *Cambrian News*, 18 March 1871.
[61] *Y Goleuad*, 9 December 1871.
[62] Ibid.

celwyddau, y meddwdod, y trais, a'r holl ddichellion anghyfiawnder a ddefnyddid mewn ardaloedd eraill yn Nghymru gan bleidwyr 'yr Eglwys' i'r diben o gau allan Fyrddau Ysgol, a chadw addysg y genedl yn eu dwylaw hwy hyd y diwedd. Nid oedd y profiad chwerw a gawsid gynifer o weithiau o nerth dichellion i gamarwain yr anwybodus, a nerth gallu i orthrymu y gweiniaid a'r dibynol, yn ddim calondid iddynt i feddwl am wynebu holl gynwrf etholiad.

[The two committees felt the strongest disinclination to appeal to the ratepayers as a whole, because they deeply abhorred the lies, drunkenness, violence and all cunning injustice that had been used in other areas of Wales by the supporters of 'the Church' in order to keep out School Boards, and to keep the control of the education of the nation in their hands to the end. The bitter experience they had witnessed so many times of the power of cunning to mislead the uninitiated, and the ability of power to oppress the weak and the dependent, gave them no heart to face the heat of an election.][63]

Moreover, *Y Goleuad* claimed that the voluntary system placed a burden on the managers and subscribers of Nonconformist voluntary schools which should be borne by the ratepayers as a whole, and that the British school managers had neither the endowments nor the other resources available to Anglican school managers to fulfil their duties. The decision of the Education Department to sanction a School Board for the parish was roundly condemned by the Anglican leadership in Bangor. Yet the greatest condemnation was reserved for the Nonconformist leaders for what were claimed to be the underhand methods used by them to secure the establishment of a Board. Despite the justifications offered in the pages of *Y Goleuad* by eminent Nonconformists, such as the Revd Dr Davies and Principal Daniel Rowlands of the Normal College, the methods adopted at Bangor aroused the hostility of a significant number of the more moderate Nonconformist members as well as uncommitted voters.[64] In direct consequence of this, the first Board election in Bangor witnessed the return of an Anglican majority, whose first act was to pass a resolution condemning the way the Board had been foisted on the parish.[65]

[63] Ibid.
[64] Ibid.
[65] Ibid.

The Education Department proceeded against local wishes in Cricieth, where both a vestry meeting and a poll of the parish had resulted in votes clearly in favour of a School Board.[66] Yet the Education Department insisted that no Board was required because the town's existing National school was sufficient for the needs of the parish.[67] Nevertheless, a personal dispute between the rector, the Revd Erasmus Parry, the schoolmaster and the local landowner led to the opening of a separate school, which admitted the children of the town free of charge, and a majority of the children moved from the National school and forced its closure. As had been the case in Bangor, after creating an artificial deficiency a School Board was established to supply the educational needs of the town, but on this occasion the tactic was adopted with the support of a majority in the community.[68] This procedure was, however, sparingly used by the advocates of the Board system after the experience of Bangor. Thus, the managers of the Welshpool British School avoided the tactic and as a result the school continued in existence, although experiencing considerable financial difficulties.[69]

The town of Denbigh provides a further example of a thriving town with a strong radical presence. Denbigh was located in a rich agricultural district, and its role as the commercial centre for the area had recently been enhanced by its development as the hub of important railway connections which brought considerable traffic in goods and passengers. Economic progress was matched by political vigour in which Nonconformity was potent. The Nonconformists were clearly the leading political and commercial force in Denbigh, and the town was the political base of Thomas Gee and his powerful *Baner ac Amserau Cymru*. An ordained Calvinistic Methodist minister, Gee had occupied the position of mayor of the town in 1869 and was a leading figure in Denbigh's commercial life. Yet despite the strength of the radical influence in the politics of Denbigh, the Nonconformists were not in a strong position in terms of the provision of schools in the town. Of an estimated requirement of 1,080 school places, no more than 736 were provided, with only 300 of these at the

---

[66] *Y Goleuad*, 25 February 1871.
[67] Williams, 'Kynnersley Educational Returns', 302–7.
[68] Ibid.
[69] PRO, ED2/630.

town's British school.[70] Although the opponents of Board provision claimed that the child population had been grossly overestimated by the inclusion of the inmates of the Denbigh Lunatic Asylum in the population figures, Anglican representations to the Education Department proved fruitless, with the result that a meeting was convened by the town council to ascertain the views of the ratepayers.[71] A large majority was recorded in favour of the establishment of a Board. The establishment of the Denbigh School Board owed more to the numerical strength of Nonconformity in the town than to any political manœuvres on the part of its Liberal and denominational leadership. Yet the experiences of Caernarfon and especially of Bangor demonstrated that where a Board was considered unnecessary and an unwanted burden on the rates, the Nonconformist leadership was likely to face severe difficulties in attempting to impose a Board. Just as important, the experience in Bangor showed that in such cases the Nonconformist community could not be relied on to ensure a majority on the Board itself.

The presence of a large body of committed religious leaders was undoubtedly a contributory factor in the overwhelming victory for the supporters of the School Board in the parish of Llanycil (Merioneth), which included the market town of Bala.[72] Its Nonconformist congregations were substantial, but the most important religious influence in the town was the Calvinistic Methodist College, its presence magnified by the personal prestige of the principal, Lewis Edwards. Conversely, in St David's, where the cathedral exercised a considerable influence, the Anglican presence was still not sufficient to prevent a large majority being secured at the vestry meeting and in the subsequent poll of the parish in favour of the establishment of a Board, a result which provided considerable satisfaction for the Nonconformist leadership.[73] In other rural towns a less controversial picture emerges. Significant majorities were recorded in favour of the adoption of the Board system in Newtown,[74]

---

[70] PRO, ED2/591.
[71] Denbighshire CRO, Ruthin BD/A/488.
[72] *Y Goleuad*, 1 April 1871.
[73] *Y Goleuad*, 8 April 1871.
[74] *Y Goleuad*, 1 April 1871.

Llanidloes[75] and Dolgellau.[76] All three towns had experience of radical politics, Llanidloes and Newtown being strongholds of Chartism during the previous generation, and Dolgellau the scene of an acrimonious dispute between the town's Nonconformist leaders and the churchwardens in the previous year.[77]

The most disappointing results for the Nonconformists in the urban areas came in the coastal towns of north Wales which were emerging as centres of tourism. At Llandudno, a spirited campaign in favour of a Board failed to secure its formation,[78] although the poll of the parish resulted in a majority of only seven votes against the proposal to have a Board on a very low turnout.[79] In Rhyl a lively campaign led to the defeat of the Nonconformist leadership at the vestry meeting and in the referendum. According to the town's Nonconformists, the defeat was attributable to an 'unholy alliance' between the Wesleyans, Anglicans and farmers fearful of a heavy rate, with liberal provision of beer by the opponents of a Board being cited as a further explanation.[80] In Prestatyn, the School Board question lay dormant from its rejection in 1871 until 1893, when it was reopened following a decision of the Education Department to condemn the town's British school. Prestatyn had seen good relations between the denominations throughout the 1860s, but they gradually deteriorated after the appointment of the Revd Thomas Price in 1868. Price was regarded as a 'disturbing element' in the community and by 1893 he had succeeded in alienating the churchwardens and the schoolmaster as well as the local Nonconformists, to whom he had addressed extremely disparaging and hurtful remarks.[81] Price's personality was an obstacle to harmony with the Nonconformists and in consequence a determined effort was made in 1893 to secure the formation of a School Board. According to the propaganda sheet issued by the Nonconformist leaders in the town:

---

[75] *Y Goleuad*, 4 March 1871.
[76] *Baner*, 18 March 1871.
[77] Ibid.
[78] *Baner*, 25 January 1871.
[79] *Y Goleuad*, 4 February 1871 and 25 February 1871.
[80] *Y Goleuad*, 25 February 1871 and 8 April 1871.
[81] Flintshire CRO, Hawarden, D/L 20.

THE BATTLE FOR THE BOARDS

Cofiwch fod ein Ymneilltuaeth yn cael ei rhoddi ar ei phrawf yn y frwydr hon. Dyma gyfle bendigedig i sefyll yn wrol dros draddodiadau ein tadau a'n teidiau o blaid annibyniaeth ac ymneilltuaeth. Byddwn yn ddynion, a safwn yn ddewr o blaid rhyddid, fel y gall ein plant gael addysg elfennol bur, heb ei chymysgu a'i thrwytho gan gredoau di-fudd, a di-sail a'i dysgu mewn catechism sydd yn ffiaidd beth gennym fel rhieni.

[Remember that our Nonconformity is being put to the test in this battle. This is a glorious opportunity to stand as men, true to the traditions of our fathers and grandfathers in defence of independence and Nonconformity. Let us be men and let us stand bravely in favour of freedom, so that our children can receive a pure elementary education, without being influenced and distorted by those unbeneficial and groundless beliefs which are taught in a catechism which we as parents detest.][82]

On occasion, considerable responsibility for the failure of School Board initiatives can be attributed to the Education Department. In Conwy the assessment compiled by the Education Department precluded the establishment of a School Board. The town's estimated child population of 320 was, according to its report, adequately catered for at the Conwy National School, which held places for 392.[83] The decision ultimately rested with the members of the Conwy corporation, but on account of the hostility expressed by the ratepayers to the proposal, the matter was not even raised. Although the Revd Spinther James of Llandudno, a local representative of the Birmingham Educational League, sought to reopen the matter in 1875, claiming that the Nonconformists of Conwy were contributing a considerable amount to the maintenance of the schools yet had no voice in their management, the attempt failed and the matter was not considered again until the 1890s.[84]

Elsewhere the difficulties arose from conflicting interests within Nonconformist society. In 1877 the parish of Whitford (Flintshire), which included the town of Mostyn, witnessed considerable agitation for a School Board. Here, the Anglican and landowning interest was in a very strong position, for the parish

---

[82] Ibid.
[83] PRO, ED2/584.
[84] For further details, see H. G. Williams, 'The School Board Movement in Caernarfonshire, 1870–80', *TCHS*, 1989, p.33.

contained the country seats of Lord Mostyn, the earl of Denbigh and Sir Pyers Mostyn. All three landowners were decidedly against the formation of a Board, with Lord Mostyn and his agent, St John Charlton, being particularly active in leading the opposition to the establishment of the Board system.[85] Yet what is significant about the campaign in Whitford is that several leading Nonconformist deacons were also hostile to a Board, notably those with large property and business interests in the town of Mostyn. As Herbert Lewis commented later:

> the whole of the territorial and landowning influence was brought to bear against us, while our adversaries had the powerful support of the church, and what was of far greater importance, that of the most important and influential section of Nonconformists.[86]

This can in part be explained by the fact that the proponents of the Board were led by the Revd E. Pan Jones, minister of Rhewl Independent Chapel and a leading figure in the Congregationalist union.[87] He was renowned as an agitator amongst the miners of the north Wales coalfield, and was firmly allied with the more radical members of the local Liberal community, such as Edward Bryan and Thomas Jones. Pan Jones's depiction of Whitford as a parish 'slumbering in the clutches of deference' certainly struck a chord with the miners. In Whitford it was the working-class community which accounted for the majority of supporters of the Board and it was to its members that the leaders of the School Board movement sought to appeal. But this was not enough to achieve victory. The extreme radicalism of some of the Board's advocates, notably Pan Jones himself, alienated the more moderate element of the Nonconformist influence, a fear of increased rates combining with social deference to leave the Church as the main provider of education in the north-east coalfield to the turn of the century. The promoters of the Board might accuse those Nonconformists who had opposed their efforts of gross treachery, but Nonconformists moved by similar

---

[85] Flintshire CRO, Hawarden, Herbert Lewis Papers.
[86] Ibid.; W. Hugh Jones, 'Herbert Lewis a llywodraeth leol', in Kitty Idwal Jones (ed.), *Syr Herbert Lewis, 1858–1933* (Aberystwyth, 1958), pp.40–56.
[87] P. Jones-Evans, 'Evan Pan Jones – land reformer', *WHR*, 4 (1968–9), 143–60; E. Pan Jones, *Oes Gofion* (Bala, 1908), pp.54–90.

considerations were to be found in many towns, with consequences for Nonconformist Liberalism in Wales which will be discussed later.

Industrial areas certainly proved to be the most fertile ground for the supporters of the School Board movement. Hugh Williams, in a comprehensive survey of the pattern of School Boards in Caernarfonshire, points to the fact that it was the quarry areas that provided some of the most spectacular successes for the supporters of School Boards.[88] Meetings such as those held in Llanllyfni in Dyffryn Nantlle resulted in a considerable majority for the establishment of a Board in the vestry meeting, those opposed to the proposal failing to secure sufficient signatures even to demand a poll of the parish.[89] Similarly, overwhelming majorities in favour of Boards were recorded in the Caernarfonshire quarrying areas of Llandwrog, Llanwnda, Llanrug, Llanddeiniolen[90] and Llanberis, as well as in Blaenau Ffestiniog in Merioneth,[91] the result being that the quarrying areas had the greatest concentration of School Boards of any rural county in Wales.[92] Yet even in some quarrying villages the voluntary system continued to provide for the educational needs of the parish. Thus, in Bethesda a compromise was reached whereby National and British schools operated harmoniously for a period of twenty years.

The responsiveness of the quarrying districts to School Board initiatives was more than matched by the industrial areas of south Wales. In the anthracite mining districts of south-west Wales, large majorities were secured in favour of School Boards despite the opposition of landowners and industrialists such as the Buckley, Ashburnham and Talbot families. In Llandybïe and Llanfihangel Aberbythych (Carmarthenshire), a controversial proposal that the parishes be amalgamated for education purposes was implemented despite strong opposition from Lord Emlyn and some Nonconformists in the parish.[93] The results were not, however, necessarily a reflection of any great disharmony between the Anglican and Nonconformist camps. In

---

[88] Williams, 'Kynnersley Educational Returns', 307–16.
[89] *Baner*, 25 March 1871.
[90] *Baner*, 18 February 1871.
[91] *Y Tyst*, 10 February 1871.
[92] Williams, 'Kynnersley Educational Returns', 307–16.
[93] Ibid.

Llandybïe, as in neighbouring Llandeilo Fawr, the relationship between the National and British efforts had been generally harmonious, a pattern that was repeated in the relationship between the National and Board schools.[94] Overall, the National school sector continued to provide the education in rural areas such as Trap, while the School Board concentrated on building schools in industrial areas such as Ammanford, Saron, Carmel and Pen-y-groes. Enduring acrimony was also avoided elsewhere in the anthracite coalfield and its environs. In Loughor (Glamorgan) a School Board was established despite the attempts of the local clergy to collect subscriptions to remedy the deficiency,[95] while in Llandeilo Tal-y-bont (Glamorgan) the overwhelming strength of Nonconformity in the parish, combined with the severe deficiency of accommodation, resulted in the vicar, the Revd John Williams Jones, abandoning his opposition to a Board.[96] In Llan-non (Carmarthenshire) a determined resistance was offered by local landowners, whose view was shared by a few leading Nonconformists; but the campaign waged in favour of a Board triumphed in the vestry meeting and the demand for a poll was eventually withdrawn.[97]

A temporary defeat for the supporters of the School Board movement occurred in Llanedi (Carmarthenshire), where demographic changes meant that two schools were required at the two most extreme points of the parish. The vicar, the Revd Roger Williams, remained totally opposed to the Board system, and, insisting that agitation to establish a School Board was insulting to the efforts of his committee, he was able to resist the setting up of a Board until 1881.[98] In Llanelli and Swansea it was abundantly clear that it would be impossible to remedy the severe deficiency by voluntary means in rapidly expanding towns. A vestry meeting at Llanelli voted overwhelmingly in its favour[99] and the Swansea Corporation moved swiftly to establish a Board, while in the Swansea Valley there were successes for the

---

[94] Gomer M. Roberts, *Hanes Plwyf Llandybïe* (Cardiff, 1938), pp.125–32.
[95] PRO, ED2/607.
[96] PRO, ED2/605.
[97] *Y Goleuad*, 25 February 1871.
[98] PRO, ED2/577.
[99] *Y Goleuad*, 8 April 1871.

supporters of School Boards in Cilybebyll,[100] Ystradgynlais[101] and Rhyndwyclydach. Other parishes in the south-west witnessed more embittered campaigns. Llansamlet (Glamorgan) rejected the proposal to establish a Board and the campaign at Pembrey (Carmarthenshire) was marked by considerable acrimony.[102]

No uniform pattern can be seen in the steam coalfield further east. Parishes such as Aberystruth (Monmouthshire) recorded large majorities in favour of a Board despite the Church having made considerable efforts to supply the educational needs of the area.[103] Similarly, there were significant majorities recorded in favour of the establishment of School Boards in parishes like Cefncoedycymer (Breconshire)[104] and Llantrisant (Glamorgan).[105] Apathy towards the question of education was seen in Eglwysilan (Glamorgan), where, despite the evident needs of areas of expanding population, it took considerable effort before a Board was eventually established,[106] while in Upper Margam (Glamorgan) little effort was made to provide for the educational needs of the area for over a decade after the passing of the Act.[107] The decision to request a School Board for Merthyr Tydfil was supported by a large cross-section of political and religious opinion in the town, a fact that highlights the view of many Anglicans in south Wales that a voluntary effort to supply the educational deficiency was a forlorn hope.[108] In Dowlais, where the prospects for educational provision already looked promising, a consensus in favour of a Board also emerged. The Dowlais Iron Company had organized a system of schools based on the denominational adherence of the parents, whereby each employee had a certain amount deducted from his wages at source in order to finance a school. Roman Catholic Irish workers were involved in a similar scheme, their contributions being handed to the Catholic priest for the purpose of education. Yet the success of these initiatives

[100] PRO, ED2/603.
[101] *Baner*, 25 January 1871.
[102] *Baner*, 4 January 1871.
[103] PRO, ED2 /622.
[104] *Cardiff and Merthyr Guardian*, 18 March 1871.
[105] *Cardiff and Merthyr Guardian*, 11 February 1871.
[106] *Baner*, 13 May 1871.
[107] PRO, ED2 /608.
[108] *Baner*, 8 March 1871.

did not prevent the establishment of a School Board for the parish.[109]

Cardiff procrastinated for a long time, before eventually adopting a School Board in 1875, partly because of the hostile attitude of the marquess of Bute. Attempts to supply the growing educational needs of the young community of the Rhondda by voluntary methods were attempted but abandoned in 1878 as successive recessions in the coal trade meant that schools were at intervals deprived of the support of local coalowners.[110] In Bedwellty, the strong Nonconformist organization, most notably at Tredegar, secured the election of a Board as early as April 1871, despite the presence of a significant body of Roman Catholic voters.[111] The strength of Nonconformity in Neath, however, did not prevent the Borough Council from remaining implacably hostile to any proposal to establish a School Board, an attitude supported by a number of the town's leading Nonconformists themselves.[112] Although a School Board was eventually established there, it was due to the British schools' inability to maintain their provision rather than as a result of the borough councillors' conversion to the desirability of a School Board. In the neighbouring town of Aberafan, the Church was engaged in considerable efforts to supply the deficiency of accommodation, again in order to counter demands for the establishment of a School Board. To the disgust of the local Nonconformist leadership, the Anglican majority on the borough council rejected a proposal to establish a Board, so that only Anglican and Catholic schools operated in the town until 1885 when, as a result of agitation on the part of the Nonconformists, the Aberavon Unsectarian schools were opened to provide an alternative for the children. These continued to operate until 1893, when a combination of a new deficiency in school accommodation and a greater Nonconformist influence on the borough council led to a decision to establish a Board.[113]

These cases, however, were insignificant compared with the debate on the School Board question at Bedwas (Monmouthshire), where events were reminiscent of the evictions in the rural

[109] Ibid.
[110] PP 1881, XXXII, Mr Edwards's Report.
[111] *Baner*, 26 April and 10 May 1871.
[112] PRO, ED16/299.
[113] PRO, ED2/601; see also Eben Jones, *The Birth of the Aberavon Unsectarian Schools* (Port Talbot, 1981).

areas in 1868. The Nonconformists of the area petitioned the Education Department that, as no elementary education was provided in the parish, it was its duty to sanction the formation of a School Board. The uncompromising vicar of the parish, the Revd Augustus Morgan, was determined to avoid the establishment of a Board and, in association with Lord Tredegar, drew up a scheme of education based on the principles of the Established Church. For the Revd Richards, the local Baptist minister, the position taken by Augustus Morgan compromised any attempt to co-operate with him, and the local Nonconformists asserted that they had no alternative but to press for a School Board. It was alleged that the Church was constructing a school

> with the aim of providing a sufficient amount of school accommodation in which the church of England catechism and dogma will be taught so as to forestall the actions of Nonconformists and if possible prevent the formation of a School Board.[114]

Edwin Phillips, a leading figure in the locality, asserted in a letter of protest to the Education Department that the local Nonconformists had an objection to the catechism being taught in day schools, as the conscience clause did not provide an adequate guarantee to the community:

> You know for every one of the poor who would have the courage to go and tell the clergyman or schoolmaster, a dozen would submit to have their children taught the catechism against their wish or keep their children at home; the poor do not like to take the risk of doing what they would think to be an offence to the clergymen, employer or schoolmaster.[115]

A meeting of the ratepayers voted in favour of a Board, but a poll of the parish was demanded. During the campaign leading up to the referendum on the issue, allegations of intimidation and threatening behaviour were levied against those who opposed the proposal. P. B. Woodruff, a leading local employer, overseer of the parish and the leading opponent of the School Board,

[114] PRO, ED2/601.
[115] Ibid.

indulged in a series of recriminations against the supporters of the Board who were on his payroll. Henry Adams, a sawyer at the Machen Tinworks, owned by Woodruff, was discharged at a minute's notice and a warning was issued to other employees that those who voted for a Board would be treated in a similar manner. John Williams, a moulder at the Machen Foundry for over twenty-three years, was also dismissed, as was James Hicks, a finer at the Machen Tinworks, together with John Hill, a labourer, John Stephens, a washman, Daniel Jones, a hammerman, Joseph Rowland, a puddler, Edward Williams, a washman, and John Rees, a finer. In the case of the latter, an order was also issued evicting him from his home.[116]

Edwin Phillips mentions that the actions of the local employers and landowners were a direct consequence of the influence of the Revd Augustus Morgan on the landed interest in the area. He accused Morgan of poisoning the whole community with his venom, stating that farmers in the locality had all been issued with an instruction by their landlords to oppose a Board. Even paupers were informed by the curate and relieving officer that they would be denied relief were they to vote in favour of a Board. Phillips claimed that

> every employer of labour in this parish, the landlords who are churchmen, made it a personal matter of offence if any in their employ voted for the Board.

In his opinion the decision of the referendum to reject a Board by 136 votes to 88 was a direct consequence of the coercion exercised by local employers.[117]

The pattern in industrial south Wales was by no means uniform and, as has been noted above, there were several examples of resistance to the establishment of School Boards and of successful attempts made to remedy the educational deficiency by voluntary effort. Overall, however, the experience of the industrial areas points to an overwhelming adoption of the School Board system. Rapid urbanization, the weakness of the Anglican Church and the presence of large numbers of Nonconformist

[116] Ibid.
[117] Ibid.

employers contributed to a process which resulted in 81.9 per cent of Glamorgan children being educated in Board schools by 1899.

By 1877 Wales was beginning to overcome its deficiencies in educational provision at the elementary level. The number of schools in receipt of government grants had reached 1,122 compared with 841 in 1869. National and Church schools remained dominant, providing 558 schools or 49.7 per cent of the total number, while the 157 British schools accounted for 14 per cent of the total, and 288 Board schools, 25.7 per cent of the total. Of these, a large number offered provision in localities where none had previously existed, but this was not invariably so, as is indicated by the decline in the total number of British schools which had been transferred to School Boards or had been closed after School Boards had been established. Roman Catholic schools numbered 34 (3 per cent), leaving the remaining 85 (7.6 per cent) to be accounted for by a host of miscellaneous schools, such as parish endowed schools and locally controlled non-denominational schools. The number of voluntary schools had increased from 588 in 1869 to 677 in 1877, mainly due to the impetus given to the construction of new schools by voluntary agencies in 1870 as church leaders in particular sought to establish a school before a demand for a School Board was voiced. In terms of the provision of actual school places, however, the Board schools accounted for a more significant portion than their numbers would suggest. Of a total of 217,465 places available in 1877, the Board schools provided 64,824 (29.8 per cent) and Church or National schools provided 89,818 (41.3 per cent). The British schools provided 33,042 (15.2 per cent), the Roman Catholics 8,024 (3.7 per cent) and other schools 21,757 (10 per cent).

By 1900, shortly before the end of the School Board era, Wales had 1,709 schools. Of these, 687 were National or Church schools, 51 were British schools, and 893 (52.3 per cent of the total) were Board schools. The total number of pupils for whom accommodation was provided had reached 439,131. The voluntary school sector accounted for 152,690 (34.8 per cent) whilst the Board schools accounted for 286,441 (65.2 per cent). Throughout the period, voluntary schools were numerous, yet because of the number of pupils enrolled, they were of less significance than their numbers suggest. Moreover, by the end of the School Board era, the Board schools had clearly established themselves as the main providers of elementary education in Wales. Again, however, considerable county variations existed. While 81.9 per cent of Glamorgan children received their education in Board schools, the figure was as low as 16.1 per cent in Radnorshire:

Table 2.3 *Number of pupils in voluntary and Board schools, 1899*[118]

County	Voluntary	Board	Total	% in Bd schls
Anglesey	4149	7090	11239	63.1
Brecon	6287	7557	13844	54.6
Cardigan	4910	10749	15659	68.6
Carmarthen	11267	21646	32913	65.8
Caernarfon	13327	14163	27490	51.5
Denbigh	13854	12958	26812	48.3
Flint	17989	3906	21895	17.8
Glamorgan	23010	104471	127481	82.0
Merioneth	3427	9835	13262	74.2
Montgomery	8909	4418	13327	33.2
Pembroke	10168	9913	20081	49.4
Radnor	4280	826	5106	16.2
Monmouth	14558	31982	46540	68.7
Cardiff	8617	22122	30739	72.0
Newport	2559	10515	13074	80.4
Swansea	5379	14290	19669	72.7
Wales	**152690**	**286441**	**439131**	**65.2**

The process of establishing School Boards highlights the varied nature of local responses to the issues posed. But although each referendum raises its particular problems of interpretation, the evidence suggests a number of common elements at work. The religious census of 1851 and the statistics compiled in 1905 for the Royal Commission on the Established Church and other Religious Bodies testify to the strength of Nonconformity in every county in Wales. The figures also point to the great variety

[118] PP 1899, XX.

which existed within Nonconformity, the strengths of the Calvinistic Methodists, Baptists and Congregationalists being concentrated in different localities, although each one sought to ensure at least a presence in the majority of towns. However, it does not appear that members of any one denomination were more wholehearted in their commitment to the establishment of School Boards than the adherents of the other denominations, although parishes that were dominated by any one denomination tended to be more likely to vote in favour of a Board.[119] In seeking explanation for the decisions reached in the various localities consideration needs to be given to concerns, largely of a financial nature, felt across the religious spectrum as a whole. Their effect was to ensure that the outcome of deliberations in a particular locality was not necessarily a predictable reflection of the broad convictions of a Liberal-Nonconformist hegemony.

Especially important in determining success or failure in forming a School Board was the issue of rates. It is the issue of the increased rates liable to be charged in the parish that most frequently compromised the Nonconformists' position. The projected cost of the adoption of the Board system was the main argument deployed by its opponents, and *Bwgan y Dreth* (the rate bogey) was quoted in several campaigns and convinced many people that they should oppose the proposals. Despite the protestations of the Nonconformist leaders, highlighted in papers such as *Baner ac Amserau Cymru*, that the concerns over the rate burden were ploys used by the established orders in rural society to retain control of education, there was genuine anxiety that substantial additions could be made to the rate bill. This was accentuated as tenant farmers were affected by a decline in agricultural prosperity, with other burdens such as the tithe rates adding to their financial problems. Additionally, many were reluctant to contribute to the cost of a village school when the remoteness of their own farms meant, in their view, that it was unlikely that their children would be able to take advantage of the education offered. An examination of the structure of rateable values in Wales is required to understand this fear and to appreciate why it assumed less significance in the closing years of the nineteenth century.

---

[119] I. G. Jones and D. Williams (eds.), *The Religious Census of 1851: A Calendar of the Returns Relating to Wales*, 2 vols (Cardiff, 1975–6), pp.xii–xxxv; PP 1910, XVIII, Vol. VI.

THE BATTLE FOR THE BOARDS

Table 2.4 Rateable values per union in Wales, 1868–91[120]

County	Poor Law Union	£ value 1868	£ value 1891	% increase/decrease
Monmouth	Chepstow	100279	133809	+ 33.4
	Monmouth	119200	117470	− 1.5
	Abergavenny	82972	126137	+ 52.0
	Bedwellty	98222	197744	+ 101.3
	Pontypool	99936	151593	+ 51.7
	Newport	259569	449930	+ 73.3
Glamorgan	Cardiff	313905	1072173	+ 241.6
	Pontypridd	222035	645771	+ 190.8
	Merthyr Tydfil	367698	412711	+ 12.2
	Bridgend & Cowbridge	134983	242033	+ 79.3
	Neath	154029	184775	+ 20.0
	Pontardawe	41642	64508	+ 54.9
	Swansea	169232	354582	+ 109.5
	Gower	34764	42089	+ 21.1
Carmarthen	Llanelli	97017	166236	+ 71.3
	Llandovery	61560	66198	+ 7.5
	Llandeilo Fawr	72094	89071	+ 23.5
	Carmarthen	155291	176042	+ 13.4
Pembroke	Narberth	87739	90533	+ 3.2
	Pembroke	103912	124483	+ 19.8
	Haverfordwest	150494	152632	+ 1.4
Cardigan	Cardigan	52477	68904	+ 31.3
	Newcastle Emlyn	52523	53719	+ 2.3
	Lampeter	24782	29686	+ 19.8
	Aberaeron	25388	34296	+ 35.1
	Aberystwyth	63416	90000	+ 41.9
	Tregaron	23191	32191	+ 38.8
Brecon	Builth	40471	48023	+ 18.7
	Brecon	96968	110526	+ 14.0
	Crickhowell	55585	54387	− 2.2
	Hay	77482	79589	+ 2.7
Radnor	Knighton	79538	73843	− 7.2
	Rhayader	22023	31317	+ 42.2
Montgomery	Machynlleth	47029	53953	+ 14.7
	Newtown & Llanidloes	103456	114196	+ 10.4

[120] PP 1893–94, LXXVI, Local Taxation Returns, 1893.

THE BATTLE FOR THE BOARDS

County	Poor Law Union	£ value 1868	£ value 1891	% increase/decrease
	Forden	103417	115508	+ 11.7
	Llanfyllin	127420	132398	+ 3.9
Flint	Holywell	137295	184140	+ 34.1
Denbigh	Wrexham	174304	234648	+ 34.6
	Ruthin	88226	92333	+ 4.7
	St Asaph	137546	182645	+ 32.8
	Llanrwst	39179	50238	+ 28.2
Merioneth	Corwen	63161	74908	+ 18.6
	Bala	25113	34336	+ 36.7
	Dolgellau	46225	65508	+ 41.7
	Ffestiniog	61656	112126	+ 81.9
Caernarfon	Pwllheli	58964	68915	+ 16.9
	Caernarfon	90329	115963	+ 28.4
	Bangor & Beaumaris	134927	164250	+ 21.7
	Conwy	62471	146489	+ 134.5
Anglesey	Anglesey	49807	55584	+ 11.6
	Holyhead	57883	74000	+ 27.8

Table 2.4 gives the basis upon which local authorities determined their rates. Those unions with a high rateable value could afford to contemplate expenditure that was considerably higher than that possible where authorities had a low rateable value, because a rate of £1 would yield a greater amount than a similar rate of £1 in a union with a low rateable value. Equally, a high rateable value was associated with industry and commerce. As a result, in areas with a high rateable value, companies, including large-scale industrial concerns, would shoulder the greater part of the rate bill, while in unions with a low rateable value the burden would fall on domestic payers or small businesses. This table demonstrates that rural unions such as Rhayader, Tregaron, Lampeter and Bala suffered from continued low rateable values, despite the apparent improvement suggested by the percentage improvement, because of the exceedingly low base from which they started. Although the rateable value of the majority of rural unions had increased by 1891, there was a decline in Monmouth, Crickhowell and Knighton and only a marginal increase in Haverfordwest,

Llandovery, Newcastle Emlyn, Lampeter and Hay. However, the increase that had occurred by 1891 contributed to the ability of parishes within those unions to contemplate the establishment of a school maintained by the rates, although by then other burdens imposed by the expansion of secondary education and the expenditure incurred by the county councils, most notably on road improvements, placed further burdens on local ratepayers. The essence of the evidence, however, indicates that the great variety in rateable values is one explanation for the diversity in the responses to the question of the establishment of School Boards in the 1870s. Even within unions, the actual value of parishes differed, and consequently parishes that were similar in religious and political outlook often differed on the question of a School Board.

The threat of high rates rather than the exertion of undue influence, therefore, was the main obstacle to the creation of School Boards in the greater number of cases in rural Wales. The threat was sufficient to prevent the establishment of a Board even in areas with a determinedly radical tradition, such as Samuel Roberts's village of Llanbryn-mair (Montgomeryshire). Where a British or a non-denominational school existed, Nonconformist ratepayers showed a marked reluctance to opt for a School Board, which was considered to be the more expensive system of elementary schooling. For instance, School Boards required a clerk, usually in a paid position, to service the Board and execute its decisions, work that was undertaken without remuneration by officers of voluntary schools. Likewise, the not inconsiderable costs of the triennial election was a further burden which fell on School Boards but did not have to be met by the voluntary schools. Finally, it was easier for a Board to contemplate expenditure since it had recourse to the rates (unlike the voluntary sector, which had to collect the money before embarking on any scheme that involved expenditure), and although Board members would have to face the ratepayers at an election they had the ability to embark on expensive schemes during the triennial period. Thus, the question of rates certainly weighed in the decision of many landowners to oppose the establishment of School Boards. While there were undoubtedly some who had a political motive for wishing to maintain the monopoly of the Anglican Church in education, it is also the case that there were those who genuinely feared the effect of an increased burden on rural communities that lacked the financial wherewithal to maintain a higher rate.

The period also saw the growth of a number of settlements in the rural counties of Wales with characteristics which distinguished them markedly from the wholly rural parishes. Based either on small-scale industry or on their role as market towns, these were not as open to gentry influences as were the rural parishes. At the same time, their rateable value was increasing, for in many rural unions the greater part of the value was found in the parish which included the town, a fact that contributed to the ability of the town to contemplate a Board. Equally, it was in those towns that many of the emerging middle-class Welsh Nonconformist leaders were based. These towns boasted a developing social infrastructure which, in addition to large chapels, also included a high concentration of voluntary schools, British as well as Anglican or National. The diversity of factors affecting such small towns was reflected in the debate concerning the establishment of School Boards, giving a further fascinating insight into the nature of Welsh society in the nineteenth century.

Neither the denominational pattern nor the variation in rateable values is in itself sufficient to explain the variety of responses to the School Board question. It is important to note the potency of previous arguments among the religious groups, such as the dispute between the churchwardens and the Nonconformists in Dolgellau, fissures that were responsible for intensifying sectarian divisions. In other parishes, the behaviour of individual landowners was the cause of the acrimony. In the parish of Llandysul, the School Board contest was one of many battles between the Unitarians and the landowner, John Davies Lloyd of Allt-yr-Odyn. Lloyd had inherited the estate after it had been held in trust during his minority. A Conservative, he had been condemned from the pulpit and in the press for evicting Liberal tenants in 1870, including the Jones family at Ffynnon Llywelyn, whose subsequent suffering had received considerable attention in the press. This and the other examples of Lloyd's excesses became part of the folklore of Welsh radicalism. Tenants had been threatened with eviction unless they assisted in the building of a church. A pack of hounds had been driven through the garden of Blaenralltddu, ruining the produce, and other tenants had been warned to send their children to the National school rather than to the one kept by the Unitarian minister, the Revd William Thomas (Gwilym Marles), again on pain of eviction. A School Board was rejected despite a determined campaign on the part of Nonconformist leaders, but the campaign revived in 1875, when a School Board was established, after the inadequacy of the National school had been proved. On both occasions, the vehemence of the campaign arose partly because of the bad feeling between John Lloyd and Gwilym Marles. The minister had regularly preached sermons which emphasized the need to remove the privileges of the landed gentry and he had publicly denounced the wasteful behaviour of John Lloyd at his coming-of-age celebrations. Matters came to a head in 1876, when the landowner decreed that the lease on the chapel in Llwynrhydowen, where Gwilym Marles was minister, would not be renewed unless Marles was removed, ostensibly because the building had been used for purposes other than religious worship. This was a reference to Gwilym Marles's political sermons and his activity in pressing the case for a School Board from the defeat of 1871 until its establishment in 1875. These events gained widespread publicity and constituted a most extreme manifestation of gentry oppression, significantly with little involvement on the part of the Anglican clergy, who distanced themselves from John Lloyd.[121]

Similar experiences occurred in other areas where the landowning interest deployed the 'screw' to prevent the establishment of a School Board. In each case, it is clear that, despite the resentment engendered in 1868, a minority of landowners were yet to learn to moderate their determination to dominate their estates. Yet even in such parishes, the degree to which the 'screw' could influence the outcome of the result was limited. In Beddgelert, for instance, where a Board was adopted in a referendum by 132 votes to 122, there were serious discrepancies in the voting patterns of the four villages which comprised the parish. Nanmor voted heavily against the formation of a Board, mainly as a result of the 'screw', while

---

[121] Nansi Martin, *Gwilym Marles* (Llandysul, 1979), pp.39–55; *Y Tyst*, 3 November 1876, and D. Jacob Davies, 'Pregeth goffa M. Ll. Gwarnant Williams', *Yr Ymofynnydd*, LXIX (1968), 7–8.

Beddgelert itself and Nantgwyn were divided almost equally on the question. The fact that Rhyd-ddu recorded a decisive vote in favour of a Board determined the issue, a reflection of the steadfast resolve of the residents of Rhyd-ddu, who were able to withstand the efforts of the opponents of the Board to dissuade them from their intentions.[122] The study of particular cases also indicates that the ability of the Nonconformist and Liberal leaders to rally support for the principle of democratic control of education was considerable. The influence of local ministers of religion, coupled with the deep feeling of revulsion evident in several areas that the education of Nonconformist children was under the control of the Anglican Church, meant that it was inevitable that the divisions between the Nonconformists and the Anglican hierarchy would be exposed very clearly. Yet, whatever the views of the leaders in Welsh society, this study also demonstrates that opposition to radical politics manifested itself in the ranks of the peasant population of rural Wales.[123]

The county council elections of 1889 are further evidence that, despite the strength of Nonconformity and radical Liberalism in parliamentary elections, the pattern at a local level was far more complex. In those elections, areas such as Aberdyfi, Whitford, Conwy and even Caernarfon elected some Conservative members, despite a broad Liberal triumph. The Liberal base was far stronger in 1889 than it was during the initial phase of the School Board referenda, yet the fact remained that even then popular Conservative personalities could attract sufficient support to win a county council seat. Although there is no clear correlation between those parishes that rejected a School Board and those that elected Conservatives in 1889, there is sufficient diversity in both contests to suggest that Wales may have been intensely loyal to the Liberals in parliamentary elections when the issue at stake was the formation of a national government, but that such loyalty could not be counted on in local elections where an assortment of local factors influenced the opinions of the voters. Gladstone may have been too cautious for many Welsh Liberal leaders, yet the evidence of local elections in the

[122] *Baner*, 10 May 1871.
[123] *Baner*, 1 April 1871. Gwyn A. Williams also gives a valuable account of the attitudes of Welsh Nonconformist denominations towards the Unitarians, in Baruch Hirson and Gwyn A. Williams, *The Delegate for Africa* (London, 1995), pp.29–60.

rural strongholds of the Liberals suggests that it was he who could depend on the invariable support of the Welsh electors rather than the more radical indigenous leaders who claimed to speak for Wales.

This diversity in the attitudes of the Welsh electorate was not confined to the rural areas. In each of the towns mentioned earlier there was a large Nonconformist presence, and those towns contained some of the largest and most influential chapels in Wales. They provided the venues for annual meetings of the congregations and the ministers included men who were prominent in the activities of their respective denominations. In part, the varied response to the opportunity to establish a School Board can be attributed to the success of the opponents of the Boards in enlisting the support of the uncommitted, especially those fearful of a high rate who were not associated with any form of organized religious worship. Yet it also indicates the variations within the Nonconformist community. However prominent many of the leaders of Nonconformity were in Liberal politics in these towns, their fellow-worshippers included a significant number who, like their rural counterparts, held allegiance to a moderate form of Liberalism.

The debate concerning the desirability of establishing School Boards in the industrial communities differed greatly from the experience of the rural areas and the small towns. In the greater number of such areas it was inevitable that Boards would have to be established on account of the inadequacy of existing accommodation and the problems which arose from an ever-increasing population. As Shadrach Pryce predicted in 1870, the majority of attempts to meet the deficiencies by voluntary methods failed, and most areas opted for the School Board system.[124] The nature of these societies also explains the amenability of the industrial areas to School Boards. The mining villages of south-west Wales and the quarry villages of Gwynedd were relatively new settlements where the power of the Church was at its weakest and where few Church or National schools existed. Despite the power which could be exercised by employers over these communities, the villages were regarded as bastions of Nonconformity. These societies included families who, having

[124] PP 1870, XXII, Mr Pryce's Report.

been sturdy pillars of their causes in the rural areas, and often of a liberated spirit, had migrated to the industrial areas mainly for economic reasons though often also to escape the influence of the Church or gentry. By virtue of the fact that it was short-distance migration that characterized these villages, the population being derived from the immediate rural hinterland rather than further afield, the communities retained the Welsh characteristics of the rural areas and did not have the great mix of ethnic backgrounds and religious affiliations of working-class communities further east.[125] These were relatively homogeneous societies. Yet the ties of deference and personal loyalties which could affect the political complexion of rural areas did not exist to such an extent in a developing industrial economy, while many members of the congregations had considerable power by virtue of their business interests in the localities.

However, it would be wrong to assume that these factors created a uniform pattern in industrial communities. For instance, the degree of social influence which could be exerted in industrial areas should not be underestimated. The evictions of 1868 in the rural communities were mirrored by several instances of victimization of Liberal voters by employers in south Wales, notably in the Merthyr Tydfil area.[126] Nor were the interests of Nonconformist entrepreneurs necessarily linked to the promotion of publicly funded schools. The fear of increased rates which businessmen would inevitably face led to determined efforts on the part of several employers to avoid the creation of Boards. The pronounced Anglican affiliations of a number of the leading industrialists in south Wales were a further restraining factor. Industrial employers such as the Gilbertsons in the Swansea Valley, the Ashburnham interest in the Gwendraeth Valley and that of Dynevor in the Amman Valley revealed reservations derived from religious affiliation as well as financial objections to the creation of Boards. Their attitudes were partly responsible for the heated campaigns in areas where manufacturing industry, notably tinplate, was as important as mining in the economic life of the community. Despite the fact that some local Nonconformist businessmen were among the shareholders of

[125] Brinley Thomas, 'The migration of labour into the Glamorganshire coalfield, 1861–1911', *Economica*, X (1930), 275–94.
[126] T. M. Bassett, *Bedyddwyr Cymru* (Swansea, 1977), pp.290–1.

tinplate companies, the dominant influences were families such as the Tregonnings in Llanelli, the Ashburnham family in Pembrey and Burry Port, the Gough family in Pontardawe and the Gilbertson family in Clydach, in all cases members of either the Anglican or Roman Catholic Churches. Yet their efforts to prevent the creation of School Boards often failed owing to the strength of Nonconformity and in some cases, particularly in the Swansea Valley, the presence of Liberationist influences.[127] At the same time, the opposition of the owners of manufacturing companies was not entirely associated with their religious or political affiliation. It is noticeable that purely mining areas were more amenable to the Board system than other parishes with a more diverse economic base. This may reflect the fact that colliery owners did not face the prospect of a rate burden equivalent to that which would be faced by the owners of ironworks, tinplateworks or other large-scale operations above ground. Colliery rates were assessed on the basis of the tonnage of coal mined, and the arrangement whereby one-eighth of a ton of coal was discounted from the rate assessment meant that colliery owners never carried the rate burden that other employers faced. Unlike rural communities, however, the presence of collieries and small-scale commercial concerns meant that, while they prospered, there was a source of finance other than domestic rates, with the result that householders would not be faced with the entire burden of maintaining a School Board, provided that output was reasonably consistent. The case of Flintshire demonstrates that in those areas where the future of the coal industry was less secure, fear that the industry could fail (and cease contributing to the rates as soon as production of coal ended) was a sufficient deterrent to prevent the establishment of School Boards. In the larger towns of south-east Wales, these factors were largely absent. The growth of large centres of commercial activity, coupled with the sheer impossibility of meeting a large educational deficiency by voluntary means, generated a consensus within those towns that favoured a School Board. Moreover, it was more difficult for those groups who

[127] The Revd Thomas Levi had served as a minister in Ystradgynlais before moving to Morriston. He had been active in a dispute with the church authorities during his period in Ystradgynlais and he was also a leading propagandist on behalf of the Liberation Society.

opposed the creation of School Boards to mislead or seek to exert undue influence in such towns, given that the urban environment offered more anonymity than did rural or semi-rural villages.

The process by which School Boards came to be established in Wales was highly complex, with local circumstances and personalities having a considerable effect on the result in several areas. Despite the instances of a few parishes which saw a consensus between the Anglican and Nonconformist sections of the community, the majority of votes on the School Board question reflected a direct conflict between the two religious interests, albeit with varying degrees of acrimony. In several parishes the local Anglican clergy, gentry interests and their supporters were so overwhelmingly defeated that they abandoned attempts to oppose the operation of Boards and many took the advice of the earl of Powis and sought seats on these bodies. In a number of referenda, the local landowners did not attempt to exercise undue influence in resisting the establishment of Boards. The accusation levied in *Baner ac Amserau Cymru* that the gentry were imposing a 'screw' to prevent the establishment of Boards, while being an accurate description of the situation in several areas, did not reflect reality in the majority of cases in Wales.

Yet the Nonconformist denominations could not claim total victory and they suffered serious defeats. The manipulations which resulted in the establishment of Boards such as those of Bangor and Caernarfon generated considerable resentment in the Nonconformist community in the towns, with serious electoral consequences for the Liberal and Nonconformist leadership. At the same time, it would be wrong to assume that the whole of Nonconformist opinion was committed to the establishment of Boards, whatever the cost. The experience of small urban settlements demonstrated that, even in Nonconformist circles, the possibility of an increased rate burden was enough to generate hostility to the establishment of a School Board. The experience of south Wales illustrates that the disputes over the establishment of School Boards, while being more pronounced in the rural areas, were also in evidence in the industrial districts, the events at Bedwas being reminiscent of those which occurred in the rural areas two years previously. The key factor in these areas was that the deficiency of school accommodation was such that voluntary effort was clearly inadequate. In many respects, the debate in south Wales was to be over the policies and expenditure of the Boards rather than over the desirability of establishing the Boards themselves.

As has been indicated already, the voluntary sector was in marked decline by the end of the nineteenth century. The increasingly rigorous standards on which the Education Department insisted meant that many schools became burdened with costs they could not bear, while many landowners who had previously patronized voluntary schools found it increasingly difficult to do so because the agricultural depression had reduced their revenues. However, in large areas of Wales, especially rural Wales, education remained the responsibility of the Church to the turn of the century.

III
HIGH PRINCIPLES AT THE PARISH PUMP

The debate concerning elementary education in Wales did not end with the passing of the Forster Education Act. The issues which were raised at that time continued to be discussed in parish and School Board meetings, in public disagreements and in the pages of the press, for the remainder of the century. Together with matters such as the tithe, disestablishment, the land question, and political allegiance, education was one of the enduring issues of Welsh politics.[1] The School Boards were also part of an evolving system of local government in Wales. Throughout the late nineteenth century, the Liberal Party emphasized the principles of democracy and accountability, tenets that were particularly relevant in Wales in view of the way in which Nonconformist denominations stressed those ideas in the form of government they developed within their congregations. The concept of democracy was not confined to the extension of the parliamentary franchise. Rather it encompassed a wide range of local institutions and services. The School Boards, the County and District Councils and the Parish Councils represented a force for this democratization.[2] The Boards preceded the County Councils and the District Councils and, together with the Poor Law Guardians, constituted a remarkable apprenticeship in local democracy.[3] As such, the School Boards of Wales offer fascinating evidence of the evolution of Welsh local government, the priorities of local politicians and the attempt to reconcile high ideals with local realities.

The decades that followed the passing of the 1870 Education Act witnessed unprecedented economic developments, not only in terms of the continued industrialization of south Wales but also as swathes of rural Wales became accessible through the

---

[1] J. E. Vincent, *The Land Question in North Wales* (London, 1896), pp.1–39; K. O. Morgan, *Rebirth of a Nation: Wales, 1880–1980* (Oxford, 1981), pp.38–40.
[2] K. O. Morgan, *Democracy in Wales from Dawn to Deficit* (Cardiff, 1995), pp.1–3.
[3] J. A. Price, 'Welsh education and Welsh public life', *Cymru Fydd* II (November 1889), 593–604.

advent of the railways, a development that was crucial for the commercial life of those areas. The geographical distribution of population in Wales was changing dramatically. The industrializing county of Glamorgan saw its population rise from 317,752 in 1861 to 397,859 in 1871 and 859,931 in 1901. Conversely, the population of Montgomeryshire declined from 66,919 in 1861 to 54,901 in 1901, while that of Cardiganshire fell from 72,245 to 61,078 during the same period.[4] These demographic changes not only resulted in falling school rolls in the rural areas but also meant that the financial burden of maintaining a school was borne by a declining population. Conversely, in industrial areas, substantial in-migration resulted in overcrowded schools and pressure on resources, again with serious financial implications for School Boards. At the same time, the Welsh economy was plagued by fluctuations in prosperity, a factor which had a direct bearing on the ability of local authorities to proceed with the development of vital public services. Ambitious school building programmes had to be postponed or abandoned altogether as a result of economic uncertainties, resulting in the uneven and sporadic evolution of the education system.[5] As John Williams has demonstrated, south Wales depended largely on an extractive economy and, as was illustrated above, colliery rating, based on output rather than buildings, was assessed on a different basis from that of other industrial concerns.[6] The fact that it was output which determined the amount of rates paid by the coal-owners, the largest employers, meant that local authorities in south Wales suffered more from fluctuations in economic prosperity than did those in the industrial areas of Britain, where the presence of large manufacturing concerns ensured some consistency in the returns from the rates.

The nature of the society created by industrialization and the prolonged economic depression witnessed in the rural areas placed further strains on the resources of Welsh School Boards. Parents were periodically unable to pay the school pence, and the wish of many Boards to remit those fees rather than see a child deprived of education was both a tribute to the spirit in

---

[4] John Williams, *Digest of Welsh Historical Statistics*, 2 vols (Cardiff, 1985), I, pp.6–24.
[5] PRO, ED 16/ 384.
[6] John Williams, *Was Wales Industrialised?* (Llandysul, 1995), pp.14–36.

which many Boards administered their responsibilities and a source of considerable financial burden. From 1876 the Poor Law Guardians could decide to pay *in lieu* of needy parents, and Boards responded in various ways. Many School Boards deliberately sought to impose a high charge on the Guardians as a means of generating income which did not increase the rate burden. Schemes were also devised to take account of the levels of prosperity and poverty of various areas in determining school fees, and a system of means testing was adopted in other areas.

The School Boards undoubtedly faced problems, but the government's continued support of the voluntary schools, among which the National schools predominated, by no means assured their prosperity. The voluntary schools depended primarily on the landowning classes for their existence and, in view of the difficulties they faced, the plight of the schools became increasingly desperate. The difficult task of raising the funds to maintain a Church or National school increasingly fell on the clergy, and their efforts to attract funds from the community at large were certainly undermined by the denominational divisions in Wales. Yet it is also the case that the Anglican efforts failed to win the wholehearted support of their own adherents. The reports of the Church Congress are strewn with complaints that those who were in a position to contribute were loath to do so.[7] These problems were compounded by the fact that both the Education Department and the population in general had rising expectations in relation to the standard of education, particularly concerning the quality of buildings, equipment and more highly qualified staff, all of which placed additional demands on limited resources. The voluntary sector had no recourse to the rates to subsidize such improvements, and the Nonconformists were increasingly unwilling to subscribe to voluntary schools following the establishment of School Boards. Whereas previously the absence of any form of education other than the voluntary sector had led many Nonconformists to join in Anglican ventures for the sake of education, the situation was now reversed. The availability of another method of obtaining a school, which could be controlled by the Nonconformist majority, meant that

---

[7] *Report of the 7th Church Conference at Rhyl, 17 and 18 September 1889* (Wrexham, 1889).

Nonconformists had more to gain by undermining rather than supporting Anglican schools.

Of equal significance was the fact that new financial pressures were generated by the development of democratic institutions and the devolution of power from central government to elected bodies with responsibility in localities. Initiatives such as road improvements, bridges, asylums and other provisions again resulted in an increased rate burden on the community and also affected efforts to ensure the viability of the voluntary schools. High rates, combined with economic depression, reduced the amount of 'spare' money available for voluntary public works. As early as 1870, George Clark, chairman of the St David's Archidiaconal Board of Education, spoke of an impending crisis in the voluntary school sector because of competition from rate-aided schools and improved government standards.[8] This anxiety continued throughout the period and was reflected in the increasingly desperate tone of appeals from the Anglican clergy for financial support from local landowners.[9] Faced with these difficulties and the realization that its schools did not compete for financial support on equal terms with those of rivals, a new spirit of bitterness marked the efforts of the Church. In addition, the majority of Welsh Nonconformist parents, if offered a choice of National or Board school, would choose the latter. In Cellan (Cardiganshire), a rural village in an area where communications were difficult, the majority of parents chose to send their children to the Board school three miles away rather than allow them to attend the local National school. Conversely, members of the Anglican Church sought to emulate the efforts of the Llandysul churchmen who tried to prevent the expansion of the Board school in an attempt to force children who could not be accommodated there to attend the National school.[10] In so doing they failed to recognize that the 'religious difficulty' was a real and genuine concern for considerable numbers in the Nonconformist community in Wales at the end of the nineteenth century.[11] Yet it was also the case that Nonconformist denominations were

[8] NLW, Picton Castle Papers, 3895–7.
[9] NLW, Lucas Correspondence 3950; and Pembrokeshire CRO, D/RTM/MHE/801.
[10] NLW, T. E. Ellis Papers, 585, dated 1894.
[11] PRO, ED 16/377.

involved in blatant attempts to undermine National and Church schools. The Nonconformist denominations at Lampeter resolved to withdraw their children from the town's National school in 1875 in order to make the school economically and educationally unviable.[12] Likewise, the deacons of Adulam Chapel, Llanelli, threatened their members with expulsion unless they withdrew their children from the National school in 1898.[13]

Yet, many such disputes arose as a result of the fact that truculent personalities were able to upset the equilibrium of a community, rather than as a consequence of more basic tensions in Welsh society. The Anglican clergy were noted for their frequent reluctance to co-operate with the education authorities in implementing compulsory attendance policies. For instance, the vicar of Holywell, the Revd R. O. Williams, was criticized in 1893 for refusing to provide the school attendance committee with a list of non-attenders in his school, thereby undermining the committee's attempts at enforcing attendance.[14] In Holyhead the Church authorities denied that the education authority had any right to information pertaining to attendance at their school and in so doing succeeded in undermining years of effort on the part of the attendance officer.[15] The record of the elected authorities themselves demonstrates their willingness to stoop to unscrupulous methods in order to undermine the Church school sector. Complaints were regularly made that School Boards were prepared to allow massive arrears of school fees in order to fill their schools and empty the voluntary schools. They were accused of building schools as close as possible to existing Church schools,[16] and of utilizing the 'bottomless public purse' in order to build extravagant and well-equipped schools which outmatched those built by voluntary effort, as well as paying larger salaries to their teachers in an attempt to attract the higher quality staff.[17] In many ways such comments reflected the siege mentality of the Anglican leaders in Wales, who were faced with both loss of control over education in certain areas and

---

[12] A. L. Trott, 'The implementation of the 1870 Forster Education Act in Cardiganshire, 1870–1880', *Ceredigion*, 3 (1956–9), 207–30.
[13] *LLG*, 10 February 1898.
[14] *CDH*, 14 April 1893.
[15] *CDH*, 1 December 1893.
[16] PRO, ED2/638–640, /597–600, /613–616.
[17] Ibid.

Nonconformist agitation over disestablishment and the tithe question.[18] Yet it also reflected the fact that voluntary organizations were no longer suited to the task of providing an essential service such as education, not for political reasons but because of their financial plight.

The issue of the control of education remained a poignant one in a number of areas. In many districts where a School Board had not been demanded in the referenda of the early 1870s, a harmonious relationship had been forged between the managers of National schools and the local Nonconformist community, based on an understanding that the Church would conduct its school on a non-denominational basis in return for an agreement by local Nonconformist leaders not to continue to press for a School Board. However, the arrival of young, newly appointed clergymen often destroyed such an accord. In most instances, they regarded it as their duty to protect and assert the rights and privileges of the Church at a time when these were being challenged by the political leadership in Wales. In seeking out and insisting on observing those rights and privileges to the letter, however, many destroyed the harmony which their predecessors had developed by taking a more relaxed view of the position of the Established Church. The explanation given by the Revd D. Evans of his right to manage the Church school at Cynwyl Elfed (Carmarthenshire) revealed the attitude of many such clergymen:

> the schoolroom [was] given by a clergyman to my predecessor wherein to hold a National School in which religious instruction were essential conditions and in conformity with the teachings of the Established Church. But my predecessor in his declining years handed it over to the Board during school hours . . . Being young, I intend to receive back the schoolroom to continue it in accordance with the terms of the Deeds as a National School.[19]

A more pronounced illustration was the case of Aberdyfi (Merioneth), where a non-denominational school had been conducted from the 1860s, managed jointly by representatives of the Anglican and Nonconformist churches. In 1876 two new

---

[18] J. P. D. Dunbabin, *Rural Discontent in Nineteenth-Century Britain* (London, 1974), pp.211–31.
[19] PRO, ED2/576.

Nonconformist representatives were elected to the board, to be told that they had no legal claim to participate in the school's affairs because a deed of transfer of 1871 had ended the non-denominational management of the school and had placed it under the sole charge of the Anglican Church. The change of management had occurred on account of lack of vigilance by the Nonconformist members and caused a furore in the town in 1876.[20] A compromise solution was agreed, whereby the Anglicans would continue to manage the school but would respect its non-denominational character, an arrangement which was to last only until 1892, when an unfavourable HMI report was received.[21] In the opinion of the local Nonconformist community, much of the problem with the school was that only members of the Church of England could apply for appointment as head-teacher; this limited the choice of potential masters and could lead to a less qualified master being appointed than might otherwise be the case. An attempt by the Nonconformists to secure the transfer of the school to the School Board was rejected by the Anglicans and led to a decision to build a separate non-denominational school at Aberdyfi, which could be transferred to the Board when completed.[22] As in Aberdyfi, the Nonconformist community in Cynwyd (Merioneth) was served by a Church school which had been conducted on a non-denominational basis for a number of years, financed by a voluntary rate and managed by a popular local rector, the Revd N. P. Evans.[23] The arrival of a new rector, the Revd Lodwick Davies, in 1885 meant that the Nonconformists could no longer rely on the benign co-operation of the Anglicans in the parish and, consequently, a group of Nonconformist ratepayers resolved to withhold payment of the voluntary rate which maintained the school until they were granted a voice in its management. The managers of the Anglican school thus charged 'preferential fees' on those Nonconformist children whose parents were refusing to pay the voluntary rates. The rector's intransigence in refusing to negotiate with the leaders of the Nonconformist community

[20] *Y Goleuad*, 23 March 1894.
[21] PP 1893–94, XXVI.
[22] *Y Goleuad*, 24 November 1893.
[23] W. G. Evans, 'Canmlwyddiant T. E. Ellis A.S. a helynt Ysgol Cynwyd', *Cylchgrawn Cymdeithas Hanes a Chofnodion Sir Feirionnydd*, X (1985–9), 142–7.

prevented the adoption of a compromise solution. Despite the sympathetic attitude of the government, the Llangar School Board was prevented from constructing a school in the parish by the regulations of the Education Department, which insisted that no educational deficiency existed in the parish because of the existence of the National school.[24] Again, it was resolved to build a school by voluntary contribution and then transfer it to the control of the School Board, with a national appeal for support circulated throughout Nonconformist circles in Wales.[25] As late as 1901, the educational needs of Fishguard were supplied solely by the Established Church. Eighty-one per cent of the children who attended the National schools were Nonconformists and, in order to maintain good relations with the community, the vicar, the Revd Rees Lloyd, had chosen to avoid denominational religious instruction and to disregard the clause in the trust deed which stipulated that the master had to be a member of the Anglican Church.[26] Here again it was the arrival of a new clergyman, the Revd William Evans, which destroyed this consensus. The schoolmaster was dismissed, causing an outcry in the town and the formation of a British school.[27]

The difficulties indicated in these three examples had varied causes. In Aberdyfi, it was negligence on the part of the Nonconformists which allowed the school to fall under the total control of the Established Church; in Cynwyd and Fishguard, the Nonconformist community entered into an agreement which left them devoid of any legal rights. Yet in all three cases it was the local clergyman's determination to insist on abiding by the letter of the law that undermined the consensus which had secured an education provision appropriate to the locality. Such cases exemplified the spirit behind the warnings of Gee and others in 1870 that a School Board was needed, not because of what the Church *did* with the power which it held in areas of compromise,

---

[24] Gwynedd CRO, Dolgellau, A52 (Cynwyd Papers).
[25] Ibid.
[26] Northern Counties Education League, *Education Struggle at Fishguard, Pembrokeshire* (Rochdale, 1901). Further evidence of harmony between Nonconformist congregations and the Anglican Church is offered in J. O. Williams, *Stori 'Mywyd* (Liverpool, 1932), esp. pp.30–7, evidence which supports the assertion that personal factors were essential ingredients of the more pronounced religious conflicts.
[27] PRO, ED2/632.

but because of what the Church *could* do with such powers. Moreover, doctrinal differences between the Anglican Church and Nonconformists had evolved into bitter political conflict that included conflict over education. As John Owen Thomas commented in the *Cambrian News*, the world of the late nineteenth century was a far cry from the middle of the century:

> it certainly may seem, in these degenerate days, incredible that a clergyman of the church of England should do anything so large-minded as to co-operate with Dissenters for the promotion of education.[28]

Gentry opposition to the School Board system was also in evidence in the reluctance of certain landlords to sell land for the founding of a school; this was a recurring complaint throughout the period under consideration.[29] These disputes had two broad aspects, the first financial and the second ideological. Financial difficulties arose in the developing towns, especially in those where a single landowner had a monopoly of landownership, as Lord Mostyn did in Mostyn and the marquess of Bute in Cardiff.[30] There, the school inspectors noted, the 'gigantic monopoly' of landownership had resulted in recourse to compulsory purchase, against the wishes of the marquess of Bute, whose opposition to the building of a school was based on the likelihood that it would reduce property values in the vicinity and prove a deterrent to commercial development.[31] Market forces were not the only factors responsible for increases in the price of land. In those areas where Boards had been issued with directives from the Education Department to take immediate steps to remedy the educational deficiencies, landowners were prone to demand extortionate sums of money, because they realized that the Board would face sequestration unless it took immediate steps to build a school. Lord Dynevor refused to sell land to the Llandybïe School Board (Carmarthenshire) so as to remedy the educational deficiency in Ammanford because, in his opinion,

---

[28] *Cambrian News*, 24 November 1893.
[29] NLW, T. E. Ellis Papers, 1802. As late as 1894, H. Roberts of Dolgellau complained to T.E. Ellis that both School Boards and Nonconformist chapels were in need of legal protection to prevent landowners from refusing to sell land on account of political or religious motives.
[30] J. Davies, *Cardiff and the Marquesses of Bute* (Cardiff, 1981), esp. ch. V.
[31] PP 1884–85, XXIII, Mr Williams's Report.

the amount offered by the Board was insufficient,[32] as did Lord Emlyn in the neighbouring parish of Llanfihangel Aberbythych.[33] Neither Emlyn nor Dynevor, however, had cited principled objections to the sale of land to School Boards on the grounds of an aversion to the School Board system. Indeed, in the case of Dynevor, the contrary was true. An Anglican Conservative, he served as member and occasional chairman of the Llandeilo Fawr School Board. His political inclination was characterized by a search for consensus rather than confrontation, as reflected in the fact that the Llandeilo Fawr School Board reached unanimous decisions in every meeting except one between 1882 and 1885,[34] and although he was pledged to the voluntary schools where they existed, there was no disputing his commitment to the establishment of Board schools in those areas where the voluntary bodies had failed.

Despite complaints from the inspectorate and the Education Department at the slow pace by which the educational deficiency in Wales was remedied, the Department's own regulations were responsible for a considerable number of those delays. These regulations, for instance, precluded School Boards from taking over those voluntary schools which were in debt. As a result, Boards were unable to accept the transfer of a school and underwrite the debt, and they were on occasion faced with having to construct their own school, even though the cost of erecting a new building far exceeded the debt of the existing school. When such a situation arose in Dinorwig (Caernarfonshire) in 1873, the Department remained intransigent in the face of opposition from the existing school managers, members of the School Board and the ratepayers of the locality.[35] Similar cases occurred throughout Wales, especially where, as in Caernarfon in 1884, the insistence of the trustees on the right to use the school on a Sunday led to protracted discussions with the Department as to the desirability of transferring the building.[36] At the same time, Board members regularly complained that the recommendations made by the inspectors were inappropriate. J. W. Phillips, a

[32] PRO, ED21/814–18.
[33] PRO, ED2/ 578.
[34] *LLG*, 12 February 1885.
[35] PRO, ED2/ 585.
[36] *CDH*, 8 March 1884.

member of the Haverfordwest School Board, complained that the Board seemed powerless in the face of the demands of the inspectorate and that there was not enough scope for local discretion in the affairs of the School Board. Such complaints were indicative of the delicate nature of the evolving relationship between central and local government in relation to the administration of elementary education. Yet it is also clear that the intricacies of local circumstances were no longer accepted, either by the inspectorate or by the Education Department, as an excuse for procrastination, and that those charged with the execution of the Act in Wales were placed under pressure to ensure an increasing level of educational provision for the community.[37]

Despite the difficulties encountered by many Boards, by the mid-1870s those Boards which had successfully executed their responsibilities were making confident predictions that Wales was on the verge of an enlightened new era. Members of the Aberystwyth Board prophesied in 1873 that, because the work of the Board was nearing completion, the town would be a cleaner place, with drunkenness eradicated.[38] Llanberis[39] and Ffestiniog Boards[40] joined in this self-congratulatory spirit, as did the majority of Boards in their respective reports on their first triennial period. A combination of efficiency and competence at local level and the legislation of a Liberal government was on the verge of transforming Welsh society. Yet, as will be demonstrated presently, the issue of elementary education remained high on the agenda of local politics long after the schools themselves had been erected.

The triennial elections held for the School Boards ensured that elementary education remained a matter of public debate throughout the period covered in this study. These were among the elections which introduced Welsh society to the experience of representative government and as such they provided a crucial initiation into democratic processes in the localities. All ratepayers were entitled to vote, irrespective of whether or not they owned their properties. Women who were ratepayers in their own right

[37] NLW MS. 11552.
[38] PRO, ED2/568.
[39] PRO, ED2/ 585.
[40] PP 1877, XXIX.

were enfranchised and were able to stand for election.[41] However, the confused state of tenancy agreements meant that the electoral pattern in School Board elections was frequently erratic. Reference was made to allegations of bias on the part of local government officers in the conduct of elections, yet the most regular complaints concerned the rate book itself. Volander Jones, in a letter to T. E. Ellis, claimed that the pattern of landownership in Brecon was such that Conservative voters who owned small parcels of land in the parish were included in the rate book, and were thus entitled to exercise the vote, although they had only a tenuous connection with the parish.[42] Conversely, in Dyffryn Nantlle (Caernarfonshire), tenants who had their rates included in their rents were denied the status of ratepayers, the landowner being the sole registered ratepayer for those properties.[43] The elections were conducted on the basis of a secret ballot, as the result of an amendment to the 1870 legislation brought in by the Gladstone government partly in reaction to the events of 1868. But despite assurances about the secrecy of the ballot, common perceptions of the validity of that secrecy varied. Accusations were made that landowners were claiming a knowledge of how each tenant voted (although it was never stipulated how they might have ascertained the information), with counter-accusations claiming that a chapel 'screw' was in operation in several areas, though again it is unclear how the denominations might have been able to secure the information.

The electoral system was weighted in favour of securing representation for minority groups. As was noted earlier, under the cumulative voting system, it was possible for an elector to distribute votes among candidates as was desired, and to cast more than one vote in favour of a particular candidate. Thus, in a Board of seven members, where each elector had seven votes to give, it was possible to cast up to seven votes for one candidate. Elections were fought on denominational lines, and, while it was known for sectarian divisions to emerge within the Nonconformist

---

[41] Examples of women members were, however, rare and those women who were elected had usually married into politically influential families, such as Mrs Crawshay at Merthyr and Mrs Colby at Clydey, Pembroke.
[42] NLW, T. E. Ellis Papers 1294.
[43] UW Bangor MS 1124.

denominations during Board elections, there was a common Nonconformist slate in the majority of cases which competed against the Anglican and, in certain cases, Roman Catholic slates. In the larger towns, however, notably Cardiff and Newport, denominational affiliations were replaced by political demarcations towards the end of the century, and the period from 1870 to 1902 witnessed the development of an increasingly diverse voting pattern. As voters became more confident of the secret ballot, fears of landlord, employer or denominational pressure declined. Electors increasingly supported individuals irrespective of party or denominational affiliation. Given that the electoral system lent itself to the development of 'hung' or balanced Boards, a limit was placed on the ability of any one religious sect to achieve overall control. Denominations which were in a minority in a particular parish could seek to ensure that their candidates were returned by nominating a limited number of candidates and urging their supporters to give their votes only to those candidates. Even so the greatest beneficiaries of this system were non-sectarian candidates, usually standing as independents, and minority groups, notably the Roman Catholics and, to a lesser extent, the Unitarians. Parochial loyalties became a feature of these elections, often overcoming political and religious differences. Thus, villages supported candidates who would promote the interests of those localities, especially where the Board had been embroiled in controversy as to where a school should be sited.

The general impression during the period 1870–1902, therefore, is of an increasingly sophisticated electorate which took full advantage of the various nuances in the voting system in order to reach particular objectives. Personal and local considerations played a major part, with a wide variation between voting patterns at local and national elections. This was seen at its most pronounced in the Irish Roman Catholic communities, which voted heavily in favour of Liberal candidates at general elections because of Gladstone's Home Rule policy, but which allied themselves with the Conservatives in Board elections because of their support for denominational education.[44] As will become clear in this chapter, the Roman Catholic Irish were not the only

[44] P. B. O'Leary, 'Immigration and integration: a study of the Irish in Wales, 1799–1922', Ph.D. thesis, University of Wales, 1990, pp.211–20.

group to adopt such policies, making Board elections a fascinating phenomenon in Welsh local democracy.

Even so, the enthusiasm and acrimony which had surrounded the initial referenda for School Boards stood in marked contrast to the indifference shown towards successive elections in many parts of Wales. In Llanfihangel Ystrad (Cardiganshire), where the Nonconformist community had been involved in a long and embittered struggle against the influence of the Peterwell estate, it was surprising that insufficient nominations were received for the School Board election in 1874.[45] In Llanfair Mathafarn Eithaf (Anglesey), in the same year, no nominations were received at all.[46] This was in the second term of the School Board and the early enthusiasm had quickly died down. Many of those who had stood for election in the first instance had done so under denominational or party political compulsion rather than for educational reasons. As a result, it was inevitable that they would be daunted by the drudgery and slow, if steady, progress which was a necessary part of much local government work. Agreements between the various parties and denominations in School Board elections were a common feature throughout this period. Back-room deals accounted for unopposed returns such as those recorded in Dolgellau (Merioneth), Tregaron (Cardiganshire), Pembrey (Carmarthenshire), Llanberis (Caernarfonshire), and Llan-non (Cardiganshire) in 1874. These arrangements fall into three broad categories. The first involved an informal meeting of local political leaders to decide the composition of the Board. The second was a formal meeting of the ratepayers to determine the composition of a School Board. The third and most common form of arrangement, however, was the agreement of certain candidates to withdraw from the contest after nominations had closed, as was the case in Beddgelert (Caernarfonshire) in 1880. Arrangements such as these were often undertaken during periods of heightened political activity, notably general elections, and reflected the preoccupations of those who were otherwise engaged. Yet, similar arrangements were also made during periods of relative political inactivity, suggesting that the desire to avoid School Board contests cannot

[45] *Baner*, 6 May 1874.
[46] Ibid.

be attributed solely to the fatigue of political activists. First, the cost of School Board election contests had to be borne by the ratepayers of the parish and, as will be seen, the considerable financial burden imposed on the School Boards by the Boards of Guardians, in return for conducting the elections, was a source of much contention in nineteenth-century local government relations. Yet, the practice went wider and deeper than a quest for a financially desirable arrangement for it reflected the genuine desire in Welsh society to avoid political acrimony where possible and eschew elections that could prove to be occasions of bitterness. As has been argued already, a high number on both the Nonconformist and Anglican sides, especially in rural areas, wanted to avoid any deliberate disturbance of the equilibrium of the community. They regarded open tolerance of one another as the key to maintaining good relations in local communities, an objective which was often more important than asserting a denominational or political point. Second, the acceptance by several clergymen and Anglican leaders of one seat on the Board, in an arrangement by which all candidates would be returned unopposed rather than force a contest, was a reflection of the manner in which many of the Anglican clergy had come to accept the *fait accompli* that, despite being the Established Church, they were numerically in a minority in Wales. For many Anglicans the key point was not to enter into political posturing at local School Board elections, but to gain a single seat rather than have no candidates elected.

Reactions to such arrangements were mixed. Morgan Owen commended the practice in his report to the Education Department for 1878–9,[47] suggesting that it was a means by which acrimonious debate could be kept out of education. Others saw more ulterior motive in such arrangements. The *Carnarvon and Denbigh Herald* was the vehicle for an accusation in 1889 that the Holyhead School Board had agreed not to have a contested election in order to protect its members from the wrath of an electorate angry at the persistent incompetence of the Board in, for example, the appointment of an under-age pupil teacher.[48] Similar motives were cited as reasons why a contest should be

---

[47] PP 1878–79, XXIII.
[48] *CDH*, 28 June 1889 and 5 July 1889.

forced in Llanelli in 1883,[49] the *Llanelly and County Guardian* insisting that an election was needed because the Board had been unopposed for many years. Indeed, the paper, sickened by what it saw as the sectarianism of the Board's activities, urged support for independent candidates who would be 'square dealing and efficient men' rather than representatives of particular denominations.

Notwithstanding this pattern of agreement, School Board elections could be as acrimonious as the referenda which had created them. The Revd David Henry Davies, vicar of Llan-non (Carmarthenshire), was accused of attempting to exert undue influence on the ratepayers in his unsuccessful attempt to gain a School Board seat in 1874,[50] while in Holyhead the churchmen adopted the unprincipled action of entering into a gentleman's agreement to avoid a contest and then force a contest after the Nonconformists had withdrawn.[51] Control of the Saundersfoot School Board (Pembrokeshire) was hotly contested in 1874, when a Nonconformist victory was achieved in the teeth of attempts by the Tories to 'screw' their tenants into voting Conservative and to threaten the local Congregational minister with the loss of the lease on the chapel unless he acceded to their request to place Conservative posters in the chapel's windows.[52]

As has been pointed out already, the influence of personalities was strong in these elections and regularly accounted for unpredictable results. In 1880, for instance, the poor reputation of the Nonconformist members of Llanddewibrefi School Board (Cardiganshire) resulted in the Anglicans taking control of the Board,[53] a result mirrored at Pembrey three years later. While the *Llanelly and County Guardian* attributed the Nonconformists' defeats to the disreputable behaviour of their members, others saw loss of control by the Nonconformists as an indication of a deeper trend. The Anglicans gained control of the Llandybïe School Board in 1880 and immediately proclaimed the result as indicative of a general Anglican revival in Wales. According to 'Bwthynfab' in the *Guardian*, the result reflected the fact that the

---

[49] *LLG*, 15 March 1883.
[50] PRO, ED2/580.
[51] PRO, ED2/558.
[52] Ibid.
[53] *Baner*, 11 February 1880.

churches of Wales were now full, while the Nonconformist denominations were complaining of a decline in membership.[54] Yet, despite the jubilation of the Llandybïe Anglicans, the results were not typical. Indeed, in neighbouring Llandeilo Fawr (Carmarthenshire) the previous year, Lord Dynevor, Sir John Mansel and David Pugh, the former MP for Carmarthen, failed in their attempts to secure School Board seats despite being well-known local personalities and popular landowners, even in the eyes of ardent Liberals in the locality.[55] Mutual agreements in relation to School Boards did not cease on polling day, as is testified by the decisions of certain Boards to elect local landowners or Anglican clergymen as their chairmen. By 1875 R. Laybourne, one of the most ardent opponents of the School Board at Bedwas, was chairman of the Bedwellty School Board. In the same year, the Hon. C. H. Wynne served as chairman of the Gwyddelwern Board in Merioneth and Captain Henry Vaughan similarly at Cilcennin in Cardiganshire.[56] The Nonconformist community in Lampeter (Cardiganshire) complained of their own denomination's support for the election of the Revd Ll. Lewellin of St David's College, described as an 'overt and bigoted' Anglican, as chairman of the Board in 1875,[57] while less controversy surrounded the election of Lord Dynevor as chairman in Llandeilo (Carmarthenshire)[58] and of Viscount Emlyn in Llandybïe (Carmarthenshire).[59] The handing of chairmanships to political opponents was, even so, a matter of consternation for the more zealous exponents of the Nonconformist sensibility. Nonconformist opinion certainly condemned the practice in 1875, arguing that the prestige of the office was being conferred on the opponents of Nonconformity and the School Board system. Yet, as Arthur Trott has argued in his study of the School Boards of Cardiganshire, the inclusion of a local Anglican landowner in the work of the Board was often crucial to its success. Bestowing the chairmanship on an Anglican Conservative made it easier, it was

[54] *LLG*, 24 January 1883 and 31 January 1883.
[55] PRO, ED2/577.
[56] *School Board Directory* (London, 1876).
[57] Ibid.; Trott, 'Implementation of the 1870 Act', 215–18; for Lewellin, principal of St David's College, D. T. W. Price, *A History of St David's University College, Lampeter* (Cardiff, 1977), p.34.
[58] *LLG*, 12 February 1885.
[59] Ibid.

claimed, to acquire sites for school buildings from the chairman himself or from other members of the landowning class in the locality.[60] Such efforts reflected the political astuteness of the Welsh Liberal leadership at local level. In the same way that Forster justified his numerous concessions to his Tory opponents during the passage of the 1870 Bill, the local Liberal establishment was determined to promote as wide a degree of popular consent for their policies as possible. The inclusion of a Conservative in the figurehead position of chairman of the Board was considered a price worth paying in return for his support for the Board's policy, especially when the chairman's actions were constricted by accepting collective responsibility for the decisions of the Board. Such seemingly magnanimous behaviour was not necessarily reciprocated on the Anglican side, however. The Revd John Williams Jones, vicar of Llandeilo Tal-y-bont (Glamorgan), considered that he had been personally slighted by the decision of the Board not to hand him the chairmanship in 1873,[61] a similar attitude being taken by the Revd Hugh Jones, rector of Llanrwst (Denbighshire), leading to the resignation of both clergymen from their respective Boards.[62]

Clergymen and Nonconformist ministers comprised a significant proportion of the membership of School Boards in Wales, along with farmers, tradesmen and representatives of the professions. A survey of the occupational pattern shows a definite bias towards the middle class. In 1875, the successful candidates for the Cardiff School Board consisted of an estate agent, a merchant, a colliery owner, a surgeon, an engineer, a Catholic priest, a clergyman, an architect, a gentleman, a Congregationalist minister and an ironmonger.[63] In 1878 they were joined by a solicitor, and later members included a shipowner and a building contractor. In the same year, Aberdare School Board boasted two Baptist ministers, a grocer, two squires, a bootmaker, a vicar, a colliery owner, a colliery manager and a colliery agent, a Congregationalist minister, a Catholic priest, a gentleman, a solicitor and two miners.[64] In the rural areas, a similar pattern of

[60] G. G. Davies, 'Addysg elfennol yn Sir Aberteifi, 1790–1902', *Ceredigion*, 4 (1960–3), 359.
[61] PRO, ED2/606.
[62] PRO, ED2/579; NLW, Voelas and Cefnamwlch, B 6, 111–16.
[63] Cardiff School Board, *Triennial Report* (Cardiff, 1875).
[64] Glamorgan CRO, D/DX38 1–7, Cardiff, Miscellaneous Papers concerning Education in Aberdare.

middle-class dominance emerges. In Llangefni (Anglesey), the Board elected in 1884 included an Anglican butcher, a Calvinistic Methodist minister, a Methodist merchant, a Congregationalist merchant and an Anglican publican,[65] while the Abenbury (Denbighshire) Board elected in 1878 included two who described themselves as gentlemen, one agent and three farmers.[66] The Liberal bourgeoisie, who comprised the majority of members in Wales, included individuals such as Gwilym Evans, a commercial entrepreneur in Llanelli with a wide range of business connections who eventually became chairman of Carmarthenshire County Council. Alongside him sat David Harry, a second-generation Nonconformist coalowner. Llandeilo Tal-y-bont Board was chaired for many years by Rees Harries, a major shareholder in the local tinplate industry. Educationalists such as G. T. Clark in Merthyr, the Revd T. J. Wheldon in Blaenau Ffestiniog and the Revd John Davies in Caernarfon took a prominent role in the activities of their respective Boards, the latter two adopting a particularly progressive attitude.[67] This pattern of middle-class representation was reflected throughout Wales and, as will be seen, stimulated a concerted attempt by labour and trade union representatives to ensure working-class representation.

Nevertheless, throughout the period under discussion, the education of the working class rested in the hands of upper- and middle-class members of the community. The motives of these individuals in seeking election were varied. Clearly, a debate such as that which surrounded education in Wales, often affected by denominational concerns, was guaranteed to attract the active participation of ministers of religion, clergymen and other

[65] *CDH*, 9 August 1884.
[66] Denbighshire CRO, PD/88/1/6, Minute Book of the Abenbury School Board.
[67] T. J. Wheldon (1841–1916) was a former pupil teacher who entered the Calvinistic Methodist ministry through Bala C.M. College. He served as a member of Newtown School Board but his greatest contribution was as member and chairman of Blaenau Ffestiniog School Board. He pressed for a higher grade school at Blaenau Ffestiniog and was later instrumental in the development of County Schools as a member of Caernarfonshire Education Committee. John Davies (Gwyneddon, 1832–1904), a journalist, was active in north Wales literary circles as well as a leading figure in the public life of Caernarfon. G. T. Clark (1809–98) had an even more remarkable career. An engineer in Merthyr, his career included periods as a public health inspector, railway engineer and manager of the Dowlais Ironworks. The author of several works on archaeology and the medieval history of Glamorgan, he served as a supporter and manager of voluntary schools in Merthyr until 1870, when he became a member of the Merthyr Tydfil School Board. See relevant entries in *DWB*. B. Ll. James (ed.), *G. T. Clark: Scholar Ironmaster in the Victorian Age* (Cardiff, 1998).

religious leaders, while others were introduced to School Board work by political organizations. Many who served on School Boards also served on Boards of Guardians and were to become county councillors after 1889. Examples such as Gwilym Evans, G. T. Clark, T. J. Wheldon, Lord Dynevor and John Davies testify to the involvement of persons of prominence in numerous aspects of local government. This cannot entirely be attributed to the fact that only a limited number of people was prepared to devote time and effort to the government of the locality. Membership of the School Board offered the opportunity to take responsibility in an important aspect of the life of the community and to gain recognition as a trustworthy participant in its corporate endeavour. Reputations made as members of School Boards were important contributions to the development of personal and political support. The respect for local Liberal leaders, built up partly as a result of their performance as members of Boards, was an important contribution to the defeat of Conservative candidates by the Liberals in the County Council elections of 1889. Of equal significance was the fact that active individuals like Dynevor, Evans and Wheldon considered elementary education to be an important feature of the development and improvement of society and thus desired to be part of its management and to influence the direction and the ethos of the schools. Yet it is also noticeable that the radicalism of Liberal members was suspect. Gwilym Evans had had Unionist connections in the early days of his political activity. David Harry, a Liberal coalowner and a patron of Nonconformity in Llwynhendy (Carmarthenshire), conducted relations in the village in a manner reminiscent of the landed gentry of rural Wales. His behaviour may not have been tyrannical, but he certainly demanded a considerable measure of deference from the local community.

The implementation of the 1870 Education Act was eagerly awaited in most parts of Wales and reference has already been made to the mood of the population at large in that year. A Liberal government, pledged to radical policies, was about to deliver promises made to the Welsh Nonconformist community. Its assertive and self-confident leadership was determined to wrest control of all aspects of Welsh life from the entrenched gentry class and to replace its influence with democratic control. As has been shown, the referenda for School Boards in Wales perfectly reflected this feeling. Yet the actual performance of those Liberal leaders as members of School Boards did not match their enthusiasm for the establishment of Boards. Indeed, as will be argued in the concluding chapter, the commitment to education shown by Henry Richard, Lewis Edwards and the other national leaders was not reflected in the attitude of a large number of those charged with the implementation of the Act at local level. The Education Department regularly complained of the lassitude of Welsh School Boards, complaints which were echoed even in the pages of the Welsh Nonconformist press. The Llangurig School Board (Montgomeryshire) was heavily criticized in 1873 for having accomplished nothing since its establishment.[68] Similar criticisms were levied at the Pembrey School Board in 1876 over the expensive and cumbersome way in which it undertook surveys of the educational deficiencies of the parish without taking any steps to remedy the situation.[69] The Denbigh School Board, serving Gee's bastion of radicalism, was threatened with sequestration and dissolution unless it complied with the Department's instruction to construct a girls' school in 1893.[70] Other Boards sought to wait and see what progress neighbouring Boards would make before they built their own schools, hoping that a large school in a neighbouring parish would enable them to divert surplus pupils there. These inadequacies exercised the patience of the school inspectorate. The Revd Robert Temple noted in his report for 1874 that, while the majority of Boards had declared their intention to build schools, a large number found excuses for not doing so. He mentioned, in contrast, the immense progress made by the voluntary sector in the period from 1870 to 1874. This he attributed to the imminent deadline for voluntary agencies to complete the work and to the fact that the voluntary committees were composed of people with a zeal for education, while Boards consisted of members elected for political reasons.[71] This point was echoed by the Revd Shadrach Pryce, who complained that, while many village personalities were keen to secure seats on School Boards, they did not demonstrate a similar enthusiasm

[68] PP 1874, XVIII.
[69] PP 1875, XXIV.
[70] *CDH*, 2 June 1893.
[71] PP 1874, XVIII, Mr Temple's Report.

for the work of the Boards.[72] The inspectors were particularly critical of Boards such as that at Llanddyfnan (Anglesey), where members were accused of having a greater enthusiasm for avoiding work than for providing a school.[73] Significantly, they drew attention to the inertia of the Aberdaron School Board (Caernarfonshire), the scene of a notable contest between the local Nonconformists and Lord Penrhyn over the establishment of a School Board, and where the much-vaunted Board had managed to operate until 1877 without laying a single brick.[74] According to the Revd E. T. Watts, a situation like this arose from the fact that in his district the members who desired to provide educational accommodation were a minority on virtually every Board.[75]

The lack of commitment on the part of several School Board members was further illustrated by the high instances of non-attendance at meetings. School Boards such as those at Bangor, Newtown, Llanwrtyd Wells (Breconshire), Saundersfoot (Pembrokeshire) and Llanrhystyd (Cardiganshire) found it almost impossible to hold quorate meetings because members were loath to attend.[76] As inquorate meetings could not transact any business, a further obstacle was placed in the path of the development of an effective education system. Moreover, the image conveyed by such behaviour was anything but positive. Anglican commentators were quick to attribute this lack of interest to the fact that those elected were political representatives rather than educationists, and that they had none of that real commitment to education found in the ranks of the voluntary committees. Such loss of interest was an indictment of those who represented Liberalism in Wales.

Liberal representatives in rural Wales regularly pointed to the common interest which prevailed in rural areas. Yet, although class divisions were less pronounced there than in the increasingly class-conscious industrial areas, it would be wrong to believe that they were wholly absent. The size of the land-holdings has been cited as a justification for the view that little

---

[72] PP 1876, XXIII, Mr Pryce's Report.
[73] PP 1877, XXIX.
[74] Ibid. NLW, Voelas and Cefnamwlch, B 6, 1–20.
[75] Ibid.
[76] PP 1882, XXIII.

difference existed between tenant farmers and the labouring population in rural Wales. It is clear that Welsh landholdings were small by comparison with their English counterparts, as is illustrated below:

Table 3.1 Change in the size of farms in Wales, 1875–1895[77]

Farm size	1875	1895
1–50 acres	43403	45130
50–100 acres	10375	10980
100–300 acres	7975	8583
300–500 acres	486	438
Over 500 acres	102	67

The majority of farms consisted of less than 100 acres and a substantial number were below fifty acres, often of barren, unproductive land. To use the limited extent of the Welsh unit of agricultural production to justify a belief in the absence of class distinctions fails to recognize, however, the arguments of historians, notably David Jenkins and David Pretty, who have demonstrated pronounced differences between the social status of farmers and of agricultural labourers.[78] Pretty also points to the fact that, whereas the tenant farmers may have professed radical ideas, their enlightened behaviour did not extend to their treatment of agricultural labourers. An analysis of the referenda for Welsh School Boards indicates that the radical reputation of Welsh farmers should be questioned. It is also clear from the evidence of the performance of the farmers as members of Welsh School Boards that as a group they were far from wholehearted in their acceptance of the vision of an enlightened, progressive society that based its hope on improvement through education. As Dr John Davies has argued, the successor generation of Welsh Liberal politicians, particularly at local level, were notably loath to provide those services which they were required to provide,

[77] Williams, *Digest of Statistics*, I, pp.238–9.
[78] David Pretty, *The Rural Revolt That Failed: Farm Workers' Trade Unions in Wales, 1889–1950* (Cardiff, 1989); D. W. Howell, 'The agricultural labourer in nineteenth-century Wales', *WHR*, 6 (1972–3), 262–87; David Jenkins, *The Agricultural Community in South-west Wales at the Turn of the Twentieth Century* (Cardiff, 1971), pp.39–72.

especially in relation to public health.[79] For many Liberals of that generation it was the *tenure* of power rather than the *exercise* of power which was crucial. The same accusations can be levied against the previous generation of Liberal leaders. Criticism of the attitudes of Welsh farmers should, even so, be tempered by an acknowledgement that they operated in a difficult economic and political climate. Their commitment to Liberalism was at its height in the late nineteenth century, when the issues which loomed large in Liberal thinking also dominated Welsh politics, and their arguments did not place great emphasis on either the rights of workers or the obligation of employers. It can be reasonably argued that the cause of Welsh education suffered from this lack of commitment to the needs of the disadvantaged.

At the same time, many cases of a failure to make progress in the field of education can be explained by the financial precariousness of School Boards. They were recently created bodies whose very existence was often based on a fragile local consensus. They had been created in the teeth of Conservative opposition which was based in no small part on attempts to frighten the local community with threats of an increased rate burden. Thus, the Boards sought on all occasions to limit the rate burden as much as possible in order to counteract the Conservative accusations and prove the economic efficiency of the Board system. Just as important, the Liberal leadership was patently aware of the economic plight of those whom they represented. The small tenant farmers and *petit bourgeoisie* of shopkeepers were the backbone of the Liberal Party in Wales but they were by no means an affluent group in society. They were already labouring under an economic depression and the burden of tithes. As a direct result, Liberal local authorities were determined to keep expenditure to a minimum, both for party political reasons and out of genuine commitment to the welfare of the local community. As will be shown, the need to achieve a balance between the requirements of public expenditure and the obligation to keep the rate burden to a minimum was a major problem facing Liberal local authorities in Wales throughout this period.

---

[79] John Davies, 'Y gydwybod gymdeithasol yng Nghymru rhwng y ddau ryfel byd', in G. H. Jenkins, (ed.), *Cof Cenedl*, IV (1989), 163–7.

The School Boards were founded on a parish basis (except for the amalgamated United District School Boards), and, while in many cases the distribution of the population was such that a single school was sufficient, this was not always the case and the interests of localities within the parish might be dominant. The temptation to concentrate on a particular area or village was much in evidence, and many elected members failed to develop a wider view, concentrating on the benefits for one locality to the detriment of the area as a whole. The earl of Cawdor claimed that a narrow attitude was all too present in the minds of the members of the Llandeilo Fawr School Board and that this had a detrimental effect on education in the parish. In his opinion, the Nonconformists who comprised the majority on the School Board could think only in terms of villages while he, with his vast experience of running a disparate estate, could conceive of the interest of the entire district.[80] A similar localism was in evidence in the Llwchwr district. The town of Gorseinon developed in the late 1880s at the point of contact of three parishes, Loughor Borough, Llandeilo Tal-y-bont and Llangyfelach. All three parishes had School Boards, Llangyfelach forming part of the Swansea School Board. As the urban development at Gorseinon created a need for a school for 200 pupils, and as the children attending the school would be drawn from the three parishes, it was suggested that the three Boards should jointly fund the erection of the school and contribute to its maintenance. Both the Swansea and Llandeilo Tal-y-bont Boards agreed, yet Loughor rejected the proposal on two counts. First, it was stated that the Board already provided a school at Loughor itself while, of the other villages in the parish, Tre-uchaf was served by a National school and Pontybrenin needed the provision of a Board school so as to cater for children who would otherwise be forced to attend the National school. The Board would not, therefore, contribute to yet another school at Gorseinon. Second, the Loughor Board had a principled objection to spending Loughor ratepayers' money outside the borough of Loughor. Despite the repeated pleadings of the former two Boards, and the promptings of the Education Department, the Loughor Board remained resolute. Indeed, it was only the threat of sequestration

[80] PRO, ED2/578.

and disbandment which eventually caused the Loughor Board to relent.[81]

Such examples, mainly of a local interest, litter the minute books of School Boards throughout Wales and form the bulk of the correspondence between Welsh Boards and the Education Department. Disputes arose over the siting of schools in certain villages on the grounds that children from other villages would be forced to travel long distances to school. The Loughor example suggests that while co-operation between Boards was a fine principle, it was difficult to administer at local level. Yet these were issues of localism rather than matters of principle, and no serious conceptual arguments arose in the course of discussion. Rather, the debates distracted the Nonconformist majorities on School Boards and led to disunity and infighting. Discord and insularity gave further ammunition to the Conservative and Anglican opponents of the School Board system.

Arguments such as those in the Gorseinon area were mere distractions in the process of developing an education system. Of far greater importance were the accusations of excessive expenditure regularly levied against the Boards, and which had even greater poignancy in periods of economic depression, lending credence to Conservative attacks made on grounds of cost. A public petition was sent from Llandeilo in protest against the decision of the School Board to construct a school, at great expense, during a period of economic depression when Lord Dynevor had already agreed to extend his own school to make up the deficiency.[82] In Holyhead, the purchase of musical instruments was regarded as lavish,[83] as was the decision of the Llangadog School Board (Carmarthenshire) to hold an annual banquet for its members.[84] Accusations of profligacy were also made over the design of school buildings. While the majority of rural Boards adopted a simple design for a school – for example, the Pant-perthog School built by the Tywyn and Pennal School Board (Merioneth) – others regarded the school as a status symbol of the Board's authority. The Llanelli Board was accused of wasting ratepayers' money by insisting on the architecturally

[81] PRO, ED2/607.
[82] Ibid.
[83] PRO, ED2/579.
[84] Ibid.

elegant design for the town's Higher Grade School,[85] and similar accusations were made in Swansea, Merthyr, Newport and Cardiff, where schools such as the Roath Park Board School stood as fine architectural achievements. Expensively designed buildings were found at Swansea's Higher Grade School and the Manselton Board School in Swansea.[86] Certainly, rivalry in building plans and civic pride characterized the agenda of local municipal leaders. The Alexandra Road Board School in Aberystwyth was regarded as one of the finest buildings in the town in the 1870s, clearly indicating that the desire for architectural elegance was not confined to the industrial areas. Indeed, the design adopted by the Talley School Board (Carmarthenshire) indicates that, despite the fact that the school catered for a comparatively small number of children, the Board was determined that it should be housed in a building of some quality. As Malcolm Seabourne has demonstrated, the architects employed by the Boards often reflected the prestige which Boards felt would be derived from their schools.[87] Architects such as W. Snooke, E. W. M. Corbett and G. E. T. Laurence were pre-eminent in the design of schools. Others such as Lingen-Barker designed schools in places as diverse as Brecon, Aber-nant (Glamorgan), Lakefield in Llanelli and New Inn (Monmouthshire). Others concentrated on designing schools for Boards in particular localities. Szlumper and Aldwinckle were active in Cardiganshire, W. Turner in Denbighshire, Habershon, Fawckner and Groves in Cardiff and E. A. Lansdowne in Monmouthshire. The smaller Boards, however, generally opted for a less grandiose design than did their urban counterparts. Local builders were regularly engaged, often with disastrous consequences. The pressures of attempting to ape the grand schools of the urban areas while working within a tight budget made for an uneasy task.

The attacks on the extravagance of School Boards formed much of the substance of Conservative opposition to the School Boards of Wales during the period after their establishment. The

---

[85] *LLG*, 27 June 1889.
[86] The Dowlais Central School was built by Lady Charlotte Guest, at her own expense. I am indebted to Professor Sir Glanmor Williams for this information.
[87] M. Seabourne, *Schools in Wales, 1500–1900* (Denbigh, 1992), pp.178–9 and 190–2. For details on architects, Seabourne refers to the Biographical Files in the Royal Institute of British Architects Library; for school building, see below, pp.139–40.

charge of prodigality and the wasting of ratepayers' money on such things as banquets and subscriptions to newspapers was part of the populist campaign by the Conservative Party in opposition, in order to embarrass the established Liberal administrations. Likewise, complaints concerning the grandeur of buildings, and the decision to go for the best rather than the cheapest option, highlighted the dilemma of elected members in determining whether to put the interests of the rising generation, or those of existing ratepayers, to the fore. So seriously were such accusations taken by controlling Liberal groups that in Swansea, where there was controversy over expenditure, it was boasted that the Board had merely met the minimum statutory requirement in supplying educational accommodation, clearly in an effort to counteract the charges of profligacy.[88] Indeed, so determined were some Boards to deny accusations of extravagance that their real achievements were often obscured. School Boards throughout Wales achieved a dramatic increase in the total number of schools and in securing schools of higher quality than their predecessors. The contrast with the situation which prevailed in 1847 was stark and should not be overlooked in any analysis of the performance of the School Boards of Wales.

Since the School Board system was dominated by political representatives, it was inevitable that education and the operations of the Boards would become major issues in developing and consolidating the respective positions of political parties in Wales during the late nineteenth century. School Boards witnessed the emergence of political caucuses early in their development. Although in the early years elections tended to be fought on denominational rather than on party political lines, the Liberal members regularly combined to operate as a political group rather than as individuals, especially in the towns and particularly in marginal areas. These groups often acted to limit political damage. By meeting in private before the official meeting of the Board, controversial items on the agenda could be discussed and a Liberal policy agreed upon. The development of collective responsibility within the group meant that there was less likelihood of Liberal members opposing each other in public or voting with the opposition on a particular issue. A united front

---

[88] Swansea School Board, *Triennial Report* (Swansea, 1882).

was maintained and defeats for the Liberal leaders were avoided. Thus, when the Llangadog School Board was considering a controversial item of expenditure, the Liberal members resolved to hold the meeting in a remote area of the parish in the hope that the press would be unable to attend.[89] Likewise, the chairman's knowledge that Lord Dynevor was intending to object to an item of expenditure led him to hold the meeting of the Llandeilo Fawr Board on the afternoon of the wedding of his lordship's daughter, safe in the knowledge that Dynevor and other Conservative members would be otherwise occupied.[90]

The role of the Welsh language as a means of conducting local authority business was a further feature of the deliberations of School Boards in Wales. As Gwilym Prys Davies has shown, it was natural in a number of areas for public business to be conducted through the medium of Welsh, a practice which was sanctioned by the Whitehall authorities for Board and Parish Council meetings.[91] In certain areas this was a necessity rather than an option, for even as late as the 1880s a number of Board members were monoglot Welsh-speakers. Thus, the Waunfawr School Board (Caernarfonshire) resolved to conduct its affairs through the medium of Welsh in 1893, not as a matter of principle but in order to facilitate the deliberations of its members.[92] The policy of holding meetings in Welsh had an added benefit for those Nonconformist members who wished, for various reasons, to exclude opposition members from their deliberations. The fact that the Conservative Party drew its representatives mainly from the ranks of Anglicized gentry and clergy and the English-speaking middle class played into the hands of the Welsh-speaking Nonconformist leaders. A Conservative member of the Llanddewibrefi School Board (Cardiganshire) complained that he was being excluded from the meetings owing to the clerk's policy of sending notices of meeting and agendas in Welsh only, rendering their contents meaningless to him.[93] The practice was by no means confined to the overwhelmingly Welsh-speaking areas. Thomas Ashford complained

[89] *LLG*, 19 January 1882.
[90] PRO, ED2/577.
[91] Gwilym Prys Davies, *Llafur y Blynyddoedd* (Denbigh, 1991), pp.128–30.
[92] PRO, ED2/589.
[93] PRO, ED2/570.

of the same problem at Cwmfelin (Glamorgan), where the managers had deliberately resolved to hold the proceedings in Welsh in order to exclude him from the debate.[94] The managers, however, remained unmoved, claiming that they had conducted their affairs in Welsh for the previous eight years, with the sanction of the Merthyr School Board; were they to hold their proceedings in English, three monoglot Welsh-speaking managers would be excluded from the meeting.[95]

Particular policies of individual Boards were a further target for attacks by the Anglican members. In Cockett (Glamorgan) it was claimed that the school attendance officer paid more attention to his duties as a propagandist for the Board system than he ever did in enforcing school attendance.[96] The Bedwellty Board (Monmouthshire) was accused of ignoring the educational plight of Tredegar for sectarian reasons, while in Merthyr the Board came under attack for placing advertisements for teaching vacancies in Nonconformist journals such as *Baner ac Amserau Cymru*, *Y Tyst* and *Y Goleuad*, and deliberately refusing to advertise in Conservative papers like the *Western Mail*, in order to predetermine the political affiliations of the town's teachers. The activities of the Pembrey Board (Carmarthenshire) were claimed to be even more blatantly political. The Board was accused of refusing to sanction expenditure on schools in Conservative areas in order to divert resources to Liberal and politically marginal villages, a charge vehemently rejected by the Nonconformists on the Board, who counterclaimed that Conservative landowners needed no lessons in gerrymandering, in view of their policy of allocating key farms to their political supporters.[97] In addition to politically inspired decisions, individual Boards regularly faced accusations of open corruption. The allocation of tenders for the construction of schools was claimed to be riddled with corruption and was associated with back-handers to Board members. Similarly, tenders to supply schools with coal were said to be determined illegally in many areas. As will be demonstrated below, the most regular accusation concerned the allocation of headmasterships. The practice of canvassing Board members

[94] PRO, ED16/384.
[95] Ibid.
[96] PRO, ED16/395–99.
[97] Ibid.

was rife throughout Wales and, in a number of areas, was expected by the candidates. Attempts were made to outlaw the practice by including notices to all applicants that canvassing would disqualify the applicant from consideration. Despite the adoption of this policy, the habit continued to the extent that one Llanelli member, Gwilym Evans, complained that he was suffering from insomnia as a result of late-night visits from applicants for teaching posts.[98]

The relationship between the School Boards and other local authorities was a further problem affecting the development of the education system in Wales, particularly the relationship between the School Boards and the Boards of Guardians. This was a crucial link because the Boards of Guardians were responsible for conducting elections to School Boards. Moreover, the Guardians were responsible for issuing rate demands and collecting the revenue. School Boards and, later, the County Councils would determine the amount in the pound of rateable value which they required, and would then instruct the Guardians to demand and collect that amount on their behalf. This administrative arrangement generated friction on three counts. First, the Guardians were accused of charging excessive amounts for conducting elections to School Boards. Second, they demonstrated a marked reluctance to precept as instructed by the Boards and, third, the fact that elections were conducted by the Guardians meant that elementary education was associated with pauperism in some quarters.[99] Clearly, Boards of Guardians regarded elections to School Boards as opportunities to fill their own coffers, irrespective of the fact that it was the ratepayers themselves who had to bear the brunt of the cost of those elections. Guardians were also reluctant to charge excessive rates for fear that they, as a rate-collecting body, would face unpopularity as a result of the high rates levied by the School Boards from a public which lacked understanding of the origins of the various items on the rate demand. Whereas the Guardians had a direct relationship with the ratepayers, the School Boards' rate could be hidden in the general rate demand, thereby reducing the unpopularity of the School Boards. In certain cases

---
[98] *Llanelly Mercury*, 12 July 1894.
[99] NLW MS. 2994E.

it was undoubtedly a case of open conflict between Conservative-controlled Boards of Guardians and Liberal School Boards. Yet the situation also arose where the two authorities were controlled by the same party. Despite their strong allegiance to the Liberal Party, the organization was loose enough in certain areas to enable individual representatives to develop a stronger loyalty to the authorities on which they served, and certainly to their own electoral advantages, than to the party they represented. Rivalries between local authorities and allegations of petty corruption are the food and drink of local newspapers. Such accusations were no more prevalent in the late nineteenth century than at any other period in the history of local government. Those local authorities were, however, accountable to the electorate as no other form of local administration could be.

The staffing of School Boards was crucial to the development of an effective education system and reflected the performance of the political leaders of nineteenth-century Wales in relation to education. The position of clerk to the School Board was a key position in the administration of the system and was, in the majority of cases, of an importance at least equal to that of the chairman. In the urban areas the appointment of a clerk was facilitated by the increasing numbers of trained professionals who were available during this period. In the rural areas, however, the choice remained limited, the position often falling on ministers of religion or members of the teaching profession itself. On occasion the choice fell by general consent upon a suitable candidate, but not invariably so. The Anglican community in Llanfair Pwllgwyngyll (Anglesey) expressed doubts as to the impartiality of Morris Jones, a Nonconformist shopkeeper, as clerk to the Board.[100] More serious accusations were made in Denbigh, where the Anglican opposition accused the clerk of making gestures when they spoke in order to influence the reaction of the Nonconformist members,[101] and accusations were made throughout the period of biased clerks being appointed by individual Boards.

The tithe disturbances and wider political issues also featured in the debates of Welsh School Boards. The Colwyn Bay School

---

[100] PRO, ED2/560.
[101] *CDH*, 21 June 1889.

Board was urged to join the battle against the tithes in 1888 by refusing to pay the four-shilling tithe payment due from the Board,[102] while an anti-monarchist blow was struck in Llandybïe in 1887 when two of the Board's members refused to sign a petition to the Queen congratulating her on reaching fifty years on the throne.[103] Such instances were, however, mere posture politics. There was no real orchestrated campaign on the part of the School Boards of Wales to resist the payment of tithes, and neither were the schools used as a means of indoctrinating the children of Wales in Nonconformist, Liberal politics. Certainly, the introduction of pastoral issues such as temperance can be regarded as an attempt by the education authorities to counteract the decline in the influence of the chapels in Wales and to ensure that children who were no longer receiving a chapel-based moral education were at least receiving some in the school. But there was never a campaign on the scale of that witnessed in the Third Republic in France to indoctrinate children in republican morality. Rather, the Welsh schools kept politics firmly outside the classroom and schoolchildren were largely untouched by the political upheavals in the wider community. The success of the teaching profession in achieving this at a time when political controversy was widespread in Wales, and when the schools themselves were matters of political controversy, was a tribute to their professionalism, especially in view of the fact that a high number of teachers were themselves involved in political activity.

The 1870 Education Act was designed primarily to ensure at least a basic education for working-class children. As several studies have demonstrated, education was at the forefront of the concerns of the labour and trade union movement. The Trades Union Congress (TUC) played a leading role in the debate surrounding the Act of 1870, lending its support to the development of free, compulsory and non-sectarian schools. Education was considered a crucial force in the emancipation of the working class, not least because it could generate a demand for further social reform. The development of these ideas was followed by concerted efforts in England to secure the election of

---

[102] *CDH*, 24 February 1888.
[103] *LLG*, 12 May 1887.

Labour candidates to School Boards, early successes being recorded in Birmingham, Bradford and London.[104] This had a particular relevance to the debate on education in Wales. The degree of working-class participation in education in Wales was significant, particularly in relation to working-class involvement in the Sunday school movement. At the same time, there was a high number of company or works schools funded either jointly with employers or entirely from workers' wages.[105] Yet the idea of independent working-class action in Wales was in many ways hampered by the nature of the Nonconformist community. C. Aull-Davies has argued that the dominance of the Nonconformist chapel, particularly its role as an alternative focus for social prestige, combined with the economic factors noted above to create a situation whereby class divisions and tensions were absent from Welsh society.[106] More persuasive is the argument put forward by Ieuan Gwynedd Jones that, with the development of government agencies, both local and national, a new middle class emerged in Wales which increasingly articulated the views, concerns and aspirations of the working-class community. The fact that the working class, for a variety of reasons, accepted this leadership helps to explain the low level of direct working-class participation in electoral politics in the late nineteenth century.[107] Despite the tensions which were increasingly visible, there remained an alliance between middle- and working-class communities in Wales, based on a Nonconformity which made common cause for the promotion of shared objectives. Education formed an important element in the common objectives of the two groups, alongside other issues, notably the development of religious freedom, the extension of the franchise and the democratization of local government in Wales. The objectives of the working class during the greater part of the period under discussion mirrored those of the wider Nonconformist community, as reflected in the priorities of workers' leaders like

---

[104] B. Simon, *Education and the Labour Movement* (London, 1965), pp.121–97.
[105] L. W. Evans, *Education in Industrial Wales, 1700–1900: A Study of the Works Schools System* (Avalon, 1971), pp.298–9.
[106] C. Aull-Davies, 'Welsh nationalism and the British State', in G. Williams (ed.), *Crisis of Economy and Ideology* (Cardiff, 1987), 201–13.
[107] I. G. Jones, *Explorations and Explanations* (Llandysul, 1981), especially chs. 3, 4 and 5.

William Abraham. This alliance with the wider Nonconformist movement was manifested in the support provided by trade union leaders for the campaign for School Boards in Wales, often in the teeth of employers' hostility in such places as Bedwas and Machen (Monmouthshire).[108] In a number of cases it was the working-class leadership itself which played the greatest part in the referenda for School Boards, as in the campaign for a School Board at Whitford (Flintshire) and at Llanasa (Flintshire).[109] Yet only in a limited number of cases, as at Port Dinorwig (Caernarfonshire), could the Board agitation be said to be exclusively working class.[110] Herbert Lewis was a lawyer by profession, while Pan Jones, as a minister of religion, was firmly established in the ranks of the middle class despite his poverty-stricken background.[111] Thus, even in those campaigns which did feature working-class leaders, there remained an important alliance with the more radical sections of the Liberal Party.

As has been demonstrated, working-class support for the establishment of School Boards was not reflected in the selection of candidates for those Boards, a factor which prompted independent action by the working-class leadership in certain areas. In Blaenau Ffestiniog, a community dominated by quarry workers, denominational rivalry had declined under the chairmanship of T. J. Wheldon. Here, a determined effort was made to ensure the election of a representative of the slate quarrymen, yet his success owed as much to a recognition by the town's middle class of the desirability of working-class representation as it did to the electoral strength of the quarrymen.[112] In Aberffraw (Anglesey) in 1893 the local Liberal establishment was rocked by the success of the Labour candidate, who topped the poll.[113] Not surprisingly, however, it was the industrial areas which provided Labour candidates with their greatest successes. In Llanelli, the leader of the Tinplate Workers' Union, Thomas Phillips, secured election, though he was rejected in his bid for official support by

---

[108] See ch. 2.
[109] See ch. 2.
[110] *CDH*, 19 October 1888.
[111] P. Jones-Evans, 'Evan Pan Jones – land reformer', *WHR*, 4 (1968–9), 143–60.
[112] *Baner*, 17 March 1880; R. Merfyn Jones, *The North Wales Quarrymen, 1874–1922* (Cardiff, 1981), pp.66–71, 162–5.
[113] *CDH*, 20 October 1893.

the local Liberal Association.[114] Similarly, James Wignall secured election to the Swansea School Board in 1897 despite official disapproval of his candidature,[115] and so did Isaac Edwards in Merthyr in 1892;[116] and Labour candidates were returned in Llandeilo Tal-y-bont in 1897.[117] Yet favourable estimation of these successes for Labour candidates has to be qualified. The success of Labour in Llandeilo Tal-y-bont owed much to the dissatisfaction in the locality at the controversial school hours introduced by the previous Board; similar local issues prompted the Swansea Trades Council's determination to secure a seat. Of greater significance, however, was the fact that the majority of Labour candidates returned were active and prominent members of the Nonconformist community. Isaac Edwards and Thomas Phillips were both deacons, and James Wignall had come into prominence initially not as a Labour leader but as an evangelical preacher in the Kilvey area of Swansea.

Several of the most prominent Liberal leaders, such as T. E. Ellis and D. R. Daniel, actively promoted the cause of working-class representation on the School Boards of Wales.[118] Yet their arguments were not universally welcomed by the Liberal leadership. The *Llanelly and County Guardian*, while admitting the ability of a number of working-class leaders, remained opposed to class representation,[119] sentiments that were echoed by Gwilym Evans, who nevertheless advocated the appointment of artisans as school managers.[120] There is little evidence, however, of an anti-Labour alliance developing between Conservatives and Liberals on the School Boards of Wales, an alliance which later became a part of Welsh local government. The divisions between Liberals and Conservatives remained too great for these groups to co-operate against Labour representatives.

The policies adopted by Labour members on election to School Boards are a further indication of the alliance with the

---

[114] *LLG*, 11 July 1889.
[115] *Industrial World*, 3 December 1897.
[116] W. Harris, 'Education in Merthyr Tydfil, 1840–1912, a brief survey', Merthyr Public Library MSS.
[117] *Industrial World*, 5 March 1897 and 3 December 1897.
[118] NLW, T. E. Ellis Papers, 2852.
[119] *LLG*, 9 June 1894.
[120] *LLG*, 11 August 1892.

wider Nonconformist community. Labour members were constrained by the fact that they never achieved overall control of a Board for any real length of time and were therefore obliged to co-operate with, and persuade, mainstream Liberal members in any policy changes. Some innovative suggestions were, however, made by Labour representatives. George Colwill strongly advocated the introduction of manual and technical subjects in Swansea's schools as a means of making the curriculum more relevant and of combating the decline in interest in education which had been noted among certain working-class children.[121] The Cardiff Labour manifesto for the School Board election of 1893 included the provision of swimming baths and gymnasia at the schools and the provision of library services for schoolchildren.[122] In Merthyr, Isaac Edwards was given the unpopular post of chairman of the attendance committee, allegedly a deliberate attempt by the Liberals to reduce Edwards's popularity in the town by giving him responsibility for chasing truants and arrears of school pence. Edwards, however, demonstrated considerable aptitude in relieving some genuine cases and enabling parents of errant children to attend Board meetings by insisting that they be held on 'Mabon's Monday', the monthly holiday enjoyed by miners. Edwards scored a further success in securing the use of school playgrounds as recreation grounds for the general public outside school hours.[123] Whatever the importance of these achievements, the innovative policies of Labour members remained few. The majority shared the views of the Liberal majority on most policy issues although, in certain cases of mistreatment of teachers and attendance officers, Labour members sought to protect the interests of fellow trade unionists. Their real complaint was with the limitations of the educational ladder. Working-class leaders regarded the small number of scholarships to intermediate schools as constituting a barrier to the educational opportunities of working-class children, and they regarded with distaste the continuation of paid places at intermediate schools. These, however, were issues for national legislation and County Council activity rather than for

[121] Swansea CRO, D/7714, Minute Book of Swansea Trades Council, 3 December 1897.
[122] *Western Mail*, 4 January 1893.
[123] Harris, 'Education in Merthyr'.

School Boards. For considerable numbers of Liberal supporters the criticisms of the Labour members were petty and unimportant distractions from the great Liberal achievement of an education system. They jealously defended the system which they believed was their party's creation. As a result, Labour members' criticisms of the lack of educational opportunities were ignored, leading to a feeling of embitterment and exasperation on their part. This disenchantment over the complacency of the Liberal attitude was to contribute to the eventual weakening of the Liberal embrace in Welsh politics.

Elementary education remained a burning political issue throughout the late nineteenth century and, as has been indicated above, the arguments did not end with the referenda on School Boards. New issues, such as the role of School Boards in the tithe disturbances or the claims of the working class to representation, certainly arose towards the end of the School Board era. Yet the issues that dominated the agenda concerned economy of expenditure and the relationship with the Anglican Church, issues which remained constant throughout the period. The control of education remained a key feature in the democratization of Welsh local government. Yet in too many cases the schools became objects in political discourse. Educational arguments were often not heard, as Liberal and Conservative members argued over issues of policy which frequently had no relevance to the classroom itself. The development of the elementary education service was hampered further by economic, geographical and demographic difficulties and by individual personalities complicating the process. Yet the most pressing problem affecting the development of the system was the fundamental flaw in the management structure of elementary education. Parishes as units of government were simply too small to make effective entities despite the achievements of numerous small Boards. The limited extent of the areas administered encouraged both parochialism and a situation whereby individuals were able to disrupt the process for a variety of malevolent reasons. The transfer of elementary schools to the control of the County Councils undeniably resulted in a reduction in the ability of individuals to hold up progressive policies, lessened the influence of parochial considerations and led to the development of more strategic thinking and a more rational distribution of resources. Despite the difficulties faced by these Boards, however, and their preoccupation with issues which were of little relevance to the teaching of children, the development of the elementary education system in the late nineteenth century remains, in no small part, a tribute to the School Boards of Wales, their members and their staff.

IV
DIFFICULTY AND PROGRESS

The political and religious arguments which surrounded the creation of an education system in Wales would have been of little significance had they not been accompanied by an improvement in the standard of learning in the country and an enhancement of the skills of the population. Before the passing of the Forster Act, the concerns expressed by school inspectors regarding the provision of education in Wales fell into two broad categories. First, they criticized the fact that there were not enough schools in Wales and that there were few opportunities for children to receive even a basic education, an issue which the Act subsequently sought to address. A second, and more complex, criticism was levied against the standards and attainments of the schools, a complaint which never met with a completely satisfactory answer throughout the School Board era.

The annual comments of the school inspectors are valuable evidence in attempting to understand these issues. The Revd Shadrach Pryce complained that the majority of schools in Wales suffered from bad classroom discipline, inferior equipment and an unintelligent method of teaching, drawbacks which were reflected in the low level of attainment found among the children.[1] These remarks were echoed by fellow inspectors such as the Revd E. T. Watts and William Williams, both of whom complained of the prevalence of rote learning as opposed to an attempt to ensure that the children understood what had been learned. In addition, they claimed that there was evidence to suggest a high instance of 'cramming' within the education system in Wales and that pupils were taught only what was necessary to pass an examination. Both noted that performance in the examinations betrayed signs of a last-minute effort rather than a continuous endeavour over the duration of the year.[2] The issue of cramming caused serious concern both to the school

[1] PP 1871, XXII.
[2] Ibid., Mr Watts's and Mr Williams's Reports.

inspectors and to the wider educational community. They were reflected in the views of educationalists such as the Scottish commentator, Austin Herbert, who expressed his concern that the practice of cramming was likely to 'lead to an intellectual distaste in after life', one which he believed would not only lead to difficulties in securing a good attendance at school but would discourage the growth of a love of learning within Welsh communities.[3]

These concerns were echoed in discussions within the teaching profession itself. The National Union of Elementary Teachers (NUET) alleged that a high number of passes in examinations and a good place on the league table of schools compiled by the inspectors did not necessarily reflect good teaching. Representatives of the teachers increasingly urged that it was necessary to take a much broader view of education and attributed the deficiencies in teaching methods to the system by which payment of teachers was determined according to the results of the examination.[4] Despite the firm opinion of members of the teaching profession that the problem of cramming was attributable to 'payment by results', and the admission by the inspectorate that this was the case, HMIs remained adamant that the system should be retained. This view was held even as late as 1897, when the senior HMI, L. J. Roberts, expressed reservations at the impending abolition of the system, highlighting the fact that the more progressive educational views were yet to permeate the ranks of Welsh inspectors.[5]

Throughout the greater part of the period under consideration in this study, the system of payment by results remained in operation. As a result, dubious examination practices, such as cramming or entering only the most able candidates for examination, continued as an inevitable evil in numerous Welsh schools.[6] Apart from the constraints imposed by the prevailing system, these practices were set to remain as long as the older

[3] NLW, Llysdinam Papers, 2233; José Harris, *Private Lives, Public Spirit: A Social History of Britain, 1870–1914* (Oxford, 1993), p.88.
[4] *Schoolmaster*, 12 April 1884.
[5] PP 1897, XXVI, Mr Roberts's Report.
[6] Dubious practices such as cramming and selective examination continued after the abolition of payments by results, as schoolchildren began to be entered for scholarships for intermediate schools. However, it was ameliorated by the fact that the teacher's salary no longer depended on the examination.

generation of schoolteachers continued to teach. As late as 1895, William Williams complained that progressive ideas on teaching received short shrift in Wales, particularly among the army of non-college-trained teachers who dominated the ranks of the profession in the rural areas.[7] He also complained of the way reading was taught by the 'silent reading' method, a practice which did not ensure understanding or correct pronunciation, and which thus constituted a barrier to fluency.[8] These deficiencies should not, however, be allowed to obscure the substantial advances that were made in teaching methods between 1870 and 1902. By 1883 both HMIs, B. J. Binns and Morgan Owen, commented that the teaching in their district was becoming more intelligent, and that teachers were increasingly placing the emphasis on understanding as well as knowledge, and both inspectors expressed their conviction that the unacceptable practices would be eradicated with the passing of the older generation of teachers.[9]

The three 'basic' subjects of reading, writing and arithmetic gained the greater part of the attention of each inspector throughout this period. Initially, the standard of arithmetic in Welsh schools was often poor and HMIs such as Shadrach Pryce regularly complained of bad habits (such as the use of fingers when counting) and the failure to develop skills in mental arithmetic.[10] The standard of reading in Wales was reported to be favourable by comparison with even the better areas of England (which were not affected by the complexities characteristic of a bilingual society), although complaints were made that the reading was often monotonous. In the opinion of John Rhys, the lack of understanding was a consequence of the imposition of a foreign language on the Welsh-speaking community, a factor also cited by other members of the inspectorate, which is considered elsewhere.[11] The poor standard of writing in Wales was a further cause for concern. In general, this was attributed to the bad equipment and materials used to teach writing rather than to the teaching methods themselves. In 1877 the continued

[7] PP 1895, XXVII, Mr Williams's Report.
[8] Ibid.
[9] PP 1883, XXV, Mr Binns's Report and Mr Morgan Owen's Report.
[10] PP 1873, XXIV, Mr Williams's Report; PP 1878–79, XXIII, Mr Pryce's Report.
[11] PP 1876, XXIII, Mr Rhys's Report.

use of slates and the paucity of exercise books were cited as reasons for bad penmanship in Wales.[12] Moreover, it was felt that many of the desks being used in schools were unsuitable for educational purposes. In the opinion of William Williams, this difficulty was caused by the tendency of school managers and School Boards to commission local carpenters to make the furniture rather than adopt the more expensive option of purchasing directly from firms specializing in educational products. As a result, desks were usually not only of a similar design but also of the same size, and they took little account of the fact that pupils did not conform to a uniform size, often rendering those desks totally inappropriate for use in the classroom.[13] Despite these concerns with the standards of reading, writing and arithmetic, it was the standard of spelling and composition which caused the greatest anxiety for the inspectorate. As will be noticed later, the existence of strongly Welsh-speaking districts led inspectors such as William Edwards, Dan Isaac Davies and John Rhys to advocate the use of Welsh as a medium of instruction in some areas.[14] In those areas where Welsh was the main language the difficulties of teaching English were compounded by the idiosyncrasies of the English language by comparison with the phonetic nature of Welsh. Thus, the similar spelling but dissimilar pronunciation of words such as 'viscount' and 'discount' was likely to create confusion in young minds, while other avoidable complications, such as the unnecessary insistence that 'show' should be spelt 'shew', caused further difficulties. In Welsh-speaking areas, therefore, the children were not only expected to learn a new language, but a language with perplexing characteristics, at a time when English-language reading materials were rarely available in many areas.

The complaints about the alarming state of spelling in Wales formed part of a wider concern about the standard of grammar in general. While some schools chose to teach grammar as a specific subject, others were loath to do so. The schools that saw no advantage in detailing the rules of grammar considered the

[12] PP 1877, XXIX.
[13] PP 1884–85, XXIII, Mr Williams's Report.
[14] For details of the more sympathetic attitude adopted by school inspectors towards the Welsh language, see, for instance, J. E. Hughes, *Arloeswr Dwyieithedd: Dan Isaac Davies, 1839–1887* (Cardiff, 1984); and below, ch. 7.

subject to be confusing, a judgement that was shared by many school inspectors. In their opinion, the time would be better used in teaching the rudiments of grammar rather than in attempting to teach the more complex formations of the language, or attempting to do everything only to find that nothing was done properly.[15] The inspectors placed a greater emphasis on the need to overcome more basic faults, such as the tendency of Welsh pupils to drop the final 's' in the third person, the non-pronunciation of 'h', and the use of the single present tense for references to the past, such as 'he go to school yesterday' rather than 'he went to school yesterday'. In the opinion of the inspectors, teachers often ignored such mistakes and failed to correct them in the classroom, leading to an inability among some pupils to distinguish grammatical English from the ungrammatical form.[16]

The organization of the classroom, and the failure to use resources that were available, were further points of concern for the inspectorate. In 1871 William Williams complained that classrooms were often too large and that this resulted in bad discipline, which in turn hindered the attainments of the children. This problem was most prevalent in the voluntary school sector and in those schools which had been transferred to Board control after having previously been maintained on a voluntary basis. Such schools were often of a very primitive design and barely complied with the specifications of the Education Department; furthermore they were erected by voluntary effort with concerns of economy rather than education uppermost in the minds of those responsible for their construction.[17] These problems were not brought to an end by the establishment of School Boards. Boards were loath to sanction expenditure on new equipment. For instance, the innovation of the blackboard was regarded by the inspectorate as indispensable, yet it was not considered to be a priority in the minds of many School Boards and school managers. Again, considerations of expense and the conservative attitude prevalent among many members of Boards and management committees hindered this development. Once purchased, however, the inspectors faced the difficulty of persuading the teaching profession itself to

[15] PP 1889, XXIX.
[16] PP 1887, XXVIII.
[17] PP 1871, XXII.

use the equipment. Horace Waddington complained that too much was done verbally by the teachers, who tended not to write on the blackboard examples of what was taught.[18] Morgan Owen complained as late as 1889 that, despite the presence of a blackboard in the majority of classrooms, its purchase was rendered futile by the refusal of the teachers to use it.[19]

Schoolteachers were under immense pressure throughout this period, a fact which, as will be demonstrated, was never fully appreciated by the community, education authorities or government inspectors. The capital equipment available in a great number of schools was poor, many having to make do with old or broken apparatus which hampered the teaching of children more often than it assisted in the process. The difficulties in teaching large classes were accentuated by the way classes included children of mixed ages and different abilities. Differentiated work could be achieved in a mixed-age classroom, but the effects of keeping a child back with younger children could be detrimental, not least because of the stigma that was perceived to be attached to a child when placed in a lower-ability group, and the disruption which might be caused by those pupils. As a result, there were few teachers, except those responsible for very small schools, who could give effect to teaching concepts that emphasized a rapport with pupils and an understanding of their individual needs.

These problems inevitably generated concern regarding the standard of discipline in Welsh schools, an issue that vexed the inspectorate throughout this period. Their concerns were heightened by the worry within Anglican circles (to which so many of the inspectors belonged) that Wales was on the verge of insurrection during the more violent episodes of the tithe wars. Earlier, the Revd E. T. Watts complained of the atrocious discipline in Caernarfonshire in 1874,[20] a comment echoed by Robert Temple, who attributed the decline to the loss of interest in discipline shown by older teachers.[21] HMI Binns, in his report for 1878, sounded a more optimistic note, stating that the majority of teachers were now slowly asserting their authority

[18] PP 1877, XXIX, Mr Waddington's Report.
[19] PP 1889, XXIX, Mr Morgan Owen's Report.
[20] PP 1874, XVIII, Mr Watts's Report.
[21] Ibid., Mr Temple's Report.

over their pupils, with a majority of teachers avoiding severe tactics. He maintained, however, that the continued prevalence of whimpering and general untidiness in the classrooms of his district were not conducive to imposing good discipline in future.[22] Horace Waddington claimed in 1880 that, while individual discipline was good, class discipline left much to be desired,[23] and Mostyn Pryce asserted that the key place for instilling good discipline was in the infants' classes, because practices learned there would be remembered in the later school career.[24] The cases of indiscipline noticed in reports included the efforts of boys at Ffairfach Board school who were in the habit of burning gunpowder on the seat of the boys' lavatories;[25] although their punishment was relatively lenient, the majority of misdemeanours were punished severely with few concessions being made to the more liberal school of thought.

The issue of gender division was a matter of little relevance in rural areas and therefore its importance was confined to urban Wales. The majority of the inspectorate were firmly of the opinion that schools should be divided into separate departments for boys, girls and infants, and where this was impractical the boys ought to be separated from the others. Of the inspectors, it was the Revd E. T. Watts who argued the case with the greatest fervour. Having first raised the issue as early as 1871,[26] he returned to the same theme in 1881, claiming that the moral condition of the country was being endangered by mixed schools:

> Though it might be impossible to prove to a demonstration that a mixed system of education is injurious to morality, I beg to record my conviction that the familiarity contracted in many of our mixed schools is not calculated to promote it. And even if my apprehensions on the score of morality are groundless, other arguments may be advanced in favour of separate departments for girls, whose force, I think, is irresistible.[27]

Despite the promptings of the Revd Watts, however, the cost of such division was considered prohibitive by the majority of

[22] PP 1878, XXVIII, Mr Binns's Report.
[23] PP 1880, XXII, Mr Waddington's Report.
[24] Ibid., Mr Mostyn Pryce's Report.
[25] *LLG*, 5 October 1885.
[26] PP 1871, XXII, Mr Watts's Report.
[27] PP 1881, XXXII, Mr Watts's Report.

School Boards in Wales, particularly those which served rural areas or where economic fortunes regularly fluctuated.

The condition of the school buildings was a further problem highlighted by the inspectorate. Malcolm Seabourne has illustrated, in his excellent study of the design and specifications of the schools, that Welsh schools often differed considerably from the standard pattern of those in England.[28] The quality of the majority of buildings erected before the passing of the 1870 Act was considered to be appalling in many cases, with many schools which were deemed efficient in the survey of 1870 barely passing the set standard, and even then only after considerable expense was incurred in improving them. With the passing of time, the problem became increasingly acute, particularly with regard to the non-rate-aided voluntary schools. Education Department guidelines were ignored on numerous occasions by the managers, who felt helpless in the face of the higher standards being imposed by the Department. Indeed, it was often the threat of withdrawal of a grant from a school, and the financial repercussions of not improving the premises, which motivated many managers to make essential improvements to their schools. These problems were not confined to the voluntary sector, however. Although William Williams noted the superiority of Board over voluntary schools, there were many shortcomings in the design of Board schools.[29] William Edwards commented in 1881 that many of the difficulties were created when School Boards, on grounds of economy, insisted upon giving the contract for the design of a school to local builders rather than to professional architects.[30] Although the designs of schools did improve, most notably after Boards adopted the practice of employing professional architects, many defects remained unaltered. William Williams noted that cloak-room facilities in the rural areas were often atrocious, with no room to dry wet clothes in winter, a matter of particular concern as many children had to undertake long journeys to school and were affected by shortcomings that clearly had a detrimental effect on their health. The condition of privies was again reported to be unsatisfactory in the majority of cases, a problem

[28] M. Seabourne, *Schools in Wales, 1500–1900* (Denbigh, 1992), pp.178–216.
[29] PP 1877, XXIX, Mr Williams's Report.
[30] PP 1881, XXXII, Mr Edwards's Report.

compounded by the fact that they were the regular targets of child vandalism.[31]

The continued existence of private or adventure schools in certain areas remained a problem because of the inferior quality of the education which they provided. They nevertheless remained popular among certain parents. HMI Binns, in 1874, noted the tendency to refuse to allow children to attend Board or National schools for fear that they might encounter the rougher elements of the community. The adventure schools, where the children were often referred to as 'Master' this or 'Miss' that and treated with reverence, pandered to the pretensions of some parents, while detrimentally affecting the education of their children. Although these schools did gradually disappear, they were responsible for blighting the education of many children in late nineteenth-century Wales.[32]

The despondent comments included in the HMI reports undoubtedly concentrated on the deficiencies rather than the successes of Welsh education. There were children who developed a great love of learning, not least because of the self-denying efforts of committed teachers. The quality of teaching was, on occasion, a matter of warm commendation. For instance, the Revd Shadrach Pryce noted in 1883 that strenuous efforts were being made in the Llanfynydd school (Carmarthenshire) not only to teach the rudiments of reading but also to instil a love of learning in the pupils, both in order to facilitate the teaching and to encourage learning in later life. Much of the success at Llanfynydd, it was claimed, was derived from the varied and interesting reading material which was offered to the children. According to Pryce, schools would do well to emulate the example of Llanfynydd and introduce works such as *The Vicar of Wakefield, The Swiss Family Robinson, Sandford and Merton*, or *A Voyage in the Sunbeam*. Pryce expressed his conviction of the need to encourage a broader educational ethos:

> a lad may forget his English grammar and geography and even the higher arithmetic he learnt. There is nothing in his daily life to make him recur to these subjects after leaving school, but this does not apply to reading. If he has been taught to read well and to love reading, his education and mental

[31] PP 1889, XXIX, Mr Williams's Report.
[32] PP 1874, XVIII, Mr Bancroft's Report.

improvement will not cease with his school days, but he will daily increase his stock of knowledge. A taste for reading implanted in the mind of a child will, when he leaves school for the workshop, prevent that waste of knowledge which at present there is so much reason to deplore.[33]

It was in these cases that it could truly be said that education, rather than schooling, was being provided.

Although the purpose of elementary education was to teach sufficient basic knowledge to equip a child for adult life, the Education Department also envisaged a more varied curriculum. Class subjects and specific subjects were intended to supplement the basic subjects of reading, writing and arithmetic and thus contribute to a broad elementary school curriculum. Specific subjects were introduced in 1871 and initially brought a sum of three shillings for every pupil who achieved an acceptable mark in two subjects in the annual examination. Examination in specific subjects was, however, limited to children in the upper three standards of each school. Class subjects were introduced in 1875 and provided a sum of four shillings for every pupil who achieved a satisfactory standard. Unlike specific subjects, however, class subjects were taken by every pupil. The majority of schools opted for an ambitious programme of class and specific subjects.[34] Of the class subjects that were allowed, it was English, geography and elements of science that were chosen by most schools. The teaching of music was also popular in the schools of Wales, a trend that was commended by the school inspectors. HMI Binns in his report for 1874 noted that children demonstrated a measure of delight at being examined in the subject, especially in the singing section of the examination, in contrast to the feeling of dread which characterized their expressions when other subjects were being examined.[35] According to HMI Robert Temple, the teaching of music was particularly relevant in Wales, given what he considered to be the natural musical abilities of the Welsh nation.[36] Indeed, an overall survey of the

[33] PP 1883, XXV, Mr Pryce's Report.
[34] PP 1880, XXII. Class subjects included topics such as English, geography, history and elementary science, while specific subjects included algebra, animal physiology and domestic economy.
[35] PP 1874, XVIII, Mr Binns's Report.
[36] PP 1874, XVIII, Mr Temple's Report.

comments of the inspectorate throughout the period from 1870 to 1902 indicates that music was the only subject on which the inspectors gave a resounding tribute to the teaching staff and to the attainments of the pupils. The term 'music' has to be qualified, however. In the main, music was equated with singing, both in the minds of teachers and school inspectors. Few schools grappled with the problem of enabling pupils to read music other than the sol-fa method of teaching singing, and there was little development of instrumental music in Wales. In general, the music of the schools of Wales reflected that of the Nonconformist community, the emphasis being laid on participation and choral work rather than on appreciation, composition or orchestral activity.

Other supplementary subjects were not taught to the standard desired by the inspectorate, however. The standard of attainment in geography was a constant cause of concern. Moreover, the contents of the geography curriculum were also being questioned. HMI Binns complained in 1878 that schools did not give enough attention to Wales or to the colonies and the British Empire and that too much attention was being given to European countries.[37] Geography could become a highly relevant and popular subject when properly taught. These lessons provided the basis for valuable knowledge in a society which was becoming increasingly integrated into world economic markets and dependent upon foreign trade. Studies of soil quality and climate were highly relevant to pupils in rural areas, while geological surveys of south Wales would obviously benefit pupils who were destined to spend their working lives in the coal industry. The popularity of the subject was certainly strengthened by the broad variety of topics that it covered and by the fact that it offered an opportunity to visit local places of interest, a policy that was strongly advocated by the school inspectorate. Yet, despite the laudable ambition of many schoolteachers to make elementary education as broad as possible, the want of intelligence and lack of understanding that had been evident in the teaching of basic subjects were also apparent in these subjects. Horace Waddington commented that the children of Newport had a vague idea of the names of the rivers of Africa,

[37] PP 1878, XXVIII.

yet had no knowledge of the 'name of the large town at the mouth of the river Usk in Monmouthshire'; a similar situation arose in Cardiff when the question was asked 'what is the name of the large town at the mouth of the river Taff in Glamorgan'.[38] The dilemma highlighted the perpetual need to balance what was desirable and what was possible to achieve.

The teaching of domestic economy in the schools of Wales was a further innovation keenly recommended by the inspectorate. As early as 1871 the Revd Shadrach Pryce noted that such a development would exert a beneficial influence on living conditions in Wales.[39] The Revd E. T. Watts considered that the absence of a knowledge of domestic economy, and particularly of the principles of hygiene and budgeting, were among the most serious defects of the Welsh as a nation, and of its mothers in particular, and expressed his opinion that the introduction of the subject in the schools would overcome the long-standing bad practices of Welsh women.[40] Although strongly advocated by the inspectorate, the introduction of domestic economy was an expensive venture which few School Boards could contemplate other than in the higher grade schools. In the majority of cases it was confined to sewing, with specially appointed part-time sewing mistresses taking the subject. The increase in knowledge of basic hygiene and the ability to control a domestic budget owed little to the success of the education system and more to an application of the skills gained in the elementary schools to the traditional knowledge already existing in the community itself.

The pressures caused by the ambitious programme of education envisaged by the Education Department were felt by some inspectors to be an obstacle to success in the basic subjects. Complaints were made that teachers seemed so determined to impress the Department by introducing as broad a curriculum as was possible that they adopted an over-ambitious scheme of study. In part, however, this desire on the part of teachers reflected the ostentatious programme promoted by the inspectorate itself. For instance, the Revd Herbert Smith, in his report for 1871, had advocated the introduction of subjects such as map drawing, English literature, grammar, English history and

[38] Ibid., Mr Waddington's Report.
[39] PP 1871, XXII, Mr Pryce's Report, and PP 1874, XXVIII, Mr Temple's Report.
[40] PP 1881, XXXII, Mr Watts's Report.

geography into the curriculum, as was advocated by the Education Department.[41] Robert Temple strongly advocated the introduction of mechanics and agricultural economics in the schools of eastern mid-Wales and was disappointed at the lack of response from the schools. In his opinion the school curriculum had been allowed to become far too narrow and did little to broaden the horizons of the pupils.[42] The practical experience of the implementation of the Act, however, led to the emergence of a consensus that such developments hindered the main objective of the schools, which was to teach basic subjects and instil a sound knowledge of the rudiments of reading, writing and arithmetic. John Rhys stated that subjects such as English literature and grammar were inappropriate in elementary schools and resulted in an over-burdened school curriculum. He believed that the introduction of these subjects by so many schools reflected a feeling that this would impress the school inspector rather than inculcate genuine interest in the subjects among the pupils.[43]

The danger of excessive pressure in schools began to feature prominently among the concerns of educationists. Yet their anxieties were often ignored by the Education Department as the trifling worries of a minority of theorists with little practical experience of teaching, an attitude which continued to be reflected in the Education Department's loyalty to the specific subjects long after the evidence was clearly pointing to their superfluity. Welsh inspectors gradually admitted that the views expressed by Herbert Smith had been impractical. Robert Temple warned in 1874 that undue pressure was leading to several cases of epilepsy among scholars in his district, and that many pupils were being pressurized not only in school but also in the home. In his opinion, the health of many children was being 'sacrificed to the Moloch of parental ambitions'. The Department, he insisted, should always bear in mind that the regulations and curriculum intended for elementary schools were for children rather than the students of Balliol College.[44] By the late 1880s, a strong body of opinion had emerged within the ranks of

[41] PP 1871, XXII, Mr Smith's Report.
[42] PP 1873, XXIV, Mr Temple's Report.
[43] PP 1876, XXIII, Mr Rhys's Report.
[44] PP 1874, XVIII, Mr Temple's Report.

the school inspectorate which was firmly of the view that the introduction of elaborate and complex subjects was more harmful than beneficial to the development of education, and that those practices were contributing to the unbearable pressure which was being felt by both teachers and pupils. Influenced by this opinion, the amendments contained in the Mundella Code of 1888 led to a decline in the number of schools introducing the specific subjects, the majority of schools now concentrating on a more limited range of subjects, such as physical education, music, geography and domestic economy.

The School Boards of Wales were aware of the fact that, despite the qualified success of the elementary schools, the Welsh education system remained incomplete. Larger School Boards sought to address one aspect of this problem by establishing higher grade elementary schools during the 1890s, a development which became a feature of the major towns of Wales. These schools were intended for the older pupils and, drawing a significant portion of their funding from the Department for Science and Art rather than the Education Department, they concentrated on technical and practical subjects as well as more advanced forms of the instruction given in the elementary schools. Higher grade schools were established in centres such as Colwyn Bay, Caerphilly, Ogmore Vale, Bargoed, Pontardawe, Port Talbot, Merthyr, Pontypridd, Rhondda, Swansea, Llanelli, Ffestiniog, Abersychan and Newport, and they rapidly gained a status superior to that of the elementary school.[45] As Gareth Elwyn Jones has demonstrated, working-class leaders in Wales came to regard these schools as offering the best opportunity for the pupils whose interests concerned them, a view which was reinforced by the notion that the intermediate schools had failed to provide sufficient opportunities for those children.[46]

A further development was the establishment of adult continuation classes by the School Boards. These were held in

---

[45] W. G. Evans, 'Education and the needs of an industrial community, decision-making in Victorian Llanelli', *Carmarthenshire Antiquary*, 28 (1992), 71–8.
[46] G. E. Jones, *Controls and Conflicts in Welsh Secondary Education, 1889–1944* (Cardiff, 1982), p.7; D. M. Lewis, 'Addysg gweithwyr Cymru', *Y Geninen* (April 1886), 105–6.

the elementary schools outside school hours and were a source of additional remuneration for the schoolteachers who engaged in the ventures. This was an important and visionary concept. It saw the schools created by the Act not merely as means to extend the advantages of education to children, but as centres of learning which were appropriate as cultural and educational facilities for the whole community. By encouraging the adult population to make use of the school, it was hoped to increase popular awareness of the value of education, and thus generate a love of learning among the parents which could then be passed on to the children. At the same time, the classes held in elementary schools were akin to the university extension movement of the time and, although there is little evidence of a co-ordinated alternative system of education, their existence nevertheless points to an appreciation of the value of adult education and to a vision of educational opportunities being extended as widely as possible. However, adult continuation classes, particularly those organized by School Boards, were not received with the enthusiasm which the originators of the idea had anticipated. In Wales, in particular, the schools were not the first organizations to offer educational opportunities for adults, for work had already been done through the Nonconformist chapels and particularly within the Sunday school movement. Its long-standing achievement in terms of the teaching of reading, writing and basic arithmetic to the adult population was one of the greatest achievements of Nonconformity and made similar efforts by the continuation classes superfluous. Thus it is hardly surprising that, according to Shadrach Pryce's report for 1883, the adult continuation classes had declined and many Boards were refusing to sponsor such ventures.[47] In the opinion of the inspectorate, a major defect was the placing of adults in the same classes as teenagers, a practice which had fostered a feeling of humiliation in the minds of many adults. Instruction in these classes was of such a rudimentary nature that its rejection was well-nigh inevitable. The classes were seen as pointless and repetitive, merely revisiting ground that had already been covered elsewhere.

As a result of these deficiencies, attempts were made to develop a more advanced curriculum for the continuation

[47] PP 1883, XXV, Mr Pryce's Report.

classes, although the changes were not implemented until the mid-1890s. In his report for 1895, William Williams noted that the classes had become more popular after the Education Department allowed greater curricular freedom and that the addition of technical and vocational subjects, such as bookkeeping, shorthand, geology and agricultural economics, had also been of great benefit.[48] Yet the continuation classes failed to develop a broad curriculum and they were open to the accusation of failing to allow sufficient freedom of enquiry. Continuation classes were a pastime for a minority of the population. A combination of the long hours of work endured by most of the adults at work with the multitude of other cultural attractions in late nineteenth-century Wales, not least the almost nightly activities centred upon the Nonconformist chapels, compounded by the coming of diversions such as music halls and theatrical activity, rendered the continuation classes less popular in terms of public participation. Moreover, the development of political consciousness, and increasing disillusionment with the staid politics of Liberalism among the younger generation, meant that the non-political and highly constrained curriculum of the continuation classes lost its appeal. Adult education activity switched increasingly to the halls and institutes which were emerging throughout Wales at the turn of the century, to the disappointment of those who had hoped that, by concentrating the classes on government-sponsored elementary schools, they could have been kept free from political or religious ties.[49]

Continuation classes and higher grade schools emerged in Wales at the same time as the county schools established themselves as local centres of excellence. These schools were regarded as a great success of Welsh Liberal society, yet their impact on the elementary school sector was not altogether beneficial. Their foundation was accompanied by an annual competitive entrance examination and, as a result, considerable impetus was certainly given to the efforts made in the elementary school. Although some teachers, such as John Jones, the master of Halkyn School in Flintshire, were reluctant to enter the children of labourers for examination as late as 1901 (on the spurious ground that the

[48] PP 1895, XXVII, Mr Williams's Report.
[49] PP 1917–18, XV.

parents of those children would be unable to maintain them in education beyond the statutory school-leaving age),[50] achieving a high pass-rate became a matter of personal prestige for many teachers. Moreover, several Boards and school managers were offering increased remuneration for good results in the scholarship examination, thus providing a further financial incentive to creditable performance. In addition, a high rate of success in entering candidates for the county scholarship was regarded by the teaching profession as crucial to gaining positions as masters of the larger elementary schools. These laudable effects of the Intermediate Education Act on the efforts made within the elementary school did, however, create problems. While acting as a stimulus for many teachers, it also resulted in a tendency to concentrate on a minority of able pupils who were likely to pass the scholarship examination, and consequently the neglect of the majority of children. This raised the question of the desirable age at which children should move from one school to another. The examiner of English in the county schools, Professor McNeile Dixon of Birmingham, warned that the transfer should be undertaken as early as possible because the elementary schools were failing to achieve the high standards that were required, a comment that was doubted by HMI Leggard in his report for 1899.[51] The practice of withdrawing pupils who had qualified for entry to the intermediate schools, while in many ways beneficial to those particular children, meant that the elementary schools did not develop the specialist teaching for eleven- to fourteen-year-olds that would have benefited those pupils who were precluded from entering for the scholarship by virtue of domestic financial circumstances.

It is also the case that the intermediate schools not only looked to the English public schools as an inspiration for the curriculum, but were also in many ways better suited to England where the middle class was far more developed than in Wales and where more parents could afford the financial commitment that became incumbent on the parents of children who attended intermediate schools, including the parents of candidates who had

[50] Flintshire CRO, Hawarden, DGR 1305.
[51] William McNeile Dixon was Professor of English at Mason College, Birmingham. PP 1899, XX, Mr Leggard's Report.

won scholarships to the schools.[52] Intermediate and higher grade schools also had a direct effect on the life of elementary schools. Many of the abler, older pupils were withdrawn from the elementary school to attend the larger institutions, thus depriving the school of the influence of the abler pupils (who were important as role models for younger children) and also reducing the pool of potential pupil teachers. Equally important, the loss of these more able children reduced the number of pupils whom the teacher could enjoy teaching, thus depriving that teacher of the opportunity to indulge in innovative and intellectually stimulating work. Consequently, there was a tendency for the more gifted elementary teachers to seek appointments in the emerging intermediate schools, depriving the elementary sector of many of its best teachers.

As a result of the development of the education system, Wales was provided with elementary, higher grade and intermediate schools as well as adult continuation classes. Inevitably, there would be tensions between the various institutions.[53] Partly as a result of the staggered manner in which the system had developed, there was a lack of clarity about what form of education should be provided by each institution and, therefore, much unnecessary duplication. There was insufficient co-operation between the teachers of intermediate and elementary schools and a failure to recognize that they had common aims which could only be achieved through concerted effort.[54] Moreover, as will be considered below, the apparent abundance of educational institutions did not mean that the multifarious educational needs of Wales were wholly satisfied.

The education system was developed during a period of unprecedented industrial expansion in Wales. Employment patterns changed rapidly and the continued migration from rural to industrial communities created a need for a versatile workforce able to adapt to a variety of occupations. Educational commentators were aware of the need for an education system capable of producing workers with skills and knowledge which

---

[52] Jones, *Controls and Conflicts in Welsh Secondary Education*, p.7.
[53] W. G. Evans, *Educational Development in a Victorian Community: A Case Study of Carmarthenshire's Response to the Welsh Intermediary Education Act 1889* (Aberystwyth, 1990), pp.22–45.
[54] PP 1899, XX, Mr Leggard's Report.

would be beneficial in an industrial economy. At the same time, the views of the parents and of the pupils themselves are an important guide to analysing the response to the schooling provided. Inevitably, the most serious criticism of the education system in Wales is found in the work of activists, many of whom had particular grievances against the system. The fact remains, however, that the ethos and aims of the education system of Wales came under increasing scrutiny as the era of the School Boards came to a close.

As was noted above, HMI Robert Temple detected an innate conservatism regarding the school curriculum, reflected in a tendency to add subjects to the curriculum rather than to reconsider the curriculum as a whole. There was a widespread feeling that the schools of Wales were remote from the life of the community and had little relevance to the future life of the pupils. Notice has already been taken of the quaint nature of the geography curriculum, and there was a comparable tendency for history to be taught as a list of battles, kings and queens. Often the history curriculum made no reference to the history of Wales, so that even important local landmarks, which could have been used as a means of stimulating children and arousing their interest, were ignored by the teachers. In rural Wales it was felt that the curriculum was relevant only for the urban areas, generating a distaste for the rural areas in the minds of the pupils, as has been shown by Pamela Horn in her studies of education in the rural districts of England.[55] Likewise, a feeling existed in industrial south Wales that the curriculum had no relevance to a rapidly expanding industrial economy.[56] A view emerged that the school curriculum, particularly its advanced elements, was designed for the urban society of the home counties rather than for areas such as Wales, and that it sought to generate multitudes of clerks rather than craftspeople, pen-pushers rather than pick-workers. These issues were recognized in Wales. Schools were criticized for being preoccupied with administration and with a mechanical form of teaching. In addition to the normal complaints of a failure to ensure that

---

[55] T. Elias, 'The difficulties of rural schools in Wales', *NUET Conference Handbook* (1933), pp.97–115; Pamela Horn, *Education in Rural England* (Dublin, 1978), pp.146–50.

[56] Harris, 'Education in Merthyr Tydfil, 1840–1912, a brief survey', Merthyr Public Library MSS.

pupils understood, rather than simply learned, there were other demands for schools to become brighter, more welcoming places where children would be afforded the light and outlook that were unavailable in drab and poverty-stricken homes.[57] Furthermore, the 1870 Act was blamed for failing to provide sufficient resources to enable schools to purchase equipment or employ expert staff and thus to enable Wales to develop a more practical form of education that would equip the child with the skills essential in adult life.[58]

By the late 1890s this question of the need for a more relevant school curriculum began to be addressed. The revision of the Education Code undertaken by Arthur Acland resulted in a more progressive form of education which was also better geared to the aim of generating a child population that would feel at home in an industrial or rural economy, rather than one designed simply to produce Oxford graduates or Education Department clerks.[59] The Liberal, Nonconformist-influenced Boards sought to use this increased curricular freedom. The issue of temperance was a key element in the programme of radical leaders in Wales, drink sharing a pre-eminent place with the landowners among the demons identified by the Nonconformist denominations.[60] Thus, Welsh School Boards entered the campaign against the drink trade by introducing lessons on the evils of alcohol and over-indulgence. Despite opposition from the Conservative members and, in a number of cases, considerable public hostility, Boards throughout Wales introduced this subject, citing, as justification, the fact that there was a proven link between drunkenness, poverty, truancy and slow educational progress.[61] Other subjects were also introduced, notably lectures on the 'evils of bastardy' and the importance of thrift, in an attempt to mould the character of the rising generation. Thus, School Boards were attempting to move away from the mere

[57] T. Rees, 'Addysg Cymru', *Cwrs y Byd*, VI (May 1896), 100–5.
[58] T. Rees, 'Addysg elfennol ym mharthau gwledig Cymru', in T. Stephens (ed.), *Cymru: Heddyw ac Yfory* (Cardiff, 1908), pp.195–7.
[59] Acland worked in close co-operation with T. E. Ellis in an attempt to formulate a coherent strategy for educational development in Wales. Their initial thoughts can be traced in a joint article in *CDH*, 3 October 1890; Gillian Sutherland, *Policy Making in English Education* (London, 1973), pp.319–21.
[60] W. R. Lambert, *Drink and Sobriety in Victorian Wales, 1820–1895* (Cardiff, 1983), pp.115–56.
[61] *CDH*, 25 October 1889.

teaching of the rudiments of education and seeking to develop pastoral work as part of their responsibilities. The same ethos was seen in the development of the eisteddfod movement, regularly associated with schools, and in attempts to make greater use of local examples in explaining national phenomena in subjects such as history and geography. These curricular innovations reflected the concerns of the Nonconformists and were an attempt to promote a virtuous lifestyle.[62] The image of Wales would be that of the progressive, democratic but above all cultured *gwerin* depicted by O. M. Edwards. Yet, as has been pointed out by others, notably David Jones and Russell Davies, the Nonconformist image differed substantially from the reality of nineteenth-century Wales.[63] The 1851 religious census demonstrated that 40 per cent of the Welsh community were not in attendance at any place of religious worship on the chosen Sunday and it is likely that a significant proportion of those associated with Nonconformist denominations found themselves unable to adhere to the prescribed mode of living.[64] Yet, quite apart from the illusions of the Welsh Nonconformist leadership, it is clear that the lifestyle urged in the schools of Wales constituted an attempt to develop a new code of behaviour. A similar philosophy surrounded the educational policy of Republican France in the same period, whereby the schools were regarded as a tool for the development of a democratic and moral peasant society. The experience of Wales never reached the level of the French model, yet both were inspired by a similar view of society and a comparable awareness of the importance of education as a means of moulding the national culture.

Historians of education in Wales have constantly emphasized the particularities of the Welsh and Nonconformist view of education. Towards the end of the period considered in this

[62] David Jenkins refers to two distinctive lifestyles prevalent in the rural areas of south-west Wales which he categorized as *Buchedd A* and *Buchedd B*. The groups were not mutually exclusive nor hostile to each other. However, a marked contrast did exist between the mode of living of those whose lives revolved around the Nonconformist chapel and its associated cultural activities and those whose lives revolved around more worldly pursuits (David Jenkins, *The Agricultural Community in South-west Wales at the Turn of the Twentieth Century* (Cardiff, 1971), pp.216–18).

[63] D. J. V. Jones, *Crime in Nineteenth-Century Wales* (Cardiff, 1992), pp.30–55; Russell Davies, *Secret Sins: Sex, Violence and Society in Carmarthenshire, 1870–1920* (Cardiff, 1996), esp. chs. 3, 4 and 5.

[64] I. G. Jones and David Williams (eds.), *The Religious Census of 1851: a Calendar of the Returns Relating to Wales*, 2 vols. (Cardiff, 1975–6).

work, commentators such as Professor Thomas Rees prided themselves on the creation of an education system which provided opportunities for children to pursue their education from the elementary school, through the intermediate school and to the University of Wales, matters that will be discussed further in a later chapter.[65] Those who were active in promoting the establishment of the education system in Wales proclaimed the need for an arrangement which would take account of the particular requirements of Wales and which would assist social, economic and political progress in Wales. Their pronouncements emphasized these factors as they campaigned for a structure capable of addressing the educational needs of the nation. J. Gwynn Williams, in an analysis of the university movement in Wales, refers to a consciousness of the role and duty of the University of Wales in Welsh life.[66] His studies also demonstrate the fact that the Liberal and Nonconformist community in Wales were propagating the Benthamite concept of middle-class leaders elected by a franchise of enlightened and educated working-class voters. Welsh leaders were interested in providing education above the elementary level to children from a wider social group than was being provided for in England, and in many cases succeeded in doing so. Yet the system which they created only succeeded in providing opportunities for a minority of exceptionally gifted or fortunate children. Those who designed the system failed to address the needs of children, particularly those of the industrial areas, who continued to be unable to gain access to educational opportunities. Indeed, Welsh Liberal educationists tended to ignore the concerns of the industrial areas and, for men such as O. M. Edwards and T. E. Ellis, the idealized form of Welshness was to be found in the countryside rather than the towns. Their vision of the education system was geared to provide opportunities for the able sons of Welsh-speaking tenant farmers, whose appetite for education had been whetted in Nonconformist circles and who had a modicum of financial means to enable them to continue with their studies. This vision, however laudable, had the tendency of overlooking the needs of a growing industrial population and,

[65] T. Rees, 'Addysg Cymru', *Cwrs y Byd*, VI (May 1896), 100–5; see ch. 9.
[66] J. Gwynn Williams, *University and Nation, 1893–1939*, T. Jones Pierce Memorial Lecture (Aberystwyth, 1992).

indeed, of less fortunate groups in rural Wales, such as the children of labourers and servants. It must also be recognized that the opportunities that were provided by the education system in many ways undermined their perception of Welshness. The opportunities that were made available to Welsh children enabled them to pursue notable careers in a variety of spheres. Yet, invariably, their careers took them away from the villages in which they had been nurtured and thus deprived those localities of the contributions of their most able and articulate products. Inevitably, this weakened the vitality of life in rural Wales, and ironically so, for the Liberal elysium was based on the notion of a spirited and energetic village culture.

Others have pointed to the fact that the shortcomings of the education system stemmed from the failure of those responsible for its creation to be more appreciative of the distinctive needs of Wales. As Gareth Elwyn Jones has argued, Wales was given the same arrangement for education as that given to England despite the fact that in Wales factors such as the absence of a large middle class and the dominance of Nonconformity had created a society very different from that of England.[67] The failure of the Liberal and Nonconformist leaders in Wales to recognize the need to take account of the special circumstances of Wales in responding to the provisions of the Elementary Education Act has already been noted. Yet, quite apart from the protests at the failure to recognize specifically Welsh administrative requirements in 1870, Wales did not seek to address its distinctive educational requirements when it was presented with the opportunity of changing the curriculum following the reforms undertaken by Arthur Acland during his period at the Education Department between 1892 and 1895. Wales did not witness an attempt to develop a distinctive approach in the curriculum of either elementary or intermediate schools. For the majority of Welsh children, any idea of Welsh nationality came from the home and the chapel rather than from the school, a fact which was even more pronounced in the experience of those pupils who graduated to the intermediate schools. Science remained a neglected subject at both elementary and intermediate levels;

---

[67] G. E. Jones, 'What are schools in Wales for? Wales and the Education Reform Act', *Contemporary Wales*, II (1988), 83–97; Owen Prys, 'Addysg elfennol yng Nghymru', *Cymru Fydd*, II (February 1889), 63–73.

despite the awareness of the need to develop technical and practical education, and to elevate these disciplines to enjoy parity of esteem with arts subjects, no positive steps were taken to do so. Whereas the Scottish education system was geared towards science, particularly engineering and medicine, and therefore assumed a distinctive characteristic, the Welsh education authorities remained unconvinced of the benefits to be gained by investment in the equipment and expertise necessary to teach these subjects successfully. As a result, another important avenue by which Welsh nationality could have been developed remained uncharted. At the same time, as G. W. Roderick has indicated, technical education was not sufficiently encouraged in a period when the productivity and competitiveness of the economy in south Wales were failing to match those of growing economies elsewhere, a feature which was to have wide repercussions.[68]

The failure to address these issues stemmed, partly, from the way in which Anglican schools continued to provide elementary schooling for a significant proportion of Welsh children. The concepts that were espoused by Nonconformist Liberals had limited resonance for members of the Anglican Church, many of whom leaned towards a conservative social vision. The development of a distinctive approach in Wales was hampered by the absence of a unified body to co-ordinate elementary education in Wales in the way the Central Welsh Board was to do for intermediate schools after 1896. Wales lacked the administrative distinctiveness that Scotland, for instance, enjoyed, and neither the court of the University of Wales nor the body of school inspectors in Wales took on this role. An equally important factor, however, was the failure of Welsh leaders themselves to make practical suggestions as to how Wales's education system could address the needs of the nation. Their concern remained with the machinery rather than the objectives of the schools, and as a result a clear void existed that no other body was equipped to fill.

Indeed, the issue of the nature of educational provision did not gain prominence until O. M. Edwards began to question the

---

[68] G. W. Roderick, 'Education, culture and industry in Wales in the nineteenth century', *WHR*, 13 (1986–7), 438–52.

ethos and methods of Welsh schools in 1909–11, when important questions were raised concerning the curriculum and the emphasis the schools placed on examination. Edwards was certainly not a lone voice, but his comments were not a reflection of any great movement for reform of the education system and they attracted a great deal of condemnation even in 1910. Despite the fact that the Welsh Intermediate Education Act was hailed as a great triumph which recognized the need for separate legislation for Wales, the schools that were created could have been designed for English counties and were noted for their reluctance to admit to any Welsh characteristics. Significantly, there were few parents or public leaders who advocated reform, the majority simply rejoicing in the creation of a system.

This failure to take cognizance of Welsh characteristics in intermediate and higher education had clear implications for the elementary sector. The degree to which a certain curriculum can be changed in an elementary school is limited and it may be assumed that there was a consensus in favour of the teaching of basic skills such as reading, writing and arithmetic. However, as was noted above, many elementary schools developed an English ethos, partly due to the influence of HMIs such as Shadrach Pryce in the 1870s and 1880s. Those attitudes were reinforced by the English ethos of the intermediate schools, which were regarded by many in the elementary schools as epitomizing the best in education, with the inevitable result that some elementary schools sought to emulate the Englishness of intermediate schools, a feature which, as will be shown, was of relevance to the debate concerning the Welsh language.

A further factor is that the existing system was widely accepted by the leaders of the emerging working-class movement in Wales. A movement led by individuals such as William Abraham, inextricably linked to the Liberal and Nonconformist forces in Wales, was likely to take pride in what was regarded as the great achievement of that society. In England the relationship between the working-class movement and the establishment was not as strong as that which existed between the working class and the emerging Liberal-Nonconformist establishment in Wales. Yet, as Brian Simon demonstrates, few radical, working-class representations were made with regard to the education system. In the main, it was issues such as free education, secular education and the development of higher grade schools that were the main clarion calls.[69] The real differences arose over the speed at which measures should be implemented rather than a radically different agenda. As a result, another potential criticism of the emerging education system was not articulated.

An overall survey of the educational standards of Wales at the end of the School Board era points to considerable advances in pupil attainment, teaching methods and in the quality of the fabric of the schools in Wales. A more realistic and relevant curriculum was being developed which took account of the need to avoid excessive pressures in schools. The leaders of Liberal opinion in Wales were convinced that the Welsh now had access to an education system which was complete, with every child being given the opportunity for education and, through education, for social mobility. Yet, as will be argued in a later chapter, the reality was very different from the perceptions of the leadership. The education system had undergone a transformation from its situation in 1870, yet the condition of education – the fabric of the buildings, the methods of teaching and the attainment of children – remained below the highest level. Social and economic factors, as well as educational reasons, accounted for these difficulties.

---

[69] Brian Simon, *Education and the Labour Movement* (London, 1965), p.123.

V
'TO EDUCATE AND NOT TO PROSELYTISE'

The 1870 Education Act coincided with other efforts, undertaken throughout the western world, by which the state came to replace religious bodies as the main providers of education. In Wales, the argument lay not simply between the proponents of provision by the state and provision by religious bodies, but also among the religious bodies themselves. The response to the Forster Bill in 1870, and the vigorous debate that ensued concerning the manner in which legislation might be accommodated to the religious affiliations of Welsh society, highlighted the fact that the relationship between the Nonconformist bodies and the Established Church remained tense. The denominational configuration of Wales was such that the tension created by sectarian complexities would not necessarily be removed by the greater measure of state involvement in education now introduced. For, as the religious census of 1851 revealed, on the basis of those present at the morning service, Anglican worshippers accounted for 100,953 (28.4 per cent) of all worshippers compared to 254,147 (71.6 per cent) in the main Nonconformist denominations, a gap that was considerably wider according to the evening figures.[1] Admittedly, there was a noticeable moderation in the pronouncements of the leaders of religious and political opinion in Wales following the passing of the 1870 Act. Yet it is also clear that the tensions that manifested themselves at that time did not disappear on the passing of the Act. This chapter will examine the way in which the arguments that were rehearsed in 1870 continued to occupy the minds of the leaders of public opinion in Wales for the remainder of the century. It will consider the experience of those areas where the Anglican Church remained the provider of elementary education, focusing on the debate between those members of the Church of England who wished to insist on a dogmatic adherence to the principle that the schools should be conducted on a strict Anglican basis, and those who urged a more pragmatic solution that involved compromise

---

[1] John Williams, *Digest of Welsh Historical Statistics*, 2 vols (Cardiff, 1985), II, pp.352–3.

with the Nonconformist majority in Wales. At the same time, the chapter will analyse the debate within the Nonconformist community in Wales, a discourse which offers important evidence concerning its convictions and inclinations.

A distrust of the intentions of the Anglican Church in relation to religious instruction constituted the basis of the Nonconformist reservations regarding the 1870 Act. Nonconformists believed that there was genuine reason to be fearful of the intentions of the Anglican Church, mainly over the danger that it would insist on the provision of a form of religious instruction that, adhering to the principles of the Established Church, would include the Church catechism and other features that were unacceptable to the Nonconformists.[2] It was considered that in the Church schools the conscience clause arrangements, introduced by the Cowper-Temple amendment as an attempt to uphold the rights of those with a principled objection to a particular form of religious instruction, would not provide sufficient protection for the Nonconformist majority in Wales.[3]

These fears were to be in some degree ameliorated in the following years, but the views of the Nonconformists had to take account of the fact that the Anglican adherents in Wales were not altogether agreed on a more accommodating approach to educational issues. Their unity was undermined by the fact that their more zealous members, notably those associated with the Church Defence League, continued to advocate the inclusion of the catechism in all schools, and objected to any compromise that did not adhere strictly to the principles governing Church schools. The Church Defence League was an extreme Anglican organization that had initially been established to co-ordinate the campaign against the disestablishment of the Church but had rapidly expanded its activities to other spheres, including education. Its opinions were propounded in its journal, *Amddiffynnydd yr Eglwys*, where it was asserted that the Anglican Church, by virtue of its 'superiority' as the Established Church, was the only religious denomination which had a moral authority to provide religious instruction. It was claimed that the Church had a right to assert its creed in all schools and many

---

[2] See above, chs. 2 and 3.
[3] D. Cadvan Jones, 'Addysg grefyddol yn ein hysgolion dyddiol', *Y Diwygiwr*, LVI, No. 5 (May 1891), 142–6.

were to come to the same conclusion as the Revd J. K. Lloyd of Nerquis, who contended that an instruction in the religious principles of the Established Church was vital in the mid-1880s as Gladstonian legislation threatened the very 'foundations of the constitution'.[4]

The views expressed in *Amddiffynnydd yr Eglwys* in favour of an Anglican form of religious instruction were totally unacceptable both to the Nonconformists and to the more moderate leaders of Anglican opinion in Wales. Indeed, the extremist tones of the journal would indicate that Welsh Nonconformist fears that the conscience clause would not be honoured were well-founded. The more moderate Anglican leaders in Wales sought to distance themselves from the League by adopting a more realistic proposal which acknowledged the strength of the Nonconformist denominations and sought to develop a curriculum of religious instruction that was acceptable to each denomination. Of equal significance were the views represented by Lord Emlyn, who warned that denominational rivalry should not be allowed to prevent people from all denominational backgrounds from attempting to develop a simple form of religious instruction that was appropriate for children and acceptable to all creeds. Representatives of more moderate opinion in the Anglican Church sought to revive its fortunes by means of a reform which could attract Nonconformist members to their ranks. Moreover, they accepted the need to emphasize common ground with Nonconformists rather than to concentrate solely on battles concerning issues that divided the religious bodies. As was noted earlier, acrimonious disputes were avoided in a number of areas through the moderation that was displayed by both sides. The fact remained, however, that in those areas where the Church continued to be responsible for the local school, the Nonconformist denominations relied on the goodwill of the Anglican community to prevent the provision of an excessively Anglican form of religious instruction. Goodwill was a matter which varied according to personal temperament and inclination.

In those areas where School Boards had been established, the Boards themselves were responsible for determining the religious

[4] Flintshire CRO, Hawarden, D/Pol 15.

policy of each school under their jurisdiction. This local autonomy resulted in the development of a lively local debate concerning the desirability of religious instruction and what form that instruction should take. The discussion was influenced by the religious bodies, the teaching profession and the official representatives of the Education Department, the HMIs. The last-named group no longer had the responsibility of examining religious instruction, yet their comments do reflect official perceptions of the religious and social divide in Wales. Invariably, HMIs sought to impress upon both the Education Department and local school authorities the need for the introduction of some form of religious instruction, albeit with the inclusion of a conscience clause, while at the same time they sought to discount the extent of religious divisions in Wales. The Revd E. T. Watts, for instance, stated that he was unaware of any real religious difficulty in the Caernarfonshire area, comments that were also reflected in the sentiments of the Revds Henry Smith and B. J. Binns.[5] The chief inspector noted in his report for 1877 that religious teaching should be given in accordance with the beliefs of the majority of the people, and he urged the clergy to refrain from any attempts to turn Board schools into Church schools by infiltrating the School Boards. In his opinion, a more sensible proposal would be to strive for a system of religious instruction which was acceptable to all sides and which did not give preferential treatment to the religious views of one section as opposed to another.[6] Certain inspectors did appreciate the faith of Welsh Nonconformists in the Sunday school movement. HMI Robert Temple, writing in 1874, noted the excellent organization achieved in the Sunday school,[7] yet the official opinion was that, although they maintained high standards, the Sunday schools could not provide an adequate framework for the provision of religious instruction to all Welsh children. Indeed, it is clear that, despite the fact that the inspectorate did not recommend religious instruction, they were not convinced of the benefits of secular education.

The teaching profession was also wary about religious instruction. As a body they served the School Boards, and

[5] PP 1871, XXII.
[6] PP 1877, XXIX.
[7] PP 1874, XVIII, Mr Temple's Report.

teachers were inevitably tied to whatever policy was adopted by those Boards. Yet the profession was divided, and the division between those advocating non-denominational schools and the proponents of secular schools was reflected in the ranks of the teachers. Organizations representing teachers, notably the local branches of the National Union of Elementary Teachers, were loath to become involved in the controversy. The main concern of the NUET was to avoid any development which would increase the workload of the teachers even further. The Llanrwst (Denbighshire) branch protested vigorously against any proposal to examine religious instruction, as this would reduce the time available to teach core subjects and could involve the teachers in bitter sectarian conflicts.[8] This approach was also reflected in the debates of the union's Llandybïe and Llandeilo Fawr (Carmarthenshire) branch, which was not convinced that a scheme of religious instruction could be devised that was acceptable to all denominations, despite its being in favour of the introduction of some form of moral education.[9] The guarded response of many teachers to this question is certainly understandable. They had no desire to become embroiled in sectarian debates and they had a professional duty to maintain a working relationship with parents who had differing views, while at the same time they had a duty to uphold whichever policy was adopted by the School Boards. Yet, as with the school inspectors, the majority of members of the teaching profession considered that the functions of a school should include the provision of moral instruction based on Christian principles.[10]

Despite the significance of the views of both HMIs and the teachers, the key factor in the debate was the position taken by the Nonconformist denominations themselves. Welsh Nonconformists were engaged in a continuing debate concerning the merits of introducing a form of religious instruction in the schools. Yet, as will be demonstrated in this chapter, that debate signified a much deeper argument. It concerned the nature of the relationship between the state and the individual, and the

---

[8] *Schoolmaster*, 5 March 1889.
[9] *LLG*, 12 March 1891.
[10] José Harris, *Private Lives, Public Spirit: A Social History of Britain, 1870–1914* (Oxford, 1993), p.178.

dialogue was to have a considerable influence on the Nonconformist view of state involvement in the life of the individual.

During the passage of the 1870 Act, the opposition in Parliament was led, initially, by Henry Richard who steadfastly opposed the introduction of religious instruction in the day schools; he did so on libertarian and Nonconformist grounds. He declared a principled objection to the provision of any form of religious instruction which was supported by financial assistance from the state, and expressed his conviction that the efficiency of the Sunday school meant that the introduction of religious instruction to the schools of Wales would be superfluous.[11] Yet his argument in favour of secular schools was rejected and, although he accepted the Forster compromise, he remained convinced that the failure to adopt a more resolute approach in 1870 was one of the factors that contributed to the defeat of the Liberals in 1874.[12] However, despite the fact that Henry Richard regarded himself as the tribune of Welsh Nonconformist opinion in Parliament, his views on the issue of religious instruction in schools were not shared by the body of Welsh Nonconformity. From the introduction of the Bill a debate emerged between those figures who advocated a system of wholly secular schools, leaving the provision of religious instruction to the discretion of the parents and to the well-organized and influential Sunday school movement, and others who saw a need for the provision of a certain amount of religious instruction on a non-denominational basis within the day schools.[13] This latter view gained support with the passing of the years as the Nonconformist community became increasingly aware that a generation was in danger of being lost to Christianity because of the way in which it was educated without reference to the word of God. For, as the secular schools gained in importance, the Sunday schools declined. Many of the less deeply religious adherents of the Sunday school movement, whose main reason for attending had been to become literate and numerate rather than to gain Biblical

---

[11] Henry Richard, *Letters and Essays on Wales* (London, 1884), pp.25-35.
[12] This was a theory influential within the more radical circles of the Liberal Party. It attributed the defeat to the fact that the turn-out of voters was less in 1874 than in 1868, Liberals being the most prominent among non-voters. This, it was argued, was due to the failure of the Liberals to motivate their followers by the implementation of a bold, radical policy when in office.
[13] NLW MSS 11650.

knowledge, withdrew their support for the Sunday schools, a trend which led to a decline in religious knowledge, fervour and observance in Wales.[14]

The debate was maintained by figures such as Evan Williams, the secretary of the Merthyr Education Campaign, who was vociferous in opposing those within Welsh Nonconformity who argued in favour of the introduction of a non-denominational system of religious instruction in the day schools. Williams did so on grounds similar to those stated by Henry Richard, namely, that it was morally unjustifiable to advocate a system of compulsory education unless the provision was secular in character, adding that in his opinion those urging any alternative to the secularist model were insulting the efforts and capabilities of the Sunday school movement in Wales. Crucially, however, he took the view that the concept of non-denominational religious instruction was unattainable and that some groups would have an objection to whichever scheme was adopted. The objections were numerous. The Church catechism was not acceptable to Nonconformists. The doctrine of the Trinity was denied by the Unitarians. The Jews did not accept the teachings of the New Testament, and the Catholics did not accept the standard translation of the Bible.[15] Those religious groups were all represented to some degree in Wales and all were ratepayers who, given the introduction of religious instruction in the schools, might be financing the teaching of religious principles with which they disagreed. The practicalities of arranging a curriculum of religious instruction also vexed those opposed to its introduction. Many areas were considered 'marginal' in terms of religious and political affiliation, and in those localities the control of the School Board was uncertain. As a result, the School Board could be governed by Anglican or Catholic representatives. The alliance of the Roman Catholics with the Liberals over the issue of Irish Home Rule was not apparent in elections to School Boards, where the commitment of the Catholics to denominational education was their overriding consideration. The influx of a large number of Catholics, mainly Irish, into areas such as Merthyr, Newport and Cardiff and, to a lesser extent, Swansea,

---

[14] R. Tudur Jones, *Hanes Annibynwyr Cymru* (Swansea, 1962), p.240.
[15] *Y Tyst*, 20 March 1871.

Tredegar and Ebbw Vale, created a possibility that their influence would mean that Nonconformists were denied control of the School Boards.[16] The prospect of Anglicans and Catholics entering into an alliance on the School Board and determining the syllabus for religious instruction was viewed like a thousand nightmares by Welsh Nonconformist leaders, fearful of the teaching of doctrines which were considered objectionable.[17]

The sentiments expressed by the proponents of secular education did gain a significant measure of support. *Y Goleuad* was initially sympathetic to the concept of secular schools, as indeed was the doyen of Welsh Calvinistic Methodism, Dr Lewis Edwards. *Y Goleuad* upheld the Liberationist doctrine that the Bible was above the authority and interference of the government, and that as a result legislation which dealt with religious matters should not be passed.[18] The provision of religious instruction in schools created by the government was therefore unacceptable. Even so, the prospect of an alliance with atheists, and the maintenance of schools in which no form of religious teaching was allowed, was one that appalled a considerable body of Nonconformist opinion. The leaders were also embarrassed by the way in which the Anglicans were continually pointing to the divisions among Nonconformists and what they regarded as the 'unholy alliance' between evangelical Nonconformists and atheists over the question of religious instruction. Allegations were made that, in its hostility to the Church, the Nonconformist community in Wales was prepared to sacrifice any form of religious teaching. Writing to John Johnes of Dolaucothi, John Griffiths, archdeacon of Llandaff, crystallized the attitude of many Anglicans:

> I do not believe that either Mr Gladstone or Mr Forster, both religious men, wished to introduce a system of secular instruction . . . The most melancholy feature in the case is the readiness of the Dissenters to sacrifice all their religious principles to their hostility to the church.[19]

---

[16] P. B. O'Leary, 'Immigration and integration: a study of the Irish in Wales, 1799–1922', Ph.D. thesis, University of Wales, 1990, pp.211–20.
[17] *Y Tyst*, 20 March 1871.
[18] *Y Goleuad*, 12 August 1871.
[19] NLW, Dolaucothi Correspondence 3791.

Faced with such charges, Nonconformist leaders such as Dr Lewis Edwards began to urge a reconsideration of the attitude of their denominations. Principal of Bala Calvinistic Methodist College, a noted theologian and a keen educationist, Edwards had been instrumental in the establishment of several voluntary British schools; he was acutely aware of the opportunity that elementary education provided for the creation of a well-educated, articulate society and the maintenance of a vigorous ministry. To this end, he was a passionate believer in the creation of an education system, yet he discarded the arguments for secular education that he himself had advocated in Aberystwyth in 1870. Lewis increasingly believed that the exclusion of the Bible and the adoption of a policy of confining religious instruction solely to the Sunday schools were likely to result in a significant proportion of Welsh children being excluded from acquiring Biblical knowledge because their parents did not attend any religious institution.[20]

Similar points were raised in the Congregationalist paper, *Y Tyst*, which related the issue of secular schools to the problem of declining congregations and stated that the policy had implications for religious observance and morality in Wales:

> Dadleuir yn dyn y dylai yr holl ysgolion newydd fod yn *secular*. Wel, pa beth fydd effaith hynny? Yr ysgolheigion a *orfodir* i fyned i'r ysgolion hyny ydynt blant anwaraidd y dref, y rhai a fegir yn awyrgylch anfoesoldeb yn swn rhegfeydd a llwon annuwiol, yn yr ymarferiad a lladrad a phob math o ddrygau ac aflendid. Cedwir Gair Duw a phob moeswers ddyrchafol o'u cyrhaedd hwy y rhai y mae arnynt fwyaf o'u heisiau, tra y dysgir y gwersi hyny i'r plant mwyaf ffafredig, y rhai nad oes arnynt eisieu y cyfryw bethau.

> [It is tightly argued that all the new schools should be secular. What will be the effects of this? The scholars who are compelled to attend those schools are the unruly children of the town, the ones who are reared in an atmosphere of immorality, among curses and ungodly oaths, in committing theft and all manner of misdemeanour and uncleanliness. The word of God and every uplifting lesson in manners would be kept from them, the ones who are in greatest need of such lessons, while those lessons

---

[20] T. C. Edwards (ed.), *Bywyd a Llythyrau y Diweddar Barch Lewis Edwards* (Liverpool, 1901), p.445.

will be taught to the most favoured, the ones who are in least need of such things.][21]

These comments reflected another view, often asserted by the leaders of Anglican opinion, that while the Nonconformists were engaged in titanic efforts to construct chapels, the policy of excluding the Bible from the day school was undermining the community that could sustain the chapels.[22] In consequence, papers such as *Y Tyst* declared their support for a system of religious instruction, but one from which the catechism and all other denominational traits were excluded. In the opinion of *Y Tyst*, the Nonconformists of Wales had more to fear from atheism than from sectarianism, asserting that the only two religious groups which could not be accommodated were the Catholics and the Jews, who were unlikely to send their children to rate-aided schools and who could be covered by the conscience clause were they to attend.[23] As a correspondent in *Y Goleuad* stated, the transmitting of religious knowledge to the children of Wales could no longer be left to the Sunday school movement owing to the decline in adherence to it:

> Dywedir fod darpariaeth ddigonol a chyflawn am bob hyfforddiant moesol a chrefyddol, yn Nghymru, o leiaf yn yr Ysgolion Sabbothol, ac yn yr addysg deuluaidd a gyfrenir gan y mwyafrif o rieni ein gwlad, ond a chydnabod yr oll a honir ar y mater hwn gan y rhai a dueddant i wthio pob math o addysg grefyddol o'r ysgolion dyddiol, y mae y ffaith fod dymuniad hyd yn oed yn Nghymru am roi gorfodaeth trwy gyfraith y tir ar rieni difater ac afler i anfon eu plant i'r ysgol ar yr wythnos, yn brawf fod yn ein gwlad rai dosbarthiadau o bobl ag ydynt yn ammharod ac yn anghymwys i roddi yr addysg foesol a chrefyddol i'w plant ag sydd yn angenrheidiol i'w paratoi i gyflawni eu rhan fel aelodau o gymdeithas. Hefyd os esgeulusir anfon y plant i'r ysgolion ar yr wythnos, a ydyw yn debyg y gofelir eu hanfon dan addysg ar y Sul?
>
> [It is said that there is sufficient and complete provision for moral and religious instruction, at least in Wales, in the Sunday schools, and through the familial education which is provided by the majority of parents in our

---

[21] *Y Tyst*, 4 March 1870.
[22] *Report of 10th Church Conference at Newtown, 14 and 15 September 1893* (Welshpool, 1893).
[23] *Y Tyst*, 4 March 1870.

country, but even admitting all that is asserted on this matter by those who tend to exclude all forms of religious instruction from our day schools, the fact that there is a desire, even in Wales, to make it compulsory by the law of the land for indifferent and negligent parents to send their children to school during the week, proves that there are certain classes of people in our country who are unwilling and unqualified to give their children the moral and religious education to prepare them to fulfil their role as members of society. Is it likely that children who are not sent to school during the week will be sent to Sunday school by their parents?][24]

The same paper warned against expecting too much from the Sunday school movement, given the little time available for the Sunday schools to undertake their responsibilities, and declared its conviction that, despite the deep and serious theological and doctrinal divisions which existed between the various Protestant denominations, agreement could be reached on a curriculum which was suitable for children.

The debate on the question of religious instruction continued to occupy the minds of members of the Nonconformist community in Wales throughout the 1870s and 1880s.[25] Indeed, HMI Waddington complained in 1880 that the Cardiff Board members took little interest in any matter other than religious instruction, lamenting that they did not attach as great an importance to issues such as attendance and good management.[26] With each Board responsible for its own policy, the debate was fought largely on a localized level and its outcome was heavily influenced by local political and religious circumstances. In Henry Richard's Merthyr Tydfil, the School Board discussed, in 1873, a resolution from Mrs Crawshay which sought to introduce Bible readings on the grounds that she could not be party to the exclusion of the Bible from the schools of the town. The attempt was supported by Charles James, who felt that, while acknowledging the wonders attained by Nonconformist and Episcopalian organizations in getting hold of children for

[24] *Y Goleuad*, 16 April 1870.
[25] See, for instance, Daniel Rowlands, 'Addysg grefyddol yn yr ysgolion dyddiol', *Y Traethodydd*, XLI (October 1886), 431–53; R. Iwan Jenkins, 'Addysg elfennol: enwadol ai anenwadol?', *Seren Gomer*, X (October 1889), 60–4, 115–20; E. Edmunds, 'Addysg Feiblaidd yn yr ysgolion dyddiol', ibid., XII (January 1891), 27–30; E. K. Jones, 'Addysg Feiblaidd yn yr ysgolion dyddiol: yr ochr arall i'r cwestiwn', ibid., XII (March 1891), 81–6; J. P. Williams, 'Addysg Feiblaidd yn yr ysgolion dyddiol', ibid. (March 1891), 165–70.
[26] PP 1880, XXII, Mr Waddington's Report.

religious teaching once a week, they could not ignore the fact that there were thousands who were never reached, and never would be reached, as far as religious knowledge was concerned, unless provision were made in the Board schools.[27] The decision of the Merthyr Board to recommend the introduction of religious instruction was considered to have been a major factor in the defeat of Mrs Crawshay in the Board election of the following year. Her failure to secure re-election meant that in Merthyr, at least, the Nonconformist majority remained hostile to the introduction of Biblical instruction, although, equally, her defeat could also be attributed to her individualist conduct on the School Board.[28] For the majority, the fear that a Roman Catholic or Anglican majority elected to the Board might impose a by-law leading to denominational teaching was sufficient reason to avoid the introduction of any form of religious instruction. The view of Nonconformists, such as the Revd Sonley Johnstone and the Revd J. P. Williams, that nothing could justify a corporate body legislating on religious matters, triumphed.[29] The arguments propounded in the Merthyr School Board were repeated in School Boards throughout Wales with differing conclusions. No unified policy on religious instruction was developed, although an increasing number of Boards came to abandon or amend secularist policies and opt for non-denominational alternatives, in response to both the decline in Nonconformist adherence and the diminishing strength of the Sunday school movement itself.[30]

The debate was defused by the gradual emergence of a consensus on the form of religious instruction that was appropriate in the day schools. As early as 1872, the Bangor School Board adopted a non-denominational system of religious instruction, comprising the reciting of the Lord's Prayer, the reading of extracts from the Bible and hymn singing at the start and end of the day.[31] A similar policy was introduced in Swansea, although it was stipulated there that the teacher should make no comment on any of the portions of the Scriptures which

[27] *Merthyr Telegraph*, 11 July 1873.
[28] Ibid., 13 April 1874.
[29] Ibid., 11 July 1873.
[30] For interesting parallels with England, see E. Biagini, *Liberty, Retrenchment and Reform* (Oxford, 1992), p.209.
[31] PP 1873, XXIV.

were read.[32] Other Boards allowed teachers to make comments of an explanatory nature on what had been read to pupils but expressly forbade the staff from making any comment of a 'doctrinal nature'. In Aberdare, the Board resolved not to allow any reading of the Bible or hymn singing owing to the influence which certain choices could be said to exert, resolving instead merely to allow a recitation of the Lord's Prayer at the beginning and end of each day.[33] Gradually, Boards that had adopted secularist policies revised their attitudes. In 1888 the Llandudno Board changed its policy so as to allow the schoolmaster to purchase a Bible to be read at the beginning and end of each day, insisting that the teachers refrain from any comment on what had been read.[34] In Caernarfon, where a secular policy prevailed until 1889, a feeling of exasperation at the moral condition of the town's children, together with a concern for the declining numbers attending the town's Sunday schools, induced a decision on the part of the Board to implement a scheme of non-denominational instruction on the model adopted by the Liverpool School Board.[35] The comments of the Revd Owen Davies crystallized the new outlook of many Nonconformist leaders:

> the future welfare of the whole kingdom depends upon the moral training of the children. The Sunday schools have done glorious work in this direction but the short time at their disposal is hardly sufficient to do the work satisfactorily. The bulk of the parents in this locality would like their children to be taught elementary Bible knowledge.[36]

As the mainstream of Nonconformist opinion moved away from the secular position, however, certain influences within the community sought to uphold these convictions. *Y Celt*, edited by the regular dissident E. Pan Jones, was the medium for a determined effort to reiterate the Liberationist arguments against the introduction of the Bible:

---

[32] Swansea CRO, E/SB 71/2, Minute Book of Swansea School Board, 1873.
[33] Glamorgan CRO, Cardiff, Miscellaneous Papers concerning Education in Aberdare.
[34] *CDH*, 27 January 1888.
[35] *CDH*, 3 January 1890.
[36] Ibid.

Os ydym i ddwyn y Beibl i fewn i'r ysgol ddyddiol, rhaid i drethi y wlad fyned i'w ddysgu ac, os ydyw y trethi i fyned i ddysgu y Beibl, rhaid i'r ysgolfeistr orfodi y plant i'w ddysgu, a byddis felly yn dysgu gair Duw trwy orfodaeth cyfraith y wlad, yr hyn gredai i sydd yn hollol groes i ysbryd Cristionogaeth.

[If we are to introduce the Bible to the day school, the taxes of the country must go towards the teaching of it and, if taxes are to be used to teach the Bible, the schoolmaster must compel the children to learn it, thus the word of God would be taught through the compulsion of the law of the land, something I believe to be totally contrary to the spirit of Christianity.][37]

Even so, these arguments were becoming the battles of the past by the turn of the century. The new generation of Liberal and Nonconformist leaders, despite continuing to fight the battles of Nonconformity on the political field, regarded the secularizing influences which were becoming increasingly evident as a greater threat than any obstacle to religious instruction based on denominational divisions. Many concurred with the sentiments expressed by 'Ymneillduwr', who urged that the principle of secularism had been taken much too far:

Tybia Mr Lewis a chwithau [*Y Celt*] fod egwyddorion Ymneilltuaeth yn gwahardd dysgu crefydd ar draul y trethi, ond tebyg yr addefwch ill dau y gellir cospi dynion ar draul y trethi am ymddygiadau anghrefyddol, megis lladradau, ymosodiadau etc. Onid mwy Cristionogol fyddai defnyddio yr arian hyny i gyfranu addysg grefyddol iddynt i'w cadw rhag y fath droseddau? . . . ni ddylid peryglu diogelwch cymdeithas, drwy fagu cenedl anfoesol ac aflywodraethus, er mwyn boddio mympwyon ychydig penboethiaid sydd a'u cydwybodau heb eu goleuo.

[Mr Lewis and yourselves [*Y Celt*] [would] assume that the principles of Dissent prohibit the teaching of religion, funded by the rates, but you will both probably admit that men can be punished for irreligious behaviour, such as thefts, assaults etc., with the cost falling on the rates. Would it not be more Christian to use that money to provide them with religious instruction that would keep them away from such crimes . . . society's safety should not be jeopardized by nurturing an immoral and

---

[37] *Y Celt*, 25 March 1892.

ungovernable nation, in order to satisfy the whims of a few hot-heads whose consciences have not been enlightened.][38]

By the mid-1890s, the majority of the leaders of Welsh Nonconformity had been converted to some form of religious instruction. Thomas Gee, who had been influenced by his own experiences of seeing the godless urchins of Denbigh remain untouched by either school or Sunday school, published 'Awgrymiadau i Fesur Newydd ar Addysg' in 1896.[39] In his article he proposed a series of new measures, the most important of which was that religious instruction be given on Friday afternoons, with a minister of each denomination being allowed into the school to provide instruction for children of those denominations, a pattern that had been advocated in Ireland in order to overcome Roman Catholic distrust of the education system. The scheme did gain some support in Wales, from moderate Anglicans such as David Howell, vicar of Gresford, and Archdeacon John Griffiths, as well as from Nonconformists who realized that the measures would indirectly give official recognition to Nonconformist ministers by establishing a legal right to provide religious instruction.[40] Yet the overall response to Gee's proposals was less than favourable and they failed to attract support from any substantial body of opinion. The Liberal *Manchester Guardian* considered that the scheme would merely perpetuate the undesirable sectarian divisions which it considered to be the 'curse of Wales'.[41] Likewise, the *Cambrian News* concluded that it was a 'shameful thing that children cannot be taught to do justly, to love mercy and to walk humbly with their God without denominational rivalry'.[42]

In view of the amount of local discretion that existed in the provision of religious instruction in the schools of Wales, much of the debate was largely irrelevant except in its influence on individual members of particular Boards. The varied pattern

---

[38] *Y Celt*, 19 December 1890. Henry Lewis (1847–1923), a leading Congregationalist in north Wales, was active as a promoter of UCNW, Bangor, and other educational work. He had been prominent among those who sought to develop a non-denominational form of religious instruction.
[39] *Baner*, 12 August 1896.
[40] For the reaction, see *Baner*, 26 August 1896.
[41] *Manchester Guardian*, 20 August 1896.
[42] *Cambrian News*, 21 August 1896.

revealed in the reaction of the Nonconformist-dominated Boards mirrored the disparate nature of opinion in the country as a whole. Moreover, the acrimony which had surrounded the creation of Boards in several districts induced a cautious policy in the early years. The religious policy of several Boards was influenced by a deliberate attempt to avoid too rigid an adherence to Nonconformist principles in order not to offend Anglican and Catholic opinion.

Despite an inclination towards relaxing the secular policy, there remained the difficulty of obtaining suitable teaching material. Most religious textbooks were the products of one or other denomination and were therefore unacceptable for use in school. At the same time, the introduction of religious instruction created divisions regarding the selection of Biblical extracts and the choice of hymns. While many hymns (including some of those of the Anglicans) were common to all denominations, examples such as 'All things bright and beautiful', with its mention of the preordained order of the lord in his castle and the poor man at his gate, caused consternation in democratically minded Liberal and Nonconformist circles in Wales. With these difficulties in mind, a detailed syllabus for religious education was drawn up by Henry Lewis, who had been closely associated with the advancement of the University College of North Wales. His proposal encouraged the adoption of the Liverpool School Board scheme for religious instruction, emphasizing biographical knowledge of the Old Testament and a thorough knowledge of the life of Jesus from birth to ascension, including His parables and teachings. Lewis's programme emphasized adherence to the exact word of the Bible without conceding any reference to interpretations or meaning, the field in which the vast majority of doctrinal divisions arose. The objective was to give children sufficient grounding in Biblical knowledge to satisfy two different aims: ensuring that children were educated in the Christian faith and truths, and enabling them to have sufficient knowledge of the basic Gospel to understand the more complex interpretative points which might be made by their respective ministers of religion or clergy.[43] Although the proposals did not secure unqualified support in Wales, they nevertheless provided a firm

[43] UW Bangor, Belmont Papers.

framework within which teachers and School Boards could agree on their own schemes and, by the end of the School Board era, despite the protestations of Pan Jones, a consensus had emerged in favour of a form of religious instruction.

The fact that the several denominations abandoned their advocacy of secular education is one example of the complex nature of Nonconformist society in Wales in this period. Undoubtedly, its conversion was influenced by the perceived decline in the moral and religious condition of the Welsh people, yet the change of heart concerning religious instruction can also be seen as an attempt to resist the more general secularization of Welsh society. R. Tudur Jones and others have argued that the period from *c.*1890 onwards saw a marked decline in Welsh theology, with a distinctly adverse effect on the quality and efficacy of preaching and an increased tolerance of secular trends.[44] According to this view, a more liberal form of theology developed which, in conjunction with social changes (illustrated by the conspicuous consumption of the late Victorian era), contributed to a serious decline in moral and religious standards in Wales. Rather than challenge the new society and reiterate fundamental doctrinal creeds, Nonconformity is seen to have adapted to, and in some cases accepted, the new order, thus further accentuating the decline. The debate between those who regarded Nonconformity's adaptability to the 'world' as a strength and those who regarded it as a factor contributing to the decline of religious observance in Wales is not an issue that need be pursued here, for the allegedly casual attitude towards preaching and theology cultivated in some minds was not reflected in the denominations' stance towards education. Indeed, the opposite pattern emerges, with evidence that Nonconformist leaders made a determined effort to combat the decline of religious feeling in Wales by insisting on a greater provision of religious instruction in schools. The pages of *Y Tyst, Y Goleuad* and other papers indicate that a new attitude was emerging, namely that, with increasing numbers of children denied any

---

[44] R. Tudur Jones, *Ffydd ac Argyfwng Cenedl: Cristionogaeth a Diwylliant yng Nghymru, 1890–1914*, 2 vols (Swansea, 1981–2), I, pp.86–120, 154–71.

moral education at home, and the materialistic attitudes prevalent at the time, a trust in secular schools was deemed inadequate.

The fact that the Nonconformist bodies only gradually accepted the need for some form of religious instruction, and the vigorous debate that was generated by the issue, were related to the philosophical influences on the politics of Welsh Nonconformity. To understand this debate it is important to note the liberationist background of many of the country's Nonconformist leaders. They had been advocates of a voluntarist system of instruction whereby denominations and individuals were responsible for the creation of schools. Experience had resulted in their becoming reconciled, first, to the principle of government grants to assist with the establishment and the maintenance of a school and, later, to the compromise enshrined in the 1870 Act. The reluctance of many early Nonconformists to accept government assistance testified to their wariness of the state. The concept of the rejection of state involvement in the life of the individual was an important feature of the Calvinist theological tradition that had been espoused by the early leaders of dissent in Wales, most notably by John Elias and Christmas Evans. Both men emphasized individual salvation and rejected any idea that the state should shoulder social responsibility. Unsympathetic to the advancement of democratic government, they favoured a political quiescence within an established order. This influence certainly waned in the decades preceding the 1870 Act as Nonconformists adopted a progressively radical political outlook. As minority dissent became majority Welsh Nonconformity, and as the organization of the chapels became more democratic and responsive to the needs of a larger congregation, the denominations became reconciled to the concept of the involvement of the state in the provision of opportunities for social improvement. This certainly included education; the extent of the change in outlook was reflected in the erosion of hostility to government grants between 1847 and 1870. However, the precise nature of the connection between education and religion was not entirely resolved. The liberationist principles which were promoted by Henry Richard and Evan Williams during the 1860s disputed the role of the state in promoting any particular form of religious belief. The liberationists may have been prepared to concede the principle of government involvement in the provision of basic education, but they were not yet ready to concede the principle of state involvement in the religious instruction of the children, since this would create a new association between the state and a form of religion when their objective was to deny the state any involvement with religion. liberationist principles, rather than faith in the Sunday school, constituted the major factor in the commitment of leaders such as Henry Richard to the principle of secular schools. The strength of the Sunday schools in Wales was acknowledged, yet Richard and others who shared his conviction did not demand a separate approach to Wales on account of that strength. Rather, they advocated a system of secular schools for the whole of England and Wales, despite the fact that, apart from in some urban areas, the Sunday school was not strong in England.

The factor that exercised the most powerful influence on the leaders of Welsh opinion was the massive transformation that Welsh society underwent in this period. Industrialization inevitably created new social pressures. With the continuing change in economic fortunes associated with that process, Welsh society became far more mobile as the migration of workers to and from urban areas continued. Rural society was gradually integrated in a much wider, less parochial environment as rail communications in particular linked rural towns and villages to larger centres of industry and commerce. As the new society emerged in Wales, the focus of Welsh Nonconformity also changed. The bulk of the membership of the denominations was increasingly found in the chapels of the industrial areas of south Wales, and although chapels in rural towns continued to exert a disproportionate influence in the counsels of Nonconformist denominations, the need for an adjustment to changed circumstances came to be recognized. The industrial communities presented the Welsh Nonconformist leadership with new challenges and indeed an appreciation that the priorities of Welsh Nonconformity had to change. An acknowledgement that industrial communities might be lost to the denominations was joined with a realization that these communities had to be held if Nonconformity was to survive as a guiding force in Welsh society. The practical difficulties of organizing a Sunday school provision capable of responding to the needs of a growing population in industrial areas, and the need to bring the Christian message to each child by whatever means was available, played a large part in Welsh Nonconformity's abandonment of its opposition to the introduction of religious instruction in the day schools.

The Nonconformist denominations did not adopt the undiluted liberationist viewpoint on the desirability of a minimalist relationship between the state and its people, and this was to have considerable impact on the political movement in Wales during the late nineteenth century and in succeeding decades. Even in terms of the provision of religious instruction, Welsh Nonconformists came to accept the need for some state involvement and it was accepted that the state could provide a form of religious instruction acceptable to all faiths. The battleground thus changed in the late nineteenth century and the matter in contention was the need to remove the preferential treatment accorded to certain religious groups. The concept of an Established Church remained abhorrent to the minds of Welsh Nonconformists, who did not flinch from their conviction of the need for disestablishment.

Yet in accepting state provision in education, Welsh Nonconformity was adopting a principle that countenanced a wider role for the state than orthodox liberal principles would allow. The Welsh Nonconformist movement was gradually adopting a viewpoint that acknowledged the role of the state as a servant of the people and therefore conceded the validity of state involvement in the life of the individual. This rejection of undiluted liberalism coincided with a new emphasis within Welsh Nonconformity that was increasingly sceptical of the individualist religion of an earlier generation. The doctrine of personal salvation remained a powerful influence, yet it was now part of a broader faith that embraced a more socially inclined belief that acknowledged the needs of society, and recognized that those needs should be met on a collective rather than an individual basis. This development was facilitated because Nonconformity had become the faith of the masses rather than of a small minority and because it was increasingly prominent in promoting political action. A new generation of Welsh Nonconformist leaders was more inclined to address problems of poverty, economic instability and provision for the poor rather than place their emphasis wholly on personal salvation and a hope of eternal life, and they looked to the emerging democratic framework provided by the extension of the franchise and the democratization of local government as the means to accomplish that mission. Welsh Nonconformity was able to reconcile itself to such concepts in part because, abandoning its erstwhile rejection of state intervention, it accepted the notion of the state as a provider of certain services, and among these education was of cardinal importance. The debate over religious instruction in the schools is thus an indication of that modification in outlook, which was a crucial factor in the debate on social provision that exercised the denominations during the Edwardian period and later. The debate testifies to the way in which the priorities of Nonconformity changed as the denominations became increasingly confident and aware of their role and responsibilities, not only in spiritual matters but also in articulating the concerns of the nation.

VI
THE WELSH LANGUAGE

In 1870 Wales acquired a system of elementary schools that was identical to that provided for England. The legislation by which it was created took no account of the different religious and political experience of Wales. Another fundamental issue, that of language, was also ignored, even though Welsh was, at the time the policy was formulated, a language spoken by a very substantial proportion of the people. According to the calculations of E. G. Ravenstein, 71.2 per cent of the population of Wales was able to speak Welsh in 1871. The language was noticeably strong in Cardiganshire (95.5 per cent), Merioneth (94.4 per cent), Carmarthenshire (94 per cent), Anglesey (93.1 per cent) and Caernarfonshire (92.9 per cent); Radnorshire (4 per cent Welsh-speaking) was heavily Anglicized, but the other border counties of Monmouthshire, Breconshire, Flintshire and Montgomeryshire included a significant Welsh-speaking population. By 1901 the position had undergone considerable change. Slightly less than half of the population of Wales (49.9 per cent) was able to speak Welsh. In Monmouthshire Welsh-speakers accounted for 13 per cent of the total population, and in Glamorgan they accounted for 43.5 per cent, and, while the language remained strong in Carmarthenshire, Cardiganshire, Merioneth, Caernarfonshire and Anglesey, its general position had been considerably impaired.[1] Yet throughout the period considered in this study, the language remained a matter with which those concerned with the implementation of the Act of 1870 had to contend, and the precise issues which arise will be considered in this chapter. It will examine the way in which the climate of opinion on language issues changed during this period, and it will assess the response of the agencies concerned with education in Wales in the late nineteenth century. It will consider whether the Board schools were responsible for undermining the Welsh

---

[1] John Williams, *Digest of Welsh Historical Statistics*, 2 vols (Cardiff, 1985), I, pp.86–7. Dot Jones, *Statistical Evidence relating to the Welsh Language, 1801–1911* (Cardiff, 1998), pp.223–4. I am indebted to Dot Jones for her assistance with these figures.

language, as was continually claimed by critics of the 1870 Act, and whether the failure to make adequate provision for the Welsh language thwarted educational progress.

Those who drafted the 1870 Act failed to acknowledge the distinctive linguistic considerations in Wales, yet this was not due to any ignorance of the existence of the language. Welsh had featured prominently in the deliberations of the Commission of Inquiry on Education in Wales in 1847.[2] Yet in the heated debate which followed its publication, the language never acquired the importance of the moral, educational and political issues that were highlighted. Neither was the Welsh language a major concern in the controversy concerning the details of the 1870 Act. As was noted earlier, Welsh Nonconformist leaders saw their arguments with the proponents of the Forster Act as part of a wider concern for the Nonconformist community in England and Wales, and as a result there was little incentive to address specifically Welsh grievances. However, during the period after 1870, most especially after 1880, the language issue came to the fore as the political and social discourse changed from being a debate centred on Nonconformist demands made on general liberationist grounds to one more securely grounded in the Welsh experience. The Welsh language was to prove crucial to this debate.[3]

The failure to recognize the linguistic differences in Wales reflected broader perceptions of the Welsh language in 1870. It was not accorded any status as a medium of official business; Welsh was not the language of genteel society, nor of the expanding commercial and industrial world, and neither was it the language of academia and learning. Indeed, the domain of the Welsh language was increasingly limited to domesticity and religious worship and it was regarded, essentially, as a hindrance rather than an advantage to personal advancement and social progress. Thus, it was English that was accorded the status of the language of education in schools which ensured that all pupils left fully proficient in English and able to take full advantage of

---

[2] PP 1847, XXVII, Report of the Commissioners of Inquiry into the State of Education in Wales, 1847. See also above, Introduction.

[3] The Liberation Society under the secretaryship of Henry Richard insisted that those demands made by Welsh Nonconformist leaders should equally be applied to the Nonconformists of England.

the opportunities that that language could bring. Indeed, what is noticeable is that few voices were raised to proclaim the need to promote the Welsh language for its own sake, and the majority of those engaged in the discussion accepted that English was the superior tongue. Rather, the greater part of this period was spent debating the best means by which competence in English could be achieved, notably whether the 'direct method' of teaching English (whereby English was the only medium of instruction) was preferable to using Welsh as a tool in the teaching of English. The debate also considered the extent to which Welsh should be the informal language of the school; whether, for instance, it should be allowed in the playground or during informal conversation between teacher and pupil when the teacher was carrying out pastoral work. Finally, the debate considered the desirability of introducing the Welsh language as a subject for study like geography, history or English literature.

The issues raised in the course of the debate were broached in the period before the passing of the Education Act. Welsh was rarely a means of instruction in the voluntary schools that emerged between 1847 and 1870, although the extent to which it was used as a means of teaching English and enforcing discipline varied. Language policy cut across the normal denominational divisions that affected educational policy in Wales. The Nonconformist managers of British schools, such as the Rhondda Colliery schools or the Taibach Company schools, were as committed to emphasizing the use of English as were the Anglican managers of the National schools at Llanystumdwy (Caernarfonshire) or Llanuwchllyn (Merioneth).[4] The language policy adopted in these widely different areas was in part a reflection of the continued influence of the attitudes expressed in the Blue Books of 1847. For a large body of opinion in Wales, it was the Welsh who should change their language so as to gain access to the broad culture in which English was the necessary medium and in order to become assimilated with the incoming tide of English-speakers.[5]

---

[4] Ceri Lewis, 'The Welsh language', in K. S. Hopkins (ed.), *Rhondda Past and Future* (Rhondda, 1975), p.211; A. L. Evans, *The History of Taibach and District* (Bridgend, 1981), pp.122–6; W. George, *My Brother and I* (London, 1958), p.40; W. J. Gruffydd, *Owen Morgan Edwards: Cofiant* (Aberystwyth, 1938), pp.48–50.
[5] NLW MS 5744C.

These attitudes created the climate in which Welsh was excluded from the schools, with the result that instruction was rendered almost meaningless to a large number of children. O. M. Edwards recalled his experience of school as one of deep discomfort in an alien environment, where proceedings were conducted entirely through the medium of English.[6] Edwards also stressed his personal experience of the 'Welsh Not' in the school at Llanuwchllyn (Merioneth). The 'Welsh Not' was a wooden block that was hung around the neck of any child caught speaking Welsh in the classroom and was intended as a badge of shame. Edwards held that the practice, conceived as a means of eradicating the Welsh language, also encouraged divisions and disharmony within the classroom and further afield.[7] The testimony of O. M. Edwards highlighted an identifiable cause of the decline of Welsh. His evidence is supported by other commentators, such as T. Gwynn Jones[8] and Henry Jones,[9] both of whom referred to the existence of the 'Welsh Not'. Reference to the 'Welsh Not' has been a necessary ingredient in the comments of those who had grievances against the education system of their childhood, although the numbers who could testify to personal experience of the practice were limited. Moreover, allegations concerning its use have been deployed to explain why many spurned the Welsh language in the last decades of the nineteenth century.[10] In addition to the evidence offered by Edwards on the basis of his own experience in Merioneth,[11] there is some indication that it was used in rural Carmarthenshire in the late 1860s,[12] yet the extent of its use, and its efficacy, have to be questioned. Individual log books such as that of Trap School

[6] Wynne Ll. Lloyd, 'Owen M. Edwards (1858–1920)', in Glanmor Williams et al. (eds.), *Pioneers of Welsh Education* (Swansea, n.d.), pp.83–99.

[7] Gruffydd, *Edwards*, pp.71–3.

[8] T. G. Jones, 'Bilingualism in the schools', in John Ballinger (ed.), *National Union of Teachers Souvenir of the Aberystwyth Conference, 1911* (London, 1911), p.249.

[9] H. Jones, *Old Memories* (Cardiff, 1922), p.31. This illustrates the prominent position given to the 'Welsh Not' in the literature of Wales in the nineteenth century. Careful consideration of this subject is given by E. G. Millward, 'Yr hen gyfundrefn felltigedig', in *Cenedl o Bobl Ddewrion: Agweddau ar Lenyddiaeth Oes Victoria* (Llandysul, 1991), pp.183–9. Millward highlights the fact that, as in the evidence found for this study, the 'Welsh Not' was a feature of the era before the 1870 Act, rather than a product of the system created by Forster.

[10] Jones, 'Bilingualism in the schools', pp.249–50.

[11] Gruffydd, *Edwards*, pp.71–3; O. M. Edwards, *Clych Adgof* (1908; 1921 edn.) pp.16–18.

[12] Carmarthenshire CRO, log book of Trap School, C/Ed 571.

(Carmarthenshire) indicate that whereas 'impositions' for speaking Welsh were used in the 1860s, the success of the method was limited. The master recorded in October 1866 that he had 'endeavoured to have English spoken by the senior class . . . which have been rather successful', a comment which indicates that, despite the use of 'impositions', English was not spoken in the school without considerable exertions on the part of the master. Moreover, the evidence of log books points to the fact that the 'Welsh Not' was usually a visual symbol, adopted when a child entered school for the first time, to impress upon the child that English was the language of the school. Certainly, its use was never the result of any policy of the Education Department. Its application appears, indeed, to have been limited to a minority of schools and, from the evidence of the log books, its use diminished in the period which followed the passing of the Forster Education Act. The 'Welsh Not' may offer an easy explanation of the decline of Welsh, yet to accept that argument would mean discounting the fact that opposition to the Welsh language reflected underlying social attitudes rather than any specific language policy. These attitudes prevented the Welsh language from being given an esteemed place in the education system long after the use of the 'Welsh Not' had been abandoned. At the same time, however, attitudes towards the place of the language in education were themselves increasingly diverse.

The period from 1870 to 1902 witnessed a radical reconsideration of the views of the intellectual community in Wales, mainly as a consequence of the cultural and national reawakening of the 1880s. Allied to these developments was the emergence of a greatly enhanced status for the language in academic circles, with a substantial number of scholars, in Wales and further afield, influenced by *Lectures on Celtic Philology* by Sir John Rhys, published in 1885.[13] These developments were an intrinsic element in what T. Gwynn Jones described as a renaissance of Welsh letters during this period. Welshmen educated at the English universities and on the continent had begun to take an active interest in Welsh literature while in exile, and this generation was becoming increasingly influential in Welsh public

---

[13] J. Rhys, *Lectures on Celtic Philology* (London, 1885).

affairs.[14] This influence, moreover, was now increasingly located in Wales, centred mainly in Cardiff, as contrasted with the previous generation of intellectual leaders who had been largely based in London. The expansion of the professions in Wales, particularly higher education, meant that people of ability had the opportunity to remain in Wales, something which had been denied to their predecessors.

Moreover, there was, certainly by 1885, a new trend in the argument over the role of the language in education. Enlightened opinion on the language question was changing. In the late 1870s, the Honourable Society of Cymmrodorion began to consider the role of Welsh in education and the society eventually commissioned a major study of the issue in 1884.[15] A new interest in the Welsh language was clearly in evidence, and those who represented this initiative sought to prove that Welsh had intrinsic merit as a medium of education. Attention to the role of the language in education was furthered by the Revd D. Jones Davies, the rector of North Benfleet, Essex, who set the direction of a new argument over the language with the publication, in 1882, of *The Necessity of Teaching English Through the Medium of Welsh*, a tract which remained of crucial importance to the debate even in the next century.[16] His argument was reinforced by Professor Thomas Powel, professor of Welsh at Cardiff, who addressed the Cymmrodorion on 'The Advisability of the Teaching of Welsh in Elementary Schools in Wales' in 1884.[17] Even earlier, at the Cardiff Eisteddfod of 1879, a prize was offered for 'An Essay in the Propriety of Maintaining the Cymric Language not simply for the Strengthening of Welsh Nationality but also for the purpose of aiding the English student in acquiring the language'.[18] Further impetus to the practical implications of this new trend was given by the establishment of the Society for the Utilisation of the Welsh Language as an Instrument of Education in Wales and

---

[14] Jones, 'Bilingualism in the schools', p.251.
[15] Cited in J. E. Southall, *Wales and Her Language* (Newport and London, 1902), pp.110–37; R. T. Jenkins and Helen M. Ramage, *History of the Honourable Society of Cymmrodorion, 1751–1951* (London, 1951), pp.212–15.
[16] Southall, *Wales and Her Language*, pp.263–7. B. L. Davies, 'A right to a bilingual education in nineteenth century Wales', *THSC*, 1988, 133–51; *Y Cymmrodor*, V (June, 1882), 1–3.
[17] *Y Diwygiwr*, 39 (June 1884), 179–84.
[18] Ibid.

Monmouthshire at the Aberdare Eisteddfod of 1885.[19] This body derived its support mainly from the ranks of the Cymmrodorion, most notably Marchant Williams, Isambard Owen, Beriah Gwynfe Evans and John Griffiths.[20] The title itself had significant implications for the role of the language. Whereas the Welsh title, Cymdeithas yr Iaith Gymraeg (The Welsh Language Society), was shorter and suggested a stronger commitment to the Welsh language, the leadership of the movement was determined to adopt a pragmatic approach to the promotion of the language. The introduction of Welsh in schools was advocated as a tool to ensure that children gained a better understanding of English, thus constituting a variation on the argument in favour of the 'direct method' of language teaching. To endeavour to ensure that what was taught in school was understood by the children was a perfectly laudable aim. Yet it was also the case that many of those who were most prominent in promoting the use of the Welsh language as a medium of instruction were convinced of the merit of teaching Welsh for its own sake. The society attracted appreciable support, its adherents including leading members of both Nonconformist and Anglican denominations, the principals of Aberystwyth, Bangor and Cardiff University Colleges, as well as a sympathetic response from political leaders such as Henry Richard.[21] The society never attracted a large membership and it did not articulate any groundswell of opinion in Wales; its membership was derived mainly from the Cymmrodorion, the majority of whom were still living outside Wales.

The undoubted importance of the Language Society was that it included members of sufficient influence to ensure that greater sympathy was extended to the Welsh language, and it acted as an effective pressure group that won several important concessions from successive governments.[22] The tenor of the argument

---

[19] Davies, 'A right to a bilingual education in nineteenth century Wales', 133–51.
[20] Ibid.
[21] Significantly, however, the leaders of the Welsh Language Society initially viewed Richard's appointment to the Cross Commission with some suspicion. Davies, 'A right to a bilingual education'; I. G. Jones, 'Henry Richard ac iaith y gwleidydd yn y bedwaredd ganrif ar bymtheg', in G. H. Jenkins (ed.), *Cof Cenedl*, III (Llandysul, 1988), 117–50.
[22] For a detailed assessment of the Welsh Language Society, see J. Elwyn Hughes, *Arloeswr Dwyieithedd: Dan Isaac Davies, 1839–1887* (Cardiff, 1984). The career of Beriah Evans is examined in J. E. Edwards, 'Beriah Gwynfe Evans, ei Fywyd a'i Waith, ynghyd â mynegai dethol i Cyfaill yr Aelwyd' (Ph.D. thesis, University of Wales, 1989); J. E. Lloyd, 'Cymdeithas yr Iaith Gymraeg: trem ar hanes y mudiad', *Y Llenor* (Winter 1931), 207–14.

emphasized by the society's leading figures was expressed by Isambard Owen, who asserted that the exclusion of Welsh was resulting in deep-seated effects on Welsh children. In his opinion:

> Is it calculated to conduce to the formation of habits of self-confidence and self-respect in the children of Wales that the first lesson impressed upon them when they enter school should be this, that their own native language is a thing to be straightaway forgotten and despised . . . Is there then no danger that the lesson should be transferred in the child's mind from the language itself to its associations, and become in effect a lesson of contempt and distrust for his parentage, his home, his religion, his nationality, and himself?[23]

Owen's impassioned plea was given intellectual weight by the detailed (and equally earnest) research work that was undertaken by John Southall. His investigations included pioneering studies of language sphere and function and popular attitudes towards the language. An Englishman resident in Newport, Southall learned the language and was active in promoting and publishing a host of Welsh literary works. In his opinion a bilingual community had distinct advantages and, crucially, he believed that migrants to Wales should be encouraged to assimilate in the Welsh-speaking community rather than expect the Welsh to adopt the English language. By teaching Welsh in school, he argued, the education system would assist this process of assimilation.[24] Furthermore, he advocated the introduction of Welsh as a means of securing a more intelligent teaching of English and the development of an aptitude for other languages.[25] Southall pointed to the fact that successful teachers were already making use of the language and he asserted that its general introduction would result in little additional work.[26] The existing system, he argued, had 'lamentably failed' except in a minority of cases, and all that had been achieved was a parrot-like knowledge of English in the majority of elementary schools. Thus, bad English was often learned in the elementary schools,

[23] PP 1887, XXX, Minutes of Evidence.
[24] Southall, *Wales and Her Language*, pp.167–70.
[25] Ibid.
[26] These issues are discussed in W. G. Evans, 'The "bilingual difficulty", the Inspectorate and the failure of a Welsh language teacher-training experiment in Victorian Wales', *Journal of the National Library of Wales*, XXVIII (1993–4), 325–34.

while the Welsh learned in the Sunday schools was often ungrammatical and the teaching methods dreary and unnatural. Welsh was becoming disused and many children were becoming ashamed of their native tongue. The introduction of the system that he proposed would create a thorough love for higher education and science, and would ensure a full command of a beautiful and expressive language as well as providing a classical education. It would keep alive the Welsh national spirit, and Welsh literature would be a great beneficiary. The introduction of Welsh would sharpen the intellect of the children and would enable them to comprehend the intricate Welsh that was heard from the pulpit, thus improving the mental and the moral condition of the people. The arguments deployed by Southall reiterated those that were regularly advocated by the Welsh Language Society in favour of the use of Welsh. However, the key element of his thesis was that bilingualism was a virtue in itself and that attempts to assimilate Wales totally in the English-speaking world were undesirable and should be resisted.[27]

It was in this climate that the Welsh Language Society emerged as an effective pressure group which sought to change the attitudes of those with influence over educational policy in Wales. No group was more central to this process than the school inspectors. The inspectorate constituted a key element in the structure of the education system, not only because of the way in which their reports could influence the policy of the Education Department but also because of their wider role in moulding the views of teachers and school managers. As a group they were not considered sympathetic to the Welsh language. Goronwy Jones, writing in 1893, criticized their antipathy and attributed blame for the Anglicized nature of education firmly to the school inspectors,[28] comments that were to be reiterated by others such as the Llanwyddelan School Board.[29] The inspectorate was certainly aware of the exacting difficulties that were caused by the language of education not being the first language of a very great number of Welsh children. As early as 1871, William Williams, the inspector for British schools, complained that the quality of the reading of many pupils was low and too

[27] *Y Celt*, 23 September 1892.
[28] NLW, T. E. Ellis Papers, 1067.
[29] NLW, T. E. Ellis Papers, 3646.

mechanical, and that they had little understanding of what they read, a difficulty which he attributed to the fact that Welsh was habitually spoken in the homes of a high proportion of the pupils.[30] Yet, despite acknowledging the existence of a language issue, neither Williams nor other inspectors, such as Horace Waddington or the Revd Herbert Smith, were prepared to contemplate admitting Welsh into the schools of Wales. Indeed, it was only John Rhys, the inspector for the Denbigh district, who advocated such a measure and he did so throughout the greater part of the 1870s.[31] Significantly, Rhys had the rare distinction of being an inspector who had actual experience of teaching children, from his period as a pupil teacher at Pen-llwyn (Cardiganshire) and later as a trained teacher at Rhos-y-bol (Anglesey).[32] In his opinion, the failure to use Welsh in order to facilitate the teaching of English was adding unnecessarily to the work of the teachers. Indeed, he claimed that, owing to the pressure on time created by this policy, other features of the curriculum, such as spelling and pronunciation, were neglected. In his report for 1876 he blamed the failure to use the Welsh language for the atrocious spelling problem in his district, which implied that Welsh teachers had an impossible task in attempting to make their schools as efficient as those of England and Scotland.[33]

The views expressed by John Rhys were in sharp contrast to those of the Revd Shadrach Pryce, the inspector for rural Carmarthenshire and an avowed opponent of the introduction of Welsh to the elementary school.[34] A Welsh-speaking Anglican clergyman, Pryce considered the Welsh language to be useless in educational terms. He noted an absence of Welsh technical terms and also the difficulty of teaching arithmetic in Welsh given the complicated Welsh numbers system by which ninety-six was rendered as one-on-fifteen-on-four-twenties and seventy-nine became four-on-fifteen-on-three-twenties. Moreover, he also rejected the argument in favour of utilizing Welsh in order to secure a better understanding of English. Such a practice, he

[30] PP 1871, XXII, Mr Williams's Report.
[31] PP 1876, XXIII, Mr Rhys's Report.
[32] Above, ch. 2 n. 8.
[33] PP 1876, XXIII, Mr Rhys's Report.
[34] W. G. Evans, 'Gelyn yr iaith Gymraeg, y Parchedig Shadrach Pryce, A. E. M., a meddylfryd yr arolygiaeth yn oes Fictoria', *Y Traethodydd*, 149 (1994), 73–81.

argued, would merely contribute to confusion in the minds of pupils; in his opinion, the best schools were those from which Welsh was excluded altogether, and he emphasized the need to introduce an English-only policy in the playground as far as possible.[35] Pryce argued that the most effective way to learn a language was through total immersion in that language, rather than through the use of another, and he noted that better examination results were achieved in those schools which insisted that pupils should speak nothing but English. He denied the assertion that children were 'lost' in school when faced with an education conducted totally through the medium of English, and stated his belief that children were especially apt at learning a new language in a relatively short period of time. The pass rate in the annual examination was highest in the Welsh-speaking areas of his district, proving his argument that the language difficulty was a myth. Furthermore, there was greater intelligence in the upper standards of those schools where Welsh was excluded, and he expressed disapproval of any furthering of the tendency to permit Welsh in the infant classes. However, the practical difficulties that were cited by Pryce reflected his bias against the Welsh language; he was convinced it had no intrinsic value. In his estimation, the sooner Welsh was 'stamped out of the school' the better its educational standard would be. By 1883 he confidently predicted that the language of the rising generation would be English and he gloried in the fact that the children of his district were beginning to use English in daily conversation even though their parents continued to speak Welsh.[36]

The hostile views of Shadrach Pryce were representative of those of the older generation of school inspectors who shared the mentality common since the 1847 report, that Welsh should be eradicated. Those views stood in increasingly marked contrast to more positive attitudes, most notably among the younger generation of Welsh inspectors. This latter group was personified by William Edwards, the inspector for Merthyr Tydfil, who declared in 1887 that he was convinced of the desirability of implementing proposals to use the Welsh language as a tool of

---

[35] PP 1878–79, XXIII, Mr Pryce's Report.
[36] PP 1883, XXV, Mr Pryce's Report.

education.[37] Edwards held that it was nonsense to exclude from local schools the language habitually used by a large section of the community, and he regarded Welsh as an indispensable medium in securing educational progress in Welsh-speaking areas. The adoption of a bilingual policy, he argued, would ease the process by which children could acquire a third or fourth language, as was increasingly common on the continent. In his view, Welsh would complement rather than displace English in the daily life of Wales. He dismissed the argument that the scarcity of Welsh-speaking teachers would make the introduction of Welsh impossible, and maintained that in most Welsh-speaking areas the majority of teachers were in any case fluent in the language.

The sub-inspector for the same district, Dan Isaac Davies, went further in his report for the same year.[38] He mentioned the case of the Gelli-gaer Board area, where Welsh had been introduced on an experimental basis as a subject for study, and where children from English-speaking homes had achieved the best results in Welsh. Davies stated that there was no scarcity of Welsh-speaking teachers and noted several examples of English-born teachers learning the Welsh language. Where Welsh was taught, he noted a significant improvement both in the general intelligence of the children and in their knowledge of English grammar.[39] Dan Isaac Davies and William Edwards pointed to the increasing tendency to appoint Welsh-speaking public officials in Wales, a development which would generate a need for articulate and educated Welsh-speakers, while at the same time they emphasized that the introduction of Welsh would not occasion the abandonment of English, but would rather ensure that the children of Wales were capable of understanding English and not merely of speaking the language.

In 1889 William Williams, the chief inspector with responsibility for Wales, declared his support for a more sympathetic treatment of the language. Nevertheless, he insisted that this was in order to ensure a more intelligent teaching of English,

[37] PP 1887, XXVIII, Mr Edwards's Report; W. G. Evans, 'O. M. Edwards's enlightened precursors: HMIs and the Welsh language in the late nineteenth century', *Planet*, 99 (1993), 69–77; idem., 'The "bilingual difficulty"', 325–34.
[38] Davies was already committed to the introduction of Welsh to the elementary schools (D. Isaac Davies, 'Cymru ddwyieithog', *Y Geninen*, IV (July 1885), 208–12).
[39] PP 1887, XXVIII, Mr Davies's Report cited in Mr Edwards's Report.

acknowledging, as he saw it, the bad standard of English spoken in Wales and the failure of Welsh children to distinguish between Welsh and English idioms.[40] HMI Bancroft, in his report, noted that any intelligent teacher would necessarily use Welsh in teaching English. For him, there were undeniable benefits from using Welsh where it was the language of the majority of the population, and there were good reasons for selecting Welsh as an optional subject for study.[41] HMI A. G. Leggard in 1899 criticized those examiners in the intermediate schools who failed to recognize that, for many pupils in Wales, English was a second language. Certainly Leggard was aware of the need to encourage English in Wales:

> Welsh children should not merely learn bookish English, but they should be encouraged from the infant school upwards to talk in the foreign tongue about things that interest them – their homes, their games, their pet animals – and when a vocabulary is acquired, simple rules of grammar will gradually be deduced, and the children will be trained in due course by speaking correctly to write correctly.[42]

Yet he also encouraged the use of Welsh and he was anxious to promote an awareness of literary Welsh and an 'acquaintance with the best poetry and prose of native writers'.[43] Moreover, he advocated the introduction of Welsh as a medium of instruction rather than simply as a means of improving the teaching of English.[44]

It is clear that the attitudes of the inspectorate towards the Welsh language underwent a significant change during the late nineteenth century, with a more sympathetic disposition emerging towards its end. The advocates of an enhanced role for the language, notably William Edwards and Dan Isaac Davies, were representative of the new generation of inspectors in Wales, Nonconformist in religion, Welsh in outlook and with a significant degree of sympathy with the ideas of the *Cymru Fydd* movement. The fact remained, however, that the majority of

---

[40] PP 1889, XXIX, Mr Williams's Report.
[41] Ibid., Mr Bancroft's Report.
[42] PP 1899, XX, Mr Leggard's Report.
[43] Ibid.
[44] Ibid.

inspectors during this period were English in origin and language, and the development of a more sympathetic attitude to the language was really attributable to the influence of such inspectors as A. G. Leggard and R. J. Alexander. The conversion of these men to the need for the introduction of Welsh was essentially based on educational arguments rather than any linguistic, political or cultural commitment to the native language. Crucially, however, the pro-Welsh outlook of a significant number of school inspectors influenced opinion and policy in the Education Department. A more benevolent attitude to the Welsh language was adopted by official bodies. It was an attitude that was yet to permeate the wider community in Wales.

Both the Liberal Party and the Nonconformist denominations made much of the linguistic divide in Wales. The failure of the Church to make provision in Welsh was cited as one of the reasons for its rejection by the people of Wales, while at the same time its Liberal leaders regularly denounced the gentry for their adoption of the English language and an English lifestyle. The Nonconformists were widely regarded as the custodians of the Welsh language, partly because the pulpit was the venue for some of the most polished orators in the language. Yet the Nonconformist leaders had no single view of the role and importance of the Welsh language. A number of prominent figures, such as Lewis Edwards, regarded the language as a secondary consideration, a matter to be left to the Sunday school movement in Wales and one which did not merit the attention of the day school.[45] Thus, Welsh was to be placed alongside religious instruction as the responsibility of the Sunday school, where no compulsion could be exercised, and regarded as a language suitable for the home and religious worship, but not as a language for business. These views reflect an outlook prevalent among Nonconformist leaders. It was during this period that Lewis Edwards became increasingly aware of the desirability of building English-medium Nonconformist chapels in Wales and he was particularly active in urging Welsh chapels in south Wales to turn to the use of English in order to attract a wider congregation, reflecting that in his estimation the message of Nonconformity was more important than the language in which it was delivered. Candidates for

[45] Ibid.

the ministry in theological colleges throughout Wales were receiving their training through the medium of English at a time when the majority of them were being prepared to take charge of Welsh-speaking congregations.[46] Moreover, the adoption of an English mode of living by many Nonconformist ministers, especially the most prominent figures among them, is increasingly noticeable in this period. For many children of the Welsh manse, virtually the only contact with the Welsh language occurred during the Sunday and weekday services.

Notwithstanding these differences of emphasis among the leaders of Nonconformity in Wales, the majority adopted an increasingly sympathetic attitude towards the language. In April 1886 the Congregationalist *Y Tyst* stated that it was essential that Welsh should be utilized in the teaching of English,[47] and four years later *Y Goleuad* welcomed the change in the attitude of the Education Department on the issue of the Welsh language. Indeed, *Y Goleuad* became increasingly vociferous in its condemnation of those pastors who conducted their daily lives through the medium of English while being responsible for Welsh-speaking chapels. According to the paper, no good would come from this emulation of the clergy and gentry by the Nonconformist ministers of Wales.[48] The Revd E. Pan Jones, a representative of the more determinedly radical section of Welsh Nonconformity, demonstrated his sustained enthusiasm for the cause of the Welsh language in the pages of *Y Celt*.[49] He criticized those teachers who refused to implement the permitted scheme for teaching Welsh, and recommended that any anti-Welsh majorities on School Boards should be ousted through the ballot box.[50] These sentiments attracted the support of Principal Michael D. Jones, who declared his total support for the views expressed by John Southall.[51] Likewise in April 1893, 'Eliphas', writing in *Y Celt*, stated that, unless apathy towards the language was overcome, it would inevitably decline owing to the falling

---

[46] R. T. Jones, *Yr Undeb* (Swansea, 1975), pp.102–10; T. M. Bassett, *Bedyddwyr Cymru* (Swansea, 1977), pp.347–9.
[47] *Y Tyst*, 23 April 1886.
[48] *Y Goleuad*, 10 April 1890.
[49] P. Jones-Evans, 'Evan Pan Jones – land reformer', *WHR*, 4 (1968–9), 143–60.
[50] *Y Celt*, 6 March 1891 and 21 April 1893.
[51] *Y Celt*, 23 September 1892. For Michael D. Jones (1822–98), Principal of the Independent College, Bala, see *DWB*, pp.495–6.

away of the influence of those institutions which had traditionally been the backbone of the language, notably the chapels and the literary societies.[52]

The change of emphasis that was apparent in the Nonconformist denominations must be placed in the context of the debate concerning religious instruction, an issue that has been discussed in chapter 5. The evidence of the initial debate concerning the 1870 Act indicates that Welsh Nonconformity envisaged a limited role for the school in this sphere. Individuals such as Lewis Edwards and Henry Richard had at first great faith in the ability of the Sunday school to provide religious instruction and with it instruction in Welsh. Significantly, however, Edwards was to be converted to the principle of allowing non-denominational religious instruction in the day schools, a change of view that was attributable to the decline of the influence of the Sunday school. The fact that, as part of this reconsideration of his views, he did not also advocate the wholesale introduction of Welsh in the day school would indicate a less than wholehearted commitment to the preservation and promotion of the language. By the last two decades of the century, the equivocations of the period after 1847 were finally being set aside but, as we have seen, with less than unanimity in Nonconformist Wales.

This lack of clarity on the part of the Nonconformist leadership was reflected in the opinions of the Liberal Party. Liberal leaders such as George Osborne Morgan, the Liberal victor in Denbigh in 1868, had demonstrated an awareness of the issues. Morgan, for instance, was aware of the need to appoint Welsh-speaking judges and to allow trials in Wales to be conducted through the medium of Welsh. Those views should not, however, be taken to reflect a desire to promote Welshness in public life. Rather they stemmed from a wish to remove the injustice of trials being conducted in a language with which the participants were unfamiliar. Furthermore, the introduction of Welsh in legal proceedings was regarded as a temporary necessity that would be ended when education had ensured that all Welshmen were proficient in English.[53] On the other hand, the national

---

[52] *Y Celt*, 21 April 1893.
[53] H. T. Edwards, 'Y Gymraeg yn y bedwaredd ganrif ar bymtheg', in G. H. Jenkins (ed.), *Cof Cenedl*, II (1987), 119–52.

reawakening to which reference has been made clearly influenced Liberal thinking in Wales and was given political expression in the Cymru Fydd movement in the Liberal Party in Wales, not least because of the connections between some of the leaders of Cymru Fydd and organizations such as the Welsh Language Society and the Honourable Society of Cymmrodorion. The influence of the more avowedly Welsh approach of Cymru Fydd was reflected in the deliberations of the North Wales Liberal Federation, which committed itself in 1888 to the campaign for the utilization of the Welsh language.[54] The resolution which formed the basis of the Federation's policy was proposed by representatives of the Llangar School Board, stating:

> fod y gynhadledd hon yn llongyfarch Cymdeithas yr Iaith Gymraeg ar y llwyddiant sydd wedi dilyn ei hymdrechion i gael gan y llywodraeth i awdurdodi cyfundrefn o addysg Gymraeg yn ysgolion elfennol y Dywysogaeth, ac yn dymuno annog Byrddau Ysgol ac awdurdodau addysgol eraill i fabwysiadu mor fuan ag sydd yn ddichonadwy y cynlluniau addysgol a gymhellir gan y Gymdeithas ac a awdurdodir gan y Côd Newydd.

> [That this conference congratulates the Welsh Language Society upon the success of its efforts to secure the government's authorization of a system of Welsh education in the elementary schools of the Principality, and urges the School Boards and other education authorities to adopt as soon as possible those educational schemes advocated by the Society and permitted by the New Code.][55]

The influence of the Federation in turn permeated the ranks of Liberal members of the School Boards in Wales and led to significant changes in the policies of a number of them. In 1888, the School Board in Bangor, a town that was witnessing increasing Anglicization, resolved to introduce Welsh as a specific subject in its schools, not least because of the fear that lack of Welsh was a factor dissuading children from the rural hinterland from attending school;[56] similar policies were adopted by members of the School Board at Caernarfon[57] and Ffestiniog.[58]

[54] *CDH*, 21 December 1888.
[55] Gwynedd CRO, Dolgellau, A52, Papers of Llangar School Board (n.d.).
[56] *CDH*, 13 July 1888.
[57] *CDH*, 9 March 1888.
[58] *CDH*, 21 December 1889.

However, despite the evidence of a growing commitment to the language on the part of School Boards in north Wales, it was in the heavily Anglicized areas of the south-east that the most determined effort to promote the Welsh language was made. Originally the introduction of Welsh lessons was an experiment undertaken by the Gelli-gaer School Board (Glamorgan). Welsh was later introduced by the Mynyddislwyn and Bedwellty School Boards in neighbouring Monmouthshire.[59] In both these cases, a mandate for the introduction of Welsh had been secured at the election to the Board,[60] later reinforced by referenda held to ascertain the views of parents on the desirability of introducing the language; an overwhelming majority was recorded in favour of its introduction in both areas.[61] The Merthyr Tydfil School Board also sought to promote the Welsh language through its pioneering work in the development of Welsh textbooks, thus overcoming the objections to the introduction of Welsh on the grounds that the reading material available was inappropriate. In an introduction to these volumes, the Merthyr Board declared:

Dywed calon Cymru y dylid cadw y Gymraeg yn fyw. Nis gellir hyn heb ei dysgu yn fore i'r plant. Bu ysgolion ein gwlad yn hir gaeëdig yn erbyn iaith y genedl; ond bellach, mae y drysau yn agored i'w derbyn i fewn a theg yw nodi iddi yr un safle â'r iaith Saesneg. Mae Bwrdd Ysgol Merthyr Tydfil yn argyhoeddiedig o hawliau y Gymraeg, ac wedi penderfynu ei dysgu yn yr holl ysgolion o dan ei llywodraeth.

[The heart of Wales dictates that Welsh should be kept alive. This will not happen unless it is taught to the children at an early age. The schools of our country have long since been shut against the language of the nation; but now, the doors are open to receive it, and it is only fair to award it the

---

[59] Sian Rhiannon Williams, 'Iaith y nefoedd mewn cymdeithas ddiwydiannol: y Gymraeg a chrefydd yng ngorllewin Sir Fynwy yn y bedwaredd ganrif ar bymtheg', in G. H. Jenkins and J. B. Smith (eds.), *Politics and Society in Wales, 1840–1922* (Cardiff, 1988), pp.47–60.
[60] NLW, T. E. Ellis Papers, 1946.
[61] For a detailed assessment of these cases see Southall, *Wales and Her Language*, p.387. The result of the referendum at Mynyddislwyn, for instance, recorded 1,275 votes in favour of teaching Welsh, 146 against, with 117 abstentions. The teaching of Welsh in Glamorgan and Monmouthshire also attracted the interest of T. E. Ellis, as testified by his correspondence with Southall, NLW, T. E. Ellis Papers, 1947. The campaign to introduce Welsh in the Anglicized areas of Wales was supported by such figures as Llewelyn Williams, editor of the *South Wales Daily Post*, who supported the policy not only as a means to cultural revival but also for political purposes (*Y Celt*, 19 May 1893).

same status as the English language. The Merthyr Tydfil School Board is convinced of the rights of the Welsh language and has determined to teach it to all schools under its authority.][62]

These efforts occurred in areas that had witnessed considerable immigration from outside Wales. The Mynyddislwyn Board, for instance, covered the villages of Crymlin, Aber-carn and Ynysddu, while Bedwellty covered Blackwood, Rhymney, Tredegar and Ebbw Vale. While Thomas Jones argued that the decline of the Welsh language in these areas occurred with the coming of the Board schools, the Boards themselves can hardly be held wholly responsible for the decline.[63] Certainly, the evidence demonstrates that the decline of the Welsh language cannot be attributed to a deliberate policy on the part of the School Boards of excluding the language from their schools. Indeed, where the language faced its greatest threat of being overwhelmed by the influences of the Anglicizing forces, School Boards endeavoured to promote and protect it. At the same time, while it is true that this policy was revealed in its most emphatic form in the south-east, School Boards in the more strongly Welsh-speaking areas of the west and north were in general terms equally well disposed to protecting the language.[64] This was illustrated by the insistence of a large number of Boards on the appointment of Welsh-speaking teachers in those villages where Welsh was habitually spoken by a majority of the population. Moreover, the fact that these policies were not reversed after School Board elections indicates at least a degree of popular acquiescence in the policy.

Despite the official policies of the Boards, however, implementation of their intentions was fraught with difficulty. The Bedwellty Board, for instance, abandoned its policy because it lacked a staff that was proficient in the Welsh language,[65] and in Llanelli (Breconshire) the Board declined to undertake a survey of the wishes of parents because of its fear that an affirmative vote would result in the Board being committed to a policy which was impossible to implement.[66] Thus it is clear that,

[62] Merthyr Tydfil Public Library, Education Collection, 1895.
[63] T. Jones, *Rhymney Memories* (Newtown, 1938), pp.43–8; Edward L. Ellis, *T.J.: A Life of Thomas Jones CH* (Cardiff, 1992), pp.12–13.
[64] NLW, T. E. Ellis Papers, 1946.
[65] Ibid.
[66] Ibid, 1947.

despite the positive pronouncements of several School Boards, few were prepared to exert themselves in an effort to implement the policy.

As was noted earlier, the School Board movement failed to secure control of education in large areas of Wales, most notably in rural areas. As a consequence, the provision of education in those areas was undertaken by schools controlled by the Anglican Church, often under the patronage of the landed gentry. Neither group was regarded as naturally sympathetic to the Welsh language and, as was noted above, both groups were derided as positively anti-Welsh by the tribunes of Liberalism and Nonconformity in Wales. These allegations certainly reflected a reality in many cases. Several landowners had sufficient Welsh to converse with their tenantry about mundane matters, but Welsh continued to be regarded as the language of the peasantry and working class and it was never accorded a place in polite society. Thus, according to O. M. Edwards, the wife of the local landowner who controlled Llanuwchllyn school (Merioneth), while being prepared to use the language in order to be understood, did so with considerable displeasure and disdain.[67] Rachel Howard, writing to Betha Johnes of Dolaucothi, dismissed the language, contemptuously contrasting the uselessness of Welsh with the positive advantages that were to be gained from a knowledge of Latin or German.[68] A more overtly political explanation for abandoning the Welsh language was also proposed:

> There is no doubt that the Welsh language helps to keep the Welshmen secluded from the good things of the world . . . the Scotch have got rid of Gaelic, much to their advantage. In Ireland Erse is fostered for political purposes, and I fear that it is to a certain extent the case also in Wales, and not to the benefit of our party.

Control of the vernacular press by 'extreme radicals' was cited as a further reason for opposing any support for the Welsh language.[69]

[67] O. M. Edwards, 'The Welsh Not', reprinted in M. Stephens (ed.), *A Book of Wales* (Cardiff, 1987), pp.55–7.
[68] NLW, Dolaucothi Correspondence, 6977, 30 August 1885.
[69] Ibid., 11765.

This image of Conservative landowners in Wales hostile to the language ignores the development of a more positive outlook, partly in response to the broader national developments in Wales in this period. As Hywel Teifi Edwards has demonstrated in his studies of the Eisteddfod in this period, the landowners of Wales were willing patrons of Welsh culture both locally and nationally, and many were actively involved in the Honourable Society of Cymmrodorion.[70] Although their involvement ensured that a significant part of the proceedings at various public events was conducted through the medium of English, and that official business was also transacted in English, the Welsh gentry did demonstrate their encouragement of the cultural movements of Wales. Leading landowners such as Lord Penrhyn and the marquess of Bute declared their regret at being unable to converse through the medium of Welsh, the latter going as far as to employ a Welsh tutor for his son.[71] Indeed, so strong was the support for the language expressed by Lord Dynevor in his address to the Llandeilo Eisteddfod that Dan Isaac Davies confidently predicted enlisting his support and envisaged his becoming a member of the Welsh Language Society.[72] This increasingly sympathetic attitude towards Welsh culture was in many ways a reflection of the influence of the national revival witnessed within Wales in the 1880s.[73] The commitment of certain landowners to the language in education, however, was partly a reflection of their direct knowledge of the difficulties encountered in teaching through the medium of English in Welsh-speaking communities; this knowledge derived from their experience as school managers and, in some cases, as members of School Boards. Yet, at the same time, it reflected a wish on the part of Welsh landowners to be re-assimilated in local communities. The divisions between the landowning gentry and the local communities permeated the religious, political and social spheres, yet the linguistic divide could be overcome without having to compromise over a matter of principle such as the

---

[70] H. T. Edwards, *Gŵyl Gwalia: Yr Eisteddfod Genedlaethol yn Oes Aur Victoria, 1858–1868* (Llandysul, 1980), pp.352–60.
[71] Southall, *Wales and Her Language*, pp.206–10.
[72] D. I. Davies to B. G. Evans, Cardiff Central Library MSS 3/553, Beriah Evans Papers, 12 September 1885.
[73] Rhys Morgan, 'Yr iaith Gymraeg yn ei chysylltiad ac addysg', *Y Geninen*, XV (June 1897), 99–102.

tithes, disestablishment or the land question. The need for Welsh landowners to promote and adopt the Welsh language in order to rebuild relations with local communities was highlighted by David Williams at the Episcopalian Congress in Swansea in 1889. According to Williams:

> Bishops and Barons . . . have expelled the Welsh language from their drawing-rooms; . . . and have shut the heart of the nation against them, that they shall no longer be rulers of her people . . . These natural leaders of the people, because uneducated, and perversely ignorant of the language, have abdicated their proud position and allowed the people to be led by those who had no business to be leaders of the people at all . . . It is the Welsh-speaking portion of the community, under the spell of their weekly and monthly periodicals, who wield the political power in the Principality; and it is impossible to gain their confidence by ignoring their language.[74]

He argued that the landowners of Wales needed to be at the vanguard of the Welsh-language movement in order to prevent Welsh political leadership from 'falling into the hands of those influenced by mob politics'.[75] The support won from landowners was an important achievement for the Welsh Language Society as it sought to broaden its appeal and ensure a cross-party consensus in favour of admitting the language into the schools of Wales and, crucially, to ensure that this was not regarded as yet another Nonconformist demand but rather a matter of a genuine and widespread concern.

The attitude of the clergy was as varied as that of the landowning class. As managers of local National schools, the views of the local clergy had a direct bearing on their position within the schools. According to the Revd Daniel Lewis, rector of Merthyr Tydfil, in his evidence to the Cross Commission in 1888, the introduction of Welsh in the schools was a dangerous and undesirable proposal. Lewis warned that Welsh was

---

[74] Southall, *Wales and Her Language*, pp.210–11. H. M. Vaughan, *The South Wales Squires* (London, 1926), examines the view of the squire as alien in Welsh society, but concentrates on the land question and disestablishment as the two main issues on which criticism might be levied and makes little reference to divisions caused by language.
[75] Cited in Southall, *Wales and Her Language*, p.211.

unsuitable as a language for education because of the lack of a standard grammar and its poverty as a literary language:

> the language is a spoken one; it has really no body of literature of its own. Those who are skilled in its literature are men who cannot speak the language, generally speaking, freely.[76]

He considered that the introduction of Welsh in order to teach English was likely to discourage the habit of thinking through the medium of English, something which would act as an obstacle to fluency of expression in that tongue. He had not come across any parent who desired that Welsh should be taught in the schools and, especially in view of the sparseness of Welsh literature, which in reality consisted of nothing but 'very feeble poetry', any attempt to do so would be a waste of valuable teaching time. Despite an intervention on the part of Henry Richard, a member of the Commission, who reminded his constituent that there were in existence fifteen Welsh-language newspapers, twenty-four Welsh periodicals, four Welsh quarterlies as well as numerous books, Lewis maintained that these were merely imitations and translations of English works:

> these writings are not the productions of Welsh thought, but English thought, served up in the Welsh language, and therefore they cannot be regarded as native literature.[77]

Lewis declared that the Welsh language merely reinforced provincial attitudes in Wales and that it was an obstacle to integration with England. While he did not wish death on the language, he believed it had no practical use. His argument was supported by other prominent churchmen such as the Revd Thomas Briscoe, incumbent of Holyhead and chancellor of Bangor cathedral, who claimed that Welsh was a 'useless acquirement' and that the bilingual difficulty did not exist in reality.[78] Canon M. J. Bevan, in a letter to the Education Department, made a similar point. He disputed the statistical accuracy of the numbers of Welsh-speakers, claiming that categories such

[76] PP 1887, XXX.
[77] Ibid.
[78] Ibid.

as 'habitually speak Welsh' had been deliberately misunderstood and accorded a wide meaning in order to support the nationalist argument on the language question.[79]

Many figures among the Anglican clergy and the landed gentry took a more positive attitude towards Welsh in the late nineteenth century. Yet the fact remains that those who did adopt this approach were a minority. As a group, the Anglican and landowning elements continued to reflect the views of those who emphasized the importance of acquiring a knowledge of English at the expense of Welsh. Many Nonconformist leaders failed to emphasize the desirability of strengthening the position of Welsh, creating a situation whereby none of those groups responsible for the administration of education in Wales was wholeheartedly committed to the survival of the language.

As a result, only tentative steps were taken to strengthen the position of Welsh in education. The measures that were recommended occurred mainly as a result of the recommendations of the Cross Commission, which included a consideration of the language as part of a broader inquiry into the operations of the 1870 Education Act. The Commission, which included Henry Richard among its members, became a focus for the debate concerning the Welsh language in education. The Welsh Language Society was determined to use the opportunity to press the case for the language, with Beriah Gwynfe Evans, Dan Isaac Davies, Dr Isambard Owen, Archdeacon John Griffiths and Thomas Marchant Williams presenting evidence. Beriah Evans mentioned his experience as a pupil teacher at Beaufort (Monmouthshire) and as master of British and later Board schools in the Llangadog (Carmarthenshire) area. He contended that the aims of the society were to ensure a more effective education system for Wales and denied that it was motivated by any subversive political objectives. Employing statistics, he argued that the Welsh language remained the language of everyday communication in the majority of Welsh rural districts, with the exception of the marcher districts and south Pembrokeshire, while in the industrial areas of south Wales 55 per cent of children spoke Welsh at home, notably in the Rhondda,

[79] PRO, ED 92 /8 file on the introduction of the Welsh language in the elementary schools of Wales, 23 April 1885 (letter from Bevan).

Swansea and Merthyr districts, even Cardiff having a significant Welsh-speaking population. The ease with which immigrants to the coalfield were assimilated into the Welsh-speaking community was also noted. The Dyers, Grays, Hayters, Wrights, Irvings, Murrays, Hicks and so on were soon integrated, so much so that as a rule their children increasingly chose to speak Welsh in preference to English. In the opinion of Beriah Evans, it was disgraceful that the wealth of literary works available in Welsh was ignored and not studied either in the elementary schools or in any other educational establishment in the principality, especially when it was considered that the majority of the population of Wales conducted their cultural and religious life through the medium of Welsh.[80]

For his part, Dan Isaac Davies noted that, while the people of Wales were determined that religious instruction should be the prerogative of the Sunday schools, there was considerable resentment that the latter should be burdened with the teaching of Welsh as well. Indeed, so much of the time of the Sunday schools was taken up with the teaching of grammatical Welsh that Biblical knowledge was in danger of decline. He cited the fact that, while concessions were made to Gaelic in Scotland (including permitting a certain amount of literary studies through Gaelic) and even greater concessions made to Irish in Ireland, there were no such provisions for the Welsh language. He supported the argument of Beriah Evans that English immigrants into Wales were becoming assimilated and, although admitting that the language was in decline in certain parishes, he asserted that these were rural areas which were experiencing a decline in population, while the Welshness of the expanding industrial parishes was being strengthened. Acknowledging that many working-class parents in Wales were of the view that English should be taught and Welsh disallowed in school, he reminded the committee that where workers were insisting on appointing their chosen company doctor, they invariably insisted on a Welsh-speaker, something which he predicted would be an increasingly common feature, with Welsh-speaking public officials being in great demand as well.[81]

[80] PP 1888, XXXVI, evidence of B. G. Evans.
[81] Ibid., evidence of D. I. Davies.

Isambard Owen stated that the Welsh language was the language of the majority of the population in a great number of areas and that in reality few inspectors were opposed to its use in the schools of Wales,[82] a point reiterated by Thomas Marchant Williams.[83] According to Archdeacon John Griffiths, the Welsh-medium Anglican services which he was attempting to introduce in the diocese of Llandaff were gaining considerable popularity. He pointed to the continent where it was commonplace for the working class to be proficient in two or more languages, and declared his support for the teaching of grammatical Welsh: 'if the language is to be taught at all then it should be taught intelligently'. Furthermore, he stated his conviction that Welsh would survive as a vibrant language unless it came under deliberate attack.[84]

The outcome of this pressure was a rare agreement between the majority and minority reports produced by the Cross Commission, both of which recommended an enhanced status for Welsh in education. Yet, despite the positive recommendations of the Commission, granting Welsh a role as a specific subject in the school curriculum, progress in implementing these recommendations was slow. In 1891 Welsh was adopted as an optional subject which could be taken by children in the upper standards of schools, with a further concession in 1892 whereby a more formal curriculum was introduced. This was to be divided into three stages, each of which would include formal grammar, translation from English to Welsh and from Welsh to English, and a piece of dictation. The learning of a Welsh verse and an item of composition in Welsh were also added in the later stages of the scheme. In 1893, Welsh received further recognition when it was adopted as a class subject, thus allowing its introduction in classes throughout the school. This was an important concession in so far as Welsh became a grant-earning subject and teaching Welsh was of remunerative benefit to the teacher. The provision that 'the instruction generally may be bilingual' meant that the language could be part of the daily life of the school, and subjects such as geography and history were to place greater emphasis on their Welsh dimensions. These measures gained general

[82] Ibid., evidence of Isambard Owen.
[83] Ibid., evidence of T. M. Williams.
[84] Ibid., evidence of the Revd John Griffiths.

approval in Liberal Wales. D. P. Williams, of Llanberis School Board, welcomed the proposals as a means of ensuring that children had an understanding of both languages,[85] and the *Carnarvon and Denbigh Herald* commented:

> It is, of course, gratifying to learn that Mr Acland approves of a common-sense method of utilising the Welsh language in elementary schools, so that children may acquire a real and not a mere parrot-like knowledge of English. What is not so satisfactory is that the country is left in ignorance as to whether this approbation of the principle is anything more than a mere 'pious opinion'. Is Wales to have a special Code; Or are her needs to be met with a few trumpery foot-notes and marginal references? Mr Acland entertains enlightened views as to the training of teachers; but so far as we learn from his speech, he has not yet appreciated the fact that scarcely anything has been done to train the elementary teachers of Wales to utilise the language and to impart a knowledge of the history of the Principality.[86]

Clearly, there was much still to be done, but one remarkable feature of the reaction within the Liberal and Nonconformist journals is the unanimity with which they welcomed the proposals of the Cross Commission. While many of those who welcomed the development failed to safeguard the language in their own homes, it is nevertheless revealing that the majority did feel obliged to make public declarations that reflected the ethos of the national reawakening witnessed at the time.[87] In many ways this was a cultural reflection of the political change which had affected Welsh Liberalism by the same period. The concept of integration in a wider British state had been a major influence on the generation of Liberal leaders who were prominent in the debate over elementary education in 1870. By the late 1880s, however, Liberal leaders increasingly emphasized the need for policies to address the specific aspirations and needs of Wales.

The opinions of the policy-makers inevitably affected the views of teachers and parents. Yet it is also the case that neither group was a passive force and the inclination of many parents to support the Anglicizing efforts of the schools hampered efforts to

---

[85] *CDH*, 28 April 1893.
[86] *CDH*, 18 November 1992. For Acland, below n. 104.
[87] *Y Goleuad*, 22 May 1890.

elevate the status of Welsh in education. The importance of parental support was acknowledged by both sides in this debate and both claimed to have the sympathy of the parents. The reports of the inspectors during the earlier period indicate that parents were anxious for their children to learn English, a sentiment that was particularly strong among monoglot Welsh-speakers.[88] Shadrach Pryce regularly reminded the Education Department that parents in his district shared his hostility to the introduction of Welsh,[89] a point that was also made by HMI J. Bancroft, who noted little enthusiasm among the parents or teachers of north Pembrokeshire for the introduction of Welsh.[90] In his opinion, the prevailing wisdom was that parents felt capable of teaching Welsh to their children and preferred that the school should concentrate on those subjects which they were not able to teach themselves.[91] The evidence offered by Pryce has to be considered in the light of his avowed distaste for the Welsh language. Bancroft, however, was more sympathetic to the language and he had supported those teachers who used Welsh as a means of teaching English. The key feature is the change that Bancroft noted in the late 1890s, when a definite increase occurred in the number of schools that had introduced Welsh, a development that had considerable support among parents.

Parental acquiescence in the introduction of Welsh was also reflected in the results of the referenda in Bedwellty and Mynyddislwyn in Monmouthshire. In the latter cases, support for Welsh can to some degree be linked to the backlash against extraneous ethnic groups which were blamed for increases in crime, drunkenness and fornication, most notably the Irish community.[92] The prevalence of this large community of English speakers had also resulted in the south-east becoming a bilingual community at a much earlier period than areas further west.

[88] PP 1883, XXV, Mr Pryce's Report.
[89] Ibid.
[90] PP 1889, XXIX, Mr Bancroft's Report; the opposite impression was, however, gleaned by natives of the area such as T. E. Nicholas (D. W. Howell, *T. E. Nicholas: People's Champion* (Swansea, 1991), pp.6–7).
[91] PP 1889, XXIX, Mr Bancroft's Report.
[92] S. R. Williams, *Oes y Byd i'r Iaith Gymraeg* (Cardiff, 1992), especially chs. 1 and 2. The anti-Irish prejudices prevalent in certain communities have also been considered in detail in P. B. O'Leary, 'Immigration and integration: a study of the Irish in Wales, 1799–1922' (Ph.D. thesis, University of Wales, 1990).

Consequently, the parents of the south-east were not fearful that the introduction of Welsh in the schools would prevent their children from learning English, a fear which was present to a considerable extent in areas further west. Thus, a combination of hostility to immigrant communities, a fear that the Welsh language would be submerged by the strength of English, and the absence of an obsessive fear that children would remain monoglot Welsh-speakers, could result in a more sympathetic attitude towards the language among parents in the most Anglicized areas of Wales. Correspondingly, a less positive outlook was manifested in more thoroughly Welsh-speaking districts. In those areas, the Welsh language was often associated with the working-class community, while those who aspired to an elevated social position habitually sought to emulate the English of the gentry and, increasingly, of the professional class in Wales. This consolidated the image of Welsh as a language associated with the lower classes, a factor which contributed to its decline.

Throughout this debate it was the teaching profession that was faced with responsibility for reconciling an education system that assumed that proficiency in English was the test of success with a community that had its own language. Accepting that the medium of instruction was English, many teachers were faced with the enormous task of attempting to teach children who understood little of what was being said. This problem, in turn, exacerbated the already great difficulties they encountered in securing a good attendance on account of the alien nature of the school in so many communities. In many ways the position of the Welsh language in the schools of Wales depended on the attitudes of the teachers themselves. HMI Watts, himself no enemy of the introduction of the Welsh language, felt obliged to remind the teachers of his district that English had to be the main language of instruction in school. The Welsh language received sympathetic treatment from teachers such as David Thomas, who considered that any system which punished children for speaking Welsh was 'grotesque' and who declared his sympathy for the development of a separate school curriculum for Wales. So farcical was the situation, he insisted, that pupils were being punished for speaking Welsh in school, while the letter explaining the reasons for the punishment was written in Welsh for the benefit of monoglot Welsh-speaking parents.[93] Tom Elias, headmaster of Rhydlewis School (Cardiganshire), claimed that it was the language which gave the children of Wales their distinctive sense of identity:

> A nation, when it loses its language, is cut off from its past. To a Welshman, it is in the Welsh language that are incorporated national traditions; to him it joins the present to the distant past, and conserves the history of the nation and its thought. It is, in a way, a part of his own life.

But educational reasons were also cited by Elias in his justification of the introduction of Welsh to the classroom. Speaking of the average Welsh boy, he said:

> When he comes to school first he is generally shy and diffident; he has not mixed with strangers, and lacks self-assurance; he is wholly monolingual. English words and phrases convey nothing to him; and for the first year or two the medium of instruction is Welsh alone, it being the only way through which his mind can be reached.[94]

The National Union of Elementary Teachers (NUET) gave considerable attention to the language issue throughout the period, issuing regular entreaties to the Education Department that the standards imposed by the inspectorate in examining Welsh schools should be less exacting in view of the prevalence of the Welsh language.[95] The efforts to promote its use as a means of improving standards in Welsh schools did, however, gain the support of a significant section of the teaching profession. Elements in the NUET demonstrated a sympathetic attitude. Robert Wild, an officer of the union and himself an Englishman, emerged as one of the most effective campaigners on behalf of the introduction of Welsh,[96] and the views which he promoted were reflected in declarations such as that issued by the Llandybïe and Llandeilo Branch of the union which in 1884 called for the use of Welsh to be allowed in order to assist the teacher, a resolution that was determinedly argued by the branch

---

[93] D. Thomas, 'Reminiscences of a school inspector', in W. Ll. Davies (ed.), *National Union of Teachers Souvenir of the Aberystwyth Conference 1933* (Aberystwyth, 1933), p.146.
[94] T. Elias, 'The difficulties of rural schools in Wales', *NUET Conference Handbook* (1933), pp.136–7.
[95] *Schoolmaster*, 28 December 1872 and 18 January 1873.
[96] NLW, T. E. Ellis Papers, 1151.

chairman, Beriah Gwynfe Evans, and its secretary, Frederick Smith.[97]

The favourable approach indicated by these teachers did not reflect a universal attitude on the part of teachers on the issue. David Thomas complained that Welsh was excluded from the schools where he taught in Carmarthenshire,[98] William George testified that no Welsh was heard at the school in Llanystumdwy,[99] and similar experiences were recorded of schools in the heart of the Welsh-speaking areas of Caernarfonshire, where the pupils were said to have been astounded to learn, only upon his retirement from the school, that the schoolmaster was a fluent Welsh speaker.[100] The teachers of the Lampeter and Aberaeron area strongly objected to any attempt to introduce Welsh in the classrooms of Wales. A meeting held in October 1885 called for a movement to counteract the activities of the Welsh Language Society, claiming that the parents were overwhelmingly in favour of excluding Welsh and stating that the direct method was the most appropriate way of learning English.[101] According to the Revd Daniel Lewis of Merthyr, these differing attitudes were the result of the political pressures exerted on the teachers of Wales. In his opinion, support for the introduction of Welsh shown by those teachers who were in the employment of the Merthyr Board was a result of the pro-Welsh views of its members, for the teachers in the National school, who were 'free' to express their real opinions, declared their opposition to such a policy.[102]

A survey of the attitudes of teachers conducted by the Honourable Society of Cymmrodorion in 1885 posed the question 'Do you consider that advantage would result from the introduction of the Welsh language as a specific subject into the course of elementary education in Wales'; a total of 628 replies showed 339 in favour, 257 against and 32 uncommitted.[103] These figures clearly demonstrate that, while a small majority of

[97] *LLG*, 30 October 1884.
[98] Thomas, 'Reminiscences of a school inspector', p.146.
[99] George, *My Brother and I*, p.40.
[100] I. B. Griffith, *Atgofion* (Denbigh, 1972).
[101] Lampeter and Aberaeron NUET Branch to B. G. Evans, Evans Papers, Cardiff Central Library.
[102] PP 1887, XXX, minutes of the evidence of the Revd Daniel Lewis.
[103] Ibid., Appendix of written evidence from the Society for the Utilisation of the Welsh Language.

teachers did consider that benefit would flow from the introduction of Welsh, there remained a significant portion who remained hostile to such a proposition, an attitude which gains significance when it is considered that the introduction of the Welsh language into the schools was left much to the discretion of the teachers themselves. For the majority of teachers, however, the introduction of a few hours of Welsh in each week in the form of an optional subject was considered sufficient instruction in the language.

Inevitably teachers were placed in an invidious position, regularly subjected to pressures from both sides of the debate. The demands of school inspectors, official guidelines, school managers and parents meant that teachers were loath to commit themselves to either side. Moreover, the difficulty of teaching large numbers of children, often compounded by problems relating to school attendance and lack of parental support, meant that Welsh was regarded as yet another unwanted encumbrance. The views of the teachers had to take account of the fact that, at least until the early 1890s, they operated in a climate where much depended on an annual examination that was primarily concerned with proficiency in English. For teachers who laboured under difficult conditions, the most important aim was to ensure that children satisfied the examiners. In such circumstances they could not afford to become preoccupied with the underlying effect of the education system on the Welsh language.

At no point did the policy of the Education Department deliberately seek to eradicate the Welsh language from the schools of Wales; indeed, both William Hart-Dyke and Arthur Acland were ready to make important concessions to the language.[104] This was especially so in the case of Acland, who argued for the introduction of Welsh for its own sake and not simply as a means of teaching English. As Gareth Elwyn Jones

---

[104] William Hart-Dyke (1837–1931) was the Conservative vice-president of the Committee of Council on Education from 1887 to 1892. Arthur Herbert Acland (1847–1926) served in the same post from 1892 to 1895. During their stewardship radical reforms were undertaken on matters that were not obviously contentious in political and religious terms, such as the school curriculum, the terms and conditions under which teachers worked and regulations governing the relationship between HMI and the profession.

has demonstrated, too much of the blame for the decline of the Welsh language has been placed on the 'enemy without', the external agencies such as the Education Department.[105] The evidence points to a considerate approach on the part of the Department on the issue of the Welsh language, with official policy depending very much on the submissions which were made by the Welsh representatives themselves. Welsh never sustained a deliberate attack from official agencies to the extent witnessed by other minority languages in Europe, notably Gascon and Breton in France,[106] or the experiences of the Sami and Finnish languages under Norwegian rule.[107] Yet neither was there a great commitment to the Welsh language, on the part of either official agencies or the political leadership in Wales itself. It is important to note that the concessions that were made to the Welsh language occurred nearly twenty years after the passing of the 1870 Act, by which time the outlook of Shadrach Pryce had become entrenched in the minds of many teachers, parents and policy makers. Thus it was that even in those areas of south-east Wales, where School Boards did seek to teach Welsh, the experience of pupils such as Thomas Jones was that of a school that was conducted entirely through the medium of English.[108] As Hywel Teifi Edwards has stated, no political leader in Wales at the time was prepared to make the Welsh language a 'resignation issue'. In his opinion, even the leaders of the Welsh Language Society were too ready to compromise and their goals were too limited.[109] In some ways this indifference can be attributed to the decline of the Welsh language which was not statistically recorded before 1891 and this may account for the lack of urgency in relation to the language. The Welsh language never assumed the immediacy of issues such as the tithes, disestablishment and the land question, and although the new generation of Liberal leaders was more aware of the issue, no political leader made it a central feature of his political testament

---

[105] G. E. Jones, 'What are schools in Wales for? Wales and the Education Reform Act', *Contemporary Wales*, II (1988), 83–97.
[106] V. Rogers, 'Brittany', in M. Watson (ed.), *Contemporary Minority Nationalism* (London, 1990), pp.67–84.
[107] K. Eriksen in J. Tomiak et al. (ed.), *Schooling, Educational Policy and Ethnic Identity: Comparative Studies on Non-dominant Ethnic Groups* (New York, 1991).
[108] Jones, *Rhymney Memories*, p.52.
[109] Edwards, 'Y Gymraeg yn y bedwaredd ganrif ar bymtheg', 144–6.

during the period under consideration here. This attitude, which made the issue of the language a secondary consideration, prevailed until the alarming figures of the census of 1921 created a new sense of urgency. Undoubtedly, the issue was complicated by the fact that a significant group of Liberal and Nonconformist leaders were committed only to the utilization of Welsh rather than to the development of an education system that would nurture and cherish the language. The debate on the place of Welsh in education provision in elementary schools illustrates broader sensibilities in Welsh society, where indifference rather than outright hostility characterized the approach of the majority of the population to the question of the language. Welsh-speaking communities remained aware that acquiring English was the most important goal for their children, and the prevalence of this view ensured that, in the period considered in this study, the Welsh language never gained an assured place in the system which catered for the basic needs of Welsh society.

VII

'I CAN LEARN HIM BETTER MYSELF AT HOME'

The Education Act of 1870 ensured that each child had access to a place at a school. It did not stipulate that children would be required to attend the schools. Even though attendance came to be required, initially by the resolution of school authorities in the localities and then by legislation, absences from school remained a problem throughout the period considered in this study. In the case of numerous children, education formed no part of their experience as they failed to take advantage of the school places made available to them. Among many more, attendance at school was irregular, and these absences were due to more than truancy on the part of the children themselves. For the master who bore responsibility for the school, in rural and industrial society alike, a scrupulous attentiveness to the accuracy of the school register was an essential part of the daily routine and any oversight on his part was likely to incur the censure of those to whom he was responsible. The master's problems extended far beyond the accuracy of the record, however. This chapter will examine the problems faced by masters and authorities alike in establishing a practice whereby a full and regular attendance might be secured in the schools of Wales.

The attendance figures for 1877 offer a good indicator of the level of school attendance. By then the arguments that had initially surrounded the establishment of School Boards, and those concerning related issues such as the location of schools, had abated in most areas. Whichever agency was responsible for fulfilling the educational need of the locality had had ample opportunity to do so, and facilities were by then available for the overwhelming majority of Welsh children. Furthermore, the community had been subjected to continuous efforts to impress upon it the value of school attendance, either through the efforts of the local School Board or, from 1876, through the School Attendance Committees that had been established by the Poor Law Guardians in those areas that did not have a School Board.[1]

---

[1] Gillian Sutherland, *Policy Making in English Education* (London, 1973), pp.87–90, 125–44.

Yet despite these efforts, average attendance remained poor. Anglesey secured an average attendance of 53.5 per cent, Breconshire 57.5 per cent, Caernarfonshire 56.8 per cent, Cardiganshire 53.7 per cent, Carmarthenshire 67.2 per cent, Denbighshire 68.5 per cent, Flintshire 55.8 per cent, Glamorgan 65.2 per cent, Merioneth 63.3 per cent, Monmouthshire 57.8 per cent, Montgomeryshire 63.7 per cent, Pembrokeshire 53.8 per cent and Radnorshire 45.8 per cent. Attendance figures were slightly higher for Board schools, yet even those figures did not indicate an overwhelming thirst for schooling. Anglesey Board schools attracted an average attendance of 55.6 per cent of the children, Breconshire 72.6 per cent, Caernarfonshire 57.5 per cent, Cardiganshire 54.1 per cent, Carmarthenshire 77.6 per cent, Denbighshire 56.2 per cent, Flintshire 90.7 per cent, Glamorgan 55.6 per cent, Merioneth 58.4 per cent, Monmouthshire 59.5 per cent, Montgomeryshire 87.2 per cent, Pembrokeshire 52.5 per cent and Radnorshire 46 per cent. Although there were a number of Church and National schools that did secure a good attendance, notably in Denbighshire which achieved an attendance of 83.6 per cent, the figure was as low as 45.5 per cent in Radnorshire. The British schools found it equally difficult to secure attendance, although some notable successes were scored in Cardiganshire (71 per cent), Glamorgan (74.5 per cent) and Merioneth (76.6 per cent).

A significant improvement in average attendance was discernible by 1900. Attendance had increased to 71.8 per cent in Anglesey, 75.8 per cent in Breconshire, 75.3 per cent in Caernarfonshire, 75.5 per cent in Cardiganshire, 78 per cent in Carmarthenshire, 73.8 per cent in Denbighshire, 76.7 per cent in Flintshire, 78.9 per cent in Glamorgan, 77.1 per cent in Merioneth, 77.1 per cent in Monmouthshire, 77.0 per cent in Montgomeryshire, 73.9 per cent in Pembrokeshire, and 78.0 per cent in Radnorshire. In a further important development there was now less difference between the levels of attendance secured in the voluntary schools and those in the Board schools. For instance, the voluntary schools of Anglesey succeeded in attracting 70.3 per cent of children, Breconshire 75.8 per cent, Caernarfonshire 73.3 per cent, Cardiganshire 75.7 per cent, Carmarthenshire 75.8 per cent, Denbighshire 74.5 per cent, Flintshire 77.3 per cent, Glamorgan 78.8 per cent, Merioneth

74.1 per cent, Monmouthshire 76.7 per cent, Montgomery 76.7 per cent, Pembrokeshire 75.8 per cent and Radnorshire 79.3 per cent. The following discussion examines the gradual increase in average attendance in Wales and considers why, even in 1900, almost a quarter of Welsh children were absent from school at any given time. It examines the factors that occasioned poor attendance and considers the accuracy of the notion of a nation eager to embrace educational opportunities in the light of the apathy, if not hostility, to education, which was demonstrated by a significant number of people in Wales.

The process of securing school attendance was initially hampered because the 1870 Act was silent on the issue. Although William Forster intended that attendance should be made compulsory, he did not include this intention in the Act, not least for fear of arousing the hostility of the Conservative opposition.[2] The 1870 Act did make provisions that enabled School Boards to draw up local by-laws to compel attendance at their own schools, but this was a formula soon found to be inadequate, on account of the reluctance of several Boards to propose such unpopular local legislation and the fact that School Boards did not exist in many areas of the country. The unhappy state of affairs created by the omission of compulsory attendance from the legislative provision led the Conservative government, elected in 1874, to enact the Sandon Act in 1876. This compelled the Poor Law Unions to establish School Attendance Committees to oversee attendance in those parishes where no School Board existed, and these were granted the same powers as the School Boards to implement local by-laws to this effect. The Sandon Act also stipulated for the first time that it was the duty of each parent to ensure that their children received some elementary education, although there remained a reluctance to insist that this education had to be gained at a recognized and efficient school. Establishing parental responsibility was a clear departure from the view that legislation on education should be enabling rather than compelling in nature and, despite the objections of the more extreme libertarians, the change was greeted with a considerable measure of support. The proposal to make school attendance in areas not administered by School Boards the responsibility of the

---

[2] M. Sturt, *The Education of the People* (London, 1967), p.305.

Poor Law Unions was more controversial. It was criticized on the grounds that it perpetuated the dual system of voluntary and Board schools, that it was a dogmatic policy aimed at avoiding the creation of School Boards in every parish, and that it was a policy which was likely to create the impression of a connection between schools and the Poor Law by linking school attendance to the Boards of Guardians.[3] Despite these criticisms of the legislation, the amendment introduced by A. J. Mundella in 1880 retained the existing administrative system while amending the Acts so as to compel School Boards and School Attendance Committees to establish by-laws to ensure that every child in the country received an education up to the age of ten. In addition, those clauses in the Factory Acts which allowed the employment of children, and which had been used in attempts to circumvent the Sandon Act, were to be superseded by the provisions of this Act. It did not, however, make any provision for free education, which was not brought about until 1891, although the Guardians were able to pay the fees of pauper children.[4]

Each item of legislation concerning compulsory attendance received close scrutiny in Wales. On the one hand, the policy was in tune with the Nonconformist emphasis on the virtue of education. Equally, however, it was examined closely because of the delicate issues that were raised by any proposal to compel Nonconformist children to attend the schools of the Anglican Church. Henry Richard and the leaders of Welsh Nonconformity had made compulsory attendance under a system of universal School Boards a central feature of their proposals in 1870, yet their arguments had been rejected by Forster, who remained convinced that the best means of ensuring a good attendance at the schools was to persuade the parents of the benefits of education. Rejection of the need to establish legal compulsion was reflected in the official view, as reflected in the thoughts of the Revd Shadrach Pryce in his report for 1871. Pryce predicted that Welsh parents would be persuaded of the

[3] Ibid., p.344.
[4] Ibid.; Sutherland, *Policy Making in English Education*, pp.163–9, 322–7; W. G. Evans, 'Addysg rydd neu ailwaddoli'r hen "Estrones", Cymru a Deddf Addysg 1891', *Y Traethodydd*, 147 (1992), 12–19; idem., 'Free education and the quest for popular control, unsectarianism and efficiency: Wales and the Free Elementary Education Act, 1881', *THSC*, 1991, pp.203–32; idem, 'T. E. Ellis, M.P., and the Free Elementary Education Act, 1891', *Journal of the Merioneth Historical and Record Society*, XI (1990–3), 446–58.

value of schooling as they had been of the value of the Sunday school, and he had great confidence in the sufficiency of local by-laws.[5] HMI William Williams, writing in the same year, was less confident. In his opinion no sense of 'moral mission' would be sufficient to attract children to school and he advocated a legal framework to compel attendance because he feared that the most neglected children would never benefit from the education system.[6] His scepticism about the propensity of Welsh parents to send their children to school is justified, not only by the attendance figures but also by the evidence of the log books of individual schools. The log book of Trap School for the 1860s, a school which fell within the district that was inspected by Shadrach Pryce, indicates a fluctuating rate of attendance. The normal difficulties in securing attendance caused by adverse weather and illness were compounded by other factors. Thus, the master of the school, Evan Harry, noted circumstances such as the annual procession of the Ivorites Club, quarterly meetings of religious bodies, the *cymanfa ganu* (singing festivals held in Nonconformist chapels), sales of stock, the local eisteddfod and the need for child labour on farms and in the local woollen factory to explain his failure to secure a better attendance.[7] Distractions such as these, with their daunting effect on the conduct of the school, would be noted with assiduous care and despairing concern in the log books of countless masters in the years following the legislation of 1870.

Appreciating the prevalence of such practices, the Nonconformist press saw a need to mount a vigorous campaign to convince Welsh parents of the benefits of education. *Y Goleuad* declared:

> Y mae gan rieni plant i gofio nad oes gobaith i'w plant allu gweithio eu ffordd ymlaen yn y byd i gael sefyllfa weddol anrhydeddus ymysg eu cyfoedion . . . heb iddynt roi heibio y syniad y gwna ychydig o addysg y tro. Profiad y rhai sydd a wnelont â dwyn ymlaen ysgolion dyddiol y Dywysogaeth yw mai pell yw y rhieni yn gyffredinol o gredu y mawr bwys i'r plant gael bod yn gyson dan addysg eu hathraw.

---

[5] PP 1871, XXII, Mr Pryce's Report.
[6] PP 1871, XXII, Mr Williams's Report.
[7] Carmarthenshire CRO, log book of Trap School, C/Ed 571.

[The parents of Wales should remember that there is no hope of their children getting on in the world so as to secure a comparatively honourable position amongst their peers . . . unless they forget the idea that a little education will be sufficient. The experience of those who are responsible for the day schools of the Principality is that parents in general are reluctant to believe that it is important for children to be regularly under the instruction of their teacher.][8]

These views were reinforced by the experience of administering the attendance by-laws in the period preceding the Sandon Act, and by the reluctance of some School Attendance Committees and School Boards to use their powers to make attendance by-laws in the period from 1876 to 1880. Nevertheless, although there was a widespread consensus in favour of the provisions of the 1880 Act, religious factors continued to create obstacles in generating a consensus in support of school attendance legislation. An editorial in *Y Goleuad* attacked the proposals of 1880 as being unfair to Nonconformists because they compelled attendance in schools which taught religious principles with which the parents disagreed, a situation denounced by the paper as morally indefensible. Its own answer lay in the creation of a system of School Boards that would be responsible for education in every parish and in the ending of the voluntary principle in education. The paper was also concerned with the provision to enable the Boards of Guardians to remit the fees of those unable to pay, because it reduced non-fee-payers to the humiliating level of paupers and at the same time, it created a situation whereby denominational schools could be receiving money from the local rates,[9] a portent of the outcry which accompanied the legislation of 1902.

The administrative and political deterrents to good attendance contributed to a problem that had deeper roots in the fabric of Welsh society. Nowhere was this more apparent than in the rural areas where, as was noted above, rates of attendance tended to be lowest. Attendance in those areas that relied on upland sheep farming was hampered by the fact that a significant proportion of the population lived in remote settlements, usually a

---

[8] *Y Goleuad*, 12 January 1878.
[9] *Y Goleuad*, 26 March 1871.

considerable distance from the nearest school. The condition of the roads provided a further obstacle to good attendance, as well as contributing to the difficulties faced by attendance officers in undertaking the task of visiting non-attenders. The school inspectorate was aware of these problems. In 1871 HMI the Revd E. T. Watts reported that in several areas of Caernarfonshire and Anglesey the distance travelled by some children was such that their parents were obliged to find lodgings for them in close proximity to the school, and meet the costs thereby incurred, a situation which he felt was even more unacceptable because of the children's young age.[10] Even as late as 1894, when communications had improved considerably, cases of non-attendance were reported that clearly arose from the lack of communications in rural areas. For instance, five children from the rural hinterland of Holyhead were reported never to have attended a school, not from indifference but because no school existed within six miles of the home.[11] The geographical and demographic problems were not confined to the rural areas, however. HMI Monro complained in 1887 that, on account of the rapid industrialization of south Wales, a massive influx of children had taken place, with the result that a large proportion of the child population was not known to the local authorities. This gave rise to large-scale truancy.[12]

School buildings were a further obstacle in the way of securing good levels of attendance. Malcolm Seabourne has demonstrated that there were considerable improvements effected in the design and fabric of school buildings during the period from 1870 to 1902, mainly owing to the insistence by the Education Department on improved standards of construction, heating and ventilation.[13] Yet in many instances the problem of damp, cold and pest-infected schools remained. This was especially so in the voluntary schools, none of which received any assistance from the rates. Also relevant was the reluctance of several Boards, most notably those in the rural areas, to authorize expenditure on heating and other measures that would contribute to the comfort of a school, except in the most dire weather conditions.

[10] PP 1871, XXII, Mr Watts's Report.
[11] *CDH*, 10 November 1893.
[12] PP 1887, XXVIII, Mr Monro's Report.
[13] M. Seabourne, *Schools in Wales, 1800–1900* (Denbigh, 1992), pp.174–7.

These factors compounded the geographical problems, and it is certainly the case that the uncomfortable condition of many schools acted not only as a disincentive to good attendance but also as a contributory factor in the spread of illness and disease, again with an adverse effect on attendance figures.

A further distressing reason for the absence of children from schools was genuine poverty. In Caernarfon, for instance, it was claimed that some children were so badly clothed that they could not be allowed into the school building for fear of contamination, while a number of parents would not allow their children to venture from home because of their shameful clothes.[14] Other cases of poverty affecting attendance were noted in areas such as Bedwellty, where in 1887 the School Board was compelled to suspend its efforts to enforce school attendance because of the acute depression in trade in the locality. Significantly, this reason was accepted by the inspectorate as sufficient explanation for the Board's decision, an unusual example of compassion shown by men who were noted for their rigid attitude on the question of attendance.[15]

Allied to the problem of poverty was the fact that economic pressures meant that many children had no alternative but to seek employment, often illegally. Again, this problem was most pronounced in the rural areas, where the requirements of the agricultural calendar, together with the farmers' inability to afford hired labour, meant that children's help at certain times in the year was often indispensable. Seasonal work, which was particularly available in rural and coastal areas, had a serious effect on school attendance at various times of the year. Crow-scaring, harvesting, potato planting and barking were forms of work normally undertaken by children which had serious effects on school attendance.[16] The practice influenced the policy of the education authorities, such as the Holywell School Board, which resolved to close its schools during the autumn of 1877 rather than make a futile attempt to entice children to school during the harvest period.[17] Other Boards faced more prolonged periods of habitual absence. In 1894, Tywyn and Pennal School

[14] *CDH*, 11 January 1889.
[15] PP 1887, XXVIII, Mr Edwards's Report.
[16] Carmarthenshire CRO, log book of Trap School, C/Ed 571.
[17] Flintshire CRO, D/KK/975, papers of Holywell School Board, 13 September 1877.

Attendance Committee was prompted to instruct its attendance officer to be particularly watchful of the Aberdyfi golf links in the summer months as part of its concern about illegal employment.[18] Some children were reported to be required to undertake domestic tasks throughout the year in order to relieve adults for other duties. Illegal employment regularly vexed the school inspectorate. HMI the Revd Herbert Smith, in his report for 1873, complained that large numbers of boys were being illegally employed underground, as well as in the works and factories throughout the industrial areas of Wales.[19] Indeed, so prevalent was the practice of children of school age working in the iron industry that Merthyr Tydfil schools became overcrowded in 1875 when there was a strike in the locality.[20]

The Factory Acts allowed a certain amount of child employment, yet they often conflicted with local attendance by-laws and this led to protracted legal arguments as to whether the Factory Acts or the School Attendance by-laws had the greater authority. Conflicting rulings by different judges on the matter did little to clarify the position, and the issue only became clear with the statutory powers embodied in the Sandon Act of 1876. Even then, School Boards remained empowered to issue exemptions according to their discretion, which would allow children to be excused from school to undertake certain essential tasks. These powers did not end the complaints of both teachers and school inspectors concerning the over-willingness of certain Boards and Attendance Committees to accommodate requests for exemption certificates; accusations were made that many local employers who sat as members of those authorities were themselves eager to employ cheap child labour.[21]

Issues such as demographic distribution, the inaccessibility of remote hamlets and the poverty of Welsh society in the nineteenth century were all factors that could be accepted as genuine impediments to attendance. Yet it is also the case that the very nature of Welsh society produced some avoidable obstacles to school attendance. The commitment of the Nonconformists to

---

[18] Gwynedd CRO, Dolgellau, Tywyn and Pennal School Attendance Committee Records, A/11/26, 1894.
[19] PP 1873, XXIV, Mr H. Smith's Report.
[20] *Merthyr Telegraph*, 20 February 1875.
[21] *Schoolmaster*, 27 June 1874; PP 1873, XXIV, Mr H. Smith's Report.

education was a noted feature of this period, yet their tradition of organizing Sunday school activities during the week became a matter of contention when the question of attendance was raised in School Boards and Attendance Committees throughout Wales. In 1897, for instance, the schoolmaster at Llanfynydd (Carmarthenshire) was faced with continual absences as a result of excursions and various other activities organized by local Nonconformists.[22] In common with the practice throughout Wales, these were arranged on school days, and the problem was exacerbated by the lack of an agreement among the organizers to hold their events on the same day, with the result that considerable problems arose in compelling attendance. The absence of a significant number of pupils meant that many teachers abandoned the day's lessons, to the detriment of those children who were present. Moreover, the children of more affluent parents regularly attended the annual outings of more than one chapel, registering an absence from school on each occasion. Other deterrents to attendance indicate that for a large group of children and, indeed, parents, schooling was a low priority. This is shown by the experience of the attendance officers in Llanelli who found that children would loyally insist on attending funerals in the town, irrespective of whether they knew the deceased or not.[23] Other distractions such as market days, the coming of a fair, club processions, tithe sale demonstrations and elections were also blamed by commentators throughout the land for the problems they faced. Significantly, truancy was not a problem confined to children from drunken and careless homes and many of the offspring of pious Nonconformists were among the most persistent offenders.

Difficulties such as these were inevitably going to arise in a period when a new ethos was being encouraged in a society in which children had not previously been required to attend a school. Yet the unavoidable problems created by the nature of the community were deepened by the shortcomings of parents, employers and official agencies. Indeed, both the School Boards and the School Attendance Committees were regularly criticized by the inspectorate and educational commentators for their

[22] Log book of Llanfynydd School (consulted at the school).
[23] *LLG*, 15 March 1888.

failure to manage an effective attendance policy, although the criticisms were more pronounced in the case of the School Attendance Committees. The difficulties facing the School Boards were aggravated by the knowledge that these Boards had been created amidst great acrimony and many of their leading members were anxious to avoid intensifying the unpopularity of the School Board system by insisting on a strict attendance policy. In addition, many Board members, most notably those representing the Anglican interest, were said to be at best lukewarm and at worst hostile to the introduction of compulsory attendance.

The agencies charged with enforcing school attendance must also share the blame for the alarming rate of truancy that affected most parts of Wales, especially in the early period. School Boards often allowed a variety of factors to prevent the implementation of a good attendance policy. The cost of enforcing attendance was undoubtedly high, and this was cited by numerous Boards to excuse their failure to operate a more effective policy. Boards, especially those in the rural areas, were notorious for their long and protracted deliberations about whether to institute legal proceedings against non-attenders.[24] In 1878 the Cardiff School Board admitted its failure, but its members remained reluctant to initiate legal proceedings against the parents of non-attenders.[25] In those areas where prosecutions were attempted, the results were often derisory. In 1880, out of twenty summonses issued in the parish of Aberystruth (Monmouthshire), only three resulted in penalties. In Llanishen (Glamorgan) in the same year, only one of ten parents summoned was fined, while in Penarth the figure stood at nine out of eighty-one summoned.[26]

Sectarian and denominational struggles invariably entered into the debate over compulsory attendance. In 1873 a dispute arose in Carmarthen between the vicar, the Revd Latimer Jones, and the Board, concerning the decision of the Board to remit only the fees of those paupers attending the town's Board schools, thus depriving the poor of the choice of attending the

---

[24] PP 1871, XXII, Mr Watts's Report.
[25] *Second Triennial Report of Cardiff School Board* (Cardiff, 1878).
[26] PP 1880, XXII, Mr Waddington's Report.

Anglican school.[27] These difficulties were compounded by the objections of Nonconformists to sending their children to Anglican schools, an issue that was raised continuously in the pages of the Nonconformist press.

The failures of the School Boards and Attendance Committees to secure an improvement in the attendance pattern generated considerable debate in educational circles in Wales. In 1891 the Education Department issued the Caernarfon Board with a threat of sequestration unless there was an immediate improvement in school attendance in the area.[28] This was despite a concerted effort by the *Carnarvon and Denbigh Herald* to draw attention to the 'truancy-loving urchins' who roamed the streets by day untroubled by the efforts of the Attendance Officer.[29] In the Llanelli area, the measures imposed by the Pembrey School Board to encourage attendance were said to be so feeble that the real work was done more through the influence of the sermons of local ministers of religion than through the efforts of the attendance officer,[30] while the Llanelli Board was threatened with sequestration over the poor state of attendance in the Gwendraeth Valley;[31] in areas such as Llanbadarn Fawr, in Cardiganshire,[32] or the Vale of Clwyd,[33] attendance at school was reported to be rarely in excess of 50 per cent.

The nature of the school attendance service contributed in no small measure to the difficulties faced in securing good attendance. School attendance officers regularly complained of their low remuneration and of the thankless and difficult task that they were expected to perform. The residents of Skewen complained that the refusal of the Neath School Attendance Committee to appoint more than one attendance officer to cover the entire Neath Rural District meant that the officer was unable to visit the town more than once a month.[34] Moreover, the committee refused to pay him travelling allowances which meant that he

[27] PRO, ED2/575.
[28] *CDH*, 6 February 1891.
[29] *CDH*, 11 October 1889 and 25 October 1889. The paper made strenuous efforts to persuade the Board of the merits of a ragged school, but the Board remained singularly unconvinced of the desirability of erecting such an establishment.
[30] *LLG*, 3 May 1883.
[31] PRO, ED16/378.
[32] E. G. Bowen, *A History of Llanbadarn Fawr* (Aberystwyth, 1979), pp.111–12.
[33] *Schoolmaster*, 10 November 1883.
[34] PP 1884–5, XXIII.

was forced to walk the entire area of the Neath and Dulais Valleys in search of truants, a situation that rendered his efforts wholly ineffective.[35] Another complaint was the tendency of some Boards to appoint part-time attendance officers, which was not conducive to an effective attendance policy. In Chancery (Cardigandhire), efforts to secure good attendance were said to have been hampered by a farm labourer who was appointed as attendance officer, because the refusal of his employer to release him to carry out those duties during the hours of daylight made his endeavours useless.[36] Furthermore, there is ample evidence that attendance officers were regularly ignored or treated with contempt and ridicule by the community. In Bangor, the efforts of the attendance officer to persuade the master of the National school to co-operate with his efforts led to his being assaulted by the master, Mr Gotts, and having to be admitted to hospital,[37] while in Pembrey the tribulations of the attendance officer were noted as being a source of considerable merriment to the villagers.[38] These problems with personnel were related to the nature of the individuals who were often appointed to these posts. For many School Boards the key criterion in the appointment of attendance officers was the expense which would be incurred, and accordingly they sought to ensure that the cheapest candidate be awarded the position, a complaint highlighted by each inspector in the reports for 1889.[39]

Matters were not helped, either, by the attitudes of the magistrates to the question of school attendance, and they must bear a considerable responsibility for the failure to execute the relevant by-laws. They were invariably men of social standing, usually Anglican and normally Conservative in politics, even in strongly Liberal areas. Many were undoubtedly lukewarm if not hostile to the provisions of the 1870 Education Act and, as was evidenced in the Nonconformist press, they often demonstrated a

---

[35] The Neath and Dulais valleys were served by the Neath Board of Guardians, which, under the 1876 Act, constituted the School Attendance Committee for those areas devoid of a School Board. The area was geographically large, but the real problem was the scattered nature of the villages and the mountainous terrain.
[36] PRO, ED2 /568.
[37] *CDH*, 13 December 1889.
[38] *LLG*, 2 April 1885.
[39] PP 1889, XXIX.

lack of enthusiasm for attempts to compel attendance at Board schools. HMI C. T. Whitmell, writing of the Cardiff district in 1887, advocated a radical reform of the magistracy, including the introduction of the elective principle: 'Not until magistrates are elected, and so made responsible to public opinion, do I expect any great general improvement.'[40] He complained of the 'culpable negligence' of the magistrates in enforcing attendance, comments that concurred with those of HMI R. J. Alexander and HMI Loftus Monro.[41]

The tardiness of magistrates in fulfilling their responsibilities was also evident in rural areas, where the bench was dominated by landowners who considered the provisions of the Forster legislation, and especially the subsequent amendments to compel attendance, as unwanted intrusions into the rural areas which were devised by legislators unfamiliar with the nature of the community and which threatened the social equilibrium. Thus, in October 1885 the members of the Llandeilo Fawr hunt took a day's hunting in the full knowledge that a local school would be forced to shut for the day because the boys would be engaged in coursing. More blatant examples of the attitudes of landowners were found in the courtrooms. The bench at Tywyn (Merioneth) petty sessions infuriated the Llanfihangel y Pennant School Board. A prosecution brought against two regular non-attenders was thrown out of court as a result of the failure of the monoglot Welsh-speaking attendance officer to complete the relevant documentation. In a protest to the education department, the Board claimed that W. R. M. Wynne was engaged in a deliberate attempt to undermine the work of the Board; at the same time, his insistence on an English-speaking attendance officer threatened to deprive the Board of a faithful and efficient officer.[42]

Cases which came before the bench demonstrated not only a politically motivated desire on the part of magistrates to undermine the work of School Boards, but also the influence of a paternalistic responsibility which many magistrates felt towards their communities. It was reflected in a reluctance to impose

[40] PP 1887, XXVIII, Mr Whitmell's Report.
[41] Ibid.
[42] PRO, ED2/616, 26 April 1888.

severe fines in cases of known poverty, although local knowledge that child labour was necessary to enable families to avoid serious hardship contributed to this lenient attitude. The nature of the law itself was not conducive to a universal policy of compulsory attendance. As the only element of compulsion was that School Boards and Attendance Committees were required to formulate School Attendance by-laws which had to be sanctioned by the Education Department, the system of operating by means of local resolution rather than through a unified national enactment created numerous anomalies. As a result, many magistrates managed to take advantage of local discretion to avoid imposing harsher penalties on habitual offenders. The Welsh press was inundated with examples of complaints of the leniency demonstrated by the magistrates towards non-attenders, most notably in Pembrokeshire,[43] Caernarfonshire[44] and Anglesey.[45] Considerable variations existed in the size of the fines levied by the magistrates, and, although members of some benches did show a willingness to impose fines on non-attenders, there remained much disparity in the degree to which payment was insisted on. In the Ruthin area the magistrates were accused of considering their duties complete when they had imposed the fines. They saw no reason why court officials should be burdened with the task of ensuring that those fines were paid, with the result that the work of fine collection was added to the duties of the attendance officers, many of whom faced even greater contempt in trying to collect the impositions.[46] There was a marked reluctance among magistrates to imprison even the most persistent offenders, leading to complaints such as those made by the Caernarfon attendance officer that the threat of imprisonment was no deterrent to many parents of the most habitual non-attenders.[47] As with Board members, political and commercial reasons were cited as influencing the decisions of magistrates, especially at election times. The school inspectorate was very much aware of the difficulties of persuading magistrates to adopt a more rigorous attitude on the attendance question. Yet, despite

[43] Ibid.
[44] Ibid.
[45] Ibid.
[46] *CDH*, 28 April 1893.
[47] *CDH*, 11 December 1891.

these promptings, the attitudes of the magistrates continued to be a cause for concern. Indeed, the situation was deemed so serious by 1881 that William Williams, exasperated by the attitudes of local magistrates, demanded that stipendiary magistrates should be appointed to consider all questions of school attendance.

The difficulties experienced by the attendance officers reflected popular defiance of their authority and the lack of support they received even from the Boards and attendance Committees which they served. The constabulary was expected to assist attendance officers in the execution of duties, especially in the collection of fines imposed by magistrates. Yet the constabulary was noted for its careful awareness of the demarcation lines between its own duties and those of the attendance officers. Complaints were made by attendance officers that the police merely reported sightings of truants and made no effort to apprehend them. There was little, if any, co-ordination of the activities of the two agencies, and consequently there was a marked failure on the part of the police to provide the attendance officers with the assistance which they required to carry out their duties successfully.[48] These difficulties, combined with the attitudes of the magistrates, resulted in an attendance officer service which was demoralized, ridiculed and sorely ineffective.

The fact that attendance officers were not drawn from among the most respected members of society clearly hampered their work. Significantly, however, members of the teaching profession itself were also on occasion accused of adding to the difficulties, especially in the rural communities of Wales. The problem of bad or indifferent teachers was cited by HMI Bancroft to account for the attendance problems in rural Pembrokeshire.[49] Undoubtedly, the rural areas suffered unduly from low attendance, not least because of their failure to attract better-qualified teaching staff as a result of the isolation that was felt by many rural teachers and the lower wages they were paid; such problems were compounded by the reputation of rural Boards for failing to support their employees. There are examples of teachers who were careless, drunk, idle and

---

[48] This concurs with the evidence offered by Biagini that many working-class parents resented the intrusion of the state in the relationship between the parent and the child (E. Biagini, *Liberty, Retrenchment and Reform* (Oxford, 1992), p.200).
[49] PP 1884–5, XXIII, Mr Bancroft's Report.

occasionally sadistic;[50] such traits inevitably contributed to the difficulty of persuading children to attend school. What was ultimately responsible for the endeavours of many teachers to overcome the problem of truancy was a realization on their part that poor attendance contributed to the difficulties that they faced in securing favourable examination results and, consequently, a larger government grant. The teachers at Llwynhendy (Carmarthenshire) complained bitterly of the detrimental effect that irregular attendance was having on the standards attained in their school and also on morale and discipline. Significantly, they voiced their misgivings at the lack of leadership and concern which was evident in the attitudes of the school managers and the School Board.[51] The inspectors conceded the point that truancy was affecting attainment in school. In 1875 they accused habitual absentees of being responsible for creating an increased workload for the teachers and also for deterring regular attenders from continuing to attend school, since the teachers were forced to repeat work for the benefit of those not in regular attendance. Discipline in schools was further hampered by the attendance of large numbers of children who had no desire to be present and whose parents were not convinced of the benefits of education.[52] Teachers were often overworked and the insistence of several Boards that the teachers act as attendance officers, in addition to their other duties, created an unbearable burden for many of them.[53] Nevertheless, despite the problems faced by the teaching staff in relation to school attendance, the chief inspector in his report for 1897 attributed much of the increase in attendance during that year to the efforts of the teaching profession rather than to any other agency.[54] The teaching staff, he acknowledged, were, with the exception of a small minority, a hard-working and committed group of individuals, characterized by a devotion to duty.

The endeavours of both teachers and attendance officers were also hampered by the indifference, if not hostility, of many parents. A large number of parents, particularly in the earlier

[50] See ch. 8.
[51] *LLG*, 2 April 1885.
[52] PP 1877, XXIX.
[53] PP 1897, XXVI.
[54] Ibid.

period, had themselves been deprived of an education and were often unconvinced of its benefits. Apart from the fact that parents were not well disposed towards schools, the poverty that plagued many Welsh homes, and the regular fluctuations in income which characterized the majority of Welsh households during the late nineteenth century, made the need to educate a child an unwelcome financial burden, and difficulties were made worse as large numbers of children were required to pay the school pence. Yet, lack of experience and financial difficulties were not the only reasons for the antipathy of parents. Many retained a principled objection to interference in the way in which they brought up their own children. This attitude partly reflected the lack of a tradition of education in a large section of the population of Wales and many parents believed that they themselves were the most appropriate persons to educate their own children. Not unnaturally, these inclinations were most prevalent in rural areas, and reflected the unchanging nature of many rural communities. Many of those who had toiled on the land in the time-honoured way of their ancestors had received their entire education from parents and relatives and saw no reason why they could not be entrusted with the education of their own children. There was, however, considerable change in the way in which education was regarded during the period under study. By the end of the century, the majority of parents had themselves received the benefits of an education provided at school. Of equal significance was that the rural economy was gradually changing, with a decline in the self-sufficient traditions of rural communities. Yet the problems were only partially alleviated. Within urban areas, the constant in-migration of people meant that the authorities faced a difficult task in maintaining an up-to-date register of children. At the same time, numerous localities contained individuals who had little respect for educational endeavour. As the Cardiff School Board complained in 1881:

> The great exceptions [from attendance] are those who are not prone to respect any law, however much it may be designed to benefit them. They are the profligate and reckless, who abound in every large community, especially seaports, and those in whom extreme poverty has deadened every sense of obligation or responsibility.[55]

[55] *Third Triennial Report of Cardiff School Board* (Cardiff, 1881).

The efforts to convince parents of their responsibilities and to entice children to school were not helped by the lingering libertarian sentiments that influenced the more extreme members of the Conservative Party in Wales. As late as 1891, Conservatives in Flintshire denounced the efforts of the education authorities as 'atrocious and abominable tyranny', accusing the 'School Board Neros' of relentless harassment of parents of non-attenders and bearing responsibility for the creation of a rising generation that was averse to any physical work.[56] Such views were not part of the platform on which mainstream Conservatives sought to appeal to the electorate, yet they did nothing to assist what was already an extremely difficult task of bringing Welsh children to school.

The pattern of school attendance reflects fundamental differences in Welsh society. As David Jenkins has illustrated, the attitudes of parents towards the education of their children were influenced to a considerable extent by their pattern of living.[57] A diversity of outlook was apparent in both rural and urban areas, and even the most picturesque and apparently peaceful country villages had a rougher element that could cause difficulties for education authorities and other respectable members of the community. For instance, a number of 'uncivilised ruffians' caused immense problems in Llanfynydd in the autumn of 1885, when it was reported that the peace was being shattered by

> Gangs of boys, intermixed with foolish men, who delight in concentrating in groups at night, and parading the roads until all hours of the morning, amusing themselves with singing immoral and offensive songs, and making use of the most obscene language . . . It is quite dangerous for many people, especially females, to pass the roads without being molested by these groups. It was only one night last week that many of the inhabitants were roused out of their beds by the frantic freaks of two or three men who were kicking the doors, and challenging the occupants to fight.[58]

Intermingled with such people were the adherents to the *Buchedd A* mode of living, more likely to be influenced by the Nonconformist view of education as a great opportunity for economic

---

[56] Flintshire CRO, DE 3062.
[57] These issues are discussed further in David Jenkins, *The Agricultural Community in South-West Wales at the Turn of the Twentieth Century* (Cardiff, 1971), pp.12–13, 39–72.
[58] *LLG*, 1 October 1885.

and social advancement. Their commitment to the education of their children, often at great personal cost, was impressive. Shadrach Pryce noted the love of learning which existed among the Welsh population in his report for 1875 and cited the willingness of farmers and labourers to walk with him on his journeys, in order to assist him with his work, as an illustration of this commitment. Thus, it would be wrong to regard the parents of Wales as generally careless or indifferent to the education of their children. Although a certain number did demonstrate a cavalier attitude to the attendance of their offspring, a greater proportion of those parents who did not ensure their children's regular attendance were prevented from doing so by circumstances – usually severe financial and economic constraints – beyond their own control.

As a result of the genuine difficulties that were faced by many parents in sending children to school, a new movement to secure free education gathered strength from the late 1880s. Members of the inspectorate, characterized by HMI Robert Temple, were convinced that any attempt to introduce compulsory attendance without the abolition of school fees was unlikely to succeed, given the genuine poverty that existed in many areas of Wales.[59] Temple alleged that there were parents who appeared to be racked by remorse when summoned, but who made little effort to send their children to school after receiving a warning.

The fact that much of the failure to pay the school pence was attributable to large families, combined with the reluctance of members of the community to appeal to the Poor Law to receive assistance for school fees, strengthened the demand for the introduction of free education. This policy had been a feature of Nonconformist demands throughout the period leading up to the 1870 Education Act. Henry Richard had included the demand for free education among his unsuccessful amendments to the Forster Bill and had been supported in his campaign by the Nonconformist press in Wales, notably by Pan Jones in *Y Celt*, but with support also coming from the more moderate *Y Goleuad*, *Y Tyst* and *Baner*. *Y Goleuad* reflected both the pacifist and educational tradition of Welsh Nonconformity in its editorial:

[59] PP 1877, XXIX, Mr Temple's Report.

Pan y meddyliwn i ni suddo dros filiwn o bunau mewn ychydig fynudau yn ngholliant y Victoria ar dueddau Syria, y mae yn glir y gallwn yn ddiogel fforddio cyfranu hyny chwe' gwaith drosodd i amcanion uchaf bywyd cenedlaethol.

[When it is considered that over a million pounds were lost in a few minutes with the sinking of the *Victoria* near Syria, it is clear that we can easily afford to contribute six times that amount to the highest objectives of our national life.][60]

The School Boards themselves made several comments and representations on the issue of free education. The Swansea School Board argued that its introduction would improve attendance not only in terms of the removal of a financial burden but also by releasing the attendance officers for the task of securing good attendance rather than their having to concentrate on collecting arrears of school fees.[61] Attendance officers had long complained that the majority of Boards placed the burden of securing unpaid fees on their shoulders, resulting in an immense pressure on their time in what was often a futile exercise. The Swansea Board stipulated, however, that a system of free education should be introduced by increasing the grant offered by central government rather than by placing the financial burden on the local authorities. These views were echoed by the vast majority of Boards throughout Wales, although a number endorsed the policy advocated by the Holyhead School Board that the tithe money should be used for subsidizing education provision.[62] Despite the commitment of the Nonconformist community to the introduction of free education, and despite the comments of individual inspectors such as Robert Temple, the majority of inspectors remained unconvinced as to its desirability. HMI Edwards, writing in 1894, reiterated the point made on several previous occasions, namely, that the introduction of free education would not lead to an increase in attendance and that the need was for greater vigilance and effort on the part of local authorities in enforcing attendance.[63] This point was supported

[60] *Y Goleuad*, 11 August 1893.
[61] PP 1893–4, XXVI.
[62] Ibid.
[63] Ibid.

by HMI Bancroft, who argued that the poor level of school attendance in Wales was not due to the school pence which, he claimed, had never been begrudged by the people of Wales, but rather that it was occasioned by the eagerness of Welsh parents to obtain their children's earnings at as early an age as possible. By the following year, however, the chief inspector was forced to concede that the abolition of the school pence had contributed to the improvement in school attendance, especially in the remoter rural areas where the combination of poverty and ineffective administration on the part of local authorities had resulted in some of the worst cases of truancy.[64] Indeed, one of the few notes of caution was sounded by HMI Alexander: 'The total average attendance has considerably increased since free education has become an accomplished fact. This is owing principally to the number of babies who are now sent to school to the great relief of their mothers and the detriment of school discipline.'[65]

Throughout the period, the Conservative Party remained unconvinced of the benefits of introducing free education. Such a policy, it was argued, would considerably reduce public appreciation of education and diminish the stature of those associated with its provision. In addition, the party remained totally opposed to any proposal to use tithe receipts for education. A Conservative leaflet issued during the 1892 election made the cost of free education a cardinal feature of its attack on the Liberal Party and, in so doing, appealed to the baser human instincts.[66] Based on the question-and-answer model, the leaflet stated:

> Question. Who is to pay for it?
> Answer. The British Taxpayer.
> Question. Whose children is it to educate?
> Answer. Other people's children.
> Question. How long is it to be paid for?
> Answer. All your life long.
> Question. Voluntary Education. Who Pays for it?
> Answer. The squire, the parson, the school subscribers and the parents.
> Question. Whose children does it educate?
> Answer. The parent's children only.

[64] Ibid.
[65] PP 1895, XXVII, Mr Alexander's Report.
[66] Flintshire CRO, DE 3062.

Question. How long have the parents to pay?
Answer. Only while their children want it.

However, despite their initial reluctance, it was Conservative legislation which brought about the introduction of free education. In part an attempt to gain support at the subsequent general election (1892) and partly an attempt to start the process of amending the Education Acts so as to strengthen the position of the voluntary schools, the introduction of free education also reflected the degree of consensus which had emerged within both Liberal and Conservative Parties on the need for such legislation. The Act passed by the Conservative government was still attacked by the Nonconformist press. *Y Goleuad* claimed the measure constituted the introduction of a state subsidy for denominational schools by introducing a system of block grants to voluntary schools, on a capitation basis, to compensate those schools for the loss of revenue from the school fees. *Y Goleuad* also argued that the grant settlement gave preferential treatment to the voluntary schools, since the majority of schools charged less than two pence per child while the grant settlement stood at ten shillings per child. It was seen as a settlement which strengthened the financial position of the voluntary schools and was likely to lead to the perpetuation of the voluntary system; at the same time no provision was made for the placing of democratically elected representatives of the community on the Boards of Management of those voluntary schools.[67]

The arguments over school attendance exposed the extent to which the Nonconformist view of Welsh society, as espoused by Henry Richard in his *Letters and Essays on Wales*, was at variance with the general body of opinion in Wales.[68] For an appreciable portion of the Welsh population cared little for education, begrudged the school pence, cherished children's earnings and made little effort to co-operate with the authorities in securing a good school attendance. These attitudes were reinforced by the carelessness of the local authorities charged with the enforcement of attendance; these were often aided and abetted by magistrates and employers who illegally offered employment to truants. This

[67] *Y Goleuad*, 12 February 1891.
[68] Henry Richard, *Letters and Essays on Wales* (London, 1884), exemplified in e.g. letter V, 'The Intellectual Condition of Wales'.

picture has, of course, to be set beside that which reflects the views of those in Welsh society who were committed to education and prepared to make considerable sacrifices in order to ensure their children received the best possible instruction. For those parents, attendance at elementary school and the opportunities which were opening in intermediate and higher education were entirely consonant with the stated aspirations of the Liberal, Nonconformist community. Yet, despite the commitment of many families to the new educational order, the reluctant attitudes of others and the inescapable poverty which affected many, meant that only a few children were able to take full advantage of the opportunities which were being made available. However pervasive the influence of Nonconformity, the average attendance of 75.86 per cent in Welsh schools in 1899 compared unfavourably with the English average of 81.55 per cent.[69] The commitment of the Welsh people to education, a virtue on which commentators began to offer their effusive commendation even before this period, was achieved only by constant effort over a long period; the years following the 1870 legislation saw important, though by no means unqualified, achievements.

[69] PP 1899, XX, Mr Leggard's Report.

VIII
THE TEACHER IN WELSH SOCIETY

The 1870 Education Act introduced schools into parts of Wales that had previously been starved of educational opportunities. It also led to the rapid expansion of the teaching profession. In doing so it introduced a new social phenomenon to Welsh towns and villages, a group of people whose social position and working conditions were as uncertain as were public perceptions of the profession. Certainly, a number of parishes had already enjoyed the benefits brought by the presence of a schoolteacher in the village. Yet many of these were of the incompetent kind portrayed by the novelist, Daniel Owen. In *Hunangofiant Rhys Lewis*, a work noted for its portrayal of early Victorian society, Owen personifies the teacher in the character of Robert Davies, commonly known as Robin y Sowldiwr (Robin the Soldier). Davies had spent his life in military service and had fallen on hard times after losing his leg in battle. Upon his return to Wales, however, he took to drink:

> Gan nad oedd incwm y goes bren nemawr mwy na'r galwadau wythnosol yn y *Cross Foxes*, syrthiodd yr hen filwr yn fuan i amgylchiadau cyfyng. Ond yn union deg daeth ymwared i'r hen frawd . . . yr oedd Mr Brown, y person, yn ŵr dyngarol a charedig dros ben wrth ei blwyfolion, yn enwedig y rhai nad oeddynt yn hereticiaid. Ac yn gymaint â bod yr hen ryfelwr yn un o'i 'anwyl gariadus frodyr,' ac yn ŵr defosiynol, hynny ydyw, yn myned i'r eglwys bob bore Sul -yn myned ar y gwely bob prydnawn Sul, ac yn myned i'r *Cross Foxes* bob nos Sul – cymerai Mr Brown ddyddordeb neillduol yn ei amgylchiadau, ac ef oedd y cyntaf i awgrymu wrtho y priodoldeb iddo ddechre' cadw ysgol.

> [The income from the wooden leg being barely sufficient to meet the weekly calls of the *Cross Foxes*, our old soldier speedily found himself in straitened circumstances. But relief was not long in coming . . . Parson Brown was wondrously kind and charitable towards all his parishioners, especially the orthodox. And inasmuch as the old soldier was one of the 'dearly beloved brethren', and a devout man, that is to say, one who went to church every Sunday morning, to bed every Sunday afternoon, and to

the *Cross Foxes* every Sunday night, Mr Brown took an especial interest in his welfare, and he was the very first to suggest to him the advisability of setting up a school.]¹

The 1870 Act sought to ensure that teachers such as these were displaced and that those who had responsibility for children's education had some competence in their subjects. In so doing, the Act gave many parishes their first experience of a trained teacher, who was potentially a source of new ideas and a means of articulating the aspirations of Welsh peasant society.[2] In terms of absolute numbers, teachers did not account for a significant proportion of the population of Wales. In 1891, for instance, there were 9,125 elementary schoolteachers in Wales, some 0.6 per cent of the population, with an even lower proportion in rural counties like Anglesey, Montgomeryshire, Pembrokeshire and Radnorshire. Yet, as will be demonstrated in this chapter, the role and influence of the teacher far exceeded what could be expected of such a small number.

The profession underwent a marked change of personnel during this period and it must be borne in mind that, in analysing the attitude of the community towards its teachers, it is a changing cadre that is being considered. As has been shown already in the Introduction, the twenty years following the 1847 Report witnessed a marked increase in the number of teacher-training institutions in Wales. As a result of the establishment of these colleges, and the expansion of places during the period following the 1870 Forster Act, there was a wider pool of professionally trained teachers available for appointment by Welsh education authorities; they were individuals who had training in current teaching methods and educational theories as well as up-to-date instruction in subject content. However, a sample of Rhondda teachers indicates that, despite these advances in teacher training, the profession continued to include people from a variety of educational backgrounds. A clear majority of the area's teachers had received some college training. The majority of the headteachers had been trained outside Wales. Evan

---

[1] D. Owen, *Hunangofiant Rhys Lewis* (Wrexham, 1888), pp.30–1; translation from English version (Wrexham, 1915), p.39.
[2] W. G. Evans (ed.), *Fit to Educate? A Century of Teacher Education and Training, 1892–1992* (Aberystwyth, 1992), pp.1–14.

Samuel, master of Blaenllechau School in 1887, Thomas Jones, master of Cwmclydach School in 1886 and John John, master of Llwynypia School in 1896, had been trained at Borough Road Training College in London. T. T. Davies, master of Cymer School in 1882, had attended college at Manchester, and H. H. Jones, head of Dinas School in 1892, had been to Nottingham. Indeed, only a few male headteachers, such as David Evans, master of Treorchy School in 1879, who had been a student at the Normal College, Bangor, had been trained in Wales. The infants' departments were, however, dominated by teachers like Louisa Emily Jones of Blaenllechau School and Margaret Davies of Dinas, neither of whom had received training in a college. Most of those in senior positions had considerable experience, significantly in other industrial areas such as Aberdare, Pontypridd and Newport rather than in the rural areas and, despite some exceptions, it is clear that the children of the Rhondda were taught by people who had a lifetime's experience of teaching children from working-class homes.[3]

The college-trained applicants competed for posts with others who had gained certificates as a result of long apprenticeships as pupil teachers. Many of those 'Ex-PTs' were both academically able and excellent classroom teachers, having the experience which was crucial in developing an education system, particularly in those areas which remained educationally barren in 1870. However, for all the capacity of those teachers to make a valuable contribution, education authorities failed to make the most effective use of this group. The insistence on the part of larger schools on college-trained teachers (a trend which became more pronounced as the decades progressed) meant that non-college-trained teachers increasingly found their career prospects confined to small, mainly rural and often voluntary-funded schools. Thus, teachers who had received an apprenticeship in large urban schools, such as the Dowlais Central, often under the guidance of sound educationists like William Hurst, found that their career prospects diminished with the influx of college-trained teachers.[4] Their practical experience of bringing education to a community not used to schooling was therefore lost to the education service in the urban areas. Their loyalty to their

[3] PRO, ED7/8.
[4] Career of F. Smith, private knowledge.

vocation, demonstrated by their acceptance of positions in smaller schools where they were denied the remuneration paid in large urban schools, testifies to the professionalism and commitment of this undervalued group of people.

In addition to a change in the composition of the teaching profession, the relationship between the teacher and the community was influenced by the changing nature of Welsh society. Wales was witnessing the emergence of an able and increasingly assertive political and social leadership which was based, in the main, on the Nonconformist chapel. The influence of these institutions, and of the individuals associated with them, permeated not only the religious and political life of the community, but also its educational life. The Nonconformist Sunday schools and the various associated cultural and literary organizations already had their own leadership, often drawn from the ranks of those with little formal education themselves. These organizations benefited from the guidance of Nonconformist ministers of religion who, in addition to serving the religious, moral and spiritual needs of society, were important links between the locality and progressive politics during this period. The coming of members of the teaching profession to such communities bolstered this activity and increased the numbers of those who could be relied on to take a leading role in their corporate life.[5] These were educated and articulate individuals in a society which was increasingly determined to express its own character and formulate its demands, and one which had shown a hunger for education. Moreover, the period from the mid-nineteenth century to the Second World War was the golden age of local cultural and literary societies in Wales. This new form of activity supplemented rather than replaced the culture of theological discussion and it was one in which local schoolteachers were active participants. Both David Howell and David Jenkins have noted the pivotal role of members of the teaching profession in debating societies in rural Wales.[6] Another manifestation of the teachers' importance was their contribution to local government in the late nineteenth century. The democratization of local government was accompanied, in turn, by the growth of a

---

[5] D. Ff. Dafis, 'Yr ysgolfeistr a'r gweinidog', *Cwrs y Byd*, III (February 1893), 31–2.

[6] D. W. Howell, 'Farming in Pembrokeshire', in D. W. Howell (ed.), *Pembrokeshire County History*, 4 (Pembrokeshire Historical Society, 1993), pp.77–110.

plethora of organizations committed to educating the community in the means by which they could execute their new responsibilities. The press in this period is replete with references to public lectures, ranging in topics from horticulture to local government, and to more general debates on democracy. The late nineteenth century saw the development of amateur dramatic and choral societies, with teachers again featuring prominently as authors, producers and conductors. These activities were not taken up by all members of the profession, and it would be wrong to attribute the increased cultural vigour of the period to the presence of qualified teachers. A great deal of the impetus came from the indigenous working-class community. Yet the teaching profession nurtured such activity and assiduously promoted the work of these societies and, in many cases, their involvement was crucial in overcoming the hostility of the more devout elements in the Nonconformist congregations towards any cultural activity not directly associated with religion.

Unlike the Nonconformist ministry, the teaching profession was not allied virtually en bloc either to the denominations or to Liberal politics. Thus, there was a crucial difference between the links uniting Nonconformist ministers with the community, which were marked by the political dimension that stemmed from the correlation between the denominations and the Liberal Party, and the bonds between the teacher and the community. The teachers' ranks included several Anglican Conservatives, who, when employed by School Boards, tended either to avoid political activity altogether, for fear of upsetting School Boards dominated by Liberal members, or to adopt a circumspect approach to political questions. For other members of the profession, however, appointments under School Boards offered opportunities to become leading figures in the radical politics of Victorian Wales. Many had been freed from the constraints of having to keep a low political profile while employed by Anglican or Conservative managers of voluntary schools, with many relishing the opportunities and freedoms which were offered by appointments under the new dispensation. Schoolteachers became as common as ministers of religion on Liberal platforms throughout Wales in parliamentary elections, and they came to fit in with the *petite bourgeoisie* of tradesmen, farmers and minor professionals who comprised the backbone of Liberal Party organization in Wales. These opportunities increased as power was devolved by central government to elected representatives at a local level, and especially as the powers of the non-elected lords lieutenants were conveyed to elected members. This was particularly true of the establishment of district and parish councils in Wales in 1894. Teachers such as Howell Howell of Llanwnda (Pembrokeshire) gave years of service as clerks to parish councils and a disproportionately large number of teachers (out of proportion in terms of the percentage of teachers in the community to those elected) were returned to serve as members of district councils after 1894.[7]

These activities on the part of a number of teachers were not without their controversial associations, not least when many teachers began to question their allegiance to the Liberal Party after the establishment of the Independent Labour Party. At the same time, many individuals, including members of the profession itself, considered it unbecoming for a teacher, who was called upon to teach the children of supporters of all manner of political opinion, to take too prominent a part in political affairs. This was particularly true over matters such as the tithe, in which boisterous law-breaking was involved, or during angry industrial disputes. If need be, Nonconformist ministers could draw on their moral authority as men of God to justify their sympathy for law-breaking activities such as the non-payment of tithes. Teachers, however, needed to adopt an even-handed approach, especially in the classroom. Another, equally important, constraining influence was that, unlike the other groups of *petit bourgeois* Liberal leaders, schoolteachers occupied an undefined social position. As Pamela Horn has demonstrated, the teacher occupied an uncertain station in the minds of the community, unlike that enjoyed by the local doctor, minister of religion or larger farmers. As a result, many found it difficult to accept the teacher's leadership, especially in the earlier decades under study.[8]

The political positions adopted by certain members of the profession certainly caused a rift between themselves and the wider community. Teachers who openly criticized the treatment

---

[7] *Pembrokeshire County Echo*, 11 May 1905.
[8] Pamela Horn, *Education in Rural England* (Dublin, 1978), p.193.

of agricultural labourers by tenant farmers as part of a wider call for greater social concern were given little support.[9] The involvement of teachers in the activities of the Swansea Trades and Labour Council led to criticism for breaking the political neutrality of the profession, comments which were made, not least, by members of the Liberal Association who relied on those same teachers for support at election time.[10] These were, however, exceptions to the general rule. Teachers who ventured into the political arena were on the whole keen to ally with the mainstream Liberal politics of the era. They concentrated on issues such as tithe, disestablishment and the land question in the same way as did the majority of middle-class Liberal leaders. On the whole, teachers did not express criticism of the treatment of farm labourers by the tenant farmers or Liberal employers in industrial society. Despite the clear links between economic poverty and lack of progress in education, the teachers did not emerge en bloc as tribunes of social reform within the Liberal Party.

The relationship between members of the profession and their employers is an important indicator of the status and respect enjoyed by the teacher in late nineteenth-century Wales. In rural schools, particularly those operating through the proceeds of a charitable endowment or the patronage of a landowner, the relationship between teachers and their employers was inevitably placed on a personalized basis. In such circumstances, difficulties such as those that arose between the teacher and the vicar in Cricieth or in Fishguard resulted in a protracted argument in which there was no satisfactory means of arbitration.[11] In other cases, the personalized nature of the relationship between the clergyman and schoolteacher resulted in a warm appreciation of each other's talents. In the parish of Llanfynydd (Carmarthenshire), a close friendship existed between the vicar, the Revd D. Daven Jones, and the teacher, Frederick Smith.[12] The two struck up a lasting friendship which extended beyond the management of the National school. They regularly exchanged newspapers

---

[9] UW Bangor MSS 5456–86, William Jones Papers.
[10] Swansea CRO, D/77/4, Papers of the Swansea Trades and Labour Council.
[11] *Baner*, 7 January 1871; PRO, ED2/632.
[12] D. Daven Jones was the author of *The History of Kidwelly* (Carmarthen, 1908) and *The Early Cymry and their Church* (Carmarthen, 1910).

and periodicals and spent pleasant evenings engaged in convivial conversation. In other cases good relations existed between local landowners and the teacher, to the extent that the former sought to use their influence in order to protect an embattled schoolmaster. A Pembrokeshire teacher, accused of being perpetually drunk and of leaving his class in the afternoon for the attractions of drinking or hunting, was saved from the wrath of the school managers by the patronage and support of the Higgon family of the Scolton Manor estate interest.[13] In the same vein, the methods deployed by Lord Boston in dealing with complaints against the masters at his schools demonstrated an immediacy of approach, especially in dealing with unfounded allegations against particular teachers.[14] Inevitably in such personalized situations, political considerations weighed in the appointment of teachers. The Picton Castle estate was assured, in a reference written in connection with an application for a teaching post, that the candidate could be guaranteed to support the Conservative cause, indicating that as far as certain landowners were concerned the choice of schoolmaster constituted an opportunity to bring a political ally into the community.[15] School Boards were less blatantly political in their operations but were nevertheless equally prone to conflicts of personality. The master of Borth Board School (Cardiganshire) declared in a letter to the Education Department that he was in fear of his life because his relations with the chairman of the School Board had deteriorated to the point of violence.[16] Summonses for assault were issued against the chairman of the Tonna School Board (Glamorgan),[17] while in Cilcennin (Cardiganshire) the behaviour of the Board was said to be so tyrannical as to prevent it from retaining the services of a member of staff for any significant length of time.[18] Religious bigotry was in evidence at Llandovery, where the activity of the local schoolmaster in organizing concerts for the entertainment of the townsfolk upset the Board members because the events were insufficiently religious in

[13] Pembrokeshire CRO, D/Hig/130.
[14] UW Bangor, Lligwy Papers.
[15] NLW, Picton Castle Papers, 3896, 23 October 1883.
[16] PRO, ED2/568, 12 April 1896.
[17] *Cambrian*, 12 January 1899.
[18] PRO, ED2/569.

nature.[19] In Aberdare the audacity of the schoolmaster in recommending that the textbooks of a certain publisher be purchased in preference to those of another was rewarded with a severe sermon from the chairman of the Board for his impertinence in attempting to lead the members.[20] Many of these problems arose where a clash of personalities occurred or from the differing priorities of schoolmasters and Board members. In the majority of cases, those teachers who found the relationship with their employers unbearable were forced to find employment elsewhere. Others, particularly the politically influential members of the profession, often came out best in conflicts with the Board. In 1884 Beriah Evans, headmaster of Llangadog Board School (Carmarthenshire), was accused by the Board members of extravagance in his expenditure on school books, especially those in the Welsh language. Undoubtedly, his position as an experienced schoolmaster, coupled with his influence in the local Liberal establishment, enabled him to overcome the charge of extravagance and opposition to the more progressive educational methods he advocated.[21] Comparable authority, however, failed to prevent the dismissal of a teacher at Cynwyl Elfed (Carmarthenshire) whose political views, entirely at variance with those of the controlling group on the Board, led to his dismissal from the headship.[22] Other teachers, such as the master of Bryncoch school in 1880,[23] found themselves tormented by the actions of their employers; such treatment occurred particularly among those who had few formal qualifications.[24]

These problems were highlighted in the investigations of the Cross Commission into the working of the 1870 Education Act.[25] In a damning indictment of the operations of rural School Boards, Mr Williams, headmaster of Betws Garmon Board School (Caernarfonshire), urged that the powers of School Boards were excessive; their well-nigh absolute authority meant

[19] Horn, *Education*, p.193.
[20] *Schoolmaster*, 2 June 1877.
[21] *LLG*, 18 September 1884.
[22] PRO, ED21/21940, 19 July 1899.
[23] *Schoolmaster*, 23 March 1880.
[24] Gwynedd CRO, Dolgellau. A/11/27, Correspondence of Tywyn and Pennal School Board.
[25] Gillian Sutherland, *Policy Making in English Education* (London, 1973), pp.81–6.

that teachers had no alternative other than to submit to persecution and intolerable circumstances. In his opinion:

> the teacher's character and interests are too often at the mercy or whim of men who have no sympathy with education or with the promotion of social virtue -ignorant, malicious, spiteful and selfish men. There is hardly any corporate body or institution in the realm that exercises such despotic sway as the school boards.[26]

In addition to his own case, in which he claimed that he had been driven from the Gaerwen Board School (Anglesey) after seven years for not placing his grocery order at the shops of local tradesmen who sat on the School Board, he cited other examples of such treatment of teachers. One teacher had been dismissed for failing to punish children for taunting the granddaughter of a member of a School Board.[27] Another had been persecuted to the point that he felt obliged to resign his post, a decision that enabled the Board to appoint a relative of one of its members to the headship. Living and working conditions were sometimes matters of concern. The school house of the master of the Bangor Board School was reported to have been so damp that his wife had developed asthma,[28] while the master at Begelly (Pembrokeshire) was forced to work in a freezing classroom, with serious consequences for the health of both teachers and taught.[29] Yet the real complaint against the school authorities, clearly stated by Mr Williams, was that there had been no means of redressing the problems at the time they occurred. Actions of this nature, if taken at the beginning of a triennial period, could remain without remedy until the subsequent election, by which time the persecuted teacher would probably have left the area. Teachers involved in these situations had no means of appeal, for there was no tribunal to which the disaffected could take claims for unfair dismissal, a point recognized by several members of the school inspectorate. The report for 1877 stated that too many teachers were having to submit to unacceptable circumstances for fear of upsetting school managers or other influential

[26] PP 1888, XXXVI.
[27] Ibid.
[28] *CDH*, 29 May 1891.
[29] W. Morgan, *The Story of Begelly* (Llandysul, 1981), pp.61–6.

members of the community; this was echoed by the NUET in its campaigns for security of tenure. Despite the consensus of opinion among members of the profession, the inspectorate and the organized representatives of teachers, no remedy was forthcoming from the government until the Board system was replaced by Local Education Authority control in 1902.

The method adopted for appointing and promoting teachers was another source of grievance in this period. Constant allegations were made that political, denominational and nepotistic influences were at work in making appointments, while the methods of the Boards in deliberating over staffing matters were also considered unacceptable. The *Llanelly and County Guardian*, in common with other local newspapers, carried reports of meetings of School Boards at which appointments were made. The deliberations, including occasionally adverse comments from a member regarding the qualities of a particular candidate, would then be published verbatim, together with testimonials from previous employers and a breakdown of how each Board member cast his vote. Such a practice was clearly degrading for the applicants, who were forced to have their merits and blemishes exposed in public for all to read. Moreover, the parents of children, and indeed some of the older children themselves, were thus given the opportunity to read what were often uncomplimentary comments on the teacher, and free to quote such remarks in any subsequent confrontation with the individual concerned, reinforcing the widely held view that parents were doing the teacher a favour by allowing their children to attend the school. Allegations of denominationalism were also rife and again undermined the position of those teachers who had supposedly benefited as a result of the patronage of the leaders of a particular denomination. In Llanelli, the question was raised as to why the most prized teaching posts were being given to candidates from the town itself, a practice which 'Argus' attributed to the influence of certain politically influential families who were able to secure appointments for their own relatives and placemen. These assertions were given special prominence in 1890, at the time of the appointment of a headmaster for Lakefield Elementary School. Lakefield was a new school, with facilities considerably better than those enjoyed by most schools in the Llanelli area, and it was also larger than any other school in the town. Under these circumstances, the headship was a coveted position, especially among the long-serving headmasters of neighbouring schools.[30] Yet the appointment of a young and relatively inexperienced candidate in preference to a number of experienced and highly regarded local candidates caused a furore in the town. A public meeting convened to protest against the decision heard allegations that denominationalism had been a major factor in influencing the decision of the Board members.[31] As a result of this outcry, the Board was forced to rescind its original decision, the appointment was withdrawn and the post awarded to another candidate.

Not all teachers, however, were slaves to the School Boards. Allegations were made that in certain areas the schoolmasters themselves exercised greater power than members of the School Board. The Rhymney Board (Monmouthshire) was allegedly dominated by the schoolmaster who, by careful nurturing of local nonentities and the co-optation of men with little intelligence, had ensured that the Board was totally amenable to his wishes.[32] Likewise in Tonna (Glamorgan), the master was able to manipulate public opinion to such an extent that he triumphed over the Board, causing the members to resign en bloc.[33] The Pembrey School Board (Carmarthenshire) was involved in a dispute with the managers of Trimsaran school over claims that the master was exercising too much influence over the managers in his supposedly extravagant programme of refurbishment for the school.[34] Such controversies were noted by the inspectorate, which concluded that, as a result of the inactivity of both School Board members and managers, too many decisions were being made by the teachers themselves.[35] Yet, equally serious were the complaints against the behaviour of the managers of voluntary schools, and in particular the lack of constraint on the patrons of endowed schools, who were not even held accountable for their decisions by the need to submit themselves for public election. As Pamela Horn has demonstrated, many of those voluntary school

---

[30] The issue is well-reported in the *Llanelly and County Guardian* for the period from May to July 1890.
[31] Ibid.
[32] PRO, ED2/617–25, 20 May 1889.
[33] PRO, ED2/514, 12 January 1899.
[34] PRO, ED21/21952–56, 2 February 1887.
[35] See also ch. 3.

managers were as apt as their Board counterparts to behave in a dictatorial manner.[36]

The question of teachers' pay was an issue that was not satisfactorily resolved in this period. The NUET was continually having to demand increased remuneration; the problem was accentuated by the absence of a standard salary scale specified by national legislation. As a result, teachers found their pay set by local discretion, and often found themselves the victims of the denominational conflict which permeated Welsh society in the late nineteenth century. A teacher at Cwm Penmachno (Caernarfonshire) was compelled to leave the school in 1875 because the National school managers were unable to pay him following the decision of the villagers to refuse to contribute to a school over which they had no control.[37] Similar instances arose throughout the period. As late as 1894 in Tonna (Glamorgan), denominational rivalry resulted in the teachers being left unpaid.[38] As has been pointed out, the position of the teacher in the social hierarchy was uncertain, considered lower than the Victorian middle class yet awarded a higher status than the working class. This was certainly true of the self-perception of members of the teaching profession itself, many of whom were of working-class background but considered themselves socially distinct from the working-class children whom they taught, despite the fact that in periods of economic prosperity the average working-class wage regularly exceeded the average salary of a teacher. Added to this consideration was the fact that teachers were expected to maintain a certain standard of living, were obliged to be suitably attired, and needed sufficient income to purchase books and other materials in order to keep abreast of current intellectual and educational developments and to meet their own cultural inclinations.

The attitude of employers and the community as a whole had a considerable bearing on the remuneration awarded to the teaching profession. In 1883 Pembrey Scool Board was told that a member had an objection to increasing the salaries of the teachers on the grounds that he, a farmer, was making little more

---

[36] Horn, *Education*, pp.48–91, 180–1.
[37] PRO, ED2/585.
[38] PRO, ED2/610.

money than what was being paid to them; he considered this unacceptable in light of the fact that in his estimation teaching was 'an easier and less important living' than farming.[39] The issue of salaries became a preoccupation of the Pembrey School Board, as it did in the majority of School Boards in Wales. More than three-quarters of the meetings of the Boards were spent discussing salaries, with regular accusations of nepotism and favouritism being levied against members, who made their decisions without the guidance of a specified salary scale.

The reactions of the teachers who faced difficult circumstances varied. Many accepted their lot stoically. Others abandoned the profession or, more often, sought appointments elsewhere. This was frequently the case in rural areas, as may be instanced by the parish of Llanwenog (Cardiganshire), which considered itself lucky to retain the services of a teacher for longer than a year.[40] Other teachers sought to redress their plight. In December 1900 the Corwen (Merioneth) schoolteachers stated that they would not undertake any further administrative tasks until they were granted increased remuneration.[41] Likewise, the assistant teachers of Llanelli, despairing of their low salaries in 1890, complained directly to the School Board. One of their leaders, William Morgan, explained his position in a letter to the Board:

> I regret to find that my faithful endeavours to serve the Board honestly (as testified by my passes) have resulted in my salary decreasing in value. I can hardly believe that such a practical and educated body of men as compose the Llanelli School Board can suffer long their assistant teachers to be so wretchedly paid. I humbly maintain, that it is very hard indeed to expect a person, after having served his apprenticeship for four years or more, to be at the expiration of such time allowed only about 13s. per week for his maintenance. I question whether, in any of our local works, labourers are so underpaid as we assistant teachers are. Besides our position as members (in name) of a higher class of society, places us under the disadvantage of having to keep up our appearances as such, which is very trying indeed.[42]

The letter was dismissed by the members of the School Board in a flippant manner, Gwilym Evans proposing that the letter be

---

[39] *LLG*, 15 March 1883.
[40] D. R. Davies, *Hanes Llanwennog: y Plwyf a'r Bobl* (Aberystwyth, 1939), pp.83–5.
[41] Gwynedd CRO, Dolgellau, A/11 Box 25.
[42] *LLG*, 12 June 1890.

copied and hung on the wall of the Board's offices as a reminder to the members of the 'audacity of their employees'.[43] It is an incident which demonstrates the lack of concern which many Board members had for their teaching staff. However, the teachers did have a certain body of support among the general public. 'Argus', the scourge of Welsh Victorian hypocrisy, expressed his sympathy for the teachers, declaring in his critical column that William Morgan's letter was indicative of a wider discontent among the teachers of Llanelli and indeed of Wales in general. In his opinion, the salary scales adopted by the Llanelli and Pembrey Boards were so low as to make it surprising that the two Boards were able to attract any teachers at all.[44] His comments were justified by subsequent events in the town, triggered off by Morgan's letter. An assistant master in the employment of the Llanelli Board resigned his post rather than 'face starvation' owing to the low remuneration offered him,[45] while two teachers engaged by the neighbouring Pembrey Board threatened resignation in equally strong terms. As a result, both Boards were forced to abandon the controversial salary scales which they had adopted, only to return to the equally unreliable system of using discretion in individual cases in the payment of teachers.[46] Matters occasionally resulted in industrial action, as was the case in Newport in 1874[47] and Llangar in 1900,[48] when teachers resolved not to undertake additional duties, such as filling registers for Poor Law Guardians, unless they were given better remuneration. However, despite increased militancy on the part of many, especially among the younger members, the salaries paid to teachers remained, as a general rule, pitifully low, highlighting the lack of appreciation of the teacher in Welsh society.

The period from 1870 to 1902, however, also saw the teaching profession regarded as an attractive career option. Principal T. F. Roberts of Aberystwyth commented that 'there is in Wales, fortunately, little of the social blindness which fails to recognise in the profession of an elementary teacher one of the most inspiring

---

[43] Ibid.
[44] *LLG*, 17 July 1890.
[45] *LLG*, 13 January 1887.
[46] *LLG*, 13 August 1891.
[47] *Schoolmaster*, 27 June 1874.
[48] Gwynedd CRO, Dolgellau, ZA 52, Papers of the Llangar School Board.

avenues to usefulness which modern life affords'.[49] It was a comment echoed by David Thomas, who noted the affection and high regard in which the majority of teachers were held by their former pupils.[50] Mr Fyfe, vice-president of the NUET, claimed as early as 1874 that teachers were beginning to be accorded more respect than before, insisting that the status of the profession had been revolutionized compared with fifteen years earlier.[51] This is consistent with the increased stability noted in 1881, when the school inspectorate observed that the supply of teachers now matched the demand and that there was less frequent movement between schools than in previous years.[52] Such comments, however accurate at the time, disguised the real picture. While the supply of teachers did meet the demand, the relative stability within the profession which was achieved in the early 1880s owed more to the economic depression of the time (and the consequent lack of alternative avenues of employment) than it did to satisfaction felt within the teaching profession. Any upturn in economic conditions was usually accompanied by an exodus from the teaching profession, as former teachers found avenues in the emerging industrial and local government bureaucracies.

Economic fluctuations were to be seen at their most pronounced in relation to the ranks of the pupil teachers. Many genuine aspirants to the profession found that an appointment to this role was an important step. The position was often a coveted one, but became less sought after as new opportunities, particularly the prospect of higher wages in industry, depleted the ranks of those intending to enter the profession. Consequently, complaints were made that few schools could retain the services of a pupil teacher for longer than a few months as their scarcity made appointments to other schools easy to obtain. The matter was compounded by the coming of the intermediate schools which, as they mushroomed throughout Wales, provided alternative opportunities for those who might otherwise have become pupil teachers. The inspectorate was aware of the dwindling

[49] T. F. Roberts, 'Sixty years of education', *Young Wales*, III (August 1897), 145–52.
[50] David Thomas, 'Reminiscences of a school inspector', in W. Ll. Davies (ed.), *National Union of Teachers Souvenir of the Aberystwyth Conference 1933* (Aberystwyth, 1933), pp.148–9.
[51] *Schoolmaster*, 27 June 1874.
[52] PP 1881, XXXII.

supply of suitable persons. As early as 1871 it was noted that candidates were inferior in quality to their counterparts of a previous generation, despite the fact that public perception of the profession had improved during that time.[53] According to the inspectorate, the remedy was not to reduce the standard required prior to entry into the profession, but rather to increase the attractions of the profession through increased remuneration and the provision of pensions.

The question of pensions was one which generated considerable debate and agitation in the ranks of the teaching profession for several years and was a key issue for the NUET.[54] A Commission of Inquiry was set up to consider the matter, but the proposals of 1875 caused consternation among the teachers. While guaranteeing a pension based on teacher contributions for those at the beginning of their careers, the scheme ignored the needs of 'older' teachers (those employed before 1861), thereby creating a fear that this generation would face the prospect of living in old age on their meagre savings or, worse, experience poverty.[55] In 1882 the St Clears Branch of the Union attacked the differentiation between teachers and civil servants for superannuation purposes, claiming that teachers should be given the same terms and conditions as those awarded to the staff at Somerset House.[56] Local associations continued the agitation and ensured the support of several School Boards and management committees in the campaign to backdate the pensions for the older teachers. The failure of this campaign proved to be a serious blow to former members and, while the relevance of the issue declined with the passage of time, the issue of pensions contributed to the feeling in the profession that the efforts of the teacher were given inadequate recognition. This contributed further to the feeling of despondency which developed among the ranks of schoolteachers in Wales and in the British Isles generally.

The school inspectors were an educated, intelligent and experienced fraternity of educationists, yet their relationship with the teaching profession was less than fraternal and regularly

[53] PP 1871, XXII.
[54] *Schoolmaster*, 15 February 1873 and 9 December 1882.
[55] Horn, *Education*, pp.197–202.
[56] *Schoolmaster*, 8 March 1884.

verged on the hostile. David Thomas, writing of the relations he encountered, recalled that:

> When I joined the Civil Service the annual examination system was in full force, and much work of a trivial nature – although, perhaps, useful and necessary in the 'seventies and 'eighties – had to be performed by teachers and inspectors. It was only after the abolition of the 'Annual Parade Day' [the inspection] that teachers were able to devote their whole energy to the work of educating the nation's children. It was also after this hard-and-fast system had been abolished that teacher and inspector became co-workers in the field of education.[57]

In the case of many schoolteachers, often labouring in the teeth of employer and parent hostility, and having to deal with children who were at best irregular in attendance and often devoid of any inclination to be present at the school, contact with the inspectorate was the only opportunity to discuss issues which concerned them. Although there was an opportunity for a cooperative relationship, the role of the inspector as a critical inquisitor, whose duty it was to record failings in the ability of the teacher or even blemishes of character, made his visit an event regarded with trepidation by the majority of teachers. In the estimate of many teachers, the inspectors did not understand the communities in which the teachers worked, nor had they much understanding of the difficulties the teachers faced. The master at Pen-y-ffordd in Flintshire had to contend with an inspector whose notions of the capabilities of infants led him to conclude that 'the babies were poor at writing',[58] and others suffered from inspectors who treated teachers with a contempt while assuming an air of academic superiority. The obsession of inspectors with an accurate register of attendance, together with their criticisms of teachers' ignorance of the niceties of the Education Code and their comments on the lack of administrative finesse demonstrated by some teachers, reflected a lack of understanding of the life of the schoolmaster. Many teachers who failed to complete the administrative work demanded of them often laboured under severe difficulties, not least the pressure on their time. The

---

[57] Thomas, 'Reminiscences of a school inspector', 148–9.
[58] Flintshire CRO, D/NT/232.

manner in which inspections were conducted often led to disruption of classroom life. Frederick Smith complained of the inspector's behaviour after an uncomplimentary report on the Talley Board School was received shortly after his appointment in 1894. He asserted that any indiscipline was not a reflection of his performance:

> The order and discipline, owing to a fortnight's holiday and five weeks under a temporary master, had deteriorated shockingly. On the inspection day the order inside the room was very fair and never once out of my control. The inspector is largely to blame himself for constantly sending groups of children out and wanting them in again, several times, not knowing which he wanted.[59]

Teachers, however, received little support either from their employers or from the higher agencies in the Education Department. There was no appeals procedure against an adverse report, and it was not until the turn of the century that the inspectorate began to adopt a more sympathetic approach.

The inspectors were not alone in expressing disapproval of the teaching methods of the teachers of Wales. School Board members and school managers had a tendency, on appointment, to assume superior knowledge of educational issues. In Caernarfon in 1894 the vicar, the Revd J. W. Wynne Jones, asserted that the teaching methods of the local schoolmaster were directly responsible for the deterioration in the level of passes for pupil teachers, Jones having previously attacked the teacher for neglecting the majority of pupils and concentrating too much on the pupil teachers.[60]

Grievances against members of the profession on educational issues were, however, less frequent than complaints over school discipline and punishment practices. The press for this period is littered with references to assault charges against members of the teaching profession, such as a case at Mountain Ash in 1884 when one of the town's schoolmasters was fined ten shillings after magistrates had decided that the punishment he had inflicted upon a pupil had been so severe as to constitute an assault on the

---

[59] Carmarthenshire CRO, ED Bk 571/1, log book of Talley Board School.
[60] *CDH*, 7 October 1887.

child.[61] Parents, many of whom had fallen foul of local attendance by-laws, frequently blamed the regular beatings for their decision to keep children away from school. A system that relied on physical punishment as a basis for discipline inevitably created such complaints, although these diminished as Boards began to restrict the offences that were punishable by the cane. Cardiff School Board resolved in 1893 that corporal punishment should only be initiated in cases of indecency, dishonesty, lying and acts of gross insubordination, although the definition of 'gross insubordination' again created a grey area which both teachers and parents could exploit.[62]

As was so often the case in such controversies, the real problem was caused by circumstances beyond the control of the teacher, such as the increased pressure imposed on the profession. A single teacher might have the task of ensuring that large numbers of children were controlled and taught, both in rural areas (where to have one teacher bearing responsibility for the entire age range was commonplace), and in urban schools such as Dowlais Central, where it was known for one teacher to be responsible for a class of upwards of a hundred children. Apart from the excessive numbers, extension of the school curriculum had resulted in an over-burdening of the timetable and an unbearable extra workload was often imposed on the teachers. As a result, homework was an essential means of enabling teachers to fulfil the requirements of the Department, but its imposition was resented by parents who felt themselves deprived of the assistance (and often the labour) of their children in the home. Those children who, abetted by their parents, refused to complete such work, were openly defying the teacher and this threatened to undermine his or her authority. The severe punishments that followed often aroused the ire of the parents. Allegations of sadism were levied against members of the teaching profession, notably those of the older generation who were more accustomed to asserting their authority in a military style than to adopting the more persuasive methods advocated in the training colleges. These allegations were often

---

[61] *Schoolmaster*, 31 January 1884.
[62] *Sixth Triennial Report of the Cardiff School Board* (Cardiff, 1893).

accompanied by accusations of drunkenness, sometimes leading to open rebellion in the classroom. The pupils of Gilfach-goch (Glamorgan) struck against an unpopular teacher, who was accused of drunken sadism, and they succeeded in getting the master dismissed from the school. In relation to the number of teachers who lost their licence to teach, however, those convicted of sadistic behaviour were few. The most frequent reason for dismissal was incorrect registration or poor administrative methods rather than assault or drunkenness.

The issue of corporal punishment recurred in the debate throughout the period considered in this study, although there were more frequent pronouncements in the later years. For the majority of teachers, the use of the cane, or at least its presence as a visible deterrent, was an essential tool in maintaining classroom discipline. Certainly, in understanding the importance of corporal punishment in schools it is important to recognize the particular difficulties facing the Victorian schoolteacher. It was not an easy task to maintain discipline when classes regularly exceeded sixty pupils, especially when they varied in age and were of mixed ability. The difficulties faced by teachers were often compounded by a lack of parental support, a lack of interest on the part of the pupils, as well as the increased requirements of the curriculum and school administration. A firm disciplinary regime was often the only way order could be maintained in such situations, and it became crucial for teachers to assert their authority at an early stage and to maintain their control thereafter. Moreover, the Victorian home was likewise characterized by a strict disciplinary code which embraced the cane as both deterrent and a means of punishment. Members of the teaching profession remained adamant that corporal punishment had to be retained as a feature of school life. The Carmarthen Branch of the NUET objected strongly to the proposal of the Carmarthen School Board that use of the cane should be recorded. In the opinion of the NUET, the adoption of such a procedure would be time-consuming and would place the teachers in the invidious position of having to defend their actions to parents who had little understanding of the difficulties of the classroom.[63] The insistence of the teachers on the need to

[63] *Schoolmaster*, 15 July 1872.

retain corporal punishment was accepted by the majority of School Boards in Wales. Merthyr Tydfil School Board, however, sought to abandon such methods in its schools and to introduce a more liberal regime to the town's classrooms. The proposal, a product of Mrs Crawshay's progressive educational policies, was roundly condemned by the profession, which pointed to the deterioration in classroom discipline following the adoption of the policy. The subsequent failure of the Board to attract teachers was blamed on the fact that no member of the profession was prepared to relinquish corporal punishment, a state of affairs which prompted Mrs Crawshay to withdraw her resolution and enabled the Board to revert to its previous policy.[64]

Other complaints were levied against the discipline and lifestyle of the teaching profession. The pupil teachers of Ffestiniog (Merioneth) were condemned by the Board for their habit of smoking in front of their classes.[65] A teacher at Tudweilog (Caernarfonshire) was considered by the agent of the Voelas estate 'to be a little too fond of whisky', a problem which contributed to his accumulating debts to local tradespeople to such an extent that he was issued with a county court summons.[66] Despite allegations of misdemeanour on the part of some of their colleagues, the majority of teachers could and did win the loyalty and affection of both children and the wider community in nineteenth-century Wales. There was a high regard for successive teachers in the parish of Llan-non (Carmarthenshire), an attitude enhanced by the excellent academic achievements of the pupils.[67] Mr James of Clydach Board School (Glamorgan) was said to have so inspired his pupils that he was able to dispense with corporal punishment throughout his teaching career,[68] and similar instances of highly regarded teachers were noted in Cardiganshire, Pembrokeshire and elsewhere.[69] A high proportion of parents, notably those who could be classified as *Buchedd A* according to the classifications of David Jenkins, actively

[64] Ibid., 11 October 1873.
[65] *CDH*, 14 February 1893.
[66] NLW, Voelas and Cefnamwlch MSS, B10.
[67] N. Gibbard, *Hanes Plwyf Llan-non* (Llan-non, 1984), p.74.
[68] J. H. Davies, *History of Pontardawe* (Llandybïe, 1967), pp.197–200.
[69] See, for instance, E. Davies, *Hanes Plwyf Llangynllo* (Llandysul, 1905), or Davies, *Hanes Llanwennog*.

supported the teachers in their scholastic endeavours and in their efforts to maintain classroom discipline. Such an attitude meant that a number of parents regarded the decision of a teacher to impose physical punishment on a child as sufficient reason to inflict a second beating at home, and led others to insist on the completion of homework, often at great cost to themselves in the loss of necessary assistance. This parental support gathered pace as those who had been the first generation of children educated under the Forster Act became parents themselves.[70]

Teachers were aided by the social activities of the NUET. The role of the Union was all-embracing; it served as both a trade union and a professional society. In addition to holding debates on educational issues, it organized outings, social evenings and conferences for members of the profession to meet and enjoy the company of each other. Yet, throughout its early existence, the Union was plagued by the feeling among certain teachers that involvement in a trade union would reduce their status as professionals to that of industrial employees. Thus, in 1870 the Union resolved against the establishment of an accumulation fund because such funds were associated with trade unionism. It would, it was felt, 'do the moral power of a teacher no good to be associated with trade unionism'.[71] Because of this, the NUET was prevented from becoming as powerful an influence as had been envisaged by its founders, but the fact that many teachers remained aloof from its activities did not mean they were not prepared to benefit from those gains for which the union campaigned, much to the consternation of union activists. John Jenkins, president of the Denbigh and Flint area, complained in 1872 that only a minority of teachers was prepared to argue in public for a principle while others, fearful of the effect it would have on their careers, preferred to take none of the responsibility but still partake in all the benefits won by the union.[72] Although union membership increased in the last years of the century, the NUET failed to recruit a majority of teachers in Wales, while active members accounted for an even smaller proportion. Rivalries between those employed in the School Board sector and

[70] David Jenkins, *The Agricultural Community in South-West Wales at the Turn of the Twentieth Century* (Cardiff, 1971), pp.216–18.
[71] *Schoolmaster*, 12 April 1872.
[72] *Schoolmaster*, 2 June 1877.

those in the voluntary sector continued, often resulting in separate branches for the two sets of teachers. Despite these difficulties, the NUET registered substantial successes. The Welsh branches participated in national campaigns over pensions and exerted pressure over specifically Welsh matters such as a bilingual policy. Concerted efforts were made to secure the return of Welsh representatives to the National Executive who were conversant with the bilingual difficulty and to have less rigorous examinations in Wales in view of the problems associated with teaching through a medium other than the native tongue. This agitation did, however, result in strained relations with members of English branches, who argued that the difficulties they faced in overcoming strong regional dialects were as great as those being faced in Wales.

The teachers of Wales experienced a wide range of public attitudes during the late nineteenth century. Many became well-liked, even revered, members of society, able to influence the life of the school and its social environs. Yet, in line with their English counterparts, their social position remained ill-defined, and many teachers suffered persecution, lack of respect and low remuneration from communities which failed to appreciate the value of their contribution to social endeavour and achievement. In this respect, they occupied a position similar to that in which many ministers of religion found themselves, as respected leaders of communities, yet forced to tread a wary path, for ever at the mercy of a society which could demonstrate its ingratitude by exceedingly harsh criticism.

CONCLUSION:
RESTING ON LAURELS: EDUCATION AT THE TURN OF THE CENTURY

The nature of the debate surrounding education in Wales was significantly changed by the mid-1890s. Following the passing of the Intermediate Education Act and the establishment of the University of Wales, a spirit of self-congratulation and complacency prevailed among those who formed educational policy. These leaders confidently maintained that there was no Welsh child who was without the opportunity to achieve a full education from elementary to university level, given sufficient academic ability. The Liberal dream of social progress and personal advancement, by means of education and an adherence to a virtuous lifestyle, was now considered possible through the system largely created by the Liberal Party, itself a political movement influenced and invigorated by Nonconformity. The three-tier education system was hailed as the main achievement of the Liberals in nineteenth-century Wales, a success which contrasted with continuing failures in the fields of disestablishment, tithe and land. O. M. Edwards habitually referred to the University as *Prifysgol y Werin* (The University of the People), insisting that Wales had overcome generations of educational deprivation.[1] This feeling of satisfaction was evident in virtually all organs of nineteenth-century radicalism. Watkyn Wyn, often a critic of the failures of the Victorian education system, acknowledged that immense progress had been secured by the end of the nineteenth century. Writing in *Y Diwygiwr* in 1897, he noted:

> Mewn bwthynod y cynhelid yr ysgolion gynt, ond yn y plasau harddaf yn mhob cymydogaeth y cynhelir yr ysgolion heddyw, ac y mae ein hysgolion goreu wedi dod fel cartrefi mawr cyffredinol i'r plant, yn llawn dyddordeb a chysur; ac y mae yn well gan y plant fod yn yr ysgol na bod ar y stryd . . . Y mae cyfundrefn addysgol Cymru heddyw mor gyfan ac mor gyfleus ag y gellir dysgwyl ei gael braidd. Y mae yna ymdrech deg wedi ei gwneud, a

---

[1] J. G. Williams, *The University Movement in Wales* (Cardiff, 1993), p.189; see also G. H. Jenkins, *The University of Wales: An Illustrated History* (Cardiff, 1993).

thir lawer wedi ei feddianu yn enwedig yn ystod y blynyddau diweddaf hyn, a chyda gofal a doethineb y mae Cymru bellach ar safle fanteisiol i gystadlu a'r holl ynysoedd Prydeinig. Y mae dydd wedi tori ar Gymru, hyderwn yn y man y cwyd yr haul yn uwch i'r lan.

[The schools were formerly held in cottages, whereas now they are to be found in the most attractive mansions in every locality and our best schools are as a large second home to the children, full of interest and comfort, and the children prefer the school to the street . . . The Welsh education system is now as complete and accessible as can be. A good effort has been made and considerable ground gained especially in the last few years, and with care and wisdom Wales is now placed to compete on favourable terms with all nations of the British Isles. A new dawn has broken upon Wales and we trust that the sun will soon shine higher above the land.][2]

Professor Thomas Rees of Bangor offered similar comments in *Cwrs y Byd* in 1896. He compared the situation prevalent a generation earlier, when only those who had failed in all other occupations entered the teaching profession, with the modern attractions of teaching as a career.[3] Likewise, Edward Edwards, Professor of History at Aberystwyth, noted:

Our educational ladder is now complete, and Wales, which was a picture of educational chaos and misery in 1843, now possesses one of the most complete systems and machinery of knowledge that any country possesses. The Welsh boy of to-day has not to meet the obstacles of the past, and to proceed with his education and win his degree is now as easy for him (and as natural let us hope) as it is for him to breathe.[4]

The school inspectorate shared this spirit. HMI L. Jones, writing in 1899, argued that the system of education in the country was complete in that all Welsh children were within reach of educational advantages which were undreamed of at the beginning of the century.[5] The inspectors expressed satisfaction not only that the system was complete but that the policy of

[2] Watkyn Wyn, 'Addysg yn Oes Fictoria', *Y Diwygiwr*, LXII (June 1897), 185–7; R. D. Roberts, 'Education in Wales, yesterday, to-day and to-morrow', *Journal of the Liverpool Welsh National Society*, 14 (April 1898), 9–16; T. F. Roberts, 'Sixty years of education', *Young Wales*, III (August 1896), 145–52.
[3] T. Rees, 'Addysg Cymru', *Cwrs y Byd*, VI (May 1896).
[4] *Young Wales*, II (June 1896), 100.
[5] PP 1899, II, Mr L. Jones's Report.

establishing a large number of intermediate schools had made them accessible to a greater number of pupils and, consequently, attendance was less of a hardship.[6] Moreover, the chief inspector of schools for Wales, A. G. Leggard, noted that there was a unified system of education in Wales that did not suffer from the rivalries that bedevilled the system in England:

> There is here no strong line of demarcation between elementary and higher education, as is unfortunately the case in England. The scholars in the county schools are drawn in a very large degree from the elementary schools, and the county scholars in their turn are finding their way to the three constituent colleges of the Welsh University. Again, the Day Training Departments attached to each of the colleges form another link between the elementary schools and the higher seats of learning, and it is interesting to notice that the first Fellow of the new University of Wales was formerly a pupil teacher in an elementary school.[7]

Leggard also noted the commitment of the Welsh people to education:

> No system can really flourish unless it is supported by national sentiment, and unless it has won the affection of the people. In the case of Wales it is clear, I think, that education has got a real hold of the popular sympathies, just as it has in the northern part of Great Britain.
>
> This is shown in many ways, and not least by the generous contributions that have been made by a very large number of people in a poor country towards the building of the county schools and the University College.
>
> The self-denying efforts of parents also in many parts of Wales to enable their children to enjoy the benefits of a good education deserve warm recognition; and it is a significant fact that at one of the Welsh colleges, when an inquiry was made, it was found that more than one-third of the students had been sons and daughters of artisans or the labouring classes.[8]

Other commentators sounded a more cautious tone. As early as 1884, when some were claiming that the elementary education ladder at least was complete, *Seren Gomer* declared that it was not sufficient to provide a framework without enabling individuals to take advantage of it:

[6] PP 1899, XX, Mr Leggard's Report.
[7] Ibid.
[8] Ibid.

Y mae perygl dybryd i ni wrth ymdrechu cael moddion addysg i Gymru i ollwng dros gof fod gwaith mawr i'w gyflawnu er gwneyd y Cymry yn gymhwys i ddefnyddio y manteision. Ofnwn nad ydyw y genedl etto wedi dechreu dihuno i sylweddoliad priodol o werth gwir addysg, ac o'r cymhwysder gofynol i fanteisio ar foddion addysg . . . Y perygl mawr ydyw i ni gredu, ar ol llwyddo i sefydlu ysgolion a phrif-ysgolion yn Nghymru, fod ein gwaith ar ben.

[There is a great danger that in our effort to secure educational provision for Wales we forget that there is much to be done to ensure that the Welsh are prepared so as to avail themselves of the facilities. We fear that the nation is yet to awaken to an appropriate realization of the value of true education and of the aptitude necessary so as to benefit from educational provision . . . the great danger is for us to believe that, having established the schools and colleges of Wales, our work is complete.][9]

Historians for their part have examined the favourable assessment of the educational system. Dai Smith has commented on the success of the educational system in producing literate and articulate working-class leaders, those best able to represent the growing disenchantment among the workers, particularly in south Wales.[10] These were the subscribers to miners' institutes, libraries and other institutions, who were able to engage in independent political thought and reading as a result of the basic education received under the system created from 1870. J. Gwynn Williams, however, points to William Abraham's testimony that while

libraries and mechanics' institutes enlightened the people, refined their tastes and encouraged them to desert public houses, they could not instruct the children of the working class in the principles of political economy.[11]

Large gaps remained in the educational system, not least in terms of technical and mechanical education. Attempts to develop science in the elementary schools failed because of the expenditure which was necessary, and neither was Wales provided with a sufficient number of technical colleges. Indeed, as Richard Lewis's studies of adult education have demonstrated,

[9] 'S.J.', 'Addysg i Gymru a Chymru i Addysg', *Seren Gomer*, V (1884), 38–44.
[10] D. Smith, *Aneurin Bevan and the World of South Wales* (Cardiff, 1993), pp.49–55.
[11] Williams, *The University Movement in Wales*, p.198.

whatever was claimed for the Welsh educational system, there were significant areas of under-provision and lack of opportunity which, for many pupils, were at least as pronounced in 1903 as they were at the time of the writing of the Aberdare Report in 1880.[12]

As J. Gwynn Williams has demonstrated, despite O. M. Edwards's insistence on the virtues of *Prifysgol y Werin*, the reality indicated by his own survey of the social background of students was considerably different from what he and Leggard had claimed.[13] Of 231 Aberystwyth students in residence in 1892 surveyed by him, 12 were sons of gentlemen, 45 sons of clergy and ministers of the Gospel, 67 from professional families and 70 were from trade backgrounds. Only 25 were from farming backgrounds (an astonishing figure in view of the popular vision of the tenant farmers' contribution to the establishment of the University) and a mere 12 from the labouring class. The figures for Cardiff and Bangor were similar, although in both instances those towns' proximity to industrial centres boosted the number of students from labouring backgrounds. Taken together, it is clear that the greatest beneficiaries of the Liberal, Nonconformist educational dream were the offspring of tradespeople and professionals. As has been shown in chapter 3, it was this group that increasingly dominated the leadership of the Liberal Party at local level, despite the sentimental importance placed in Liberal speeches on the peasant culture of the *gwerin*.

In terms of being able to take full advantage of the education provision, the *gwerin* was never presented with an opportunity to demonstrate its full potential. Those who were able to take advantage of the whole of the educational system (from elementary to university) designed by the Liberal élite were a minority of exceptionally gifted children whose parents saw merit in education and who had some degree of financial means with which to support their children. Other parents found themselves unable to provide their children with the support that would have enabled them to progress from the elementary school. Economic factors and considerations of family size and gender played a crucial role in preventing able working-class children

---

[12] R. Lewis, *Leaders and Teachers: Adult Education and the Challenge of Labour in South Wales, 1906–1940* (Cardiff, 1993).
[13] Williams, *The University Movement in Wales*, pp.202–3.

from availing themselves of the benefits of the Liberal educational order. This was so even though many were drawn from families who lived according to the virtuous lifestyle lauded by O. M. Edwards and the tribunes of Welsh Nonconformity and whose lives revolved around effort, thrift and participation in religious and cultural activities. The system that was created by the progressive force of Liberal Nonconformity failed such families.

As a result, the elementary schools remained responsible for providing the only instruction that was received by the substantial majority of children who never entered an intermediate school, let alone the University of Wales. Those schools provided a basic training in reading, writing and counting, but they were hardly adequate as the sole source of education. Success in gaining admission to an intermediate school, by means of a scholarship, was a matter of immense pride shared by teachers and the communities they served. Teachers were in countless cases unsparing in their efforts to secure the best possible results for their pupils. At the same time, as was noted in chapter 4 and chapter 8, the opportunities that were made available to children to attend the intermediate schools weakened the position of the elementary school in two ways. They removed the most able pupils from the elementary school and, occasionally, drew the more capable teachers from the elementary classroom. At the same time, these opportunities removed the urgency to develop a curriculum for the elementary school that could provide a more complete education, despite the fact that the elementary school remained as important as ever for the majority of children. There were certainly wide disparities between schools and localities in the extent to which pupils were able to progress to the intermediate school. To the very end of the period studied, there were very many schools in which, often for social and economic rather than educational reasons, pupils with the ability to benefit from further opportunities were never, or only very exceptionally, entered for the scholarship examination.

Despite the failure to address more educational issues, elementary education continued to feature alongside matters such as the tithe, disestablishment, the land question and political allegiance as one of the enduring issues of politics in Wales. In addition to purely local concerns, a growing body of opinion questioned whether the organization established by the 1870 Act, and subsequently amended, was suitable for the needs of Wales at the turn of the twentieth century. The question was articulated in two distinct ways. First, a body of Welsh opinion, noted above, increasingly questioned the educational system. Although comparatively small in number, its Welsh critics were to raise a vociferous campaign for improved opportunities for the nation's pupils in the years immediately before the 1914–18 War and later. A second avenue by which discontent was channelled was found, some time earlier, in the efforts undertaken by central government to reappraise and amend the 1870 Act. A renewed stimulus was provided for this debate following the appointment of the Cross Commission in 1887.[14] Consideration has already been given to the opportunities which the inquiry provided for an examination of the issue of the Welsh language and the conduct and treatment of the teaching profession, yet the Commission had a wider remit. The broad scope of the inquiry caused anxiety for the Nonconformist leadership in Wales. While the opportunity for reassessment was welcomed, the nature of the Commission, appointed as a result of pressure from the Roman Catholic and Anglican influences and chaired by a high Anglican, caused alarm in Nonconformist ranks. As chairman of the Commission, Lord Cross declared his determination to ensure that, in consequence of its deliberations, the voluntary schools would be elevated to a position similar to that of the Board Schools in terms of government support, an intention that flew in the face of the views of Liberal members of the Commission such as Henry Richard and Dr Robert Dale of Birmingham.[15]

The Commission certainly faced difficulties, and its failure to reach a consensus was reflected in the publication of two minority reports to accompany the majority report. These demonstrated that despite the hope of Forster that the 1870 Act would present a compromise acceptable to all, deep divisions remained on the question of elementary education. Although the

[14] M. Sturt, *The Education of the People* (London, 1967), pp.373–7, 207–31.
[15] Robert William Dale (1829–95) was a Congregationalist minister who had been prominent in voluntary efforts by Nonconformists to provide schools before the Forster Act. He was also an instrumental figure in the development of the Congregationalists in Birmingham.

majority report included proposals such as the expansion of teacher training, a more sympathetic treatment of the Welsh language, the need for structural improvements to schools and an insistence on better-qualified staff in all schools, matters which certainly commended themselves to the Nonconformist leaders, the document made other recommendations that were totally unacceptable to the majority of elected representatives in Wales. It recommended an increase in public subsidies for the voluntary school sector, advocating rate aid for those schools whilst insisting that their management should remain in the hands of the voluntary sector. The minority report signed by Henry Richard, however, reached very different conclusions and painted a picture in which the community was excluded from the management of its school through the influence of the Anglican clergy and where teacher-training institutions were dominated by a clergy determined to promote their own religious opinions.[16]

The proposals of the majority report provoked a predictable reaction among the Nonconformists. R. Iwan Jenkins, writing in *Seren Gomer*, predicted that the majority report would not be implemented without a massive fight on the part of the Nonconformist community:

> dyledswydd holl garedigion addysg ydyw gorfodi y Senedd i osod attalfa ar draha yr offeiriadaeth a'i hysgolion, a rhoddi terfyn ar ddysgu credoau a gweddiau ar draul y cyhoedd . . . Er mai arian y cyhoedd sydd wedi dwyn traul yr ysgolion sectaraidd . . . etto . . . hawlir hwy gan yr offeiriaid megys eu heiddo personol . . . rhydd yr Ysgolion Eglwysig offeryn peryglus yn nwylaw Pristyddiaeth; archollwyd llawer i blentyn, a thrwy hyny lawer i deulu Annghydffurfiol â'r offeryn peryglus hwn.

> [It is the duty of all lovers of education to force Parliament to stop the impositions of the priesthood and their schools, and end the practice of teaching beliefs and prayers at public expense. Despite the fact that it is public money which has borne the costs of sectarian schools, . . . the clergy claim them as if they were their personal property . . . Church Schools are a dangerous weapon in the hands of the Priesthood; and many a child, and thus many a Nonconformist family, has been lost [to the Church] to this powerful weapon].[17]

---

[16] PP 1888, XXXV, Cross Report.
[17] R. I. Jenkins, 'Addysg elfennol: enwadol ai anenwadol?', *Seren Gomer*, X (October 1889).

Baner ac Amserau Cymru was also determined to enter into battle against the proposals:

> Yr amcan yr arfaethai y weinyddiaeth Geidwadol ei gyrhaedd ydoedd cadw ysgolion dyddiol nychlyd y parsoniaid, y rhai a gamenwir mor anfad yn 'Ysgolion Cenedlaethol', yn fyw, a'u codi uwch law yr angenrheidrwydd o orfod dibynu ar elusennau tanysgrifiadol cyfoethogion yr Eglwys, y rhai oeddynt o herwydd rhywbeth neu gilydd, yn myned yn fwy llawgauad y naill flwyddyn ar ol y llall . . . mae hi yn gryn gyffro a chyfyng-gynghor yn ngwersyll y parsoniaid a'r caredigion hyny i'r addysg enwadol Eglwysig sydd hyd yn hyn wedi esgeuluso gwneuthur y darpariaethau a ofynid oddi wrthynt yn eu hamrywiol gymydogaethau gan lythyren y gyfraith.

> [The aim of the Conservative government was to keep alive the languishing day schools of the clergy, the ones so wickedly misnamed 'National Schools', and to elevate them above the necessity of having to depend on the charitable subscriptions of wealthy Churchmen, subscriptions which were declining steadily year upon year . . . it is a time of commotion and perplexity for the clergy and those supporters of church denominational education who have so far neglected to make the provisions in their localities which are incumbent upon them by the letter of the law].[18]

Thomas Gee, its editor, proceeded to advocate the introduction of School Boards in all areas to replace the existing mixture of Board and voluntary schools.

The Cross Commission had sat for three years before it produced its reports in 1888. Yet it was not until 1896 that the Conservative government was able to incorporate its recommendations in legislation. The 1896 Bill was vehemently opposed, not only because it failed to address the problems that faced School Boards but also because of the way in which it proposed to enhance and safeguard the position of the voluntary schools. The controversy raised by the Bill of 1896 led the government to abandon the measure, to the relief of Welsh Liberal leaders. Relief proved short-lived, however, for the spirit of the proposals of 1896 was to be revived and incorporated in the Act of 1902. The Welsh reaction to the 1896 Bill was a foretaste of the controversy that was to surround the Balfour legislation of 1902. Daniel Rowlands denounced the 1896

---

[18] *Baner*, 27 August 1892.

proposals as inspired by the failure of the voluntary sector to compete with the Board Schools. Writing in *Y Traethodydd*, Rowlands insisted that the latter schools were over-performing as far as the government was concerned:

> Y maent yn gwneyd eu gwaith yn rhy dda, ac felly yn gosod anhawster yn ffordd ysgolion yr Eglwys i ddal cydymgais â hwynt yn addysgiaeth ein plant. 2. Nid ydynt yn dysgu daliadau yr Eglwys Sefydledig, ac felly yn gwasanaethu er dwyn y werin sydd wedi cefnu arni yn ol i'w chorlannau.
>
> [They are doing their work too well and are thus placing obstacles in the way of Church schools to compete with them in educating our children. They do not teach the beliefs of the Established Church and therefore are not calculated to bring back to the Anglican fold a people which has deserted it].[19]

Corwen parish council (Merioneth) claimed that the Bill sought to destroy the consensus embodied in the 1870 Act, stating that, in the 'interests of public Education and religious liberty', no further aid should be granted to denominational schools unless accompanied by adequate representative management and control.[20] Llandeilo Tal-y-bont Board (Glamorgan) predicted that the proposals would introduce sectarian bitterness into all local government elections and turn Board Schools into sources of religious contention and strife, and it pointed out that the real beneficiaries would be the subscribers to the voluntary schools rather than the pupils themselves.[21]

By 1896 the Nonconformists were in a position where it fell to them to defend the compromise formed in 1870, despite the fact that they themselves were unhappy at the privileges which continued to be granted to the Anglican Church under the Forster compromise. In some ways the reservations expressed in 1870 had been ameliorated by the practical experience of administering the Act, although issues such as those which arose at Cynwyd, Aberdyfi and Fishguard provided constant reminders of the inadequacies of the provisions of the Act. However, by the time the issue was debated, between 1896 and 1902, the Conservative Party was ascendant and was zealously attempting to mould

---

[19] Daniel Rowlands, 'Y mesur addysg', *Y Traethodydd*, LI (July 1896), 300–16.
[20] *Baner*, 1 May 1896.
[21] *Industrial World*, 5 March 1894.

public policy according to its own vision with little regard for the sensibilities of Welsh Nonconformists. Part of the Conservatives' platform was a determination to continue to subsidize the voluntary sector from public funds, irrespective of the opposition this engendered.[22] These developments had a crucial impact in galvanizing into action what had been, in the late 1890s, an increasingly lacklustre Welsh parliamentary leadership.[23] Concerns specific to Wales had not preoccupied Parliament since the debates over the tithe disturbances between 1886 and 1889. Although the Tithe Act of 1891 had demonstrated the determination of Welsh members to advance specifically Welsh claims and to secure legislation specific to Wales where that was shown to be necessary, few other such instances had arisen.[24] The issue of elementary education provided those Welsh members with renewed opportunities to promote Welsh grievances which were not confined to disestablishment, already the overriding Welsh political passion. Elementary education therefore became once more a marked feature in parliamentary debates, with particular expression being given to the Liberals' view of the position of Anglican voluntary schools in an overwhelmingly Nonconformist community. However, little attention was devoted to the actual structure of the School Boards and this resulted in a failure on the part of the Liberal Party, at parliamentary and local level, to develop a coherent policy for the reorganization of the elementary educational system. As has been demonstrated throughout this study, the performance of the Boards had been a cause for concern to government departments, school inspectors and indeed to the political leadership of all shades of opinion. Growing demands on the part of central government meant that Boards were finding increasing difficulty in undertaking their responsibilities. The size of the Boards varied from those such as Cardiff, Newport and Swansea, which employed a number of permanent staff, to those serviced by part-time clerks. These administrative difficulties were compounded by the parish-based structure of the educational system. As was demonstrated in chapter 2, the parish was in many cases too small and disparate to

---

[22] G. E. Jones, 'The "Welsh Revolt" revisited': Merioneth and Montgomeryshire in default', *WHR*, 4 (1988–9), 417–39.
[23] K. O. Morgan, *Wales in British Politics* (Cardiff, 1963), pp.178–84.
[24] Ibid., pp.85–7.

ensure effective administration even in 1870, and Boards demonstrated a marked reluctance to amalgamate. These difficulties were exacerbated during the remainder of the century, with demographic trends and further industrialization contributing to the feeling of unease at the performance of School Boards.[25] Indeed, as early as 1890, a conference representing the School Boards of north Wales unanimously passed a resolution calling for School Boards to be amalgamated and made co-terminous with the envisaged District Councils. D. P. Williams of Llanberis, whose experience as a member of a School Board and of Caernarfonshire County Council had convinced him of the benefits of the larger unit, claimed that such a reform would reduce the friction between personalities and villages and that in consequence all aspects of the work of the School Boards would be improved.[26]

The Education Bill proposed by Arthur Balfour in 1902 presented an opportunity to remedy those difficulties in the voluntary system which had resulted in the appointment of the Cross Commission in 1886 and which had taken over ten years to address. For the Nonconformist leadership in Wales, the Bill constituted the legislative incarnation of the antichrist.[27] Nonconformist denominations, School Boards, Liberal Associations and the denominational press condemned the proposals in the Bill. The transference of voluntary schools to the status of 'non-provided schools' was regarded as an attack on religious freedom and a means by which to force Nonconformist ratepayers to contribute to schools whose doctrine they opposed. Of equal importance, the Bill ensured the perpetuation of Anglican schools, placing them on a firm financial footing.

The reaction of the Welsh local authorities to the Balfour Act is well-documented and falls outside the remit of this study. The 'Welsh Revolt' inspired by the parliamentary leadership, particularly David Lloyd George, and undertaken by the county councils, succeeded in delaying implementation of the Act. It resulted in one of the closest parallels between government policy in Ireland and that in Wales manifested in the Default Act. Yet,

---

[25] G. A. N. Lowndes, *The Silent Social Revolution* (Oxford, 1969), pp.47–63.
[26] *CDH*, 11 April 1890.
[27] Rees, 'Addysg Cymru'; D. Rowlands, 'Y mesur addysg', *Y Traethodydd* (July 1896), 300–15.

throughout the debate, the School Boards of Wales were marginalized. The argument centred on the attitude of the county councils, as the new authorities, rather than on a need to preserve the Board system, which had few defenders except for the Board members themselves. With the exception of a certain number of 'revolt schools', the debate took place at a level which was remote from the local community in comparison with the referenda of the early 1870s. This reflected another equally important feature of the Act. Control of elementary education was no longer exercised by members of the community itself, with the result that the arguments, and sometimes disharmony, which had characterized so much of the work of the School Boards of Wales was now transferred to the more sedate county halls. Elementary education under the new system was not to feature as prominently in the concerns of local communities.

This decline in local control did, however, offer considerable advantages to the development of an education service. County councils were able to divert resources to areas which had previously suffered from low rateable value and had therefore been unable to make essential structural and material improvements.[28] The situation whereby each parish was compelled to stand alone was ended, as concepts of subsidy and prioritization came to dominate the argument. Under the new system, strategic planning led to more rational management and allocation of resources which contributed to a steady, if gradual, improvement in the level of the service.

A realization of the deficiencies that continued to affect elementary education in Wales at the turn of the century does not detract from the achievements that were secured in the preceding period. The machinery was in place to ensure that an elementary school was available to the children of each parish, and that a county school was available within reasonable distance of all but the most remote areas. The fabric of school buildings had been improved, on account both of the higher standards demanded by the Education Department and the competition which existed between the various providing agencies. This can also be said of the capital equipment of the

[28] Ken Hopkins, 'Educational administration and policy making 1889–1989', in Owen E. Jones (ed.), *The Welsh Intermediate Education Act of 1889: A Centenary Appraisal* (Cardiff, 1990), pp.43–62.

schools – desks, furnishings, teaching aids and other materials – which contributed to the improvement in educational standards. Wales was brought into contact with educational publishers and manufacturers to a greater extent than ever, resulting in Welsh children being able to overcome the difficulties consequent upon lack of resources. Yet, despite the importance and achievements of these reforms, many deficiencies, identified in earlier years, remained. The voluntary school sector was often starved of resources and, as has been demonstrated, increasingly so. The attitude of education authorities, and the need to limit the burden of the school on the community, resulted in less than satisfactory progress in a number of areas, notably in the rural localities.

The teaching profession showed positive signs of progress. Teachers were increasingly college-trained and demonstrated a progressive attitude towards methods of teaching. A more liberal regime was introduced into the classrooms, despite the fact that strict discipline remained essential in an era of large classes. A real improvement was secured in terms of basic education – reading, writing and arithmetic – and in a limited number of other subjects. Throughout this period, however, Wales modelled its entire education ethos on that of England. Despite the presence of a few lone voices, writing mainly in the heavier journals of the Nonconformist denominations, there was never a development of a specifically Welsh form of educational thought. Scotland was branching into its own brand of educational speciality, training potential scientists, medical practitioners and engineers at an early age and, equally important, elevating the status of those professions and occupations.[29] Wales, on the other hand, influenced by the English public-school cult of the 'all rounder', remained wedded to the classical idea of scholarship, without developing a comparable scientific education.

Teachers charged with effecting an improvement in the educational condition of Wales did not meet universal support or assistance. Their treatment by School Boards was hardly different from that of voluntary school teachers by trustees, and ranged from respect and support to almost total hostility. Their

---

[29] The success of the Scottish model was one which Welsh educationists watched enviously. See John Rhys to T. E. Ellis, NLW, T. E. Ellis Papers, 1753–4.

relationship with the inspectorate was not conducive to educational progress, an inevitable consequence of the role of the school inspectors as the educational inquisitors of the nineteenth century, upon whose comments a teacher's salary was based. These difficulties were compounded by the lack of respect often accorded to members of the teaching profession, their undefined social status and because, as newcomers to the community, they lacked the local ties of kinship which were so important in what remained in many cases a closed, inward-looking and parochial society.

The prevalence of the Welsh language remained an issue throughout this period and the lack of an effective policy seriously affected the efforts of the teaching profession to improve educational standards. For too long, central government and the inspectorate failed to acknowledge that the language was a major phenomenon in Welsh education; they took insufficient account of the efforts needed by both pupils and teachers to learn and conduct instruction through the medium of a language other than the native tongue. The language itself was undervalued and some of the blame for its decline can be apportioned to several agencies – the Anglican Church, the Conservative Party, the inspectorate, members of the teaching profession and parents. Yet what it is crucial to understand is that, despite the often open hostility of various agencies, their efforts to 'stamp out' the Welsh language were insufficient to bring about its decline. The real problem was the failure of society in general to place sufficient value on the native tongue and to see the merits of a bilingual society. In a bilingual community where one of the languages was not awarded any significant degree of merit, it was inevitable that English, as the new language with social prestige, would gain the ascendancy.[30] The revival of interest in the language and attentiveness to its value, as part of the wider nationalist movement of the 1880s, ensured that it became an issue in Welsh society. Yet it remained the concern of a minority, mainly an educated élite, and only occasionally became the preoccupation of the wider community. Even less attention was given by the community in general to the language in which its

[30] G. E. Jones, 'Perceptions of the Welshness of education', in Jones (ed.), *The Welsh Intermediate Education Act of 1889*, pp.149–167.

members conversed than to issues such as tithes and disestablishment, demonstrating the limited degree to which Welsh was valued. Relevant to this is the nature of the attention paid to the language. Welsh academics tended to look to the past – at the historical development of the language and literature of Wales – at a time when it was crucial that the practical needs of the language be addressed. The nineteenth century witnessed a transformation of both economy and society, and these changes gave birth to a new vocabulary, particularly to terms associated with industry and technology. Welsh was slow to adapt to these new needs and the Welsh terms which developed were often cumbersome versions of English equivalents. As a result, English words came increasingly into common usage, bastardizing the Welsh language and contributing to the decline in its perceived value.

The religious conflict of nineteenth-century Wales was also played out in the field of education. Those divisions in many ways camouflaged deeper social divisions. The Anglican Church, dominated by the landed aristocracy and a large group drawn from professional and commercial circles, was widely portrayed not only as élitist but also as a repressive force in Welsh society.[31] Yet the Nonconformist denominations were an equally complex group that included individuals with perceptions that differed greatly from the democratic and progressive ideals that were associated with those denominations. Significantly, throughout this work it is the term 'Nonconformist' that applies, rather than the more precise descriptions of Baptist, Congregationalist, Methodist or Wesleyan. It was 'Nonconformist' that was used most frequently in religious newspapers and periodicals of the period, which reflects the fact that the rivalries were increasingly between the Nonconformists as a body and the Anglican and Roman Catholic forces rather than between the Nonconformist denominations themselves. There were certainly varied emphases within the various denominations, over matters of church organization and doctrine, such as the debate within the Congregational Union regarding the nature of the constitution of

---

[31] *Report of the St David's Diocesan Conference held at Carmarthen, 27 and 28 September 1882* (Carmarthen, 1882). Delegates included Thomas Arthur Nicholas, a draper of Fishguard, John Thomas, a farmer of Mathry, D. R. Davies, a schoolmaster of Knighton, C. E. G. Phillips of Picton Castle, Rhys Goring Thomas of Plas Llannon, and Lord Dynevor.

the Welsh Congregationalists or within the Baptist Union regarding strict or open communion. Yet in terms of the contributions of the denominations to the public life of Wales, the Nonconformists were increasingly at one.[32] Their unity grew as the decades progressed and by the turn of the century the internal arguments of the Nonconformists were ones that crossed denominational boundaries. Thus, it was issues such as the moderating of High Calvinism, the rise of the social gospel and a change in emphasis from individual salvation to concern for issues affecting society as a whole, that came to dominate the debate. No particular denomination was more progressive or conservative than any other, and Nonconformity continued to be able to embrace people who maintained a variety of outlooks on political and social issues. However, given that Nonconformity was a very loose coalition, the Anglican Church was able to exploit the lack of a unified approach, for instance over the question of religious instruction in schools.

At the same time, the relative strengths of the various religious groups in Wales were changing, a factor that some attributed partly to the policy adopted by the Nonconformist bodies on the issue of education. As a correspondent in *Cwrs y Byd* claimed, there were fears that the Nonconformist denominations were losing ground in Wales because they had acquiesced in the provision of education by the state, and that both the Roman Catholic and Anglican Churches were gaining because of the emphasis they placed on using their own schools in order to instil their values in children. Indeed, Daniel Rowlands had previously questioned the very principle of local authority as opposed to denominational schools:[33]

> Maent hwy wedi cadw eu hysgolion yn y blaen, er yn dlawd iawn y rhan fwyaf, ac y maent yn llwyddo, pa ryfedd? Canys y maent yn hawio llwyddo, ac wele nyni – annibynnwyr a bedyddwyr – wedi taflu yr holl faich oddiar ein gwarau, a pha ryfedd ein bod yn colli tir i'r hyn fuom?
>
> [They have kept their schools, though impoverished for the most part, and they are succeeding, and no wonder. They deserve success because we,

---

[32] For a contemporary view of the emerging unity within the Nonconformist bodies, see, for instance, *CN*, 12 July 1889.
[33] Rowlands, 'Y mesur addysg', 300–15.

Baptists and Congregationalists, have shed the burden from our shoulders and should we be surprised that we are losing ground?][34]

The Nonconformist denominations had conceded that they lacked the resources to create their own system of schools and acknowledged that a rejection of state provision would have consolidated the position of the Anglicans in particular as the providers of education. Admittedly, they were able to embark on a massive programme of chapel building throughout the later decades of the nineteenth century, but they may have been correct in their assessment in 1870 of what they could achieve in terms of providing for education, a reflection of how the problem of resources had become less pronounced by the turn of the twentieth century. But their adherence to the argument in favour of state provision, irrespective of the issue of resources, had important implications that confronted them increasingly during the period in this study. Principal Thomas Rees noted, in his analysis of the crisis that faced Nonconformity in the years after the 1914–18 War, that an education system based on secular principles contributed to the emergence of a generation that was less likely to accept blindly the traditional Nonconformist (or, indeed, Christian) teachings. Rees believed that the adoption of state-supported education had been inevitable and that the task of Nonconformity was to persuade and convince the rising generation of its enduring values and beliefs; in order to do this the complacent attitudes of the Nonconformists would have to be removed to offset the increasingly secular tide.[35] Education was crucial to the emergence of new ideas among Nonconformists of the relationship between the individual (or a community of individuals) and the state, and the new relationship enabled Nonconformity to become an active promoter of an enhanced role for government in other fields, notably social reform, that would have been impossible had Nonconformity retained the older tradition of hostility to official intervention.

The experience of education also demonstrated that, despite the influence of the Nonconformist ethos, there remained a significant proportion of the community which did not comply with

[34] *Cwrs y Byd*, V (1895), 162.
[35] Thomas Rees, 'The crisis of Welsh Nonconformity', *Welsh Outlook*, VII (March, 1920), 57–60.

the classic depiction of the virtuous lifestyle of the Welsh *gwerin*.[36] Education remained an undervalued experience, and this was compounded by the fact that the educational ladder of opportunity was not available to a significant proportion of the community. In a society where financial considerations precluded many from continuing in education, the opportunity for personal advancement was inevitably limited. Moreover, those who did avail themselves of the benefits of education fell victim to their own success. The paucity of career opportunities in many parts of Wales, particularly in rural areas, meant that seeking employment elsewhere became unavoidable. Consequently, large areas of Wales were denied the benefit of the talents and learning of some of their most able and articulate offspring.

As was shown in chapter 1, the Liberal and Nonconformist response to legislation for elementary education was characterized by disappointment, followed by resignation and determination to use the Act to the limited extent that it allowed. The Nonconformist leadership was faced with an Act which was essentially a compromise between the conflicting claims of those advocating an end to the voluntary system and its defenders. For those radical leaders who were disappointed by the Act, the outcome was an indication of the fact that the Liberal leadership in Parliament was not representative of grass-roots opinion. They attributed the failure to adopt a more radical course to the Whiggish tendencies of many backbenchers, including several elected for Welsh constituencies in 1868, and they believed that their defeat in 1874 arose from disappointment at the failure of the government to follow a more radical programme. This estimate of the radical tribunes as representative of the majority of the Welsh community has to be qualified, however, by the evidence of the response to the 1870 Act. Wales did not witness a wholesale rejection of the voluntary principle in education. The failure of the School Board movement to secure Boards in parishes which were undeniably Nonconformist strongholds demonstrated that, for a variety of reasons, the Welsh community was not prepared to follow blindly the leadership of the more radical section, especially when financial disadvantage was

---

[36] David Jenkins, *The Agricultural Community in South-West Wales at the Turn of the Twentieth Century* (Cardiff, 1971), pp.177–218.

involved. The evidence of the referenda demonstrates that the hostility of the Welsh community to the Anglican Church and Conservative Party was not as pronounced as the leaders of Welsh Liberalism claimed, suggesting that the partial Conservative revival in Wales in 1874 was not altogether a result of abstention by radicals disappointed at the moderation of the government, but rather a reflection of a continued sympathy for the Conservative cause even among certain members of Nonconformist denominations. However, despite the existence of a residual Conservative vote, the strength of Welsh Liberalism increased during the 1880s and 1890s as issues such as disestablishment and tithes became the central tenets of the party's appeal.[37] Those campaigns provided an unequalled opportunity for political instruction in Wales, with rich dividends for the tribunes of radical policies. Whatever the inconsistencies in local voting patterns, the Liberals still expected easy victories in parliamentary elections at the end of the period under discussion here, a situation which contrasts greatly with earlier tests such as that of 1874. In part, the consolidation of the Liberal vote in Wales owed much to the manner in which the Liberals began to address specifically Welsh issues after the formation of the National Liberal Federation, such as those manifested in the Newcastle Programme. The Liberals came to be recognized as the political force that articulated the aspirations of Wales, Scotland and, indeed, large areas of England. Yet the rewards of this alignment with Liberalism were limited. The failure of the Liberal Party to address issues in England, most notably those which could galvanize support in the rural counties, resulted in successive defeats in the 1890s and, even after the exalted Liberal victory in 1906, the party demonstrated insufficient urgency in addressing issues such as the disestablishment question, thereby weakening its claim on the Welsh electorate.

At a local level, Welsh Liberals failed to demonstrate a radical zeal in the execution of their duties as the managers of elementary education. Throughout the period, denominationalism and parochialism undoubtedly bedevilled the debate as education became increasingly a matter of political conflict. Education was

[37] T. I. Ellis, *Thomas Edward Ellis*, 2 vols (Liverpool, 1948), pp.25–85; N. Masterman, *The Forerunner: The Dilemmas of Tom Ellis, 1859–1899* (Llandybïe, 1972), pp.90–114.

crucial to the Liberals' programme for Wales, constituting one of the few issues on which they could claim success, and it was an issue which united the rural and urban wings of the party, a common experience relevant to both communities and one of the few tenets of Liberal faith that were relevant to the industrial community. Yet, as has been demonstrated, there was a growing disillusionment with the education system in industrial Wales, and this became an issue as the political life of the coalfield became increasingly turbulent, not least after the establishment of the South Wales Miners' Federation in 1898.[38] The patient tribes of proletarian Wales no longer adhered unquestioningly to the leadership provided by what was increasingly regarded as a procrastinating and parsimonious *petit bourgeois* élite, with whom they had been allied, in varying degrees, since the early politicization of Nonconformity in the twenty years before the 1868 election.

The creation of the education system was, nevertheless, the greatest tribute to the leaders of Welsh society in the closing decades of the nineteenth century. The Wales of 1902 was very different from that of 1870. The influence of elementary education was one of the factors that facilitated economic progress and furthered change in social attitudes and the creation of a more sophisticated approach to the political life of the nation. The schools created as a result of the 1870 Forster Act were a crucial influence in fashioning modern Wales.

---

[38] Peter Stead, 'Schools and society in Glamorgan before 1914', *Morgannwg*, XIX (1975), 39–56.

BIBLIOGRAPHY

1. UNPRINTED SOURCES

a. National Library of Wales: Deposited Collections
Crosswood Papers.
D. R. Daniel Papers.
Dinas Powis Papers.
Dolaucothi Correspondence.
Glansevern Collection.
Glyneiddan Papers.
Harpton Court Papers.
Llwyngwair Papers.
Llysdinam Papers.
Lucas Papers.
Picton Castle Papers.
Spence Colby Papers.
T. E. Ellis Papers.
Voelas and Cefnamwlch Papers.

b. National Library of Wales MSS
714–5D, Press cuttings of Edward Griffiths, Springfield, Dolgellau.
928B, Thomas Stephens, 'Address to the Working Class on the Benefits of Education'.
2495E, Miscellaneous papers: education in Wales.
2834B, D. Samuel, articles and addresses on education in Wales.
2894, W. Hobley, essay on 'The Present State of Education in Wales'.
2994E; 2995, Official Letters, Circulars and Papers re Haverfordwest School Board, 1870–95.
2296E, Material: Haverfordwest School Board.
5744C, 'Gwerthfawrogiad Gwybodaeth o'r Saesoneg i'r Cymro': Prize essay, Pen-y-bont Eisteddfod, 1854.
6715B, Appeal for subscriptions for Bangor National Schools.
7106E, Journal kept by Nefydd: British Schools in south Wales.
7316E, Summary of attendance at Tywyn British School.
8559B, Collecting Book, including 'The Educational Difficulty at Cynwyd 1887'.
8832E, W. J. Parry, Copies of resolutions passed by Bethesda School Board.
9680E, Article by T. Sylvanus, 'Hanes Pen Llwyn a'r Cylch'.
10359E, Papers: dispute at Llanfair-juxta-Harlech School.
11011E, Papers pertaining to Thomas Gee.
11552D, Scrap book: Haverfordwest School Board.
11588D, Letters to M. Lovina Williams.
11646B, Press cuttings compiled by D. M. Lewis.
11650C, Essays by D. M. Lewis on educational topics.
11651C, Addresses by D. M. Lewis on religious instruction.
12262D, Report by N. John SAO to Coychurch School Board, 1895.
12283, Holograph essay 'Addysg yng Nghymru'.

12287B, School Board Accounts, Tregaron Union.
12330E, Material: religious instruction in schools.
12636D, Minute Book of Swansea School Board.
12907, Letters to Richard Rees.

c. Public Record Office, London

ED2/557–562	Files on elementary education in Anglesey.
ED2/563–567	Files on elementary education in Brecon.
ED2/568–574	Files on elementary education in Cardiganshire.
ED2/575–582	Files on elementary education in Carmarthenshire.
ED2/583–589	Files on elementary education in Caernarfonshire.
ED2/590–596	Files on elementary education in Denbighshire.
ED2/597–601	Files on elementary education in Flintshire.
ED2/602–612	Files on elementary education in Glamorgan.
ED2/613–616	Files on elementary education in Merioneth.
ED2/617–625	Files on elementary education in Monmouthshire.
ED2/626–630	Files on elementary education in Montgomeryshire.
ED2/631–637	Files on elementary education in Pembrokeshire.
ED2/638–640	Files on elementary education in Radnorshire.
ED5/180–201	Compulsory Purchase Files.
ED16	Local Education Authority Supply Files (Part III Authorities).
ED21	Files on individual schools.
ED92	General files on Wales.

d. Flintshire County Record Office, Hawarden
D/DM/631, Papers of L. J. Roberts, late HMI for Clwyd area.
D/E/1542/481, Correspondence: assault on pupil teacher.
D/E/3066, Verses entitled 'School Boardism'.
D/KT/26, Appeal for donations for new parochial school at Wrexham.
D/L/20, Election address to Mostyn mineworkers.
D/NT/232, Typescript: Primary school education in Pen-y-ffordd following 1870 Act.
D/POL/189, Request for financial assistance, Nerquis.
DE 3062, Pamphlet attacking state education.
DGR 1304, Complaint: sanitary condition of privies at Halkyn School.
DGR 1305, Accusation of apathy on part of managers of Halkyn School.
DL 52; DL 4, Papers: School Board agitation at Ffynnongroyw.
E/SB 1/14, Correspondence re Holywell School Board.
HL, Herbert Lewis Deposited Papers.
NC/646; NC/648, Materials: educational disagreement at St Asaph.

e. Denbighshire County Record Office, Ruthin
BD/A/484, Correspondence: Church schools at Rhyl.
BD/A/488, Correspondence attacking Denbigh Borough Council: School Board issue.
DD/DM/128/35, Paper: education prepared for Baptist Union Congress.
DD M/228/45, Extracts from *Wrexham Leader*: education.
DD/WY/5807, Correspondence: School Board agitation at Nant yr Eira.
PD/84/1/25, Correspondence: Nantglyn Schools.
PD/88/1/6, Correspondence: Rosset parish.
PD/101/1/345, Attempts to enlist charitable money for school refurbishment.

f. Gwynedd County Record Office, Caernarfon
EA/1/49 1, Correspondence: Llanaelhaearn Council School.
EA/2, Papers of Pen-y-groes School Governing Body.

BIBLIOGRAPHY

EA/2/1, General educational correspondence, 1896–1900.
ES/5, Papers: elections to Llangybi School Board.
M/923/356, Correspondence: Caernarfon School Board.
Vaynol 3044, Correspondence: Llanddeiniolen School.
XD8/4/890, Correspondence: Porthmadog School Board.
XES/5, Materials: Conwy National School.
XM/1212/209, Correspondence: education in Rhiwabon and Llanddeiniolen.
XM/5599, Papers: education at Betws Garmon.

g. Gwynedd County Record Office, Dolgellau
A/11/23, Agreement between Dyffryn Board School and Llanenddwyn School Board.
A/11/26, Rules and duties of managers under Tywyn and Pennal School Board.
A/11/27, Correspondence: Tywyn and Pennal School Board.
A/16/10, Minutes of meetings: education at Aberdyfi.
A/16/6&7, Printed leaflets: Aberdyfi School case.
A/16/51, Correspondence: Trawsfynydd School.
A/17/19, Papers of Glyndyfrdwy National School.
A/20/5, Minutes of meeting: improvements to Bryncadifor School.
A52, Papers of Llangar School Board.
D/16/12, Materials: Aberdyfi Undenominational School.
Z/A/29/6, Minutes of Llandecwyn National School.
Z/A/53, Materials relating to Mallwyd National School.

h. Carmarthen County Record Office
Bishop Papers, Letter Books nos. 1–25, excluding 20 and 23, general estate correspondence.
C/1/96, Minute Book of Cenarth School Management Committee.
C/108/1/98, Minute Books of Llanfihangel Abercywyn School Board.
C/ED/83a, Minute Book of Llandybïe School Board.
C/ED/109/1/98, Minute Book of Llangyndeyrn School Board.
C/ED/180, Llanelli Pupil Teachers' Log Book.
C/ED/181a, Minute Book of Llanfihangel Rhos-y-corn School Board.
C/ED/182–84, Log Books of Five Roads School.
C/ED/184, St Clears School Board Managers Minute Book.
C/ED/185–87, Log Books, Park Street Boys' School, Llanelli.
C/ED/188–90, Log Books, Old Road Schools, Llanelli.
C/ED/226, Log Book, Cefnarthen Evening Continuation School.
C/ED/242, Minute Book of St Clear's School Board.
C/ED/597, Minute Book of Llanwinio School Board.
C/ED/L69–79, Minute Books of the Llanelli School Board.
Castell Gorfod Papers, B181, Church–chapel conflict in Carmarthenshire.
Coedmore Papers, 2040, Claim by National School.
Ibid., 2212, Material: Cilgerran estate.
Ibid., 2752, Relationship between teacher and community.
Derwydd Papers, CA44, Miscellaneous political papers.
Dynevor Papers, Box 137, Land for schools in Amman Valley.
Ibid., Estate Letter Books 1–9, general estate correspondence.
ED/Bk 425/8, Miscellaneous folders: School Board elections etc.
Stepney Papers C 1, General estate correspondence.
Taliaris Papers 424, Estate Letter Books 1867–81.
Ibid., 447, Material: Taliaris School.
Ibid., 305, HMI Report and Log Book for Taliaris School.

i. Pembrokeshire County Record Office, Haverfordwest
D/HIG/1320–4, National school material.
D/RTM/MHE/801, Request for financial assistance, Hubberston National School.
DX 107/1, Materials: Llanfyrnach and Eglwyswrw School Board.
HDX/1177/1, Election to Llanychlwydog School Board, 1889.

j. Swansea City and County Record Office
D/7714, Material: Swansea Trades Council attitude to elementary education.
DD/GN/E/157–167, Gnoll Estate Papers.
D/D GV/36, Correspondence: Hafod School (Vivian Collection).
D/D HSV 19/7 24–26, Swansea Valley History Society, Education Collection.
D/D P 692–777, Margam/Penrice Estate Correspondence.
D/D P 913, Correspondence between Oxwich School Board and Penrice estate.
D/D XDU, Canvassing cards opposing formation of Aberavon School Board, 1893.
D/D XGB 11, Material: NUET Annual Conference, Swansea 1897.
D/D YC 1228, Ynyscedwyn Estate Correspondence.
E/SB 71/2, Minute Books of Swansea School Board

k. Glamorgan County Record Office, Cardiff
D/D A50 1–14, Various political activities.
D/D A51 1–21, Material: political situation in Merthyr.
D/D AAN, Material concerning the caning of a child.
D/D AU 304 1–4, Material concerning Aubrey family.
D/D BR 138/1–2, Prospectus of appointment to Royal Commission on Education.
D/D BR 149/3, Comments by Bruce on Gladstone Bill.
D/D BR 162/6, Comments on the Welsh Education Question 1882.
D/D BR 164/1, Speech by Bruce on subject of education.
D/DD 570 and 571/1 and 2, Correspondence: Llanfabon National School.
D/DF/F/131, Correspondence from the Committee of Council on Education.
D/DG, Material: involvement of Guest family in education prior to 1870.
D/DX38 1–7, Material: Aberdare School Board.
D/DX38 14, Compilations: Aberdare School Board.
D/DX 80/i, Material: Llantwit Major School Board.
D/DXUF 3/2, Materials concerning Aberdare School Board.
D/DXUF 3/4, Materials concerning the Appointment of Teachers.
D/DXUF 4, Reports to Merthyr Tydfil School Board.
D/XIX, Agreement to appoint Rose Davies as teacher, Aberdare National School.

l. Gwent County Record Office, Cwmbran
CE.A.80 20, Reports: school attendance at Griffithstown.
CE SB3 C 1, Papers of Aberystruth School Board.
CE SB3 C4, Papers: education in Abertillery.
CE SB53 C–1, Letter book of Llanelli School Board.
CE SB53 C–3, Correspondence and papers, Llanelli School Board.
D/361/M 1E5, Papers concerning Education Act of 1870.

m. Deposited Collections at University of Wales, Bangor
Belmont Papers, Henry Lewis's Scheme for religious instruction.
Lligwy Papers, Corrrespondence: Lord Boston's interest in education.
MSS 1124, Materials concerning Rhyd Ddu, particularly Henry Parry-Williams.
William Jones Papers 547, Correspondence: moves to establish School Board at Bethesda.

n. Deposited Collections at University of Wales, Swansea
St Davids Priory Records, especially B19: Dan-y-graig Roman Catholic School.

o. Deposited Collections at Merthyr Tydfil Public Library
'Cyhoeddiad Bwrdd Ysgol Merthyr Tydfil' (1895).
Merthyr Express Almanac and Yearbook, 1897.
Triennial Reports of Merthyr Tydfil School Board, 1873–1905.
W. Harris, 'History of education in Merthyr Tydfil, 1840–1912, a brief survey'.

p. Deposited Collections at Cardiff Central Library
Beriah Evans Papers.

2. OFFICIAL PAPERS

a. Hansard's Parliamentary Debates, Third Series.

b. British Parliamentary Papers

1847	XXVII	Report of the Commissioners of Inquiry into the State of Education in Wales.
1870	XIII	Report of the Commission on the Employment of Children, Young Persons and Women in Agriculture.
1870	XXII	Annual Report of the Committee of Council on Education.
1870	XXV	Report on the Education of Pauper Children.
1871	XVII	Report on Education in France.
1871	XXII	Annual Report, Education.
1872	I	Annual Report, Education (Appendix).
1872	X	Report on Teachers' Pensions.
1873	XIV	Annual Report, Education.
1874	XVIII	Annual Report, Education.
1875	VIII	Appendix concerning Religious Instruction and Free Education.
1875	XXIV	Annual Report, Education.
1876	XIII	Annual Report, Education.
1877	XXIX	Annual Report, Education.
1878	XXVIII	Annual Report, Education.
1878–9	XXIII	Annual Report, Education.
1880	XXII	Annual Report, Education.
1881	XXXII	Annual Report, Education.
1882	XIII	Annual Report, Education.
1883	XV	Annual Report, Education.
1884	XIV	Annual Report, Education.
1884	XIX	Report on Technical Education.
1884–5	XXIII	Annual Report, Education.
1886	LI	Report on the Dan-y-graig School controversy.
1887	XXVIII	Annual Report, Education.
1887	XXX	Minutes of Evidence, Royal Commission on Education in England and Wales (Cross Commission).
1887	XXXVI	Report on Children attending Schools in Workhouses and Separate Poor Law Schools.
1888	XXXV	Report of the Royal Commission on Education in England and Wales (Cross Commission).
1888	XXXVI	Appendix concerning religious instruction.
1888	XXXVI	Returns concerning attendance policy, fees policy and policy concerning religious instruction from various continental countries.

BIBLIOGRAPHY

1888	XXXVIII	Royal Commission on Education in England and Wales (Cross Commission).
1888	LIX	Report on Truant and Industrial Schools.
1889	XXIX	Annual Report, Education.
1890–1	XXVII	Annual Report, Education.
1890–1	LXI	Report on the working of the Free School System in America, France and Belgium; returns concerning the provision of religious instruction in Europe.
1892	XII	Report on teachers' pensions.
1892	LX	Statistical appendix.
1893	LXVIII	Statistical appendix.
1893–4	LXVIII	Statistical appendix.
1893–4	XXVI	Annual Report, Education.
1893–4	XXXIX	Report on the education system in Holland.
1893–4	LXXVI	Local Taxation Retrurns, 1893.
1893–4	LXCIII	Statistical appendix.
1894	LXVI	Statistical appendix.
1895	XXVI	Annual Report, Education.
1895	LXXVI	Statistical appendix.
1896	XXXIV	Royal Commission on Land in Wales and Monmouthshire.
1896	LXIV	Statistical appendix.
1897	XXV	Report on Education in Ireland, Denmark and Germany.
1897	XXVI	Annual Report, Education.
1897	LXVIII	Statistical appendix.
1898	XXIV	Report into the Origins of the Welsh Intermediate Education Act.
1898	XXV	Report on Education in Switzerland.
1898	LXX	Code of Regulations concerning Evening Continuation Schools.
1899	XX	Annual Report, Education.
1900	XXI	Annual Report, Education.
1900	LXV	Report on School Boards' Contractual Arrangements.
1906	XLVI	Report on Conditions in the Rural Areas (Wales).
1910	XVIII	Royal Commission on the Established Church and other religious bodies.

3. NEWSPAPERS AND PERIODICALS

Amddiffynnydd Yr Eglwys.
Baner ac Amserau Cymru.
Brecon and Radnor Express.
Cambrian.
Cambrian News.
Carnarvon and Denbigh Herald.
Cwrs y Byd.
Cymru.
Cymru Fydd.
Industrial World.
Journal of the Liverpool Welsh National Society.
Llanelly and County Guardian.
Llanelly Mercury.
Manchester Guardian.
Merthyr Express.
Merthyr Telegraph.
Pembrokeshire Herald.
Schoolmaster.
Seren Gomer.
Standard.
Western Mail.
Y Cronicl.
Y Diwygiwr.
Y Goleuad.
Y Traethodydd.
Y Tyst a'r Dydd.
Young Wales.

BIBLIOGRAPHY

4. Books Published before 1914

Ballinger, J. (ed), *National Union of Elementary Teachers, Souvenir of the Aberystwyth Conference, 1911* (Aberystwyth, 1911)
Cardiff School Board, *Triennial Report* (Cardiff, 1875).
Cardiff School Board, *Triennial Report* (Cardiff, 1878).
Davies, E., *Hanes Plwyf Llangunllo* (Llandysul, 1905).
Edwards, O. M., *Clych Adgof* (Oxford, 1908).
Edwards, T. C., *Bywyd a Llythyrau y Diweddar Barch Lewis Edwards* (Liverpool, 1901).
Griffith, J., *Cofiant y Gohebydd* (Denbigh, 1905).
Jones, E. Pan, *Oes Gofion* (Bala, 1908).
Jones, T. Gwynn, *Cofiant Thomas Gee*, 2 vols (Denbigh, 1913).
Morgan, J. V., *Welsh Political and Educational Leaders in the Victorian Era* (London, 1908).
Northern Counties Education League, *Education Struggle at Fishguard, Pembrokeshire* (Rochdale, 1901).
Owen, Daniel, *Hunangofiant Rhys Lewis* (Wrexham, 1888).
Owen, Hugh, *Deddf Addysg 1870* (London, 1870).
Report of the 7th Church Conference at Rhyl, 17 and 18 September 1889 (Wrexham, 1889).
Report of the 10th Church Conference at Newtown, 14 and 15 September 1893 (Welshpool, 1893).
Report of the St David's Diocesan Conference held at Carmarthen, 27 and 28 September 1882 (Carmarthen, 1882).
Rhŷs, John, *Lectures on Celtic Philology* (London, 1885).
Richard, Henry, *Letters on the Social and Political Condition of Wales* (London, 1867) reprinted as *Letters and Essays on Wales* (London, 1884).
Southall, J. E., *Wales and Her Language* (Newport and London, 1902).
Swansea School Board, *Triennial Report of the Swansea School Board* (Swansea, 1882).
Stephens, T., *Cymru Heddiw ac Yfory* (Cardiff, 1908).
Vincent, J. E., *The Land Question in North Wales* (London, 1896).

5. Books Published after 1914

Bassett, T. M., *Bedyddwyr Cymru* (Swansea, 1977).
Biagini, E., *Liberty, Retrenchment and Reform* (Oxford, 1992).
Bowen, E. G., *A History of Llanbadarn Fawr* (Aberystwyth, 1979).
Cragoe, M., *An Anglican Aristocracy: The Moral Economy of the Landed Estate in Carmarthenshire, 1832–1895* (Oxford, 1996).
Davies, D. R., *Hanes Llanwennog: Y Plwyf a'r Bobl* (Aberystwyth, 1939).
Davies, E. T., *Monmouthshire Schools and Education to 1870* (Newport, 1957).
Davies, Gwilym Prys, *Llafur y Blynyddoedd* (Denbigh, 1991).
Davies, John, *Cardiff and the Marquesses of Bute* (Cardiff, 1981).
Davies, J., *Education in a Welsh Rural County* (Cardiff, 1973).
Davies, J. H., *History of Pontardawe* (Llandybïe, 1967).
Davies, Russell, *Secret Sins: Sex, Violence and Society in Carmarthenshire, 1870–1920* (Cardiff, 1996).
Davies, W. Ll. (ed.), *National Union of Teachers, Souvenir of the Aberystwyth Conference 1933* (Aberystwyth, 1933).
Dunbabin, J. P. D., *Rural Discontent in Nineteenth-century Britain* (London, 1974).
Edwards, Hywel Teifi, *Gŵyl Gwalia: Yr Eisteddfod Genedlaethol yn Oes Victoria* (Llandysul, 1980).
Ellis, Edward L., *The University College of Wales, Aberystwyth, 1872–1972* (Cardiff, 1972).
Idem, *T.J: A Life of Thomas Jones CH* (Cardiff, 1992).
Ellis, T. I., *The Development of Higher Education in Wales* (Wrexham, 1938).
Idem, *Thomas Edward Ellis*, 2 vols (Liverpool, 1948).

Evans, A. L., *The History of Taibach and District* (Bridgend, 1981).
Evans, L. W., *Education in Industrial Wales, 1700–1900: A Study of the Works Schools System* (Avalon, 1971).
Evans, W. Gareth, *Educational Development in a Victorian Community: A Case Study of Carmarthenshire's Response to the Welsh Intermediary Education Act 1889* (Aberystwyth, 1990).
Idem (ed.), *Perspectives on a Century of Secondary Education in Wales, 1889–1989* (Aberystwyth, 1990).
Idem (ed.), *Fit to Educate? A Century of Teacher Education and Training, 1892–1992* (Aberystwyth, 1992).
George, William, *My Brother and I* (London, 1958).
Gibbard, Noel, *Hanes Plwyf Llan-non* (Llannon, 1984).
Griffith, I. B., *Atgofion* (Denbigh, 1972).
Gruffydd, W. J., *Owen Morgan Edwards: Cofiant* (Aberystwyth, 1938).
Harris, José, *Private Lives, Public Spirit: A Social History of Britain, 1870–1914* (Oxford, 1993).
Hirson, Baruch and Williams, Gwyn A., *The Delegate for Africa* (London, 1995).
Hopkins, K.S. (ed.), *Rhondda Past and Future* (Rhondda, 1975).
Horn, Pamela, *Education in Rural England* (Dublin, 1978).
Howell, D. W., *Land and People in Nineteenth-century Wales* (London, 1978).
Idem, *Patriarchs and Parasites: The Gentry of South-west Wales in the Eighteenth Century* (Cardiff, 1986).
Idem, *T. E. Nicholas: People's Champion* (Swansea, 1991).
Hughes, J. Elwyn, *Arloeswr Dwyieithedd: Dan Isaac Davies, 1839–1887* (Cardiff, 1984).
B. Ll. James (ed.), *G. T. Clark: Scholar Ironmaster in the Victorian Age* (Cardiff, 1998).
Jenkins, David, *The Agricultural Community in South-West Wales at the Turn of the Twentieth Century* (Cardiff, 1971).
Jenkins, G. H., *The University of Wales: An Illustrated History* (Cardiff, 1993).
Jenkins, Roy, *Gladstone* (London, 1995).
Jenkins, R. T. and Ramage, H., *The History of the Honourable Society of Cymmrodorion* (London, 1951).
Jones, D. J. V., *The Last Rising: The Newport Insurrection of 1839* (Oxford, 1985).
Idem, *Rebecca's Children* (Oxford, 1989).
Idem, *Crime in Nineteenth-century Wales* (Cardiff, 1992).
Jones, Dot, *Statistical Evidence relating to the Welsh Language, 1801–1911* (Cardiff, 1998).
Jones, Eben, *The Birth of the Aberavon Unsectarian Schools* (Port Talbot, 1981).
Jones, Frank Price, *Radicaliaeth a'r Werin Gymreig yn y Bedwaredd Ganrif ar Bymtheg* (Cardiff, 1977).
Jones, Gareth Elwyn, *Controls and Conflicts in Welsh Secondary Education, 1889–1944* (Cardiff, 1982).
Jones, Henry, *Old Memories* (Cardiff, 1922).
Jones, Ieuan Gwynedd, *Explorations and Explanations: Essays in the Social History of Victorian Wales* (Llandysul, 1981).
Idem, *Communities* (Llandysul, 1987).
Idem, *Mid-Victorian Wales: The Observers and the Observed* (Cardiff, 1992).
Jones, Ieuan Gwynedd, and Williams, David (eds.), *The Religious Census of 1851: A Calendar of the Returns Relating to WalesI*, 2 vols (Cardiff, 1975–6).
Jones, R. Merfyn, *The North Wales Quarrymen, 1874–1922* (Cardiff, 1981).
Jones, R. Tudur, *Hanes Annibynwyr Cymru* (Swansea, 1962).
Idem, *Yr Undeb* (Swansea, 1975).
Idem, *Ffydd ac Argyfwng Cenedl: Cristionogaeth a Diwylliant yng Nghymru, 1890–1914*, 2 vols (Swansea, 1981–2).
Jones, Thomas, *Rhymney Memories* (Newtown, 1938).
Lambert, W. R., *Drink and Sobriety in Victorian Wales, 1820–1895* (Cardiff, 1983).
Lewis, Richard, *Leaders and Teachers: Adult Education and the Challenge of Labour in South Wales, 1906–1940* (Cardiff, 1993).

Lowndes, G. A. N., *The Silent Social Revolution* (Oxford, 1969).
Martin, N., *Gwilym Marles* (Llandysul, 1979).
Masterman, N., *The Forerunner: The Dilemmas of Tom Ellis, 1859–1899* (Llandybïe, 1972).
Millward, E. G., *Cenedl o Bobl Ddewrion: Agweddau ar Lenyddiaeth Oes Victoria* (Llandysul, 1991).
Morgan, K. O., *Wales in British Politics* (Cardiff, 1962).
Idem, *Rebirth of a Nation: Wales, 1880–1980* (Oxford, 1981).
Idem, *Modern Wales: Politics, Places and People* (Cardiff, 1995).
Morgan, P. T. J. (ed.), *Brad y Llyfrau Gleision* (Llandysul, 1991).
Morgan, W., *The Story of Begelly* (Llandysul, 1981).
Pretty, David, *Two Centuries of Anglesey Schools* (Cardiff, 1977).
Idem, *The Rural Revolt That Failed: Farm Workers' Trade Unions in Wales, 1889–1950* (Cardiff, 1989).
Price, D. T. W., *A History of St David's University College, Lampeter*, 2 vols (Cardiff, 1977).
Rees, D. Ben, *Chapels in the Valley: A Study in the Sociology of Welsh Nonconformity* (Upton, 1975).
Roberts, Gomer M., *Hanes Plwyf Llandybie* (Cardiff, 1938).
Seabourne, M., *Schools in Wales, 1500–1900* (Denbigh, 1992).
Simon, Brian, *Education and the Labour Movement* (London, 1965).
Smith, Dai, *Aneurin Bevan and the World of South Wales* (Cardiff, 1993).
Stephens, M. (ed.), *A Book of Wales* (Cardiff, 1987).
Sturt, M., *The Education of the People* (London, 1967).
Sutherland, Gillian, *Policy Making in English Education* (London, 1973).
Tomiak, J. J., Eriksen, K. E., Kazamias, A. and Okey, R. (eds.), *Schooling, Educational Policy and Ethnic Identity: Comparative Studies on Non-dominant Ethnic Groups* (New York, 1991).
Vaughan, H. M., *The South Wales Squires* (London, 1926).
Wallace, Ryland, *Organise! Organise! Organise! A Study of Reform Agitation in Wales, 1840–1886* (Cardiff, 1991).
Watson, M. (ed.), *Contemporary Minority Nationalism* (London, 1990).
Williams, David, *John Frost: A Study in Chartism* (Cardiff, 1939).
Idem, *The Rebecca Riots* (Cardiff, 1955).
Williams, John, *Digest of Welsh Historical Statistics*, 2 vols (Cardiff, 1985).
Idem, *Was Wales Industrialised?* (Llandysul, 1995).
Williams, J. Gwynn, *The University Movement in Wales* (Cardiff, 1993).
Idem, *University and Nation, 1893–1939* (Aberystwyth, 1992).
Williams, J. O., *Stori 'Mywyd* (Liverpool, 1932).
Williams, S. R., *Oes y Byd i'r Iaith Gymraeg* (Cardiff, 1992).

6. Articles and Chapters Published before 1914

Dafis, D. Ff., 'Yr ysgolfeistr a'r gweinidog', *Cwrs y Byd*, III (February 1893), 1–2.
Davies, D. Isaac, 'Cymru ddwyieithog', *Y Geninen*, IV (July 1885), 208–12.
Edmunds, E., 'Addysg Feiblaidd yn yr ysgolion dyddiol', *Seren Gomer*, XII (January 1891), 27–30.
James, J. D. 'Connop Thirlwall', in J. V. Morgan (ed.), *Welsh Political and Educational Leaders in the Victorian Era* (London, 1908), pp.91–108.
Jenkins, R. Iwan, 'Addysg elfennol: enwadol ai anenwadol?', *Seren Gomer*, X (October 1889), 60–4, 115–20.
Jones, D. Cadvan, 'Addysg grefyddol yn ein hysgolion dyddiol', *Diwygiwr*, 5, LVI (May 1891), 142–6.
Jones, E. K., 'Addysg Feiblaidd yn yr ysgolion dyddiol: yr ochr arall i'r cwestiwn', *Seren Gomer*, XII (March 1891), 81–6.
Jones, T. Gwynn, 'Bilingualism in the schools', in John Ballinger (ed.), *National Union of Teachers Souvenir of the Aberystwyth Conference, 1911* (London, 1911), pp.249–55.

Lewis, D. M., 'Addysg gweithwyr Cymru', *Y Geninen,* IV (April 1886), 105–8.
Morgan, Rhys, 'Yr iaith Gymraeg yn ei chysylltiad ac addysg', *Y Geninen,* XV (June 1897), 99–102.
Price, J. A., 'Welsh education and Welsh public life', *Cymru Fydd,* II (November 1889), 593–604.
Prys, Owen, 'Addysg elfennol yng Nghymru', *Cymru Fydd,* II (February 1889), 63–73.
Rees, T., 'Addysg Cymru', *Cwrs y Byd,* VI (May 1896), 100–5.
Idem, 'Addysg elfennol ym mharthau gwledig Cymru', in T. Stephens (ed.), *Cymru: Heddyw ac Yfory* (Cardiff, 1908), pp.195–7.
Roberts, J. Herbert, 'The century's progress in Wales', *Transactions of the Liverpool Welsh National Society,* 15 (January 1899), 23–39.
Roberts, T. F., 'Sixty years of education', *Young Wales,* III (August 1897), 145–52.
Rowlands, D. C., 'Byrddau ysgol', *Y Traethodydd,* XXV (April 1871), 244–50.
Idem, 'Deddf Addysg 1870', *Y Traethodydd,* XXVI (May 1871), 90–119.
Rowlands, Daniel, 'Addysg grefyddol yn yr ysgolion dyddiol', *Y Traethodydd,* XLI (October 1886), 431–53.
Idem, 'Y mesur addysg', *Y Traethodydd,* LI (July 1896), 300–16.
S. J., 'Addysg i Gymru a Chymru i Addysg', *Seren Gomer,* V (1884), 38–44.
Williams, J. P., 'Addysg Feiblaidd yn yr ysgolion dyddiol', *Seren Gomer,* XII (March 1891), 165–70.
Wyn, Watkyn, 'Addysg yn Oes Fictoria', *Y Diwygiwr,* LXII (June 1897), 185–7.

7. ARTICLES AND CHAPTERS PUBLISHED AFTER 1914

Aull-Davies, C., 'Welsh nationalism and the British state', in G. Williams (ed.), *Crisis of Economy and Ideology* (Cardiff, 1987), pp.201–13.
Davies, B. L., 'A right to a bilingual education in nineteenth century Wales', *THSC,* 1988, 133–52.
Davies, G. G., 'Addysg elfennol yn Sir Aberteifi, 1790–1902', *Ceredigion,* IV (1960–3), 353–73.
Davies, D. Jacob, 'Pregeth goffa M. Ll. Gwarnant Williams', *Yr Ymofynnydd,* LXIX (1968), 7–8.
Davies, John, 'Y gydwybod gymdeithasol yng Nghymru rhwng y ddau ryfel byd', in G. H. Jenkins (ed.), *Cof Cenedl,* IV (Llandysul, 1989), 155–78.
Edwards, Hywel Teifi, 'Y Gymraeg yn y bedwaredd ganrif ar bymtheg', in G. H. Jenkins (ed.), *Cof Cenedl,* II (Llandysul, 1987), 19–52.
Edwards, O. M., 'The Welsh Not', in M. Stephens (ed.), *A Book of Wales* (Cardiff, 1987), pp.55–6.
Elias, Tom, 'The problems of teachers in the rural areas of Wales: elementary schools', in W. Ll. Davies (ed.), *National Union of Teachers, Souvenir of the Aberystwyth Conference 1933* (Aberystwyth, 1933), pp.34–9.
Ellis, T. I., 'The development of modern Welsh secondary education', *THSC,* 1932–3, 1–39.
Evans, J. M., 'Elementary education in Montgomeryshire', *Montgomery Collections,* LXIII (1970–3), 1–46, 119–66.
Evans, W. Gareth, 'Canmlwyddiant T.E. Ellis, A.S. a helynt Ysgol Cynwyd', *Cylchgrawn Cymdeithas Hanes a Chofnodion Sir Feirionnydd,* X (1985–9), 142–56.
Idem, 'T. E. Ellis, M.P., and the Free Elementary Education Act, 1891', *Journal of the Merioneth Historical and Record Society,* XI (1990–3), 44–58.
Idem, 'Free education and the quest for popular control, unsectarianism and efficiency: Wales and the Free Elementary Education Act, 1881', *THSC,* 1991, 203–31.
Idem, 'Addysg rydd neu ailwaddoli'r hen "Estrones", Cymru a Deddf Addysg 1891', *Y Traethodydd,* 147 (1992), 12–19.

Idem, 'Education and the needs of an industrial community: decision-making in Victorian Llanelli', *Carmarthenshire Antiquary*, 28 (1992), 71-8.

Idem, 'The "bilingual difficulty", HMI and the Welsh language in the Victorian Age', *WHR*, 16 (1992-3), 494-513.

Idem, 'O. M. Edwards's enlightened precursors: HMIs and the Welsh language in the late nineteenth century', *Planet*, 99 (1993), 69-77.

Idem, 'Gelyn yr iaith Gymraeg, y Parchedig Shadrach Pryce, A. E. M., a meddylfryd yr Arolygiaeth yn Oes Fictoria', *Y Traethodydd*, 149 (1994), 73-81.

Idem, 'The "bilingual difficulty", the Inspectorate and the failure of a Welsh language teacher-training experiment in Victorian Wales', *Journal of the National Library of Wales*, XXVIII (1993-4), 325-33.

Gibson, W. T., 'Fresh light on Bishop Connop Thirlwall of St David's (1840-1875)', *THSC*, 1992, 141-58.

Hargest, L., 'The Welsh Educational Alliance and the 1870 Elementary Education Act', *WHR*, 10 (1980-1), 172-206.

Hopkins, Ken, 'Educational administration and policy making, 1889-1989', in Owen E. Jones (ed.), *The Welsh Intermediate Education Act of 1889: A Centenary Appraisal* (Cardiff, 1990), pp.43-62.

Howell, D. W., 'The agricultural labourer in nineteenth-century Wales', *WHR*, 6 (1972-3), 262-87.

Idem, 'Farming in Pembrokeshire 1815-1974', in D. W. Howell (ed.), *Pembrokeshire County History*, 4 (Pembrokeshire Historical Society, 1993), 77-110.

Jones, Gareth E., 'The "Welsh Revolt" revisited: Merioneth and Montgomeryshire in default', *WHR*, 4 (1988-9), 417-39.

Idem, 'What are schools in Wales for?: Wales and the Education Reform Act', *Contemporary Wales*, 2 (1988).

Idem, 'Perceptions of the Welshness of education', in Owen E. Jones (ed.), *The Welsh Intermediate Education Act of 1889: A Centenary Appraisal* (Cardiff, 1990).

Idem, 'Llyfrau Gleision 1847', in P. T. J. Morgan (ed.), *Brad y Llyfrau Gleision* (Llandysul, 1991), pp.2-28.

Jones, Ieuan G., 'Henry Richard ac iaith y gwleidydd yn y bedwaredd ganrif ar bymtheg', in G. H. Jenkins (ed.), *Cof Cenedl*, III (Llandysul, 1988), 117-50.

Jones, W. Hugh, 'Herbert Lewis a llywodraeth leol', in Kitty Idwal Jones (ed.), *Syr Herbert Lewis, 1858-1933* (Aberystwyth, 1958), pp.40-56.

Jones-Evans, P., 'Evan Pan Jones – land reformer', *WHR*, 4 (1968-9), 143-60.

Lloyd, J. E., 'Cymdeithas yr Iaith Gymraeg: trem ar hanes y mudiad', *Y Llenor*, 10 (Winter 1931), 207-14.

Lloyd, Wynne Ll., 'Owen M. Edwards (1858-1920)', in Glanmor Williams et al. (eds.), *Pioneers of Welsh Education* (Swansea, n.d.), pp.83-99.

Morgan, Jane, 'Denbighshire's "annus mirabilis": the borough and county elections of 1868', *WHR*, 7 (1974-5), 63-87.

Morgan, K. O., 'Democratic politics in Glamorgan, 1884-1914', *Morgannwg*, IV (1960), 5-27.

Idem, 'Gladstone and Wales', *WHR*, 1 (1960-3), 65-82.

Rees, Thomas, 'The crisis of Welsh Nonconformity', *Welsh Outlook*, VII (March 1920), 57-60.

Roderick, G. W., 'Education, culture and industry in Wales in the nineteenth century', *WHR*, 13 (1986-7), 438-52.

Rogers, V., 'Brittany', in M. Watson (ed.), *Contemporary Minority Nationalism* (London, 1990), pp.67-85.

Stead, Peter, 'Schools and society in Glamorgan before 1914', *Morgannwg*, XIX (1975), 39-56.

Thomas, B., 'The migration of labour into the Glamorganshire coalfield, 1861-1911', *Economica*, X (1930), 275-94.

Thomas, D., 'Reminiscences of a school inspector', in W. Ll. Davies (ed.), *National Union of Teachers Souvenir of the Aberystwyth Conference 1933* (Aberystwyth, 1933), pp.146-57.
Trott, A. L., 'The implementation of the 1870 Education Act in Cardiganshire 1870-1880', *Ceredigion*, 3 (1956-9), 207-30.
Webster, J. R., 'Welsh intermediate schools: creating the system', in W. G. Evans (ed.), *Perspectives on a Century of Secondary Education in Wales 1889-1989* (Aberystwyth, 1990), pp.29-42.
Williams, J. E. Caerwyn, 'Syr John Morris-Jones: y cefndir a'r cyfnod cynnar, Rhan 1', *THSC*, 1965, 167-206.
Williams, Gwyn A., 'Hugh Owen (1804-1881)', in Glanmor Williams et al. (eds.), *Pioneers of Welsh Education* (Swansea, n.d.), pp.57-82.
Williams, H. G., 'A study of the Kynnersley Educational Returns for Caernarfonshire', *WHR*, 13 (1986-7), 299-327.
Idem, 'The Forster Education Act and Welsh politics, 1870-1874', *WHR*, 14 (1988-9), 242-68.
Idem, 'The School Board movement in Caernarfonshire, 1870-80', *THCS*, 1989, 11-36.
Williams, Sian Rhiannon, 'Iaith y nefoedd mewn cymdeithas ddiwydiannol: y Gymraeg a chrefydd yng ngorllewin Sir Fynwy yn y bedwaredd ganrif ar bymtheg', in G. H. Jenkins and J. B. Smith (eds.), *Politics and Society in Wales, 1840-1922* (Cardiff, 1988), pp.46-60.

8. WORKS OF REFERENCE

Dictionary of Welsh Biography (London, 1959).
School Board Directory (London, 1876).

9. UNPUBLISHED THESES, UNIVERSITY OF WALES

Edwards, J. E., 'Beriah Gwynfe Evans, ei fywyd a'i waith, ynghyd â mynegai dethol i cyfaill yr aelwyd'. Ph.D, 1989.
George, M. V., 'An assessment of the contribution of Henry Richard to education'. M.Ed., 1975.
O'Leary, P. B., 'Immigration and integration: a study of the Irish in Wales, 1799-1922'. Ph.D., 1990.
Williams, T. I., 'Patriots and citizens: language, identity and education in a liberal state – the Anglicisation of Pontypridd, 1818-1920'. Ph.D., 1989.

INDEX

Aberaeron, 82, 209
Aberafan, 13, 76
Aberdare, 170, 245
Aberdyfi, 87, 98–100, 270
Abergavenny, 13, 82
Aberystwyth, 1, 10, 59, 103, 185, 251, 262, 265
   Nonconformist conference of 1870, 23–4, 33, 40, 166
Abraham, William, 156, 264
Acland, Arthur, 151, 154, 205, 210
Adams, Henry, 78
adult classes, 145–6, 149
Alexander, R. J., 192, 226, 234
Amddiffynnyd yr Eglwys, 159–60
Ammanford, 101–2
Anglesey, 52, 53–4, 55, 57, 59, 80, 83, 106, 111, 124, 127, 179, 188, 214, 219, 227, 246
Anglican Church and Church in Wales
   disestablishment issue, 16, 19, 23, 93, 98, 107, 211, 243, 266, 276
   dominance in school provision, 13, 16, 22, 25, 27, 32–4, 37, 39, 41–2, 45, 48–9, 51, 54–5, 65, 84, 87, 92, 97–8, 198
   High Church movement, 16, 25
   numerical strength, 20–1, 42, 158
Ashford, Thomas, 121–2
attendance officers, 65, 97, 122, 129, 219, 228–9, 233, 235
   see also non-attendance

Bala, 23, 69, 83
Balfour, Arthur, 272–3
Bancroft, J., 191, 206, 228, 234
Baner ac Amserau Cymru, 25–6, 43, 60, 68, 81, 91, 122, 232, 269
Baner Cymru, 21
Bangor, 7, 43, 66–7, 69, 83, 91, 114, 169, 185, 195, 225, 239, 246, 262
Beaumaris, 59, 83
Beckley, H. J., 64
Beddgelert, 86–7, 106–7
Bedwas, 76–8, 92, 109

Bedwellty, 82, 122, 196–7, 206, 220
Bevan, Canon M. J., 201–2
Binns, B. J., 51, 134, 137–8, 140–2, 161
Blaenau Ffestiniog 73, 83, 103, 195, 258
boroughs, 16, 47–8, 59
Boston, Lord, 63, 244
Breconshire, 11, 53–4, 59, 75, 80, 82, 104, 114, 119, 179, 197, 214
Breese, Edward, 66
Bridgend, 82
Briscoe, Revd Thomas, 201
British and Foreign School Society, 6–7, 10
   British schools, 11, 13, 43, 49, 52, 54, 54, 65, 67–8, 74, 76, 84, 100, 181, 187, 202, 214
   number of, 13, 54, 55, 79
Bryan, Edward, 72
Builth, 82
Bute, Marquess of, 76, 101, 199

Caernarfonshire, 7, 9, 12, 27, 29, 39–40, 51, 53–4, 56, 59, 64–5, 69, 73, 80, 83, 87, 91, 102, 104, 106, 111, 137, 161, 170, 179, 181, 195, 209, 214, 219–20, 227, 245–6, 249, 255, 258
Calvinism, 23, 165, 175
Cambrian News, 101, 172
Cardiff, 13, 24, 53, 76, 80, 82, 101, 105, 109, 119, 129, 143, 164–5, 168, 184–5, 203, 223, 230–1, 256, 271
Cardiganshire, 11–12, 29, 52, 53–4, 55, 59, 80, 82, 94, 106, 109, 114, 179, 188, 208, 214, 224–5, 244, 250, 258
Carmarthenshire, 7, 11, 23, 53–4, 56–7, 59, 74–5, 80, 82, 101, 106, 108, 112, 118–19, 122, 140, 162, 179, 183, 202, 209, 214, 222–4, 229, 243, 245, 248, 257–8
Carnarvon and Denbigh Herald, 107, 205, 224
Catholics, 75–6, 79, 90, 105, 109, 164–5, 167, 169, 172–3, 267
Cawdor, Earl of, 117
Central Welsh Board, 155
Chamberlain, Joseph, 22

INDEX

Charlton, Sir John, 72
Chartism, 2, 7, 70
Chepstow, 82
Church Defence League, 159
Clark, George, 96
Clark, G. T., 111–12
coalmines, 13, 76, 90, 94, 129, 281
  colliery rates, 90, 94
Collings, Jesse, 22–3
Colwill, George, 129
Commission of Inquiry on Education in Wales (1847), 2–6, 13, 31, 180
Congregationalists, 166, 276–7
  see also Y Tyst
conscience clause, 23–9, 31–2, 41–2, 77, 159–60, 167, 175
  summarized, 48–9
Conservative Party
  in Parliament, 33–4, 49, 215, 235, 269–71
  in Wales, 36, 39, 85, 87, 105, 108–10, 112, 116, 118–21, 128, 130, 151, 199, 225, 231, 234–5, 241, 275, 280
Conwy, 71, 83, 87
Corbett, E. W. M., 119
Corris, 39
County Councils, transfer of powers to, 123, 130, 147–8, 247, 272–3, 277
Cowbridge, 13, 82
Cowper-Temple, William, 25, 49, 159
Crawshay, Mrs, 168–9, 258
Criciaeth, 55–6, 68, 243
Crickhowell, 11, 82, 83
Cross Commission, see Royal Commission on Education in England and Wales (1887)
Cully, George, 11
curriculum, 9, 14, 129, 140–7, 150–2, 154–6, 164, 204, 256, 264, 266, 274
  see also Welsh language
'Cyfeillion Addsyg', 23
Cymru Fydd movement, 195
Cynwyd, 99–100, 100, 270

Daily News, 29
Dale, Dr Robert, 267
Davies, Dan Isaac, 135, 190–1, 202–3
Davies, D. Jones, 184
Davies, John, 10, 112
Davies, Owen, 170
Davies, Revd David Henry, 108
Davies, Revd J. E., 64, 67
Davies, Revd John, 111

Davies, Revd Lodwick, 99–100
Default Act, 272
Denbigh, Earl of, 72
Denbighshire, 52, 53–4, 68–9, 80, 83, 111, 113, 119, 124, 172, 188, 214
Dinas, 36
Dinorwig, 102
discipline, 14, 132, 137–8, 140, 229, 231, 246, 255–9, 274
Dixon, Professor McNeile, 148
Dolgellau, 27, 52, 70, 83
Dowlais, 13, 75
Dynevor, Lord, 101–2, 109, 112, 121, 199

Ebbw Vale, 165
Education Act (1870), 15, 20–46, 93, 104, 112–13, 125, 158–9, 179–80, 202, 215, 225, 237–8, 259, 267, 270, 279, 281
  effect on school places, 50–8, 53–4
  in Parliament, 16, 24, 30–3, 34, 39, 44, 110, 163
  summary of provisions, 16–19, 47–9
Education Act (1902), 272–3
educational standards, 6, 14, 95, 132, 132–8, 140–5, 149, 151–7, 187–9
Education Bill (1896), 269–70
Education Department, 95, 117–18, 136, 139, 141, 144–5, 154, 161, 219, 273
  and attendance, 226–7
  and establishment of School Boards, 17–18, 25, 44, 50, 52, 55–9, 62, 66–71, 92, 100–3, 271
  and teachers, 51, 255
  and Welsh language, 183, 192, 210–11
  see also Inspectorate of Schools
Edwards, HMI, 233
Edwards, Dr Lewis, 5, 23, 69, 113, 165–6, 192, 194
Edwards, Edward, 262
Edwards, Isaac, 128–9
Edwards, O. M., 152–3, 155–6, 182, 198, 261, 265–6
Edwards, Revd H. T., 39–40, 65
Edwards, William, 50, 135, 139, 189–91
eisteddfodau, 152, 184–5, 199, 217
Elias, John, 175
Elias, Tom, 208
Ellis, Revd J. W., 9
Ellis, T. E., 153
Emlyn, Lord, 73, 102, 109, 160
England, 28–30, 33, 39, 148, 156, 176, 183, 236, 260

INDEX

English language, 14–15, 135, 140–1, 144, 148, 180–1, 185–6, 188–94, 199, 201, 203–4, 206–7, 210, 212, 275–6
Evans, Beriah, 185, 202–3, 245
Evans, Christmas, 175
Evans, Gwilym, 111–12, 123, 128, 250–1
Evans, Revd Daniel, 39–40, 98
Evans, Revd N. P., 99
Evans, Revd William, 100
examinations, 8–9, 13–14, 15, 18, 141, 147–8, 156, 229

Factory Acts, 8, 216, 221
fees, 9, 17–18, 48, 94–5, 99, 230, 232–5
    remitted, 18, 94–5, 97–8, 218
Fishguard, 100, 243, 270
Fletcher, Joseph, 6
Flintshire, 52–3, 53–4, 59, 80, 83, 147, 179, 214, 231, 254
Forden, 83
Forster, W. E., 16, 24–5, 27, 30–1, 33–4, 44, 49, 110, 163, 165, 215–16, 267, 270
free schools, 21, 24, 31, 38–9, 68, 232–5
Fyfe, Mr, 252

Gee, Thomas, 26, 68, 100, 113, 172, 269
Gelli-gaer, 56, 190, 196
George, William, 209
girls, 113, 138–9
Gladstone, W. E., 27, 29, 33–4, 40, 87–8, 104–5, 165
Glamorgan, 13–14, 51, 53–4, 56, 59, 74–5, 80, 82, 94, 110, 119, 122, 196, 214, 223, 244, 248–9, 258, 270
Gotts, Mr, 225
Gower, 82
grants, 13–14, 24, 56–7, 204, 229, 233, 235, 270
    annual capitation grants, 8–9, 14, 18, 48
    for school-building, 9–10, 17
    for voluntary schools, 17, 23–4, 31, 35
    see also rates *and* rates *under* religious instruction
Green, T.W., 52
Griffith, John, 60
Griffiths, John, 13, 165, 172, 185, 202, 204
Gwynedd, 88

Harford, J. N., 35
Harries, Rees, 111

Harry, David, 111–12
Harry, Evan, 217
Hart-Dyke, William, 210
Haverfordwest, 59, 82, 83, 103
Hay, 82, 84
Herbert, Austin, 133
higher grade schools, 145, 147–9
Holyhead, 83, 97, 107, 118, 219, 233
Holywell, 83, 97, 220
homework, 256
Honourable Society of Cymmrodorion, 184–5, 195, 209
Howard, Rachel, 198
Howell, David, 172
Howell, Howell, 242
Hurst, William, 239

industry and industrialization, 5–7, 9, 11, 19, 50, 66, 71–9, 88–90, 94, 114–15, 149–50, 153, 176, 219, 281
Inspectorate of Schools, 6, 14, 18–19, 28, 48, 99, 102–3, 149, 156, 262–3, 271
    and attendance, 219, 222, 226, 232–4
    and creation of School Boards, 50–1, 56
    religious affiliations, 11, 41–2, 49, 51–3, 55
    and religious instruction, 18–19, 161, 168
    and teaching, 132–3, 135–8, 140–50, 229, 252–5
    and Welsh language, 187–92, 204, 206, 210, 275
Intermediate Education Act, 148, 156, 261
intermediate schools, 1, 148–9, 156, 252, 263, 266
    scholarships to, 129, 148–9, 266
Ireland, 28, 34, 75, 105, 164, 172, 203, 206, 272

James, Charles, 168
James, Mr (teacher), 258
James, Revd J. D., 37
James, Revd Spinther, 71
Jenkins, R. Iwan, 268
Jews, 164, 167
Johnstone, Revd Sonley, 169
Jones, Revd E. Pan, 72, 127, 170, 193, 232
Jones, Goronwy, 187
Jones, J. D., 12
Jones, John, 147

INDEX

Jones, L., 262
Jones, Michael D., 193
Jones, Morris, 124
Jones, Owen, 12
Jones, Revd D. Daven, 243–4
Jones, Revd Hugh, 110
Jones, Revd John Williams, 74, 110
Jones, Revd Josiah, 23
Jones, Revd Latimer, 223–4
Jones, Thomas, 72, 197, 211
Jones, T. Selby, 29
Jones, Volander, 104

Kendrick, G. S., 6
Knighton, 82, 83

labour and trade union movement, 111, 125–30
Lakefield Elementary School, 247–8
Lampeter, 35, 82, 83–4, 97, 109, 209
landowners, 4, 8, 17–19, 26, 28–9, 34–6, 45, 50, 92–3, 95–6, 104, 109, 112, 114–15, 115, 192, 198–200, 211, 226, 243–4, 266
  and establishment of School Boards, 60–4, 67, 71–2, 74, 84–5, 85, 101–2
  see also 'screws'
Lansdowne, E. A., 119
Laurence, G. E. T., 119
Laybourne, R., 56–7, 109
Leggard, A. G., 148, 191–2, 263, 265
Lewellin, Revd Ll., 109
Lewis, Henry, 173
Lewis, Herbert, 72, 127
Lewis, Revd Daniel, 200, 209
Liberal Party
  in Parliament, 1, 11, 20, 29, 31, 33–4, 36, 45, 49, 87, 103–5, 112, 120, 164, 192, 194–5, 211–12, 234–5, 279
  in Wales, 1, 8, 19, 28, 36, 38–9, 59–60, 64, 66, 73, 81, 87–8, 109, 111–16, 120–1, 124–5, 127–30, 147, 151, 153–4, 156–7, 170, 173, 192, 198, 205, 241–3, 245, 261, 265, 267, 271, 280–1
Liberation Society, 29, 31–2, 175–6
  see also Richard, Henry
Lindsell, H. M., 52
Lingen, R. R. W., 5
Liverpool School Board, 170, 173
Llanaelhaearn, 9
Llanarmon, 61
Llanbadarn Fawr, 10

Llanberis, 27, 73, 103, 106, 205
Llanbister, 51
Llandaff, 204
Llandeilo Fawr, 82, 226
Llandinam, 61
Llandovery, 82, 84, 244–5
Llandudno, 70
Llandysul, 85–6, 96
Llanedi, 57, 74
Llanelli, 74, 82, 97, 108, 111, 119, 197, 222, 224, 247, 250–1
Llanelly and County Guardian, 108–9, 128, 247
Llanfihangel y Traethau, 61
Llanfyllin, 83
Llanfynydd, 231, 243
Llangar, 100, 195, 251
Llanidloes, 27, 70, 82
Llanwinio, 56
Llanwrst, 83
Llanycil, 69
Lloyd George, David, 272
Lloyd, John Davies, 85–6
Lloyd, Revd J. K., 160
Lloyd, Revd Rees, 100
Lloyd, Thomas, 35–6
Loughor, 50, 117–18

Machynlleth, 23, 82
Manchester Guardian, 172
Mansel, John, 109
Merioneth, 11, 15, 27, 53–4, 55, 59, 61, 80, 83, 98–100, 106, 109, 118, 179, 181–2, 198, 214–15, 226, 250, 270
Merthyr, 22–4, 50, 53–4, 75, 82, 89, 111, 119, 122, 128–9, 164, 164–5, 168–9, 189, 196–7, 200, 203, 209, 221, 258
Miall, Edward, 29
Monmouthshire, 13–14, 53–4, 59, 75–7, 80, 82, 83, 119, 122, 179, 202, 214–15, 248
Monro, Loftus, 219, 226
Montgomeryshire, 11, 53–4, 61, 80, 82–3, 84, 94, 113, 179, 214–15
Morgan, George Osborne, 31, 194
Morgan, Revd Augustus, 77–8
Morgan, William, 23, 250–1
Morley, Samuel, 33
Morris-Jones, John, 64
Mostyn, 101
Mostyn, Lord, 72, 101
Mostyn, Sir Piers, 72
Mundella, A. J., 216

INDEX

Mynyddislwyn, 196–7, 206

Nanmor, 86
Narberth, 82
National Education League, 22, 40, 71
National Society of the Anglican Church, 6, 10, 48
  National schools, 7, 11, 13, 38, 42, 48–9, 60–1, 65, 67, 74, 79–80, 86, 88, 96–8, 181, 200, 214, 225, 249
National Union of Elementary Teachers (NUET), 133, 162, 208, 247, 249, 252–3, 257, 259–60
Neath, 13, 76, 82, 224–5
Newcastle Emlyn, 82, 84
Newport, 59, 80, 82, 105, 119, 143, 145, 164–5, 251, 271
Newtown, 69, 82, 114
non-attendance, 8, 11–12, 14, 65, 97, 122, 213–36, 217, 254
  compulsory attendance, 18, 23–4, 31, 38, 42, 48–9, 57, 215–16, 227, 232
  and legal proceedings, 223, 225–8, 235
  outside employment, 11–12, 220–1, 226, 234–5, 256
  for religious reasons, 168, 216, 218, 221–2, 224
  statistics, 213–15, 236
Nonconformity
  numerical strength, 20–1, 29–30, 34, 37, 45, 48–9, 80, 107, 152, 154, 158, 277
  provision of schools, 10–11, 13, 278
non-denominationalism, 5, 11, 19, 23–4, 26, 31, 40–3, 48–9, 54, 61, 98–100, 105–9, 160, 162, 164, 167, 169–74, 194

Oswestry, 60
Owen, Hugh, 30, 43
Owen, Isambard, 185–6, 202, 204
Owen, Morgan, 107, 134, 137

Palmer, J. P., 52
parents, 9, 18, 94, 156, 256
  and attendance, 215–17, 229–32, 234–6, 247
  attitude to education, 11–12, 14, 37, 150, 263, 265
  and religious instruction, 18, 24–5, 27–8, 31, 42–3, 49, 170
  and teachers, 256, 258–9
  and Welsh language, 201, 205–7, 210
  see also fees

parishes, 16, 47–50, 48, 57, 60, 62, 73, 105, 117, 130, 215, 271–3, 279
Parry, Love Jones, 66
Parry, Revd Erasmus, 67
Pembrey, 249–51
Pembrokeshire, 11, 52, 53–4, 59, 80, 82, 108, 114, 206, 214–15, 227, 242, 244, 246, 258
Penrhyn, Lord, 62, 66, 199
Phillips, Edwin, 77–8
Phillips, J. W., 102–3
Phillips, Thomas, 7, 13
Phillips, Thomas (trade union leader), 127–8
Playfair, Lyon, 33
polls, see referenda
Pontardawe, 82
Pontypool, 82
Pontypridd, 82
Poor Law Guardians and poor relief, 9, 18, 93, 95, 123, 213, 215–16, 218, 232
Porthmadog, 27
Portman, Edwin, 11
poverty, 7, 10–12, 50, 58, 95–6, 151, 177, 220–1, 227, 230, 234
Powel, Professor Thomas, 184
Powis, Earl of, 60–1
Prestatyn, 70–1
Price, Revd Thomas, 70
private and adventure schools, 6, 14, 50–1, 140
Prussia, 32
Pryce, Mostyn, 138
Pryce, Revd Shadrach, 41–2, 52, 56, 61, 88, 113–14, 134, 140, 143, 146, 156, 188–9, 206, 211, 216–17, 232
Pugh, David, 109
Pugh, Revd John, 10
pupils, 150–1, 166, 265–6
  access to schools, 6, 9, 261–5, 273
  and religious instruction, 18, 25, 28, 125, 170
  see also non-attendance
Pwllheli, 27, 44, 59, 83

Radnorshire, 51, 53–4, 59, 80, 82, 214–15
railways, 15, 68, 94
rates, 94, 103–4, 268
  burden of, 35, 45, 56–7, 62–3, 66, 70, 81–5, 82–3, 89–91, 96, 99–100, 123–4, 164, 170, 279–80
  as revenue, 18, 22, 24, 42, 65, 84, 90, 95

INDEX

see also under coalmines, religious instruction
Rebecca Riots, 2, 7
Rees, Professor Thomas, 262
Rees, Thomas, 278
Rees, William, 7, 26
referenda, 26, 46, 48, 59–60, 63, 66–7, 75, 77–8, 80, 81, 106, 108, 112–13, 115, 206, 280
see also 'screws'
religious instruction, 5, 14–16, 18–19, 23–45, 48–9, 96, 158–78, 194
and rates, 5–7, 21–3, 25, 28, 31–2, 36, 39, 175, 177–8, 268, 278
see also conscience clause, non-denominationalism, secularism, *and under* Inspectorate of Schools, parents, pupils
Report on the Employment of Children, Young People and Women in Agriculture (1870), 8–9, 11, 14–15
Revised Code of 1862, 8, 13–14
Rhayader, 82, 83
Rhondda, 13, 50, 76, 181, 202, 238–9
Rhos-y-bol School, 52
Rhyd-ddu, 87
Rhyl, 70
Rhys, Sir John, 52, 134–5, 144, 183, 188
Richard, Henry, 16, 29, 31–2, 33, 39, 113, 163, 168, 175–6, 185, 194, 201–2, 216, 232, 235, 267–8
Richards, Revd, 77
Roberts, J. Herbert, 1
Roberts, L. J., 133
Roberts, Samuel, 7, 84
Roberts, T. F., 1, 251–2
Roberts, William, 7, 13
Rowlands, Daniel, 43, 67, 269–70, 277–8
Rowlands, Robert, 66
Royal Commission on Education in England and Wales (1887) (Cross Commission), 200–2, 204, 206, 245–6, 267–9, 272
Royal Commission on the Established Church and Other Religious Bodies (1905), 80–1
rural areas, 5, 8–9, 19, 33, 48, 61, 83–4, 86–7, 91, 154, 218–20, 226, 228–31, 238–9, 243, 245–6, 250, 279, 281
Russell, Lord, 33
Ruthin, 12, 83, 227

Sandon Act (1870), 215, 218, 221

School Attendance Committees, 97, 215–16, 218, 220–4, 227
School Boards, 34–5, 93–121, 124, 145, 160–2, 172–3, 195–8, 233, 247, 259–60, 271–2
and attendance, 48, 97, 213, 215–16, 218, 220, 222–5, 227, 229–31
constitution, 17–18
creation of, 17, 26, 37, 41, 47–78, 89–92, 279–80
and Anglican Church, 37, 60–2, 64–5, 67, 71–2, 74, 78–9, 91
and Nonconformity, 55, 63, 69–73, 76–7, 78–9, 81, 84, 86–7, 89–91, 95–6, 98
elections to, 17, 25–6, 28, 34–5, 46–7, 84, 103–9, 246
expenditure, 102, 107, 116–20, 129–30, 136, 219–20, 225
membership, 17, 109–14, 120–3, 128–30, 164
revenues, 18, 35, 48, 81–4, 94–5, 97, 116, 123–4; *see also* grants, school pence, *and under* rates
and teachers, 99, 122–3, 241, 245–51, 255
school buildings and equipment
construction of, 8–11, 17–18, 28, 62, 97, 100–3, 109–10, 113, 118–20
numbers of schools, 13, 79–80, 80, 132
overcrowding, 13, 50, 94
quality, 13, 95, 97, 118–20, 129, 134–6, 139–40, 151, 157, 219–20, 268, 273–4
School Districts, 16–17, 47
United School Districts, 16, 57–8, 62, 73, 117
school managers, 8–9, 11, 17, 134, 229, 235, 248–9, 255, 268
school pence, *see* fees
'screws', 28–9, 34, 63–4, 77–8, 84–7, 89, 91, 104–5, 108
secret ballots, 26, 34–5, 60, 104
secularism, 19, 22, 24, 31, 31–3, 32, 37–8, 40, 163, 165–6, 169–70, 173–6, 203, 278
Seren Cymru, 60
Seren Gomer, 263–4, 268
Smith, Frederick, 243–4, 255
Smith, Henry, 161
Smith, Revd Herbert, 52, 143–4, 188, 221
Sneyd-Kynnersley, E. M., 51–2, 56
Snooke, W., 119

Society for the Utilisation of the Welsh Language
  see Welsh Language Society
Southall, John, 186–7, 193
sponsors and patrons, 9, 14, 16, 35, 95, 100
Stammers, Alexander, 13
Standard, 40
St Asaph, 83
St Clears, 253
St David's, 69, 96
Sunday schools, 4–5, 18, 32–3, 39, 44, 49, 146, 161, 163–4, 166–8, 170, 176–7, 187, 192–4, 203, 222
Swansea, 13, 51, 53, 59, 74–5, 80, 82, 90, 119–20, 128–9, 145, 164–5, 169–70, 200, 203, 233, 243, 271

teachers, 28, 51, 99, 132–4, 137, 142, 149–51, 204, 221, 228–9, 237–60, 238, 275
  appointments, 122–3, 241, 247–8
  pay and pensions, 249–51, 253, 260
  pupil teachers, 252–3, 255, 258
  quality of, 8–9, 132, 228–9, 237–8, 253, 256–7, 266, 274
  and religious instruction, 161–2, 170
  social status of, 14–15, 237, 240–7, 249–52, 258, 260, 274–5
  and training, 7–8, 13–14, 27, 51, 238, 238–9, 239, 267, 274
  and Welsh language, 190, 197, 205, 207–10
Temple, Robert, 113, 137, 141, 144, 150, 161, 232–3
tenant farmers, 12, 28, 39, 45, 81, 115, 115, 116, 198, 243, 265
Thirlwall, Connop, 13, 36–7
Thomas, David, 207, 209, 252, 254
Thomas, John Owen, 101
Thomas, Revd William, 86
tithes, 16, 19, 81, 93, 98, 124–5, 130, 211, 234, 242–3, 266, 271, 276
Toleration Act (1828), 26, 32
Tredegar, 165
Tredegar, Lord, 77
Tregaron, 82, 83
Tremenheere, Seymour, 6, 11–13, 15
Tre-wen, 29
Turner, W., 119

Unitarians, 32, 105, 164
United States, 32

University of Wales, 1, 23, 153, 173, 261, 263, 265–6
urban areas, 13, 61, 64–5, 68, 69–70, 91–2, 230–1, 239, 256, 281

Vaughan, Captain Henry, 109
vestries, 24, 35, 47–8, 55, 59, 61–3, 70
voluntary schools, 34, 47–8, 61, 166, 181
  and creation of School Boards, 17–18, 50, 62, 64, 75, 85, 97–8, 102, 269–72
  number, 79–80, 80
  revenues, 8–9, 18, 23–4, 24, 31, 35, 48, 61, 67, 84, 95–6, 235, 268, 270–1; *see also* grants, fees
  six-month grace, 17, 47, 52
  standards, 92, 113, 136
  and teachers, 241, 248–9, 260
  see also British and Foreign School Society, National Society of the Anglican Church, private and adventure schools, Sunday schools

Waddington, Horace, 138, 142–3, 168, 188
Watts, Revd E. T., 42, 45, 51, 57, 132, 137–8, 143, 161, 207, 219
Welsh Board of Education, demand for, 26–7, 122
Welsh Education Alliance, 27–8
Welsh language, 3–4, 9, 14–15, 34, 43, 52, 121, 134–5, 156, 179–212, 226, 245, 260, 267–8, 275–6
  statistics, 179, 202–3, 212
  'Welsh Not', 182–3
Welsh Language Society (Society for the Utilisation of the Welsh Language), 184–7, 195, 199–200, 202, 211
Wheldon, Revd T. J., 111–12, 127
Whitford, 71–2, 87
Whitmell, C. T., 226
Wignall, James, 128
Wild, Robert, 208
Williams, David, 200
Williams, D. P., 205, 272
Williams, Evan, 22–3, 164, 175
Williams, Mr, 245–6
Williams, Revd E., 29
Williams, Revd J. P., 169
Williams, Revd R. O., 97
Williams, Revd Roger, 74
Williams, Thomas Marchant, 185, 202, 204
Williams, Watkin, 31

Williams, William, 42–3, 51–2, 132, 134–6, 139, 147, 187–8, 190–1, 217, 228
Winterbotham, Henry, 29
Woodruff, P. B., 77–8
Wrexham, 59, 83
Wynne, Hon. C. H., 109
Wynne, W. R. M., 226
Wynn Jones, Revd J. W., 255
Wynn, Sir Watkin Williams, 60–1
Wyn, Watkin, 261–2

Y Celt, 170–2, 193–4, 232
Y Cronicl, 26–7
Y Cyfaill Eglwysig, 38–9
Y Cylchgrawn, 41
Y Diwygiwr, 261–2
Y Goleuad, 25–6, 43–4, 60, 66–7, 122, 165, 167–8, 174–5, 193, 217–18, 232–3, 235
Y Traethodydd, 27, 270
Y Tyst, 25–6, 29–30, 33, 40, 43–4, 60, 122, 166–7, 174–5, 193, 232